D1188622

*Problem and Failed Institutions*

*in the*

*Commercial Banking Industry*

**CONTEMPORARY STUDIES IN
ECONOMIC AND FINANCIAL ANALYSIS VOL. 4**

Editors: Professor Edward I. Altman and Ingo Walter, Associate Dean,
*Graduate School of Business Administration, New York University*

# CONTEMPORARY STUDIES IN ECONOMIC AND FINANCIAL ANALYSIS

*An International Series of Monographs*

*Series Editors:* Edward I. Altman and Ingo Walter
*Graduate School of Business Administration, New York University*

*Volume 1.* DYNAMICS OF FORECASTING FINANCIAL CYCLES:
Theory, Technique and Implementation
Lacy H. Hunt, II, *Fidelcor Inc. and the Fidelity Bank*

*Volume 2.* COMPOSITE RESERVE ASSETS IN THE INTERNATIONAL
MONETARY SYSTEM
Jacob S. Dreyer, *Graduate School of Arts and Sciences, New York
University*

*Volume 3.* APPLICATION OF CLASSIFICATION TECHNIQUES IN
BUSINESS, BANKING AND FINANCE
Edward I. Altman, *Graduate School of Business Administration, New
York University,* Robert B. Avery, *Graduate School of Industrial
Administration, Carnegie-Mellon University,* Robert A. Eisenbeis,
*Federal Deposit Insurance Corporation,* and Joseph F. Sinkey, Jr.,
*College of Business Administration, University of Georgia*

*Volume 4.* PROBLEM AND FAILED INSTITUTIONS IN THE
COMMERCIAL BANKING INDUSTRY
Joseph F. Sinkey, Jr., *College of Business Administration, University of
Georgia*

*Volume 5.* A NEW LOOK AT PORTFOLIO MANAGEMENT
David M. Ahlers, *Graduate School of Business and Public
Administration, Cornell University*

*Volume 6.* MULTINATIONAL ELECTRONIC COMPANIES AND
NATIONAL ECONOMIC POLICIES
Edmond Sciberras, *Science Policy Research Unit, University of Sussex*

*Volume 7.* VENEZUELAN ECONOMIC DEVELOPMENT: A
Politico-Economic Analysis
Loring Allen, *University of Missouri, St. Louis*

*Volume 8.* ENVIRONMENT, PLANNING AND THE MULTINATIONAL
CORPORATION
Thomas N. Gladwin, *Centre d'Etudes Industrielles and New York
University*

*Volume 9.* FOREIGN DIRECT INVESTMENT, INDUSTRIALIZATION
AND SOCIAL CHANGE
Stephen J. Kobrin, *Sloan School of Management, Massachusetts
Institute of Technology*

*Volume 10.* IMPLICATIONS OF REGULATION ON BANK EXPANSION:
A Simulation Analysis
George S. Oldfield, Jr., *Graduate School of Business and Public
Administration, Cornell University*

*Volume 11.* IMPORT SUBSTITUTION, TRADE AND DEVELOPMENT
Jaleel Ahmad, *Concordia University, Sir George Williams Campus*

*Volume 12.*  CORPORATE GROWTH AND COMMON STOCK RISK
David R. Fewings, *McGill University*

*Volume 13.*  CAPITAL MARKET EQUILIBRIUM AND CORPORATE
FINANCIAL DECISIONS
Richard C. Stapleton, *Manchester Business School and New York
University*, and M. G. Subrahmanyam, *Indian Institute of
Management and New York University*

*Volume 14.*  IMPENDING CHANGES FOR SECURITIES MARKETS: What
Role for the Exchanges?
Ernest Bloch and Robert A. Schwartz, *Graduate School of
Business Administration, New York University*

*Volume 15.*  INDUSTRIAL INNOVATION AND INTERNATIONAL
TRADING PERFORMANCE
William B. Walker, *Science Policy Research Unit, University of Sussex*

*Volume 16.*  FINANCIAL POLICY, INFLATION AND ECONOMIC
DEVELOPMENT: The Mexican Experience
John K. Thompson, *Mellon Bank, N.A.*

*Volume 17.*  THE MANAGEMENT OF CORPORATE LIQUIDITY
Michel Levasseur, *Centre d'Enseignement Superieur des Affaires,
Jouy-en-Josas, France*

*Volume 18.*  STABILIZATION OF INTERNATIONAL COMMODITY
MARKETS
Paul Hallwood, *University of Aberdeen*

*Volume 19.*  PROBLEMS IN EUROPEAN CORPORATE FINANCE: Text
and Cases
Michel Schlosser, *Centre d'Enseignement Superieur des Affaires,
Jouy-en-Josas, France*

*Volume 20.*  THE MULTINATIONAL ENTERPRISE: International
Investment and Host-Country Impacts
Thomas G. Parry, *School of Economics, University of New South Wales*

*Volume 21.*  POLICY RESPONSES TO RESOURCE DEPLETION: The Case
of Mercury
Nigel Roxburgh, *Management Studies Division, The Economist
Intelligence Unit Limited*

*Volume 22.*  THE INTERNATIONAL MONEY MARKET: An Assessment of
Forecasting Techniques and Market Efficiency
Richard M. Levich, *Graduate School of Business Administration, New
York University*

*Volume 23.*  TRANSNATIONAL CONGLOMERATES AND THE
ECONOMICS OF DEPENDENT DEVELOPMENT: A Case
Study of the International Electrical Oligopoly and Brazil's
Electrical Industry
Richard Newfarmer, *University of Notre Dame*

*Volume 24.*  THE POLITICAL ECONOMY OF ENVIRONMENTAL
PROTECTION
Horst Siebert, *University of Mannheim,* and Ariane Berthoin Antal,
*International Institute for Environment and Society, Berlin*

*For:*
*Joanne,*
*Alison,*
*and*
*Jessica*
*They light up my life.*

# Problem and Failed Institutions
## in the
## Commercial Banking Industry

by *JOSEPH F. SINKEY, JR.*
*Associate Professor of Banking and Finance*
*College of Business Administration*
*University of Georgia*

**JAI PRESS INC.**

**Greenwich, Connecticut**

**Library of Congress Cataloging in Publication Data**

Sinkey, Joseph F
  Problem and failed institutions in the commercial banking
industry.

  (Contemporary studies in economic and financial analysis; v. 4)
  Bibliography: p.
  Includes index.
  1. Banks and banking—United States.    2. Bank
failures—United States.    3. Bank examination—United
States. I. Title. II. Series.
HG2491.S55      332.1'2'0973      76-5760
ISBN 0-89232-005-2

*Copyright © 1979 JAI PRESS INC.*
*165 West Putnam Avenue*
*Greenwich, Connecticut 06830*

*ISBN NUMBER: 0-89232-005-2*
*Library of Congress Catalog Card Number: 76-5760*
*Manufactured in the United States of America*

# Contents

| | |
|---|---|
| *Illustrations* | *xii* |
| *Figures* | *xiii* |
| *Tables* | *xv* |
| *Acknowledgments* | *xix* |
| *Foreword* | *xxi* |
| *Preface* | *xxv* |

| | | |
|---|---|---|
| **1** | **Problem and Failed Banks: Historical Preview** | **1** |
| | 1.1 The First Problem and Failed Banks | 1 |
| | 1.2 Andrew Dexter and Farmers Exchange Bank: The First U.S. Bank Failure | 3 |
| | 1.3 Pre-Deposit-Insurance Bank Failures | 5 |
| | 1.4 Causes of Pre-Deposit-Insurance Bank Failures | 8 |
| | 1.5 Post-Deposit-Insurance Bank Failures | 15 |
| | 1.6 Causes of Post-Deposit-Insurance Bank Failures | 17 |
| | 1.7 What Is a Problem Bank? | 18 |
| | 1.8 Summary and Conclusions | 19 |

| | | |
|---|---|---|
| **2** | **Protecting the "Safety and Soundness" of the Banking System: The Role of the Banking Authorities** | **21** |
| | 2.1 Introduction | 21 |
| | 2.2 Dual Banking: The Foundation of the "Jurisdictional Tangle" | 24 |
| | 2.3 The Goal of Bank Regulation and Supervision | 26 |
| | 2.4 Achieving the Goal of Failure Prevention: Identification and Enforcement Tasks | 27 |
| | 2.5 The Role of Deposit Insurance in the Banking System | 32 |
| | 2.6 Deposit Assumptions Versus Deposit Payoffs | 34 |
| | 2.7 The Size of the Deposit-Insurance Fund | 39 |
| | 2.8 Summary and Conclusions | 40 |

**3 The Bank-Examination Process: The Importance of Bank Capital and Loan Evaluations in Identifying "Problem Banks"** **42**
3.1 Introduction 42
3.2 What Is a Problem Bank 45
3.3 Bank Capital and the Loan-Evaluation Process 48
3.4 Alternative Weighted Capital Ratios 51
   *1. The FDIC's Adjusted Capital Ratio* 51
   *2. The FDIC's Net Capital Ratio* 51
   *3. A Probability-Weighted Capital Ratio* 52
   *4. An Illustration* 52
3.5 Empirical Findings 53
3.6 The Net Capital Ratio and Recent Bank Failures 55
   *1. Large Banks and the Predictability of NCR* 56
   *2. Small Banks and the Predictability of NCR* 57
3.7 The Relationship Between Problem Banks and the Economy 57
3.8 Summary and Conclusions 62
Appendix A   1975 Bank Examination Capital Ratios 63

**4 Early-Warning Systems: Concepts and Procedures** **67**
4.1 Introduction 67
4.2 The Origins and Definition of Early-Warning Systems 68
4.3 The Purposes and Potential Advantages of an Early-Warning System 70
4.4 Some Fundamental Questions about the Concept of an Early-Warning System 72
4.5 The Multiple Discriminant-Analysis Approach 73
   *a. The Standard Two-Group MDA Approach* 74
   *b. The Outlier Techniques (Peer-Group Analysis)* 83
4.6 Alternative Systems and Research 87
4.7 Summary and Conclusions 90

**5 Financial Characteristics of Problem and Failed Banks** **92**
5.1 Introduction 92
5.2 Financial Ratios and Comparative Analysis 92
   *1. Liquidity Ratios* 94
   *2. Leverage Ratios* 96
   *3. Activity Ratios* 97
   *4. Profitability Ratios* 98
   *5. Ratio-Analysis Summary* 100

5.3 Financial Characteristics of Problem and Failed
    Banks                                                      101
    1. *Failed Banks: Data and Methods*                        101
    2. *Some "Bottom-Line" Line Measures of Bank*
       *Performance*                                           106
    3. *ROE Decomposition Analysis*                            120
    4. *The Capital Adequacy of Failed Banks*                  124
    5. *Multiple-Variable Tests of Bank*
       *Soundness: Failure-Prediction Models*                  127
    6. *Problem Banks Revisited*                               133
    7. *Identifying Large Problem Banks*                       140
5.4 Summary and Conclusions                                    143


**6  Franklin National Bank of New York: The Largest Bank**
    **Failure in U.S. History**                                **146**
6.1 Introduction                                               146
6.2 Pre-Failure Events                                         147
    1. *The Identification of Franklin as a Problem Bank*      147
    2. *The Deposit Assumption*                                152
    3. *How to Handle a Large Problem Bank*                    154
6.3 Franklin's Forty Years 1934–1974: A Brief
    Narration                                                  158
    1. *Retail Banking and Arthur Roth*                        158
    2. *Wholesale Banking and the Move into New York*
       *City: Franklin's Achilles Heel*                        160
    3. *International Banking*                                  162
    4. *Summary and Conclusions*                               163
6.4 Postmortem Analysis I: Early-Warning Based upon
    Balance-Sheet and Income-Expense Information               163
    1. *Methodology and Data*                                  163
    2. *Empirical Findings*                                    165
    3. *Summary and Conclusions*                               185
6.5 Postmortem Analysis II: Early-Warning Based
    upon Market Information                                     186
    1. *Beta*                                                  186
    2. *The Market Model*                                      187
    3. *Estimating Beta and Its Meaningfulness*                188
    4. *The CAPM and the Market Model Applied*
       *to Franklin New York Corporation*
       *1965–1973*                                             188
    5. *Section Summary and Conclusion*                        192
6.6 Summary and Conclusions                                    192
    Appendix A: Computation of Chi-Scores                      193

**7   The Demise of Other Large U.S. Banks**                                    **198**
    7.1  Introduction                                               198
    7.2  Hamilton National Bank of Chattanooga                      199
          *1.   The Roots of Hamilton's Collapse*                    201
          *2.   A Look at Some Symptoms*                             202
          *3.   Summary and Conclusions*                            205
    7.3  Security National Bank of Long Island: Our
          Nation's Largest Emergency Bank Consolidation              205
          *1.   Security: A Glamour Stock?*                          206
          *2.   Identification of Security as a "Problem Bank"*      208
          *3.   New York City: A Nice Place to Visit but
              Don't Try to Branch There from Long
              Island*                                              210
          *4.   Evidence of Security's Demise from Its Financial
              Statements*                                          210
          *5.   Summary and Conclusions*                            217
    7.4  United States National Bank of San Diego: The
          Second Largest Bank Failure in U.S. Banking
          History                                                    218
          *1.   Identification of USNB as a Problem Bank*           218
          *2.   Evidence from USNB's Financial Statements*          219
          *3.   Outlier Tests and Findings: USNB vs. the
              California Control Group*                            224
          *4.   USNB vs. the Paired Problem-Nonproblem
              Bank Sample*                                         228
          *5.   Failure-Prediction Results*                         231
          *6.   Market Information*                                 232
          *7.   Summary Inference and Implication*                  232
    7.5  Summary and Conclusions                                   232

**8   Commercial Banks and the REIT Debacle: A Three-Act
    Play (Comedic Tragedy)**                                       **237**
    8.1  Introduction                                               237
    8.2  What Is an REIT?                                           238
    8.3  Act One: Bank Financing of the REIT Expansion              241
    8.4  Act Two: The Collapse of the REIT Industry and
          the Commercial-Bank Rescue                                 246
    8.5  Act Three: The Current State of the
          REIT-Commercial Bank Debacle                               249
    8.6  Encore                                                     254

**9** **Bankers' Attitudes Toward the Bank-Examination Process and Major Issues in Banking** **256**
  9.1   Introduction                                            256
  9.2   The Typical Survey Respondent                           256
  9.3   Survey Findings                                         257
        *1.  The Bank-Examination Process and*
             *"Early-Warning" Systems*                          257
        *2.  Major Issues in Banking*                           260
  9.4   Summary and Conclusions                                 262
        Appendix: Background Information                         263
        *1.  Respondents' Job Titles*                           263
        *2.  Characteristics of the Respondents' Banks*         263


**10**  **Epilogue**                                            **268**
  10.1  Major Themes and Conclusions                            268
  10.2  Problem-Bank Publicity: Scylla, Charybdis,
        Cassandra, and Rockefeller                              269
  10.3  Bored by the Bank Flap                                  271
  10.4  Jawboning: Cookie and Capital both Start with
        "C"                                                     272
  10.5  The New Czar's Attitude Toward Problem Banks            272
  10.6  How to Use an Early-Warning System: If I Were
        Banking Czar                                            272
  10.7  Future Early-Warning Research                           274
  10.8  A Last Reflection                                       274


References                                                      275
Index                                                           283

# Illustrations

| | | |
|---|---|---:|
| First | The Search for Deep Vault | xxiv |
| Second | Dexter's Round-the-Clock Printing Press | 4 |
| Third | The Jurisdictional Tangle | 22 |
| Fourth | Ode to Bank Capital | 43 |
| Fifth | JAWS (Just A Warning System) | 68 |
| Sixth | Take Me to Your Ledger | 93 |
| Seventh | National Bank Soothsayer (NBSS) | 147 |
| Eighth | Franklin's Arthur Roth Trying to Find "21" | 211 |
| Ninth | Last National Nonproblem Bank & Trust | 233 |
| Tenth | The Accommodation Principle | 238 |
| Eleventh | A Banker's Early-Warning System | 257 |
| Twelfth | Chase's Rockefeller Between Scylla and Charybdis | 270 |

# Figures

6.1  Franklin's Business Loans and the Security Market Line     162
6.2  Risk-Return Diagram, 1969–1974                             180
6.3  Franklin's CR, 1970–1973                                    191

# *Tables*

1.1    Pre-Deposit-Insurance Bank Failures, 1865–1933    6
1.2    Average Deposit Size of Failed Banks, 1865–1933    6
1.3    Bank Failure Rates, 1897–1933    7
1.4    Bank Failures, 1930–1933    13
1.5    Failed Banks, 1934–1976    15
1.6    Ten Largest U.S. Bank Failures    16

2.1    Number and Deposits of U.S. Commercial Banks    25
2.2    Disposition of Closed Cases Under Section 8(a) of the FDI Act, 1936–1974    30

3.1    Problem Banks: Risk Classifications and Deposits    47
3.2    Alternative Hypothetical Classified-Asset Structures    53
3.3    Discriminant-Analysis Tests: 143 Problem Versus 163 Nonproblem Banks Using 1973 Examination Data    54
3.4    Large Banks and the Predictability of NCR    56
3.5    Problem Banks, 1968 IV–1976 II    59
3.6    Estimated Relationship Between the Number of Problem Banks and the Economy, 1968 IV–1976 II    61
3.7    1975 Bank Examination Capital Ratios    63
3.8    1973 Bank Examination Capital Ratios    64

4.1    Classification Results for Problem and Nonproblem Banks    78
4.2    National-Bank Peer Groups Recommended by Haskins and Sells    86

5.1    Seven-Variable Failure Prediction Model    101

5.2 Failed Banks, 1970–1975 102
5.3 Failed and Nonfailed Banks: Asset Size and Number of Offices One-Year Prior to Failure 103
5.4 Failed Banks 1970–1975: Sample Sizes Various Years Prior to Failure 103
5.5 Thirty-Seven Failed Banks: Month of Failure 104
5.6 1976 Bank Failures 105
5.7 Consolidated Report of Condition of Bank and Domestic Subsidiaries 107
5.8 Consolidated Report of Income 109
5.9 Overall Performance Measures: One Year Prior to Failure 111
5.10 Overall Performance Measures: Two Years Prior to Failure 112
5.11 Overall Performance Measures: Three Years Prior to Failure 113
5.12 Overall Performance Measures: Four Years Prior to Failure 114
5.13 Overall Performance Measures: Five Years Prior to Failure 115
5.14 Overall Performance Measures: Six Years Prior to Failure 116
5.15 Failed and Nonfailed Banks: Equality of Group Variances 117
5.16 Failed and Nonfailed Banks: Chi-Square Measures of Group Overlap 118
5.17 Failed and Nonfailed Banks: Classification Results 119
5.18 Return-on-Equity Analysis: Failed and Nonfailed Banks 1970–1975 121
5.19 Expenses of Failed and Nonfailed Banks 1970–1975 122
5.20 Schedule of Other Operating Expenses 123
5.21 Capital Ratios for Failed and Nonfailed Banks 1970–1975 126
5.22 Linear Failure-Prediction Models: Classification Results, 1969–1976 133
5.23 Coefficients (or Weights) for a Seven-Variable Problem-Bank EWS 135
5.24 A Seven-Variable EWS: Regional Data 137
5.25 Problem-Nonproblem Bank Data 139
5.26 Seven-Variable EWS for Large Banks 141
5.27 OEOI for 53 Problem Banks 142
5.28 OEOI Distribution by Identifying Agent 142
5.29 Seven-Variable Profile for Three EWS Banks 143

| | | |
|---|---|---|
| 6.1 | Franklin National Bank: Daily Borrowing from Federal Reserve | 149 |
| 6.2 | Franklin's Domestic Liability Structure | 150 |
| 6.3 | Franklin National Bank: Funds Flow (May 8, 1974 through October 7, 1974) | 151 |
| 6.4 | Franklin National Bank: Federal Funds Purchases, Certificates of Deposit, and Foreign Branch Time Deposits | 152 |
| 6.5 | T-Accounts for Franklin's Deposit Assumption | 153 |
| 6.6 | Franklin National Bank: Uninsured Deposits | 156 |
| 6.7 | Franklin's Market Share: Number of Offices and Pledged Collateral | 159 |
| 6.8 | Franklin's Market Share: Total Deposits | 160 |
| 6.9 | Six Measures of Overall Banking Performance | 166 |
| 6.10 | Franklin National Bank: Univariate Outlier Tests for Six Measures of Overall Banking Performance | 169 |
| 6.11 | Selected Expense Items as a Percentage of Total Operating Income | 170 |
| 6.12 | Franklin's Loan-Portfolio Characteristics | 171 |
| 6.13 | Examiners' Judgments of the Quality of Franklin's Loan Portfolio | 172 |
| 6.14 | Loans to Financial Institutions | 173 |
| 6.15 | Asset Composition | 174 |
| 6.16 | Liquidity Measures | 175 |
| 6.17 | Rates of Growth | 176 |
| 6.18 | Risk-Return Data and Outlier Tests, 1969–1974 | 178 |
| 6.19 | Data for Seven-Variable Outlier Test | 183 |
| 6.20 | Seven-Variable Outlier Test | 184 |
| 6.21 | Franklin's Estimated Beta 1965–1973 | 189 |
| 6.22 | Bank Stock Prices | 194 |
| 7.1 | Ten Largest U.S. Bank Failures | 199 |
| 7.2 | T-Accounts for Hamilton's Deposit Assumption | 200 |
| 7.3 | Hamilton's Operating Efficiency, 1969–1975 | 203 |
| 7.4 | Selected Expense Items for Hamilton National Bank, 1969–1975 | 204 |
| 7.5 | Hamilton National Bank: Return-on-Equity Analysis | 205 |
| 7.6 | Bank Stock Prices: Security and Moody's Averages | 207 |
| 7.7 | Security's Operating Efficiency, 1969–1974 | 212 |
| 7.8 | Security National Bank: Five Measures of Overall Banking Performance | 213 |
| 7.9 | Security National Bank: Seven-Variable Profile for Outlier Test | 214 |

| | | |
|---|---|---:|
| 7.10 | Security National Bank: Seven-Variable Outlier Tests | 215 |
| 7.11 | Security National Bank: Rates of Growth, 1970–1974 | 216 |
| 7.12 | T-Accounts for the USNB Deposit-Assumption Transaction | 220 |
| 7.13 | Important Dates in the USNB Story | 221 |
| 7.14 | Asset Size and Number of Banking Offices of the California Control Banks, June 30, 1973 | 223 |
| 7.15 | USNB's Operating Efficiency, 1969–1972 | 225 |
| 7.16 | USNB's Net Occupancy Expense as a Percentage of Total Operating Income | 225 |
| 7.17 | USNB's Interest on Other Borrowed Money as a Percentage of Total Operating Income | 226 |
| 7.18 | USNB's Ratio of Total Loans to Total Capital Plus Reserves | 226 |
| 7.19 | USNB's Return on Assets and Capital | 227 |
| 7.20 | USNB's Rates of Growth, 1970–1972 | 228 |
| 7.21 | Means and Standard Deviations of a Ten Variable Profile for the Problem and Nonproblem (Control) Banks | 229 |
| 7.22 | USNB's Ten Variable Profile | 231 |
| | | |
| 8.1 | Size and Growth of REIT Total Assets | 240 |
| 8.2 | Geographic Concentration of REIT Investments | 241 |
| 8.3 | REIT Industry Balance Sheet, 1977 | 243 |
| 8.4 | REIT Industry Balance Sheet, 1974 | 244 |
| 8.5 | Commercial-Bank Financing of the REIT Industry | 245 |
| 8.6 | Loans to Six Troubled REITs by Commercial Banks | 247 |
| 8.7 | REIT Risk Exposure of the Ten Largest U.S. Banks | 250 |
| 8.8 | REIT and New York City Risk Exposure of the Six Largest New York City Banks | 251 |
| 8.9 | A Hypothetical REIT Bank Swap: The Marginal T-Account | 252 |
| | | |
| 9.1 | Major Issues in Banking | 260 |
| 9.2 | Job Titles for Eighty-Three Survey Respondents | 264 |
| 9.3 | Total Deposits of Respondents' Banks | 265 |
| 9.4 | Branching Structure and Holding-Company Affiliation | 265 |
| 9.5 | Number of States and the Number of Respondents from each State | 265 |
| 9.6 | Survey: Attitudes Toward the Bank-Examination Process and Major Issues in Banking | 266 |

# *Acknowledgments*

I thank Edward I. Altman for suggesting that I write this book for the JAI Press' monograph series, *Contemporary Studies in Economic and Financial Analysis.* Edward J. Kane and Joanne M. (Forsyth) Sinkey each read the entire manuscript. Their comments and suggestions were invaluable and they both were a tremendous source of encouragement, as they have been throughout my career.

The research for this book was generated over a number of years and numerous individuals have made valuable contributions. Robert A. Eisenbeis and Edward J. Kane deserve special mention. Others to be acknowledged (listed alphabetically) are: E. Altman, J. Arnold, J. Boorman, S. Buser, S. Cohan, R. Dince, T. Dollar, J. Edgington, G. Gilbert, G. Gonzalez, J. Hilliard, R. Hitcock, P. Horovitz, W. Hunter, W. Longbrake, A. McCall, M. Mitchell, M. Peterson, W. Roelle, S. Silverberg, J. Verbrugge, D. Voesar, D. Walker, and W. Watson.

Computer and research assistance have been provided by J. Castner, H. Dew, J. Duffy, J. Gerdnic, S. Goldstein, P. Karnes, J. Maas, H. Merrill, J. Mitchell, W. O'Brien, and B. Shipman. The typing of the manuscript was graciously and capably performed by D. Bodiford, L. McGinnis, and C. Blizzard of the Banking and Finance Department and by M. Burger, C. Lloyd, S. Jackson, K. Myers, and E. Williams of the College of Business Administration's typing pool.

A special thanks goes to John A. Castner, Jr., who provided the artistic talent that gave shape to the ideas for the illustrations in this book. John made ten of the eleven original drawings; Lauretta Bambula sketched the remaining one. Finally, thanks again to Edward J. Kane for writing the Foreword and to Melinda Bell and David Stultz for their assistance in constructing the Index.

I thank the editors of the following publications for permission to draw upon my previously copyrighted articles. The specific credits are:

"Identifying Problem Banks: How Do the Banking Authorities Measure a Bank's Risk Exposure," *Journal of Money, Credit and Banking* (May 1978), pp. 184–193. This material is used in Chapter 3, pp. 48–57, 63–64.

"Identifying Large Problem/Failed Banks: The Case of Franklin National Bank of New York," *Journal of Financial and Quantitative Analysis,* (December 1977), pp. 779–800. This material is used in Chapter 6, pp. 163–168, 177–185, 193–194.

"The Collapse of Franklin National Bank of New York," *Journal of Bank Research,* (Summer, 1977), pp. 113–122. This material is used in Chapter 6, pp. 147–158.

"The Failure of United States National Bank of San Diego: A Portfolio and Performance Analysis," *Journal of Bank Research* (Spring 1975), pp. 8–24. This material is used in Chapter 7, pp. 218–228.

"Bankers' Attitudes Toward the Bank-Examination Process," *The Bankers Magazine* (May–June 1978), pp. 43–45. This material is used in Chapter 9, pp. 256–263.

"Problem and Failed Banks, Bank Examinations and Early-Warning Systems: A Summary," in *Financial Crises* (E. I. Altman and A. W. Sametz, eds.), New York: Wiley-Interscience, 1977, pp. 24–47. This material is used in Chapter 3, pp. 48–57, 63–64, and Chapter 6, 163–168, 177–185, 193–194.

# *Foreword*

Bank failure is a fashionable topic in the sense that, like the hem length of women's skirts, interest in it rises and falls in a cyclical pattern. But the ebb and flow of this interest is far easier to understand than changes in ladies' fashions. The public worries about bank failures only when the flow of economic information makes the threat of widespread insolvencies seem very real.

This insight leads bankers to view their continued solvency as a matter of avoiding, *not* bad policies, but bad publicity. Even for well-run banks, adequate information on the quality of assets and operating policies is notably hard to come by. Almost without exception, banks' published financial statements are exercises in cosmetic accounting, while regulators' unburnished examination reports are tightly withheld from public scrutiny. Banks' habitually self-serving record-keeping makes unfavorable information all the more damaging when it does appear. With anxious customers having much at stake and little reliable information, adverse rumors about a bank's condition can rapidly trigger substantial outflows of deposit and nondeposit funds.

When, as in 1933, such problems become epidemic, restoring public confidence becomes a political-economic problem of great urgency. At such times, fundmental changes in regulatory arrangements are adopted, sometimes only for their dramatic effect. These regulatory reforms take their place among the causes both of the subsequent economic recovery and eventually of the next banking crisis.

For example, in the 1930s, the institution of Federal deposit insurance helped to restore public confidence in the U.S. banking system. But as time wore on, it did this too well, lulling many depositors into the mistaken presumption that, except for scattered closings of small firms, bank failures were a thing of the past.

Joseph Sinkey's book takes as its focal point the series of large-bank failures in 1973–1976 that revealed the foolishness of this presumption. He investigates how—without breaching the industry code of selective nondisclosure or reforming existing regulatory incentives—regulators could have made better use of available channels of information, regulatory controls, and legal sanctions to reduce the number and dollar value of bank failures.

Sinkey builds his case with both wit and vigor, showing that information collected in routine income and condition reports could be arrayed into an effective early-warning system for identifying potential problem banks in plenty of time for the banking authorities to concentrate examination and advisory resources where and when they promise to accomplish the most good. Although Sinkey focuses on data from the past, the thrust of his analysis is forward-looking: to persuade bank regulators to redesign their systems for monitoring individual banks. Such suggestions have traditionally been resisted by Federal bank-supervisory personnel, but Sinkey's proposed reforms seem gradualist and straightforward enough. The changes he recommends can be put into place without Congressional review or authorization. Moreover, they can be interpreted as an effort to blunt the unintended subsidization of bank risk-taking inherent in the current structure of explicit and implicit costs and benefits of FDIC insurance.

Although FDIC insurance is formally limited to $40,000 per account ($100,000 for government accounts), the FDIC implicitly insures all accounts in full. To maintain confidence in the banking system, the FDIC has committed itself to a policy of failure management that minimizes losses to bank depositors and other creditors. On the cost side, the explicit fees for FDIC insurance are unrelated either to a bank's asset structure or to its nondeposit liabilities. This establishes incentives for banks to improve their bargain with the FDIC by taking on additional asset risk and reclassifying large deposits as potentially riskier nondeposit liabilities. With the marginal explicit insurance cost of such balance-sheet risk equal to zero, market equilibration requires that the FDIC impose *implicit* insurance premiums via the examination and regulatory process. It is no accident that bank examiners constitute fully two-thirds of FDIC employees.

As long as the FDIC is unwilling to adopt a risk-rated system for pricing its insurance, it must continually search for improved ways of monitoring and controlling "unsafe and unsound" bank practices. Adopting a Sinkeyesque early-warning system promises to reduce chance variations in the marginal implicit cost of balance-sheet risk to individual banks and to improve FDIC surveillance of supervisory problems generally. If a bureaucracy sought merely to optimize the performance of its mission, such a system would have been installed long ago.

Edward J. Kane
*Everett D. Reese Professor*
*of Banking and Monetary Economics*
*The Ohio State University*

# The Search for Deep Vault

# *Preface*

It is a foggy, misty morning in Alexandria, Virginia, on the eleventh day of our Bicentennial. The weather is not the kind a prospective skier likes to see, especially at 6:30 A.M. I move quietly but quickly through the house. I have only thirty minutes to get ready and I don't want to awaken our six-month-old daughter, Alison. After dressing, I sit down to my usual breakfast of grapefruit, cereal with banana, and toast with jam. Since I am rushed, however, *The Washington Post,* a regular part of my breakfast routine, is missing—it is still on the front porch.

After breakfast, I gather my outer skiing garments and head for the basement to get my skis, boots, and poles. I open the garage door and position my equipment near the door. My friend and fellow FDIC economist, Alan McCall, and Mary Jane, his wife, are supposed to pick me up at 7:00 A.M. I am right on schedule. We are going to Massanutten in the Shenandoah Mountains for a day of skiing.

After a few minutes, I start to get restless. Patience is not one of my virtues. Knowing Alan and how long it takes him to do *anything,* I am not about to blame "MJ" for their tardiness. To pass the time, I go up to the front porch to check out *The Washington Post.*

As I pick up the paper, my pulse quickens and a lump develops in my throat. Is this another Watergate-type coup for *The Post?* Look at the headline:

## Citibank, Chase Manhattan on U.S. "Problem" List

Normally, banking news doesn't turn me on this way. This is different, however, because in my research at the FDIC I am using our "problem-bank lists" in my work. Since I hadn't given the lists to anyone outside the FDIC, my main concern is whether or not someone has gotten hold of my lists, which usually are strewn all over my office. They are, after all, confidential documents in my possession and I am responsible for their safekeeping. I quickly have a vision of fecal matter hitting the fan. "Don't panic and read on," I tell myself.

The by-line reads, "Ronald Kessler, Washington Post Staff Writer." I don't know him. A few weeks later, however, he calls me at the FDIC and, after talking to me about my research (off the record and not for quotation at my request), he indicates that if I ever want to drop any confidential material in the mail to him he will appreciate it. I politely decline to be his "deep vault" at the FDIC.

As I quickly scan the story, I feel a sense of relief. The story is based upon a problem-bank list obtained from the Comptroller's Office. Later that week I call Bob Dince, then Acting Director of Research at the Comptroller's Office, to find out if he knows who "deep vault" is. He doesn't, and indicates that the atmosphere is pretty tense at the plush L'Enfant Plaza where the Comptroller's offices are located.[1] After the failures of USNB and Franklin and the emergency merger of Security (all national banks under the supervision of the Comptroller's Office), Jim Smith, the Comptroller of the Currency, doesn't need any more publicity, especially this kind. Bob Dince and Jim Smith play tennis together and Bob feels that Jim is getting a "raw deal" from Congress and the press. I agree, in part, but Smith makes some *faux pas* that Congress and the press use to hound him from office.

As I reflect on the story, I recall that Citibank and Chase are *not* on our problem-bank list. I wonder if the Comptroller knows something about those banks that we don't. He doesn't. *The Post* story summarizes the typical examiner's tale about a problem bank, that is, Citibank and Chase supposedly have a large volume of "substandard" loans relative to their capital and reserves. Such loans are the least risky and most subjective classifications that bank examiners make (see Chapter 3). *In practice*, it is mainly on this basis that banks are designated as "problem banks." Knowing how subjective such classifications are, I apply the appropriate discount to *The Post's* problem-bank story.

It is now 7:30 A.M. and the McCalls are coming up North Ashton Street. It is time to go skiing and forget about what *The Wall Street Journal* later calls "Bored by the Bank Flap."

About a month later I am back at the breakfast table, this time with *The Washington Post*. It is Friday, February 6. *The Post* has another banking story, "Problem Banks Rising," by Charles R. Babcock. Like Kessler, I don't know Babcock either; unlike Kessler, however, Babcock doesn't even call and ask me to be his "deep vault." I am crushed. *The Post's* story

---

1. The degree of tenseness is indicated in the First Illustration, "The Search for Deep Vault."

is about one of Comptroller Smith's numerous appearances before the Senate Banking Committee. Near the end of the article, Babcock reports that Senator Proxmire charges Comptroller Smith with failing to exert pressure on large banks to increase their capital. Proxmire tells Smith, "I'm not asking you to apply it ruthlessly. Apply it in a namby-pamby way. Play the violin and sing while you're doing it. Just do it." A quick-witted Smith might have responded (à la Ogden Nash):

Ode to Bank Capital
Oh bank capital, oh bank capital.
Our regulators' stricken hero.
Please don't, please don't.
Please don't go to zero.

About thirteen months later, on March 11, 1977, I am testifying before the Committee on Banking, Housing and Urban Affairs of the United States Senate. The hearings focus upon the condition of the banking system and how effectively the banking agencies have carried out their statutory responsibility to assure a "safe and sound" banking system. My conclusions to the Committee are (1) the U.S. banking system is in a relatively healthy condition and (2) the bank regulatory agencies have done an adequate job. These are conclusions Senator Proxmire *doesn't* want to hear. He is pushing legislation to consolidate the Federal banking agencies into a monolithic system. He *wants* to hear: (1) the system is in dismal shape; (2) the agencies (especially the Comptroller's office) have done an inadequate job; and (3) the reason the system is in dismal shape is *because* of the tripartite "jurisdictional tangle." Given *these* conclusions, Senator Proxmire might be able to generate enough support for his proposed legislation. Without them, his proposal would appear to be dead—breaking up (or consolidating) a "winning combination" is un-American.

I conclude my Senate statement on a lighthearted note with my "Ode to Bank Capital." Senator Proxmire, showing a lack of appreciation for my Ogden Nashism *and,* more importantly, an apparent misunderstanding of *how markets work,* responds: "If it (bank capital) does (go to zero), that is just something that will happen because of the markets and we can't do anything about it."[2] There is, of course, no need to do anything about it. In an *efficient* market, *risk-adverse* investors would not permit bank capital to go to zero (technically infinite financial leverage), or even to approach zero, without demanding compensation for the increased riskiness. As a bank's capital decreases below the industry or market

2. Unedited Transcript, Committee on Banking, Housing and Urban Affairs, March 11, 1977, lines 1–3, p. 150. (Parenthetical inserts are mine.)

norm, the risk premiums demanded by investors increase, forcing the bank to reduce its leverage (i.e., increase its capital) *or* to pay for its increased risk exposure. The market's signal for greater riskiness is a higher required rate of return.

This is a book about the "dark side" of banking in the United States, problem and failed banks. Fortunately, such institutions represent only the "tip of the iceberg"; the overwhelming majority of U.S. banks are "safe-and-sound" institutions. Like a certain soap's claim to be "99 and 44/100 percent pure," the U.S. banking industry is *almost* as clean.

My qualifications for writing this book are my educational training as a Ph.D. economist (Boston College, 1971) and my five years experience as a financial economist for the Division of Research of the Federal Deposit Insurance Corporation (FDIC).[3] During my tenure at the FDIC my research centered primarily on problem and failed banks, the bank-examination process, and the development of an early-warning system for identifying problem commercial banks. The three areas are of course closely related. That is, in striving to achieve their Congressional mandate of a "safe-and-sound" banking system, the banking authorities use bank examinations to identify so-called problem banks and try to prevent them from becoming bank failures. Computerized early-warning or surveillance systems can be used as aids in this identification process. In a nutshell, this is the focus of this book.

My publications in the *Journal of Finance, Journal of Money, Credit and Banking, Journal of Financial and Quantitative Analysis, Journal of Bank Research, The Bankers Magazine, Financial Crises,* and *Applications of Classification Techniques in Business, Banking, and Finance* attest to the quantity and quality of some of my research. In addition, I have made numerous presentations about my research at professional meetings and invited seminars throughout the United States. At the University of Georgia, I have continued to study problem and failed banks and in general the management of financial institutions. The pedagogical value of the research has been substantial; that is, studying the *mismanagement* of financial institutions facilitates communicating to students *how to manage* them.

This book should be of interest to the business, banking, and academic communities. Moreover, since Joanne, my wife (who is not a student of banking), finds the book readable and interesting (she, of course, is biased), the book may also be of interest to the general public. Regarding the use of the book in the academic community, although it is not a

---

3. To some bankers, the FDIC acronym stands for *F*orever *D*emanding *I*ncreasing *C*apital.

textbook in the fundamentals of banking, it could be used as a supplemental book for courses in commercial banking, money and banking, or financial institutions.

Joseph F. Sinkey, Jr.

Athens, Georgia

# Chapter 1

# Problem and Failed Banks: Historical Preview

## 1.1 THE FIRST PROBLEM AND FAILED BANKS

The first institution resembling what is known today as a commercial bank was established in Venice, circa A.D. 1135 [see Hildreth (1837)]. However, it was not until about the beginning of the fifteenth century that similar institutions were established in Genoa, Barcelona, Florence, and other cities in Europe. Like modern banks, some of these institutions experienced financial difficulties and were forced to close their doors. De Roover (1948), p. 3, states:

> As elsewhere, bank failures were not infrequent in Florence. In 1516, there were only three *banchi in mercato* [transfer and deposit banks] left. One of them, the Da Panzano bank, failed on December 29, 1520.

The owners of the *banchi in mercato* were called *cambiatori* (money-changers). They were local bankers who handled the transfer and deposit of funds *within* Florence.

The *banchi grossi* or "great banks" were the merchant banks of Florence. The owners of these institutions were traders as well as bankers and their business interests were international in scope. In the 1490s, there were about thirty-three of these banks located in Florence, the largest of which was the Medici bank. According to de Roover (1948), pp. 65–66, the Medici bank had seven or eight branches and about fifty employees, not including the branch managers. While the Medici bank was a giant for its time, it was minuscule compared to the Bank of America (as of 1977) with billions of dollars in deposits, thousands of employees, and over a thousand branch offices. [It is interesting to note, as Mayer does (1974), p. 11, that Bank of America, the nation's largest, began as an ethnic bank—the Bank of Italy in San Francisco.]

1

The Medici bank also had the distinction, at the time of its collapse in 1494, of being Florence's largest bank failure. The end came, not with a declaration of insolvency, but as a result of the revolution of 1494. According to de Roover (1948), pp. 64–65, a mob invaded the Medici palace and burned most of the records—the few documents that were saved bear black scars from the flames. The post-revolutionary government liquidated the bank's assets, the value of which was less than the claims of all the creditors.

Although the physical demise of the Medici bank can be linked to the fires of revolution, the performance of the bank had been declining for a number of years. The causes of the bank's decline are strikingly similar to the reasons for modern bank failures.[1] For example, Machiavelli, in his *History of Florence,* blamed the downfall of the Medici bank on the lack of managerial business ability and the princely behavior of its branch managers. Although de Roover (1948), pp. 59–65, admits that there is a substantial element of truth in Machiavelli's statement, he contends that other factors contributed to the bank's decline. First, in general, business conditions were unfavorable after 1465. For example, silver currency was depreciating relative to gold. This was important because a substantial portion of the bank's assets were valued in silver while most deposits (and interest) were payable in gold. Thus, as assets declined, owners' equity approached zero and the bank was on the verge of insolvency. Second, the bank was highly levered (in terms of fixed interest expenses) and thus vulnerable to deflationary pressures. Third, earnings were no longer being plowed back into the bank, as in earlier years, but were being used to maintain the princely status of the Medici household. This loss of capital was replaced by interest-bearing deposits which further increased the bank's leverage and risk exposure. Fourth, sound managerial policies and judgments were either nonexistent or subordinated to political considerations. Fifth, as the bank's condition began to deteriorate and new complications arose; stop-gap measures rather than long-lasting solutions were proposed. In addition, at this crucial moment the bank became more and more engaged in speculative ventures, when perhaps it should have been retrenching. And sixth, as the bank's investment opportunities (in foreign trade and exchange) became limited, it began making risky loans to princes. This policy of shifting from private banking to government finance, according to de Roover, proved to be the undoing of the Medici bank.

To summarize, problem and failed banks have existed for a number of centuries. Moreover, over these years the major cause of banks' financial difficulties—incompetent and/or fraudulent managers or directors has not changed. To underscore this point, let us now jump from the fifteenth century to the nineteenth century to examine the first U.S. bank failure.

## 1.2 ANDREW DEXTER AND FARMERS EXCHANGE BANK:
## THE FIRST U.S. BANK FAILURE

On March 25, 1809, the *Providence Gazette* reported the failure of the Farmers Exchange Bank, Glocester, Rhode Island.[2] Farmers was the first American bank ever to fail. The *Gazette* stated that the directors and managers of the bank ". . . practiced a system of fraud beyond which the ingenuity and dishonesty of man cannot go." The person responsible for Farmers' collapse was Andrew Dexter, a precursor of C. Arnholt Smith, the person responsible for the downfall of United States National Bank of San Diego (October 18, 1973).

Like Smith, Dexter was a wheeler-dealer. Dexter owned the Boston Exchange Office. The purpose of the Exchange Office, which was incorporated in 1804 (the same year that the Farmers Exchange Bank was established with an authorized capital of $100,000), was to arbitrage out-of-town bank notes by buying them at a discount and then demanding face-value payment from the issuing bank. This function apparently was regarded as useful, since it restrained inflation and checked the depreciation of circulating notes. Dexter decided to reverse the machinery of the Exchange Office, that is, to use it to delay, rather than expedite, the collection of bank notes. To do this Dexter needed a bank, so he purchased the Farmers Exchange Bank of Glocester (paying for it with the bank's own assets) and then proceeded to become, on very favorable terms, the bank's chief debtor.

Dexter's scheme was to print as many bank notes as possible (mainly in small denominations, since small-denomination notes were less likely to be redeemed) and to exchange them for notes issued by other banks. In effect, Dexter's plan was a Gresham's Law scheme, that is, to exchange his "bad" money for someone else's "good" money and then raise barriers to its redemption.

Logistically, Dexter's scheme became fairly complicated. He began by taking the Exchange Bank's note plates (or dies) to Boston and having notes printed in Newburyport for his use. The notes then were transported to Glocester to be signed by William Colwell, the cashier of the Exchange Bank. Colwell, a very loyal bank employee, worked day and night to keep pace with Dexter's printing press. As Dexter became more and more greedy, he wrote to Colwell, "I wish you would work day and night so as to sign if possible $20,000 a day." Given that Dexter was printing mainly small-denomination notes, Colwell was expected to sign between 1,000 and 4,000 notes per day. Colwell, a long-suffering Quaker who was paid $400 per annum, promised to ". . . bear my heavy load without murmur."

After the signed notes were returned to Dexter in Boston, he dis-

Dexter's Round-the-Clock Printing Press

SECOND ILLUSTRATION

counted them in exchange for other banks' notes. To prevent the notes from being returned to Glocester for redemption, Dexter tried to market the notes in distant locations. The Berkshire Bank in Pittsfield, Massachusetts, which Dexter also apparently controlled, and a bank in Marietta, Ohio, were two of Dexter's favorite market areas.

Whenever note-holders found their way to Glocester, they were given either time drafts on Dexter in Boston or put off in some manner. In this regard, Dexter, who regarded note-holders who demanded specie as villains, wrote to Colwell, "I hope you will have the goodness to remember never to pay it [specie] away except where the intention is to plague or delay the person." Thus, Colwell would spend his nights signing notes and his days trying to evade redeeming them.

Eventually, however, Colwell had to begin paying away the specie and the bank was on the verge of collapse. Dexter, greedy to the end, advised Colwell, now on the verge of a nervous breakdown, not to lose courage and sign more bills. The specie eventually was exhausted, however, and the bank was forced to close its doors with only $86.46 in cash remaining in its vault. The Rhode Island legislative report of 1809 indicated that business at the Exchange Bank was conducted ". . . as the perplexed and confused state of the books sufficiently evinces, negligently and unskillfully."

From the Medici bank to the Farmers Exchange Bank to the USNB's and Franklin's of the 1970s, misuse of banking resources by inept or dishonest managers or directors has been the major cause of bank failures (except, of course, during periods of severe economic depression). Our discontinuous journey through bank-failure history now turns to the 1860s and the establishment of the U.S. national banking system.

## 1.3 PRE-DEPOSIT-INSURANCE BANK FAILURES

The foundations for a national banking system were established with the Currency Act of 1863, which was revised extensively a year later and renamed the National Bank Act. The new act was a free-banking measure designed to establish a uniform system of commercial banking throughout the country by authorizing incorporation under Federal law. The adjective "free" simply meant that any individual or group of individuals, upon meeting certain procedural requirements specified in the statute, could start a bank. With few exceptions both Federal and state banking authorities (about one-half of the states had free-banking laws based upon New York's free-banking system established in 1839) had little discretion in granting bank charters. Thus, for the most part, new charters were approved, if the letter of the law was observed. By the 1880s the spirit of free banking was in full bloom, as evidenced by the aggressive chartering competition between the Comptroller of the Currency and state banking authorities.

The bank-failure record during this free-banking era is an interesting one. The failure record from the inception of the national banking system until the establishment of deposit insurance in 1933 is presented in Table 1.1. Over this 68-year period, 15,223 banks suspended operations. However, 6,704 of the banks (44 percent) closed their doors during the

*Table 1.1*

Pre-Deposit-Insurance Bank Failures, 1865 - 1933

| Period | National Banks Number | Deposits (millions) | State Banks* Number | Deposits (millions) | All Banks Number | Deposits (millions) |
|---|---|---|---|---|---|---|
| 1865-1920 | 594 | $ 350 | 2,514 | $ 639 | 3,108 | $ 989 |
| 1921-1929 | 766 | 363 | 4,645 | 1,206 | 5,411 | 1,569 |
| 1930-1933 | 1,385 | 1,881 | 5,319 | 3,573 | 6,704 | 5,454 |
| Totals 1864-1933 | 2,745 | $2,594 | 12,478 | $5,418 | 15,223 | $7,012 |

*Figures for the 1865-1920 period include 311 private banks and their deposits.
*Sources:* For the 1865-1920 period Bremer (1935), Table 1, pp. 27-28, all other data from Upham and Lamke (1934), p. 5.

four-year period 1930–1933. Thus, over the 64 years from 1865 to 1929, on average, 133 banks were closed each year. However, the number of failures for the 1921–1929 period averaged about 601 per year compared to about 56 per annum for the 1865–1920 period.

The average deposit size of the banks that failed during the period 1865–1933 (and various subperiods) is presented in Table 1.2. In general, the nationally chartered banks that failed during these years were about twice as large as the state-chartered banks that closed. This is not

*Table 1.2*

Average Deposit Size of Failed Banks, 1865 - 1933*

| Period | Average National Bank | Average State Bank | Combined |
|---|---|---|---|
| 1865-1920 | $ 589 | $254 | $318 |
| 1921-1929 | 474 | 260 | 290 |
| 1930-1933 | 1,358 | 672 | 813 |
| 1921-1933 | 1,043 | 480 | 580 |
| 1865-1933 | 945 | 434 | 461 |

*Deposits are in thousands of nominal dollars.
*Source:* Derived from Table 1.1.

remarkable, however, since the average national bank was about twice as large as the average state bank. The banks that failed during the years 1930–1933 were almost three times as large as the banks that closed from 1865 to 1929. Of the 9,964 state banks that failed between 1921 and 1933, 9,472 of them (or 95 percent) were not members of the Federal Reserve System, which was created in 1913. However, during the years 1921–1933 the average deposit size of state member banks that failed was substantially higher than the average deposit size of either national or state-nonmember bank failures.[3] Finally, 78.2 percent of the banks that failed during the years 1921–1933 were state nonmember banks; however, only 50.7 percent (or $3,563 million) of the failed bank deposits were accounted for by these institutions.

One of the most important failure statistics that analysts compile is the failure rate: the number of failures divided by the population of banks in operation. Bank failure rates for the 1897–1933 period are presented in Table 1.3. The average failure rate for this 37-year period was 1.78 percent. However, if the four years 1930–1933 are excluded, the average failure rate is cut in half to 0.89 percent. Over the years 1898 to 1920, the failure rate was relatively stable with a mean value of 0.31 percent and with maximum and minimum failure rates of 0.56 percent and 0.13 percent, respectively. This relatively calm period in the banking industry was followed by the volatility of the 1920s and the disaster of the 1930s.

*Table 1.3*

Bank Failure Rates, 1897 - 1933

| Period | Failure Rate* (in percent) | Range of Failure Rates | |
|---|---|---|---|
| | | Max (Year) | Min (Year) |
| 1897-1899 | 0.58 | 1.15 (1897) | 0.22 (1899) |
| 1900-1909 | 0.33 | 0.56 (1904) | 0.22 (1900, 1909) |
| 1910-1919 | 0.27 | 0.49 (1914) | 0.13 (1917) |
| 1920-1929 | 2.15 | 3.45 (1927) | 0.50 (1920) |
| 1930-1933 | 9.18 | 12.86 (1933) | 5.61 (1930) |
| 1897-1933 | 1.78 | 12.86 (1933) | 0.13 (1917) |

*Average of failure rates for individual years, where the failure rate is defined as the number of suspensions per calendar year divided by the number of active banks as of June 30 of the particular year.
*Source:* Upham and Lamke (1934, Table 3, p. 247).

From 1921 to 1929, 5,411 banks closed their doors; from 1930 to 1933, 6,704 banks suspended operations.

It is important to note that the failure rate is determined by two factors: (1) the number of failures and (2) the population base, which (in addition to being affected by the number of past failures) is affected both by the number of charters granted and by the number of consolidations or mergers. From 1897 to 1913, the number of banks tripled from 8,030 to 24,308. By 1921, the population of banks had increased by an additional 5,109 (over the 1913 level) to 29,417, the maximum reached during the 1897–1933 period. From this peak, the population of banks declined by 15,553 (53 percent) during the 1921–1933 period. In terms of absolute numbers, from 1921 to 1929, on average, 601 banks closed each year; from 1930 to 1933, on average, 1,676 banks failed each year.[4]

To summarize, in the era before deposit insurance, the typical failed bank was a relatively small state-chartered institution. In addition, as shown in a study by the National Industrial Conference Board (1932), pp. 28–45: (1) bank failures occurred more frequently in western and southern rural states than in eastern industrial states; (2) the failure rate was higher for noncity banks than for city banks; and (3) since small banks and noncity banks had higher operating expenses than large banks and city banks, they were more vulnerable to the rigors of competition and to the effects of economic and financial changes. Let us now turn to the important question of what caused these banks to fail.

## 1.4 THE CAUSES OF PRE-DEPOSIT-INSURANCE BANK FAILURES

The causes of bank failures are either internal or external to the institution, or some combination of the two factors. Internal causes are ones over which the managers and directors of the bank have *direct* control, such as loan and investment policies, insider transactions, self-serving loans, embezzlement, fraud, etc. Some forms of employee dishonesty may be difficult to uncover, but that does not absolve managers and directors from their responsibility to police and prevent such activities. Bank failures caused by internal factors can be traced to some combination of managerial ineptitude, dishonesty, or insufficient supervision by the board of directors.

External causes of bank failures are ones over which the managers and directors of the bank have little or no control, such as structural changes in the banking and economic environment. However, some external factors either should be anticipated to some degree (e.g., future interest-rate movements) or influenced to some extent (e.g., future banking legislation). Consequently, the complete bank manager is expected to offset or at least to mitigate certain adverse external events.

The distinction between internal and external causes becomes somewhat blurred when dishonesty and economic forecasting are considered because neither of the two elements fits neatly into the control-noncontrol dichotomy. However, knowledgeable bankers still are expected to show some degree of both detective and predictive skills.

When the bank-failure rate is relatively low, as it was from 1865 to 1920, internal factors probably are the major cause of bank closings. In contrast, when the failure rate is relatively high, as it was from 1920 to 1929, some combinaiton of internal and external factors may best explain the mortality rate. Finally, when the failure rate is extremely high, as it was from 1930 to 1933, major changes in economic and social parameters should be considered. With this framework in mind, let us examine the causes of bank failures for the 1865–1933 period.

On April 14, 1865, the First National Bank of Attica (New York) failed. The bank, which was a small one with total assets of $208,106 and capital of $50,000, was the first nationally chartered bank to close. (Capital-adequacy advocates should note that the bank had a capital-asset ratio of almost 25 percent.) According to Kane (1923), p. 36, the failure was caused by ". . . injudicious banking and insolvency of large debtors."

The next two national bank failures [see Kane (1923), p. 37–45] were the Venango National Bank of Franklin, Pennsylvania, and the Merchants National Bank of Washington, D.C. Venanago, with capital stock of $300,000, was closed on May 1, 1866, while Merchants, with capital of $200,000, failed on May 8, 1866. After the Merchants' failure, the House Committee on Banking and Currency undertook an investigation to determine (1) the causes of these two bank failures; (2) the amount of U.S. government money deposited in the two banks; and (3) if any additional legislation was needed to protect customers who do business with national banks. Thus, Congressional investigations into the "safety and soundness" of the banking industry, just as bank failures, are not new phenomena. They have been on the scene for over a century.

The report of the House Banking Committee indicated that each bank had a heavy business loan concentration to one particular borrower, but not the same one. Consequently, when these two business enterprises failed and defaulted on their loans, which were unsecured, the banks also failed. The managers of the Merchants Bank were characterized as being ". . . in the highest degree illegal, improvident, reckless, and dishonest" [Kane (1923), p. 38]. The Venango Bank was said to have been operated in the same manner as the Merchants Bank.

At the time of Merchants' failure, public deposits in the bank were $765,572; however, the amount of security or "pledged assets" deposited with the U.S. Treasury was only $100,000. A similar situation existed at the Venanago Bank, that is, public funds amounted to $291,467 while security was only $50,000. During the investigation of these two bank failures, the House Committee discovered that many of the banks that had converted from a state charter to a national one continued to circulate both state and federal bank notes. To prevent the "objectionable banking practices and abuses" uncovered by the House Committee, it recommended that the Comptroller of the Currency be given the power to curb improperly managed banks. Such power never was granted, however. Moreover, to permit national banks to compete with state banks, the first sixty years of the national banking system were characterized by weak or nonexistent standards and lack of supervision.

The Comptroller of the Currency in his *Annual Report of 1920* indicated that of the 594 national banks that failed between 1865 and 1920 (1) at least 345 (58 percent) were caused by criminal or unlawful banking practices; (2) 137 (23 percent) were due to injudicious banking decisions; (3) 83 (14 percent) failed because of asset depreciation; and (4) the remaining 29 (5 percent) closed for a combination of the above factors or for other reasons. To summarize, the overwhelming majority of the national-bank failures in the 1865–1920 era were caused by dishonest and/or incompetent bank managers.[5] Moreover, unless a bank was grossly mismanaged, Bremer (1935), pp. 37–38, contends that it was almost impossible for a bank to fail during this "free-banking" era, since economic prosperity tended to offset shortcomings in banking training or experience. Thus, according to Bremer, the low failure rate during this period was not a sign of the safety and soundness of the banking system but rather an "accidental occurrence."

If true, Bremer's conjecture that the low failure rate prior to 1921 was an "accidental occurrence" implies that the high failure rate for the years 1921–1929 represents an equilibratory adjustment. It arose as a delayed but natural reaction to the unlimited granting of bank charters prior to the 1920s. As a result of "free-banking," overbanking and managerial incompetency were widespread. Quite simply, there were just too many banks and the managerial wealth was spread too thinly. Until the surplus banks were purged from the banking system, it would not be in a position of rest (i.e., a state in which forces of change are not operating—equilibrium). Moreover, the regulatory environment was one in which weak banking laws and lack of supervision were the main characteristics. Thus, past events and the existing atmosphere made the banking industry ripe for a return to equilibrium via a high failure rate.

To illustrate the setting, consider the following facts. First, as of June, 30, 1920, there were 28,659 active banks in the United States, an increase of 20,329 compared to 1897. Second, according to Bremer (1935), p. 30, in 1920, 8,196 (28.6 percent) of these banks, which accounted for only 3.8 percent of total loans and investments, were located in communities with less than 500 inhabitants. For communities with less than 5,000 people, the figures were 76.5 percent (of the banks) and 21.1 percent (of loans and investments). In contrast, for cities with more than 100,000 population, the figures were 5.7 percent and 53.4 percent, respectively. Third, from 1900 to 1927 there was substantial federal "competition in regulatory laxity" to keep the national banking system "competitive" with the various state banking systems. For example, in 1900, to counter the proliferation of state banks, the U.S. Congress reduced the minimum capital requirements for a national charter form $50,000 to $25,000. And fourth, during the 1922–1931 period, two important functional changes in commercial-bank loan and investment financing came to fruition.[6] First, the relationship between bank finance and the economic activities of production and trade became more and more indirect. That is, bank credit was increasingly channeled into real markets through bond and security markets. As a result, banks had less and less control over the allocation of these funds.[7] Second, and not unrelated to the first point, there was a persistent reduction in bank liquidity throughout this period. The proportion of loans and investments originating in "self-liquidating" transactions of goods in production and commerce became smaller, as did the proportion of assets that were liquid under any security-market conditions.[8] These two functional changes made banks more sensitive to stockmarket fluctuations and to public confidence in the banking system.

Bremer (1935), pp. 54–57, conjectured that the failures of the 1921–1929 era mainly were due to the excessive number of banks established prior to 1921. To test the relationship between failure and overbanking, Bremer compared average failure rates by state for the years 1921–1929 with the number of inhabitants per bank in each state as of 1920. Bremer plotted these two groups of variables and concluded that the graph depicted an inverse relationship between the failure rate and the number of inhabitants per bank (i.e., a direct relationship between overbanking and failure). Bremer concluded that overbanking was a fundamental weakness in the banking structure of the 1920's.

To test Bremer's overbanking-failure hypothesis more rigorously, regression analysis can be applied to his data to determine what percentage of the average state failure rate for the 1921–1929 period could be explained by the number of inhabitations per bank in each state as of 1920.[9] The estimated regression equation is:

$$FR_{1921-29} = 4.76 - .57 \ (IPB)_{1920}$$
$$(.58) \quad (.12)$$

with $R^2 = .32$, $F = 22.2$, and $N = 49$, where FR = failure rate ($\overline{FR} = 2.40$ percent) and $\overline{IPB}$ = inhabitants per bank (IPB = 4,125). Figures in parentheses are standard errors. The F-statistic for the regression equation is significant at the .01 percent level and the *linear* influence of IPB accounts for 32 percent of the variation in FR. The regression slope coefficient indicates that an increase of 1,000 inhabitants per bank per state in 1920 would have reduced the 1921–1929 failure rate by 57 percentage points. Alternatively, if fewer bank charters had been granted such that IPB was 6,125 for the average state in 1920 (instead of 4,125), then the average, state failure rate for 1921–1929 could have been reduced by almost 50 percent from 2.40 percent to 1.26 percent. To summarize, these results support and extend Bremer's conclusion regarding the connection between overbanking and failure by quantifying that relationship.

The granting of an excessive number of bank charters that characterized the pre-1920s era tended to dilute both the competency and honesty of the stock of available bank managers. This was reflected in the specific causes that the banking authorities listed as reasons for bank failures during the 1920's. For example, a Federal Reserve report [see National Industrial Conference Board (1932), pp. 44–45] listed a number of causes as being important in bank closings from 1921 to 1927. Among the internal causes (which reflect incompetent or dishonest management) were listed: (1) a large volume of doubtful, slow, or past-due loans; (2) large loans to officers or directors; (3) defalcation or embezzlement; (4) excessive loans to businesses with which officers or directors were affiliated; and (5) in general, overall poor management. External causes cited were (1) heavy deposit withdrawals; (2) unexpectedly large depreciation of security investments; (3) the failure of a banking correspondent; and (4) the failure of a large debtor. Since the latter indicates an undue loan concentration, it could be listed as poor portfolio management and classified as an internal cause. Regarding the failures of national banks in 1925, the Comptroller of the Currency [see Bremer (1935), p. 99] reported that (1) 50 percent of the failures were due to inexperience and mismanagement; (2) 40 percent to unfavorable local conditions; and (3) 10 percent to defalcation.[10] Given that the test of a manager's ability is his performance under adverse circumstances, some of the failures due to "unfavorable local conditions" could be attributed to inadequate bank management.

To summarize, the potential instability built into the banking system by granting excessive charters during the pre-1920s began to materialize during the 1921–1929 period. However, the specific causes that produced individual bank failures during this period were not much different from those that led to closings during the 1865–1920 period. That is, on balance, incompetent and/or dishonest bank managers still were to blame for the majority of bank failures. The higher frequency of failures for the 1921–1929 period appeared mainly to reflect an adjustment to an overbanked structure.[11] Moreover, this structural defect primarily was due to the historical "competition in regulatory laxity" between the federal and state governments with respect to the chartering of banks. Finally, as a contributing factor, changes in economic structure made it more and more difficult for the small unit bank, which typified the banking population, to maintain its core deposits and profit margin, forcing many of them to close.

Prior to the stock market collapse of 1929, one sees little concern about the "safety and soundness" of the banking system, even though banks were failing at the rate of about 600 per year during the 1920s. According to Bremer (1935), the prevailing opinion was that ". . . the situation would correct itself automatically, and that, since only the smaller and weaker banks were involved, their elimination would eventually result in a stronger banking system" (p. 12). After the 1929 crash, however, bank failures became more widespread and public confidence in the banking system began to wane. The record of bank failures for the 1930–1933 period, presented in Table 1.4, indicates why people were concerned about the viability of the banking system. In these four years, 6,704 banks were closed and the population of active banks declined by 9,181. On average about 9 percent of the population failed each year.

Congressional concern about the failure problem first found expresssion on February 10, 1930, when the House of Representatives authorized its Banking and Currency Committee to investigate the situa-

*Table 1.4*

Bank Failures, 1930 - 1933

| Year | Active Banks (June 30) | Suspensions | Failure Rate (percent) |
|------|------------------------|-------------|------------------------|
| 1930 | 23,045 | 1,292 | 5.61 |
| 1931 | 21,123 | 2,213 | 10.48 |
| 1932 | 18,282 | 1,416 | 7.75 |
| 1933 | 13,864 | 1,783 | 12.86 |

*Source:* Upham and Lamke (1934), Table 3, p. 247.

tion. The Senate passed a similar resolution in July of that year, authorizing its Banking Committee to investigate the national banking and Federal Reserve systems. These congressional proceedings took the traditional and time-consuming form of hearings, questionnaires, and staff investigations. Thus, it wasn't until January 22, 1932, that the first substantive piece of legislation was passed, namely, the Reconstruction Finance Act. However, even this Act was only a stop-gap measure and it only temporarily reduced the failure rate. By February 1933, the banking crisis was so severe that bank "holidays" or moratoriums were not unusual. In fact, when President Roosevelt declared a nationwide banking holiday on March 4, 1933, much of the U.S. banking system was already on "sick leave."

To handle the national emergency in banking, a special session of Congress was held on March 9, 1933. On this day, an emergency banking bill was introduced, passed, and signed by President Roosevelt. The major purposes of the emergency measure were (1) to permit solvent banks to reopen and thus provide the nation with a circulating currency and (2) to prevent the hoarding of gold.[12] On March 13 the banking system began to reopen and by March 15 about 14,000 banks were back in business. In contrast, about 4,500 banks were not permitted to reopen because they were insolvent or in a condition requiring restrictions on deposit withdrawals.

With the immediate crisis abated, Congress turned its attention to more permanent banking legislation. The result was the Banking Act of 1933, sometimes referred to as the Glass-Steagall Act. The purpose of the Act was: ". . . to provide for the safer and more effective use of the assets of banks, to regulate interbank control, to prevent undue diversion of funds into speculative operations, and for other purposes (73rd Congress, 1st Session, H.R. 5661)."

Among other things, the Banking Act of 1933 provided for: (1) the establishment of a Federal Deposit Insurance Corporation; (2) separation of commercial and investment banking; (3) restrictions on the use of bank credit for speculative purposes; (4) more stringent chartering requirements for national banks; (5) prohibition of interest payments on demand deposits; (6) removal of bank directors and officers who engage in "unsafe and unsound" banking practices; and (7) branching by nationally chartered banks to be subject to the same state law imposed upon state-chartered institutions.

The provisions of the Banking Act of 1933 were designed to eliminate and prevent the recurrence of overbanking, lax supervision and regulation, lack of public confidence in the banking system, etc.—the factors which contributed to the banking collapse of 1930–1933. These factors along with a severe economic depression were held responsible for the large number of bank failures during this period.

## 1.5 POST-DEPOSIT-INSURANCE BANK FAILURES

From January 1, 1934, through September 5, 1978, 689 banks failed (see Table 1.5). However, 490 of these banks (71.1 percent) were closed over the nine-year period 1934–1942, approximately 54 banks per year. Thus, over the 35 years from 1943 to 1977, only 193 banks have failed, about 5.5 per year. With a population base of approximately 14,000 banks in any of these years, this translates into an average annual failure rate of less than 0.04 percent. [Recall (from Table 1.3) that in 1917 the failure rate was 0.13 percent.] On balance, the failure record for the past 40 years has been an excellent one, both in absolute and relative terms.

From 1934 to 1972, the average failed bank had total deposits of only $2.0 million. Separating these banks according to insurance status, the average FDIC-insured failure had total deposits of $2.2 million while the average noninsured failure had total deposits of $1.0 million. As of December 31, 1974, there were 251 noninsured banks or nondeposit trust companies in the U.S. (including U.S. possessions). These noninsured institutions accounted for only 1.7 percent of the population of 14,481 commercial banks and for only 0.95 percent of $754 billion in total deposits at commercial banks.[13]

On October 18, 1973, the United States National Bank of San Diego failed (see Chapter 7). The collapse of this bank marked the first billion-dollar bank failure in U.S. history. With total deposits of $932 million, USNB's deposits amounted to 44 percent of the deposits ($2.1 billion) in all previous failures of insured banks (512). Slightly less than one year later, on October 8, 1974, Franklin National Bank of New York failed (see Chapter 6). With total deposits of $1.4 billion, Franklin replaced USNB as "king" of the failure mountain.

Seven of the ten largest U.S. bank failures have occurred since USNB's

*Table 1.5*

### Failed Banks, 1934–1978*

| Years | Insured | Noninsured | Total |
|---|---|---|---|
| 1934-1942 | 393 | 97 | 490 |
| 1943-1978 | 162 | 37 | 199 |
| 1934-1978 | 555 | 134 | 689 |

*Data are through September 5, 1978.
*Sources: Annual Report of the FDIC* (1974), Table 121, p. 245 and FDIC Press Releases, 1975-1978.

collapse in 1973 (see Table 1.6). Horovitz (1975) has conjectured that ". . . failures of large banks (or at least worries about such problems) are going to be a permanent part of the financial picture of the future" (p. 591). Of course, without adjustments for inflation and growth in the banking system, this picture is somewhat distorted. However, there is no denying that the bank failures of the 1970s have been larger and received more publicity than past failures of insured banks. Whether or not this trend is going to be a long-run phenomenon remains to be seen.

In addition to the increased size of recent bank failures, there has been a significant jump in the number of bank failures in the past two years (1975–1976). From 1943 until 1974, only 121 *insured* banks failed, on average, less than four banks per year. (For the same period, 37 noninsured banks closed.) In contrast, in 1975, thirteen insured banks failed and in 1976 sixteen banks have closed. The year 1975 marked the first year of "double-digit" bank failures since 1942 when 20 insured banks closed. In 1977, six banks failed and, as of September 5, 1978, six banks have closed in 1978.

This recent increase in the number of bank failures and in the size of these failures, along with considerable adverse publicity concerning

*Table 1.6*

Ten Largest U.S. Bank Failures
(as of December 31, 1977)

| Bank | Year Closed | Total Deposits (millions) |
| --- | --- | --- |
| 1. Franklin National Bank, New York | 1974 | $1,445 |
| 2. United States National Bank, San Diego | 1973 | 932 |
| 3. Hamilton National Bank, Chattanooga | 1976 | 336 |
| 4. American Bank & Trust, New York | 1976 | 199 |
| 5. International City B&T, New Orleans | 1976 | 160 |
| 6. American City Bank & Trust, Milwaukee | 1975 | 145 |
| 7. American Bank & Trust, Orangeburg, S.C. | 1974 | 113 |
| 8. Northern Ohio Bank, Cleveland | 1975 | 95 |
| 9. Public Bank, Detroit | 1966 | 93 |
| 10. Sharpstown State Bank, Texas* | 1971 | 67 |

*Indicates a deposit payoff, other are deposit assumptions. Total deposits are in *nominal* dollars.
*Sources: Annual Report of the FDIC* (various issues) and FDIC Press Releases (various issues).

"problem banks" and the REIT crisis (both subjects to be discussed in later chapters), has cast the commercial-banking industry in an unfavorable light. These events have generated reactions from(among others) stockholders, depositors, the U.S. Congress, the banking authorities, and banking associations. For example, bank shareholders, who have accepted lower returns *and* lower risks (of failure and of variability of return) relative to alternative investments, have seen the value of their holdings decline and the "safety and soundness" of the banking industry questioned. As a result, both equity and debt markets have become more cautious regarding banking investments. Depositors, both individual and corporate, have wondered about the safety of their monies. In fact, several large corporations, such as General Motors and Exxon, have developed programs to evaluate the riskiness of selected banks. The U.S. Congress has reacted in its traditional manner by conducting hearings and staff investigations regarding bank failures, problem banks, bank supervision, and regulatory reform. The banking authorities have evaluated and in some instances revised their operations, most notably in the examination and supervision area where "early warning" or "surveillance" systems have been developed. And finally, trade organizations, such as the American Bankers Associations, have increased their advertising programs specifically to counteract adverse banking publicity.

## 1.6 CAUSES OF POST-DEPOSIT-INSURANCE BANK FAILURES

Prior to the 1920's, most U.S. bank failures were due to internal causes, that is, they were caused by factors or circumstances which competent or honest managers and directors could have prevented or avoided. After bank-failure equilibrium was restored to the U.S. economy in the early 1940s and since, internal factors again have been the major cause of bank failures. An FDIC study by Hill (1975), based upon 67 insured banks that failed between 1960 and 1974, indicated that three major causes have been responsible for recent bank failures.[14] First, 38 of the failures were due to improper loans to officers, directors, or owners or loans to out-of-territory borrowers. In addition, in 20 of these 38 cases, misuse of brokered funds was involved. Second, defalcation, embezzlement, or manipulation were important in 21 of the failures. And third, eight of the failures were blamed on managerial weaknesses in loan-portfolio supervision.

Hill also reports that there were several common factors usually found in these bank failures.[15] First, bank managers were characterized as "weak, disinterested, uninformed, or fraudulent." Second, internal routines, controls, and operating systems were described as being absent of insufficient. And third, in general, bank directors tended to function merely as "rubber-stamp bodies." That is, in most cases, directors did not (1) establish clear overall policies; (2) review all outstanding loans and supporting documents; (3) review cash items and overdrafts at periodic intervals; (4) use reasonable effort to get slow assets moving or to control expenditures; and (5) establish internal routines and controls or supply the necessary supervision.

On balance, strong, interested, informed and honest managers and directors usually do not permit or establish unsafe and/or unsound banking procedures and policies. In this view, it is managers who can't or won't manage and/or directors who can't or won't direct that cause problem and failed banks. As a final illustration, Hill reports that in most embezzlement cases bank managers failed to establish adequate safeguards against such manipulations and therefore afforded officers or employees the opportunity to embezzle.

## 1.7 WHAT IS A PROBLEM BANK?

Although banks with financial difficulties (i.e., problem institutions) have existed for centuries, the term "problem bank" only recently was made popular by banking authorities compiling so-called problem-bank lists. Accordingly, every financial reporter is looking for a "deep vault" so that he or she can provide his or her newspaper with a headline like "Citibank, Chase Manhattan on U.S. 'Problem' List" (*The Washington Post,* January 11, 1976). This section presents only a brief introduction to the FDIC's concept of a problem bank. (Across the three Federal banking agencies, this idea is basically the same.) Chapter 3 develops the concept of a problem bank in more detail.

The banking agencies have interpreted their "safety and soundness" mandate as one of failure prevention.[16] By identifying banks with the highest failure risks, so-called problem banks, the banking agencies hope to achieve this goal. The FDIC's Division of Bank Supervision identifies three classes of problem banks that are separated according to examiners' perceptions of failure (or insolvency) risks. Banks that are perceived as having at least a 50 percent chance of requiring FDIC financial assistance in the near future are classified as "potential payoffs" (PPOs). Banks that appear to be headed for PPO status unless drastic changes occur are referred to as "serious problems" (SPs). And finally, banks that have significant weaknesses, but a lesser degree of vulnerability than PPO or SP banks, are called "other problems" (OPs).

In a recent letter from former FDIC Chairman Wille to Senator Proxmire, the FDIC's general guidelines for identifying SP and OP banks were described:

SERIOUS PROBLEM: This category usually includes banks in which the nature of volume of weaknesses and the trends are such that correction is urgently needed. The net capital and reserves position of such banks (i.e., their book capital and reserves less supervisory adjustments for *all* adverse asset classifications, nonbook liabilities and shortages) is likely to be substantially negative. In addition, management is usually rated Unsatisfactory or Poor. Representing the greatest area of financial exposure to the Corporation, "Serious Problem" nonmember banks necessarily receive the most concentrated FDIC attention and supervision.

OTHER PROBLEM: Generally, a bank may be designated an "Other Problem" bank if net capital and reserves are nominal or a negative figure. However, the adequacy of net capital is not the only criterion for the Other Problem designation. There will be some banks whose net capital and reserves are positive figures but which, nevertheless, belong in this problem bank category because of excessive loan delinquencies, a rapid rate of asset deterioration, significant violations of law or regulations, and unusually low "adjusted" capital position (i.e., book capital and reserves less all assets classified Loss and 50 percent of all assets classified Doubtful), an undesirable liquidity posture, pronounced management deficiencies or other adverse factors. Generally speaking, management has been rated Unsatisfactory, with a rating of Fair or Satisfactory the exception.[17]

## 1.8 SUMMARY AND CONCLUSIONS

Problem and failed banks are not new banking phenomena. The historical record indicates that such institutions have existed since commercial banks were first established in the twelfth century. Moreover, except for periods of structural imbalance due to overbanking and severe economic depression, the major cause of problem and failed institutions, weak and/or dishonest bank managers and/or directors, basically has remained unchanged. The form of the weakness or dishonesty has varied, depending upon the shortcomings or deviousness of the managers and directors, but the driving force has not changed. The first U.S. bank failure in 1809 was due to ". . . a system of fraud beyond which the ingenuity and dishonesty of man cannot go." Since then, however, weak, disinterested, uninformed, and fraudulent bankers (of which there are very few) have been accepting Andrew Dexter's gauntlet. The next chapter of this book focuses upon the regulatory and supervisory environment in which the banking authorities try to minimize the financial difficulties created by the Andrew Dexters of the banking industry.

## NOTES

1. Chapter 6 of this book scrutinizes the collapse of Franklin National Bank of New York, the largest U.S. bank failure. The decline and fall of the Medici and Franklin banks had several similar characteristics.

2. This section paraphrases Hammond's account of the Exchange Bank's demise; quotes are from Hammond (1957), pp. 172–177.

3. The average size of failed state-member banks derived from Upham and Lamke (1934), Table 7, p. 250, was: $2,471,000 (1921–1933), $562,000 (1921–1929), and $4,133,000 (1930–1933). For comparative purposes, see Table 1.2.

4. Figures in this paragraph and the previous one are derived from Upham and Lamke (1934), Table 3, p. 247.

5. The record of state-bank failures for this period is not as detailed. However, Bremer (1935), p. 38, contends that a similar situation regarding failures undoubtedly existed in the state banking systems.

6. For a detailed discussion of these changes, see National Industrial Conference Board (1932), pp. 72–110.

7. The REIT-commercial bank crisis of the early 1970s was characterized by a similar type of indirectness (see Chapter 8).

8. According to the National Industrial Conference Board (1932), "self-liquidating" referred to the proportion of loans and investments which arise ". . . out of producer's and merchant's transactions in goods and, because of those goods, is self-liquidating within a brief period . . ." (p. 78).

9. Readers who are not familiar with regression analysis may want to skip this paragraph. The data for this test are from Bremer (1935), Table 14, p. 55.

10. The causes of state bank failures were of a similar nature [see Bremer (1935), pp. 99–100].

11. According to Secrist (1938), the bank failures during the 1925–1932 period were the price paid for allowing "free" competition in banking.

12. For more detail, see Bremer (1935), pp. 18–19.

13. As of December 31, 1974, there were 168 noninsured banks of deposit (15 of which had 39 branches for a total of 207 offices) located in 27 states. The states and number of banks are: Colorado (61), New York (29), Illinois (15), Iowa (7), Texas (7), Massachusetts (5), Pennsylvania (5), Washington (5), Georgia (4), Maine (4), Minnesota (3), North Dakota (3), Missouri (2), Ohio (2), Oregon (2), Rhode Island (2), Tennessee (2), and one each in Arkansas, Connecticut, Florida, Indiana, Kansas, Kentucky, Michigan, New Hampshire, North Carolina, and Oklahoma. Unless otherwise noted, figures in this section are derived from FDIC *Annual Reports* (various issues).

14. Hill's study updated an article by Slocum (1973).

15. In addition to these general factors, Hill (1975), pp. 1–2, describes 41 specific acts that contributed to the insolvency of these 67 banks. The extreme end of the failure spectrum was characterized by a bank whose managers and/or directors were guilty of 21 internal and external manipulations.

16. Congressional oversight and recent hearings on problem and failed banks reinforce this interpretation.

17. This letter was dated February 5, 1976 (copies are available from FDIC's Office of Information). Regarding PPO banks (ones that could fail in the near future), the letter stated that no specific guidelines are used. See Wille (1976).

Chapter 2

# Protecting the "Safety and Soundness" of the Banking System: The Role of the Banking Authorities

## 2.1 INTRODUCTION

Addressing the 1974 American Bankers Association Convention in Honolulu, Hawaii, on October 21, 1974, Arthur F. Burns, Chairman of the Board of Governors of the Federal Reserve System, described the United States system of bank regulation as follows:

> ... [O]ur system of parallel and sometimes overlapping regulatory powers is indeed a jurisdictional tangle that boggles the mind. There is, however, a still more serious problem. The present regulatory system fosters what has sometimes been called "competition in laxity." Even viewed in the most favorable light, the present system is conducive to subtle competition among regulatory authorities, sometimes to relax constraints, sometimes to delay corrective measures.

When lecturing about the U.S. system of banking regulation, professors frequently begin by asking students to design a bank-regulatory framework. To date and to their credit, so the story goes, not one student has proposed the "jurisdictional-tangle-that-boggles-the-mind" system. Moreover, if a student does propose the current regulatory model, he or she is destined to flunk the course. Chairman Burns (1974), a former professor, states:

> ... I have no doubt that if we were setting out today to create a system of bank regulation where none existed before, we would arrive at something other than the present structure. Much of our present regulatory

21

## The Jurisdictional Tangle

FEDERAL RESERVE SYSTEM

50 STATE BANKING AGENCIES

NONMEMBER BANKS

COMPTROLLER OF THE CURRENCY

BHCs

MEMBER BANKS

NATIONAL BANKS

DUAL BANKING

FDIC

SEC

JURIS-DICTIONAL TANGLE PIPE & TOBACCO CO.

JAC 78

THIRD ILLUSTRATION

framework can be understood only by reference to historical developments in our country.

Two issues are intertwined here: (1) the jurisdictional tangle and (2) competition in laxity. While it is true that the current regulatory framework lacks a logical foundation and is unduly complicated (i.e., it is a "jurisdictional tangle"), the fact of the matter is that, since 1933, the structure has maintained the confidence of the banking public—the ultimate test of the "safety and soundness" of a banking system. This suggests that (to date at least) any "competition in laxity" has not been very harmful to the system. In contrast, there is no question that "competition in laxity" had a significant adverse effect on the stability of the banking system prior to 1933. For example, according to Bremer (1935):

> . . .[T]he evidence does not support the view often advanced in the past that divided jurisdiction has prompted healthy competition between the national and state systems, and has resulted in raising the standards of banking and the practice of management. The fact is that the competition for banks and resources has necessitated repeated relaxations of the banking laws [p. 95] . . . [which] . . . resulted in lowering the level of banking operations generally, and gradually undermined the soundness and safety of the banking system [p. 98].

In those days, the "competition in laxity" was blatant; today, Chairman Burns sees it as being "subtle" in the form of relaxed constraints and delayed corrective actions.

Although Burns (1974) did not give any examples of "subtle competition in laxity," several come to mind. Most notably was the competition (which at times was not very subtle) between the Federal Reserve and the Office of Comptroller of the Currency during the period November 16, 1961, to November 15, 1966, which marked the reign of James J. Saxon as Comptroller.[1] Comptroller Saxon believed that a little competition among the banking agencies would benefit the public in the long run. According to Hilkert (1964), the kernel of the controversy was whether or not bank supervision should have been substantially relaxed at that time. "Mr. Saxon seems to be saying it should, and the [Federal Reserve] System is saying that it shouldn't" (p. 4). Saxon's "liberal" attitude towards chartering, branching, and other banking activities was based upon the premise that macroeconomic stabilization policy was effective enough to permit freer competition in banking. Depending upon one's perspective, Saxon's five-year reign may have represented an era of "competition in laxity" or, according to Robertson (1968), a period in which ". . . bank regulation changed in many ways to fit the needs of the 20th century" (p. 158).

Regarding the "delayed-corrective-actions" aspect of "laxity in competition," the failures of USNB of San Diego and Franklin National Bank of New York are potential examples. In USNB's case, there was evidence that the integrity of the bank-examination process had been compromised (see Chapter 7), while, in Franklin's case, the Fed's subsidy and the length of time it took the FDIC to arrange a deposit assumption were suspect (see Chapter 6).

The purpose of this chapter is to look at the U.S. system of bank regulation. The "jurisdictional tangle" presently consists of fifty state banking agencies and three federal ones, the office of the Comptroller of the Currency, the Federal Reserve System, and the Federal Deposit Insurance Corporation. To unravel the "tangle," we begin first with a look at the concept of "dual banking."

## 2.2 DUAL BANKING: THE FOUNDATION OF THE "JURISDICTIONAL TANGLE"

Over the years, banking laws and traditions have established that the states and Federal government *together* shall be overseers of the public interest as it relates to banking.[2] Thus, the notion of states' rights in banking is not mere tokenism. Individual states have authority to grant charters, establish branching restrictions within their state boundaries, and examine and supervise state banks. This dichotomy between state and Federal regulation has been labeled as "dual banking," hence the term "dual-banking system." This term, however, is misleading, since it does not begin to suggest the "jurisdictional tangle" that results from tripartite Federal regulation.

In its most narrow sense, dual banking refers to the fact that a commercial bank may be chartered by either the Federal or state governments. Thereafter, banking institutions primarily are supervised by their respective chartering authorities. If this was the extent of the "jurisdictional tangle," the system would not be too complicated. However, on top of the dual-banking system, the Federal bureaucracy imposes its deposit-insurance and reserve-system structures.

The most common argument in favor of the dual-banking system has been that it fosters competition by providing bankers, with freedom of choice (or "meaningful" choice) regarding their regulatory authority. Supposedly, this safeguards against inequities in either chartering or regulation. Put another way, bankers are free to embrace the more "liberal" banking authority.

The Federal chartering agency for commercial banks is the Office of the Comptroller of the Currency. Federally chartered banks are referred to as "national" banks. National banks are required by law to become members of the Federal Reserve System and to obtain deposit insurance from the FDIC. To obtain this insurance, the Comptroller must certify to the FDIC that, among other things, the bank's future earnings prospects and the "convenience and needs" of the community have been considered and will be served.[3] In addition to being the chartering authority for national banks, the Comptroller's office is responsible for supervising and examining national banks and for approving all new branches and mergers in which the acquiring bank holds a national charter. Regarding would-be branching by national banks, state law prevails.

National banks may expand in a state only to the extent permitted by state law. As of year-end 1975, there were 4,744 national banks with 21,074 offices and total deposits of $450 billion, 58 percent of total deposits in all insured commercial banks.

The state chartering authorities for commercial banks are the banking agencies in each of the fifty states. State-chartered banks are referred to as "state" banks. State banks are *not* required to join the Federal Reserve System nor to obtain Federal deposit insurance. If a state bank joins the Reserve system, it must be insured by the FDIC. To obtain this insurance, the Fed certifies to the FDIC that the bank meets the deposit-insurance requirements. For state banks that choose not to join the Federal Reserve but wish to be federally insured, the FDIC conducts its own deposit-insurance investigations. As of December 31, 1975, there were 9,910 state-chartered banks, 8,595 (87 percent) of which were insured but not members of the Federal Reserve. These banks are referred to as "insured-nonmember" banks. Only 1,046 state banks (10 percent) were members of the Reserve system as of year-end 1975. These banks are referred to as "state-member" banks. The remaining 269 state banks (3 percent) were not associated in any way with the Federal banking bureaucracy. These banks are referred to as "noninsured" (commercial) banks. The number and deposits of all commercial banks as of December 31, 1975, are presented in Table 2.1.

State banking authorities are responsible for examining and supervising state banks and for approving all new branches and mergers in which the acquiring bank has a state charter. Federal banking au-

*Table 2.1*

Number and Deposits of U.S. Commercial Banks
(December 31, 1975)

| Type of Bank | Number of Banks | Number of Offices | Total Deposits ($ billions) |
|---|---|---|---|
| National | 4,744 | 21,074 | 450 |
| State-Member | 1,046 | 5,452 | 143 |
| Insured-Nonmember | 8,595 | 18,042 | 187 |
| Noninsured* | 269 | 348 | 12 |
| Total | 14,654 | 44,916 | 792 |

*Includes nondeposit trust companies.
*Source: Annual Report of the FDIC* (1975), Tables 101 and 104.

thorities, the Fed in the case of state-member banks and the FDIC in the case of insured nonmember banks, also are responsible for regulating their respective state banks. Thus, in terms of examination, supervision, branching, and mergers, Federal and state regulatory powers are parallel and sometimes overlapping and therefore result in some duplication of effort. On the positive side, the overlap does serve a checks-and-balances function. For example, regarding merger decisions, Federal authorities only render decisions if the state authority indicates its approval. However, since the antitrust statutes are Federal laws, Federal denials overrule state approvals. Regarding the examination of state banks, considerable duplication of effort does occur, even though some field or on-site examinations are conducted jointly. In the states of Georgia, Iowa, and Washington, the FDIC recently experimented with a "selective-withdrawal" program whereby it accepted the states' examination reports in lieu of its own on-site inspections. Although the experiment appears to have been successful, the program has not been adopted permanently and the FDIC, as a final check on the program, is going to return to examining banks in those states.

The "jurisdictional tangle" is still more intense since the regulation of holding companies and Edge Act corporations must be considered. These institutions primarily are regulated by the Federal Reserve System. However, some states also have laws relating to bank holding companies.

To summarize, it should be clear that the U.S. system of bank regulation is an extremely complex apparatus, one which has a multiplicity of substructures rather than a simple duality. Chairman Burns (1974) regards the "jurisdictional tangle" as ". . . the most serious obstacle to improving the regulation and supervision of banking . . ." (p. 267). Although simplistic beauty tends to be a highly regarded virtue, complexity is not necessarily a vice. This is especially true if the more complex system appears to work. Those who believe that the system of bank regulation has not worked well, especially recently, would like to see the system overhauled and streamlined. In contrast, those who think the system has performed relatively efficiently feel that only minor changes in the regulatory and supervisory functions (as opposed to structural ones) are needed. In 1976 legislative infighting, advocates of structural reform were defeated; they claim, however, that the war is not over.

## 2.3 THE GOAL OF BANK REGULATION AND SUPERVISION

According to Santayana, "Those who cannot remember the past are condemned to repeat it." Since the memory of the banking chaos of the 1930–1933 era should be with us for some time to come, we hope that its replication can be avoided. Today it is widely recognized that it is the task of macroeconomic stabilization policy (i.e., monetary and fiscal policy) to prevent severe economic depression. Thus, bank failures due to severe contractions in the money stock and bank credit are not the province of bank regulation and supervision.

The goal of bank regulation frequently has been stated in somewhat nebulous terminology as "maintaining the safety and soundness of the banking system" or "maintaining (depositors') confidence in the banking system." Since 1933, the implementation of the "safety-and-soundess" mandate has focused upon minimizing the number of bank failures. The objective has been achieved mainly by (1) constructing barriers to entry and (2) closely supervising the quality of banks' assets. The goal of bank regulation is not to prevent *all* bank failures. Moreover, the banking authorities recognize that banking is a risk-taking business. In fact, recent nondiscriminatory policies such as equal-credit opportunity and anti-redlining may encourage greater risk-taking in banking. That is, since it is illegal to deny credit solely on the basis of age, sex, marital status, race, color, or creed or to deliberately not make funds available to certain geographic areas, bankers, fearful of potential lawsuits, may adopt less restrictive lending policies and take on *greater expected risk.* However, as long as this greater expected risk is compensated for by *greater expected return,* risk-averse bankers (and regulators) should be satisfied. Finally, within this limited failure-prevention framework, the banking authorities have attempted to promote some banking competition by permitting banks, among other things: (1) to manage their liabilities, (2) to establish holding companies, and (3) to branch and merge relatively freely. Moreover, relaxing some banking regulations has been aimed more at promoting innovation and growth than "competing in laxity" (among the banking agencies).

To summarize, the goal of bank regulation has been one of limited failure prevention.[4] By restricting the number of banks and preventing existing banks from taking "excessive" risks, the banking agencies expect to maintain a safe-and-sound banking system and thereby preserve depositors' confidence in the system.

## 2.4 ACHIEVING THE GOAL OF FAILURE PREVENTION: IDENTIFICATION AND ENFORCEMENT TASKS

To achieve their goal of failure prevention, the banking authorities primarily (1) restrict entry into the industry and (2) monitor existing banks to see that they are operated in a "safe-and-sound" manner. Limited entry is maintained via the federal and state chartering laws which require, among other things, that prospective earnings and/or the "convenience and needs" of the community merit granting a charter. Since very few bank charters are granted without Federal deposit insurance, the deposit-insurance system provides a Federal check on the granting of state charters. In addition, since nationally chartered banks must join the Federal Reserve System and since member banks must be insured, the FDIC also acts as a check on the granting of national charters (see the section on "dual banking" presented above).

Since bank charters are not granted to persons deemed unqualified to run a bank, even if other factors would justify issuing one, restricted entry automatically tends to limit the number of failures that ordinarily would arise in the absence of such restraints. Restricted entry, however, is a double-edged sword which also tends to limit the exit of marginally efficient banks from the industry, ones that would not survive in a freer system. On balance, the U.S. Congress and the banking authorities have concluded that the benefits of restricted entry far outweigh the costs. Thus, regulated entry is one of the major weapons used by the banking authorities to prevent bank failures and maintain confidence in the banking system.

Once a bank is established, the banking authorities try to see that it is operated in a "safe-and-sound" manner (the problem-identification task). This task focuses upon identifying banks with undue or excessive risk exposure. To determine the riskiness of individual banks, detailed on-site bank examinations are conducted on a regular basis (i.e., about once a year). The purposes of a bank examination are:

1. To determine asset quality;
2. To determine the nature of liabilities;
3. To ascertain compliance with laws and regulations;
4. To evaluate controls, procedures, accounting practices, and insurance;
5. To evaluate management and its policies; and
6. To determine capital adequacy.[5]

In conjunction with constraints imposed by market forces (e.g., by uninsured depositors), by managers and directors, and by stockholders, supervisory judgments based upon the results of on-site bank inspections determine the appropriate degree of "safety and soundness" or risk for individual banks.

Bank examinations are the identification or diagnostic part of bank supervision. Once "poor" asset quality, "inadequate" capital, violations of laws and regulations, and other weaknesses have been uncovered, the banking authorities must try to correct these deficiencies (the enforcement task). In this area, the banking authorities have two basic enforcement powers. On the one hand, they employ moral suasion and threats of legal action to attempt to get bankers "voluntarily" to correct supervisory-perceived weaknesses. However, since bank managers and directors may differ with bank supervisors on the extent of a bank's financial difficulties or weaknesses, "jawboning" may not always be an effective enforcement weapon (although usually it is). In cases where more stringent enforcement powers are needed, the banking authorities may, among other things: (1) issue cease-and-desist orders to stop unsafe and unsound banking practices (Section 8(b) of the FDI Act); (2) remove or suspend bank officers and directors (Section 8(e) of the FDI Act); and/or (3) terminate deposit-insurance coverage (Section 8 (a) of the FDI Act).

To illustrate the "jawboning" aspect of supervisory enforcement, consider the following excerpt from a *Memorandum to File* (August 12, 1976) by an FDIC Regional Director regarding insider transactions at two banks dominated by the same two individuals.

> My goal is to cause to be removed from both banks all or a major portion of the insider related loans of [names deleted] and I am willing to participate in whatever enforcement action is necessary to achieve this. At the same time, I believe that we now have the best chance of achieving our goal by keeping [names deleted] as "alive" as possible and under rather heavy pressure. There is no doubt that they are very scared at the moment and I believe they will make every effort to move the major portion of the related loans. It is unlikely that they could make any more effort along that line even with a Cease-and-Desist Order hanging over them. In the meantime, both banks appear to be observing the resolution placed, at our suggestion, on the minutes of directors' meetings held earlier this year, to the effect that no further credit would be extended to [names deleted] or their interests.

To illustrate more extreme enforcement action, consider the FDIC's recent handling of the First State Bank and Trust Co., Rio Grande City, Texas.[6] In August 1975, the FDIC had evidence that the bank was in an unsafe-and-unsound condition primarily due to an excessive amount of loans to its controlling stockholder and persons associated with him. Accordingly, the FDIC initiated formal enforcement action against the bank. By April of 1976, the situation still had not been rectified and the FDIC and the bank agreed that if the bank did not correct the condition to the FDIC's satisfaction within ninety days, either the FDIC or the bank could terminate the deposit-insurance agreement without further proceedings. On subsequent examination, the FDIC determined that the unsafe-and-unsound condition still existed, and using the April agreement, it accepted the bank's voluntary termination of its insured status. On November 17, 1976, deposit-insurance coverage was terminated at the bank. The mandatory legal notification of noninsured status was made on November 5, 1976. On November 19, 1976, two days after deposit insurance was terminated, the bank failed. The closing of the bank was attributed, in part, to illiquidity caused by deposit withdrawals following the November 5 notification of intent to terminate insurance coverage. The deposits of the failed bank were assumed by the newly chartered First National Bank of Rio Grande City, which opened for business on November 29, 1976.

From 1936 until 1974, the FDIC initiated 224 actions to terminate the insured status of banks charged with unsafe-and-unsound banking practices or violations of laws and regulations.[7] Of these 224 cases, 220 of them have been closed as of December 31, 1974. The outcomes of these 220 cases are presented in Table 2.2.

Since termination of deposit insurance (or the mere threat of such action) supposedly is the most powerful weapon in the FDIC's enforcement arsenal, it is important to understand both how such proceedings are initiated and carried out and how effective is the weapon.

*Table 2.2*

Disposition of Closed Cases Under Section 8(a)
of the FDI Act, 1936 - 1974

| Disposition | Number | Percent |
|---|---|---|
| 1. Corrections Made | 95 | 43.3 |
| 2. Banks Absorbed or Succeeded by Other Banks* | 73 | 33.2 |
| 3. Banks Suspended Prior to Setting Date of Termination of Insured Status by FDIC | 37 | 16.8 |
| 4. Insurance Terminated, or Date for Termination Set** | 13 | 5.9 |
| 5. Formal Written Corrective Program Imposed and 8(a) Action Discontinued | 1 | 0.4 |
| 6. Cease-and-Desist Order Issued and 8(a) Action Discontinued | 1 | 0.4 |
| Total Cases Closed | 220 | 100.0 |

*Indicates that 64 of the 73 absorptions were with the financial aid of the FDIC.
**Indicates that nine of the thirteen banks suspended operations prior to or on the date of termination. Three of the banks continued in operation and one suspended operations four months after insurance was removed.
*Source: Annual Report of the FDIC* (1974), Table 8, p. 17.

Proceedings for termination of deposit insurance begin with an order from the FDIC for the bank to correct the specified unsafe or unsound practices or violations of laws and regulations within some designated time period. If the weaknesses are not corrected, then, following an administrative hearing at which the bank may respond to the FDIC's charges, the FDIC's Board of Directors may issue an order to terminate the bank's deposit insurance.[8] If a bank's insurance is removed, insured deposits at the time of termination continue to be insured for a period of two years. However, new deposits accepted after the termination date are not insured.

To determine the effectiveness of the termination-of-deposit-insurance weapon requires some standard for measuring "success." Using the relatively narrow standard of "corrections made" (see Table 2.2), the weapon has an effectiveness or success rating of 43.3 percent, based upon cases in which an actual termination order was issued. However, using a broader definition of success to include, not only "corrections made," but any disposition which eliminates the bank's weaknesses (even if it eliminates the bank), the effectiveness rate is 217 out of 220 or 98.6 percent. Alternatively, under this standard, an unsuccessful 8(a) action is one in which the bank continues to operate as an uninsured institution. As indicated in the notes to Table 2.2, only three banks out of 220 have remained in existence after their deposit insurance was removed, hence the effectiveness ratio of 217/220.

To summarize, the consequences of past 8(a) actions have been fairly clear: either the problem was corrected or the bank was driven out of existence.

Another component of the effectiveness of 8(a) action is the mere threat of such action. However, since the FDIC does not keep formal records of instances in which this type of leverage was employed, its impact cannot be measured. Given the apparent effectiveness of 8(a) action, the mere threat of such action probably is successful in achieving the desired regulatory response.

In addition to termination-of-deposit-insurance proceedings, the banking authorities have other enforcement powers that they may initiate against so-called problem banks.[9] First, cease-and-desist proceedings (Section 8(b) of the FDI Act) may be initiated to stop alleged violations or unsafe-and-unsound banking practices. Second, removal proceedings (Section 8(e) of the FDI Act) may be initiated against bank officers or directors who engage in unsafe-and-unsound banking practices or who violate laws, rules, regulations, or final cease-and-desist orders. And third, suspension proceedings (Section 8(g) of the FDI Act) may be initiated against officers, directors, or other managerial personnel if they are charged (in an information, indictment, or complaint issued by a

U.S. Attorney) with a felony involving dishonesty or a breach of trust. In such cases, the person is prohibited from participating in the affairs of the bank and suspended from his or her position. Although it is not mandatory, a person found guilty of the charges usually will be subject to removal proceedings. However, a verdict of not guilty or other disposition of the charges does not eliminate the possibility of removal or prohibition proceedings thereafter.

During 1974, the FDIC undertook the following enforcement actions against insured nonmember banks: (1) three 8(a) termination proceedings, (2) four 8(b) cease-and-desist proceedings, (3) one 8(e) removal proceeding, and (4) three 8(g) suspension proceedings.[10]

To summarize, the banking authorities strive to achieve their goal of failure prevention primarily by (1) restricting the number of charters that are granted and (2) closely regulating and supervising existing institutions. Until very recently, the identification of banking problems was solely the province of the traditional on-site bank examination (see Chapter 3). Today, however, the banking authorities are complementing that process with "early-warning" or "surveillance" systems based upon detailed analyses of a bank's balance-sheet and income-expense data (see Chapter 4). The purpose of these systems is to identify banks whose prior financial reports suggest the possibility of a problem situation.

## 2.5 THE ROLE OF DEPOSIT INSURANCE IN THE BANKING SYSTEM

The so-called deposit-guaranty section of the Glass bill of May 1933 provided for the establishment of a Federal deposit insurance corporation. On June 16, 1934, the Federal Deposit Insurance Act was passed and later amended by the Banking Act of 1935. The purpose of the FDIC was to provide for the speedy liquidation of failed banks and to protect the deposits of small savers against losses due to bank failures.[11] Originally, a "small" saver was one with a deposit equal to or less than $2,500; today, $40,000 is the definition of "small." Obviously, if a bank does not fail, its depositors do not incur losses. Thus, from the beginning, failure prevention was one of the FDIC's major goals. As explained in the previous section, regulation and supervision are the means for achieving this goal. Once a bank fails (i.e., is declared insolvent by its chartering agency), the FDIC usually functions as its receiver or liquidator. (The FDIC receivership appointment is a statutory requirement for all national banks but optional for state banks.) To protect the depositors of failed insured banks the FDIC usually arranges either a deposit payoff or a deposit assumption. A deposit payoff simply involves paying off *insured* deposits in a bank that is closed and being liquidated; a deposit assumption involves the absorption (with the FDIC's financial assistance) of a failed bank's *total* deposits by a viable insured bank. The purpose of this section is to look at the important role that deposit insurance plays in the U.S. banking system.[12]

One of the most important functions of deposit insurance is to maintain depositors' confidence in both the money supply and the banking system. The money supply provides a means of payment (circulating currency and demand deposits or checking accounts) for economic transactions while the banking system provides a multitude of financial services including administration of the payments mechanism. Confidence in the monetary mechanism and financial institutions is vital for a healthy economy. Deposit insurance plays an important part in maintaining that confidence.

Macroeconomic stabilization policy and deposit insurance have been two of the most important structural innovations in the U.S. economy since the Great Depression. Recently, however, stabilization economists met their Waterloo at the "battle of stagflation." According to the Phillips-curve trade-off, galloping inflation, racing at a double-digit pace, would be collared by the reins of unemployment and put out to pasture in the fields of recession. However, when the horse never broke stride as it jumped the unemployment hurdle, the jockey economist, wearing Keynesian colors, was stunned and thrown off. This defeat was a psychologically devastating one, especially for members of the business community who perhaps missed the question mark in Samuelson's (1970) section heading "Requiem for the Business Cycle?" As a result, businessmen's expectations and confidence in macroeconomic stabilization policy were shattered. In fact, much of the sluggishness associated with the recovery from the 1974 recession has been attributed to businessmen's lack of confidence in the economy and more specifically [as Chairman Burns has argued] to fears of inflation.

At the same time (1974–1976), the banking system was having its own Waterloo. The frequency and size of bank failures had increased; so-called problem banks were making news headlines; and the REIT-commercial bank fiasco caught some of the largest banks in an embarrassing position (i.e., with their financial pants down around their ankles). As a result of these difficulties and others, bankers and the banking authorities recognized that it was time to retrench. Bank of America, the nation's largest bank, set the tone when it publicly announced that it was moving to increase its liquidity. In addition, on August 19, 1976, the Federal Reserve Board reinforced its 1976 "go-slow" signal (with respect to bank-holding-company expansion) when it dramatically announced that since Bankers Trust Co., the nation's seventh largest bank, was "experiencing financial difficulties," the expansion proposal from its parent company was being denied.

Throughout this period of banking difficulties (1974–1976), it generally was recognized that the FDIC was the banking agency cast in the least unfavorable light. The Office of the Comptroller of the Currency and its chief, James E. Smith, received the most adverse publicity and pressure from the Senate and House banking committees. Smith eventually resigned as Comptroller. Over at the Fed, Congress, Ralph Nader, and others were inquiring about such things as (1) the subsidy to Franklin National Bank of New York prior to its failure; (2) the rapid expansion of the holding-company movement; (3) the so-called Fed's secrecy; (4) "problem-bank" lists; (5) the workings of monetary policy and, of course, (6) Wright Patman's favorite, auditing the Fed. At the FDIC, the mood was one of cautious optimism. Chairman Wille was making relatively impressive appearances before the Congressional committees and the FDIC had not been embarrassed yet. In fact, Chairman Wille even made a few offensive moves. For example, when Congress was clamoring for the right to see the agencies' so-called problem-bank lists, he released some detailed but general information regarding the FDIC's problem-bank list. While this information was not what Congress really wanted (i.e., they wanted the names of individual banks on the list), it did silence some of their thunder.

During this turbulent period of economic and banking difficulties, if the public's confidence in the economic and banking systems had been less strong, serious financial difficulties might have developed. Fortunately, this confidence hardly was shaken. Let us now examine some of the aspects of the deposit-insurance system which are a major factor in the public's high confidence. We begin with the FDIC methods of protecting depositors.

## 2.6 DEPOSIT ASSUMPTIONS VERSUS DEPOSIT PAYOFFS

The FDIC employs two principal methods to protect depositors in failed insured banks (1) deposit payoffs and (2) deposit assumptions. In a deposit-payoff case, the FDIC directly reimburses or pays off *insured* depositors; in a deposit-assumption case, the FDIC financially assists in the absorption or assumption of the failed bank by another insured bank.[13] Based upon recent FDIC experience, payments to insured depositors usually have begun within five to seven days after a bank's closing. In an assumption transaction *all* the deposits of the failed bank (including the uninsured ones) are absorbed by the assuming bank, that is, a deposit assumption provides 100 percent deposit insurance. Thus, in a deposit assumption, uninsured depositors receive the same protection as insured depositors. (A deposit assumption is not costless to depositors, however, since established bank-customer relationships are severed.) In contrast, in a payoff, uninsured depositors do incur losses. First, they *may* lose part of their deposit principal; however, since the FDIC has a deposit-recovery rate of 99.5 percent, such losses usually are small. Unfortunately, such recoveries are not instantaneous. For example, as of year-end 1974, the FDIC still was actively involved in the liquidation of twenty-five deposit-payoff banks with estimated additional recoveries of approximately $32 million, with the earliest liquidation dating back to 1964. In effect, uninsured depositors lose interest payments on their outstanding uninsured deposits for the length of the recovery period. In addition, without access to their funds, alternative investment opportunities are lost. Thus, when a failed bank is paid off instead of being absorbed by another bank, uninsured depositors are discriminated against vis-à-vis insured depositors and, most importantly, they incur financial losses.[14] In addition, since a deposit payoff means the disruption of banking services and relationships plus the inconvenience and cost of establishing new services and relationships, even insured depositors would prefer (in most cases) an assumption to a payoff. One exception that comes to mind regards possible adverse affects from the future exercise of the assuming bank's increased monopoly power, in which case insured depositors would prefer a payoff to an assumption.

From the depositors' point of view, a deposit assumption clearly is preferred to a deposit payoff. However, the FDIC is bound by law to select either a payoff or an assumption on the basis of minimum expected cost or risk to the deposit-insurance fund. The FDIC's Annual Report (1974), p. 3, states:

> Whenever, in the judgment of its Board of Directors, the Corporation's risk or losses will thereby be reduced, the Corporation is authorized to assist financially in the absorption of an insured bank in financial difficulty by another insured bank.

This statement reflects the FDIC's interpretation of Section 13(e) of the Federal Deposit Insurance Act (i.e., ". . . reduce the risk or avert a threatened loss to the Corporation . . ."). In making the decision between a payoff or an assumption, an important FDIC policy consideration has been not to contribute more cash towards an assumption than would be required to pay all insured depositors up to the legal limit (currently $40,000).

In arranging a deposit assumption, the FDIC attempts to establish a uniform basis for competitive bidding by more than one bank. Since the FDIC, as receiver of a closed bank, has a fiduciary obligation to the owners and creditors of the failed bank to realize the maximum value for the bank's business, a competitive bidding process is desirable. However, in some cases, it may be impossible to find enough eligible or willing banks to ensure such competition. It is important to distinguish between the eligibility screen and the willingness factor. The willingness of banks to enter the bidding process will be a function of the quality of the failing bank's assets; the size of the failing bank relative to the size of the potential acquiring banks; and the viability and availability of resources of the potential acquiring banks. In contrast, the eligibility screen mainly will depend upon state laws regarding branching and holding companies; monopoly-power and antitrust considerations; and the viability of the potential acquiring banks. The sifting of the eligibility screen was dramatically illustrated in the case of the Franklin National Bank of New York (see Chapter 6). First, banks outside the State of New York were not eligible, because of restrictions regarding interstate branching and, second, many of the banks within the state would have been unacceptable to the Justice Department because of the anticompetitive effects of such an acquisition.

To summarize, the number of realistic deposit-assumption candidates may not be very large, especially in cases when the failing bank is quite large (e.g., Franklin) or the quality of the failing bank's assets is very poor (e.g., Sharpstown State Bank, Texas). When a small- or medium-sized bank has very poor asset quality, the assumption risks and costs are quite high and the FDIC usually pays off such a bank. It is highly unlikely, however, that a very large bank would have such poor asset quality so as to create a deposit-payoff condition (i.e., high deposit-assumption risks and costs). Finally, the possibility of a trade-off in applying the eligibility screen could arise, especially in the case of a billion-dollar bank. For example, rather than force the FDIC to pay off a very large bank, the antitrust or state branching laws might be bent a little.

Banks interested in acquiring a failed bank submit sealed bids to the FDIC. Prior to bidding, the potential acquiring banks will be informed by the FDIC about the dollar amount of "clean" assets (i.e., low default-risk assets) they will be expected to purchase from the failed bank's asset portfolio; whether or not the FDIC will indemnify the bank against losses that result because of the assumption; and other aspects of the agreement. Assuming that all the bidding banks are "eligible," the FDIC accepts the highest bid.

Since most failed banks have certain "bad" assets in their portfolios, which potential acquiring banks naturally are not interested in assuming, almost all deposit assumptions have been arranged with the financial assistance of the FDIC.[15] In general, the amount of FDIC financial assistance (FA) equals the assumed liabilities (AL) minus the "clean" assets (CA) minus the purchase premium (PP). That is,

$$FA = AL - CA - PP. \tag{2.1}$$

Holding AL constant, the amount of financial assistance varies directly with the "cleanliness" of the bank's assets and the size of the purchase premium. Using DP to denote the amount of cash requiced to pay off all insured depositors, decision rules for choosing between a payoff and an assumption can be expressed as follows:

$$\text{If } FA > DP, \text{ pay off the bank.} \tag{2.2}$$

$$\text{If } FA \leq DP, \text{ arrange an assumption.} \tag{2.3}$$

Since a deposit assumption is less costly and disruptive to *both* depositors and the FDIC, rule (2.3) favors a deposit assumption even if FA = DP.[16]

It is interesting to note how the financial community supposedly perceives decision rule (2.2). According to the "market place," the payoff rule (2.2) does not apply to "large" banks, where large presumably means billion-dollar failures such as Franklin and USNB. Since 9 of the 10 largest bank failures (see Table 1.6) have been absorbed by other banks and since only four of the last twenty-nine bank failures have been payoffs (the largest of these four had total deposits of $23.9 million), perhaps there is some substance to this conjecture. However, despite these facts, the FDIC has not stated that it never will pay off a "large" failed bank.

The chances of the FDIC's paying off a large bank can be seen more clearly by combining equations (2.1) and (2.2) to yield

$$FA = AL - CA - PP > DP. \tag{2.4}$$

The chances of FA being greater than DP, other things equal, are greater the smaller that CA and/or PP are. Therefore, for cases in which CA and/or PP are relatively small, a deposit payoff is more likely. When are CA and/or PP likely to be small? In cases where fraud or misconduct have been pervasive, three related factors are likely to exist. First, the dollar amount of "dirty" assets is likely to be large. Second, potential acquiring banks are likely to be less interested in assuming the failed bank because of the risks involved. And third, as stated in the FDIC's 1974 *Annual Report,* p. 3,

> . . . the FDIC may decide that the indemnities that would have to be given to the assuming bank as protection against unknown or undetermined liabilities of the failing bank involve too much risk to the Corporation, even allowing for the premium which the assuming bank would pay for the sound assets and the liabilities it assumes.

The first point indicates that CA is likely to be small; the second that PP is likely to be small or perhaps zero; and the third that the FDIC explicitly considers indemnity costs (which can be treated as an increase in AL or a decrease in PP, either way these costs increase FA relative to DP). Since the chances of fraud or misconduct being pervasive at a "large" bank are relatively small, it is *unlikely* that the FDIC would ever be faced with a deposit payoff under these circumstances. This is different, however, from stating that the FDIC *never* will pay off a "large" bank.

In addition to fraud-type cases, the FDIC may encounter circumstances in which, because of size or legal (e.g., branching, holding company, antitrust, etc.) restrictions, the *effective* purchase premium (PP) is zero. In other words, there are simply no *eligible* buyers for the failed bank. In such cases, the FDIC has three alternatives: (1) to pay off the failing bank; (2) to appeal to Congress for statutory exemption to handle the case; or (3) to provide financial assistance to keep the bank from failing (this alternative which has not yet been mentioned is discussed below).

The present FDIC statutory requirement of minimizing costs to the deposit-insurance fund makes the choice between a payoff or an assumption a fairly mechanical although complex process. Horovitz (1975) has argued that this process is particularly inappropriate for handling the failures of large banks because of the broader social issues involved (e.g., the possibility of financial panic, the loss to uninsured deposits, etc.).[17]

In addition to the payoff or assumption options, the FDIC may either provide financial assistance to a failing bank or establish a Deposit Insurance National Bank (DINB). Under Section 13(c) of the FDI Act, the FDIC can financially assist an insured bank to remain in operation if it can establish that (1) but for the assistance, the bank is in danger of closing *and* (2) the bank is essential in providing adequate banking service to the community. The key to meeting the statutory test is, of course, the second requirement, since enough bail-out money can prolong any ailing bank's life (e.g., Franklin).[18] As of December 31, 1974, the FDIC has used 13(c) action on only three occasions. The first was in 1971 to assist a small minority-owned bank, Unity Bank in Roxbury, Massachusetts. In 1972 (and again in 1976), Bank of the Commonwealth of Detroit was given financial assistance. And in 1974, American Bank and Trust of Orangeburg, S.C. (a one-bank town) was provided with a short-term loan to keep it afloat until a deposit assumption could be arranged. While the Unity and AB&T cases clearly appeared to meet the "banking-service" test, other factors such as local banking structure, number of banking offices in ghetto areas, and "confidence" in the banking system were considered in the Commonwealth case. The FDIC's "liberal" interpretation of Section 13(c) in the Commonwealth case could lead other bankers to expect similar treatment when their banks are experiencing financial difficulties.

A fourth alternative available to protect depositors is for the FDIC to organize (charter) and operate a Deposit Insurance National Bank (DINB) to take care of the emergency banking needs of a community (see Section 11 of the FDI Act). A DINB, which provides only limited banking services, is permitted to operate for only two years before it must be closed or taken over by another bank or by new owners. It is designed to bridge the gap between the closed bank and what is hoped to be a new bank established and capitalized by the local community. The FDIC disposes of a DINB either by offering capital stock in the bank for sale or by transferring its business to an insured bank within the community. Former stockholders of the failed bank have their first opportunity to purchase such stock.

From 1935 to 1976 the FDIC has organized and operated only five DINB's. These were at Bradford, Pa. (1935), at Dell City, Texas and Newport News, Va. (both in 1964), and at Kansas City and St. Thomas, Virgin Islands (both in 1975). The DINB in Kansas City replaced the Swope Parkway National Bank, a ($9.4 million deposit) minority-owned institution. On December 18, 1976, the FDIC transferred the remaining business of this DINB to Laurel Bank of Kansas City, since there was not enough interest in the community to establish a new bank. As of this writing, the FDIC is working with interested groups in the Virgin Islands regarding the disposition of that DINB.

Because of limited FDIC resources, a DINB only is practical in the case of a relatively small bank. In addition, from a practical standpoint a prospective DINB must be in a very weak financial condition and not be attractive or legally obtainable by another bank.

## 2.7 THE SIZE OF THE DEPOSIT-INSURANCE FUND

The banking difficulties of the 1970s have caused many people to worry about the adequacy of the FDIC's deposit-insurance fund. As of December 31, 1974, the insurance fund ($6,124 million) was only 0.73 percent of total deposits ($833 billion) and only 1.18 percent of insured deposits ($530 billion). With such low coverage ratios, the nominal figures do appear to be inadequate. However, the nominal figures are seriously misleading for a number of reasons. First, as any insurance business, the FDIC depends on the law of large numbers to smooth out the number of failures that are likely to occur in any one period. Second, it is the task of macroeconomic stabilization policy to prevent what Gibson (1972) calls "depression" failures (i.e., widespread failures due to a sharp economic downturn). Just as homeowners insurance would not be adequate to protect homeowners in the event of a nationwide disaster, the deposit-insurance fund cannot protect depositors from widespread "depression" failures. The job of the deposit-insurance fund is to protect the public from nondepression or "normal" bank failures. So the relevant question is whether or not the fund is adequate enough to protect depositors from individual bank failures or smaller disasters short of widespread depression failures. Two points are important here. First, even though a bank may fail, the value of its assets is never zero or anywhere near that value. Failed banks always have a substantial amount of "clean" assets that can be liquidated or assumed by another bank. Thus, the FDIC disbursement required to protect depositors usually is substantially less than the face value of the bank's assets. And second, the U.S. Treasury is committed to supply the FDIC with "hurricane" money in the event of a disaster that would challenge the deposit-insurance fund. On balance, the FDIC deposit-insurance fund seems adequate for handling "normal" bank failures.

## 2.8 SUMMARY AND CONCLUSIONS

The role of the banking authorities in protecting the "safety and soundness" of the banking system focuses upon the goal of failure prevention. By restricting entry into the industry and examining the performance and operations of existing banks, the banking authorities have been able to maintain a relatively stable banking environment over the past forty-three years. Given the complexity of the "jurisdictional tangle" that characterizes the U.S. banking system, this could be viewed as a remarkable accomplishment.

## NOTES

1. See Robertson (1968), pp. 159–162, for a discussion of this controversy between Saxon and the Fed.

2. The evolution of the present regulatory framework is best understood from historical perspective, see Hammond (1957) or Robertson (1968).

3. The factors to be considered in the certification are listed in Section 6 of the FDI Act.

4. For a recent statement of the FDIC's objectives of bank regulation, see Barnett (May 3, 1976).

5. Bank Examiners' Orientation Course, FDIC (1973), (mimeographed notes). The bank-examination process is reviewed in detail in Chapter 3.

6. See *FDIC New Release,* PR-99-76 (November 28, 1976). Available from the FDIC's Office of Information, Washington, D.C., 20429.

7. Such action is authorized under Section 8(a) of the Federal Deposit Insurance Act. Prior to 1936, no termination-of-deposit-insurance proceedings were initiated.

8. The FDIC's Board of Directors has three members, the Chairman of the FDIC, the Director of the FDIC, and the Comptroller of the Currency.

9. These actions are initiated by the bank's respective regulatory agency (see Section 2.2 above). Termination of deposit insurance, however, only can be done by the FDIC.

10. *Annual Report of the FDIC* (1974), pp. 14–18.

11. Although the government has protected the small saver from losses due to bank failures, it has done little to protect those savings from being eroded by inflation, see Kane (1970).

12. This section looks mainly at how the deposit-insurance system works and its role in the banking system. See Mayer (1965), Gibson (1972), Horovitz (1975), and Leff (1976) for evaluations and proposed reforms.

13. When a very large bank fails, the assumption could be divided among a number of banks. For example, in the case of Franklin National Bank of New York (see Chapter 6), the FDIC considered the possibility of a multi-bank absorption. The final arrangement, however, was a one-bank assumption.

14. In a payoff, insured depositors also incur financial losses because of the lag between failure and payoff (usually five to seven days). However, these losses are relatively small compared to those incurred by uninsured depositors and therefore are ignored.

15. From 1934 to 1976, the FDIC has arranged 232 deposit assumptions; only three of them have been without the Corporation's financial assistance. The largest of the three banks, which also was the most recent one (1962), had only $3 million in deposits. See *Annual Report of the FDIC*, (1963), p. 42 and (1976), p. 279.

16. Since an assumption saves the FDIC the administrative cost of actually paying off insured depositors, an absorption is, other things equal, less costly than a payoff to the FDIC. The administrative expenses, which in a large failed bank are quite substantial, involve such things as verifying deposits and offsetting assets, writing checks, and making the payoffs.

17. On a broader basis. Horovitz (1975) argues that the present regulatory structure and set of laws and procedures are not optimal for handling large-bank failures.

18. The bail-out in Franklin's case was, of course, provided by the Fed's discount window and not by FDIC 13(c) action, see Chapter 6.

Chapter 3

# The Bank-Examination Process: The Importance of Bank Capital and Loan Evaluations in Identifying "Problem Banks"

Ode to Bank Capital

Oh bank capital, oh bank capital.
Our regulators' stricken hero.

Please don't, please don't,
Please don't go to zero.

## 3.1 INTRODUCTION

During October of 1977, Citicorp, the parent holding company of Citibank (the second largest U.S. bank), announced it would repurchase on the open market three million of its 128 million in outstanding common shares, less than 2 percent of its total dollar capital. By January 19, 1978, the repurchase plan was completed. Since Citicorp shares were trading in the low 20s over this period, (the 1977 high was 33½), the repurchases cost roughly $65 million, approximately ten weeks of the corporation's earnings. Citicorp's rationale for the repurchase scheme was to enhance its "... ability to access capital markets in the future." That is, repurchases decrease the number of shares outstanding, thereby increasing earnings per share and reducing *total* dividend costs. Other things being equal, the lower total cash dividends will over time gradually replenish the reduced common stock via increased transfers of net income to individual profits. In addition, Citicorp is counting on debt conversion, exercise of stock options, and a projected 10–15 percent annual earnings growth to augument its capital base.

In a letter dated December 16, 1977, the Comptroller of the Currency, John G. Heimann, criticized Citicorp for shrinking its capital base. Heimann wrote, "Since one of the major functions of equity capital is to provide a cushion against unforeseen occurrences, any reduction in equity capital, be it of the bank or its inseparable partner—the holding company—is of concern to me." In addition, Heimann expressed concern about (1) the *timing* of the reduction; (2) the fact that Citicorp ". . . does not appear to be overcapitalized"; and (3) Citicorp's earnings projections (". . . it is always possible (they) will not be realized.") From the *regulator*'s point of view, the first and third points appear to be appropriate criticisms; however, the second one is shrouded in the mysterious concept of capital adequacy. At present, none of the banking agencies

Ode to Bank Capital

FOURTH ILLUSTRATION

have the *direct* authority to prevent banks from reducing their equity capital; they must be content to jawbone, i.e., *F*orever *D*emanding *I*ncreasing *C*apital (FDIC). Oh bank capital, our regulators' stricken hero.

From Citicorp's vantage point, it was simply taking advantage of the depressed equity market. Moreover, the repurchase was only a small percentage of its total capital base. The plan made economic sense and basically was a sound managerial decision. All rational traders try to buy at the lowest possible price and to sell at the highest.

Both the Comptroller and Citicorp have valid arguments in this controversy, which can be traced to the regulatory focus upon bank capital as the major indicator of a bank's risk exposure. (The impact of Congressional oversight upon the banking authorities' capital-adequacy policies must not be overlooked.) Will Citibank now be classified as a "problem bank"? What is a problem bank and how are a bank's financial difficulties uncovered? What role does bank capital play in the problem-identification process? These are some of the questions addressed in this chapter.

The bank-examination process is the primary supervisory technique for identifying banks with financial difficulties. Bank examinations focus primarily on the quality of a bank's loan portfolio relative to its capital. With respect to bank capital, loan evaluations, and problem banks, this chapter contrasts banking authorities' words against their deeds. The banking agencies recognize (in words at least) that identifying banks experiencing financial difficulty is a multidimensional problem. However, it appears that, in practice, de facto differentiation between "problem" and "nonproblem" banks depends primarily on a bank's "net capital ratio." This produces a working defintiion of a problem bank as one with a large volume of "substandard" loans relative to its capital and reserves. Still, even this unsubtle definition identifies failing banks in advance of their death throes and allows authorities to help to rescue some of them.

We develop these themes in seven sections. The first section further explains the FDIC's concept of a problem bank (see also Section 1.7 of Chapter 1). In the next section, we clarify the roles played by bank capital and loan evaluations in the bank-examination process. Alternative weighted capital ratios used in identifying "problem banks" (and a new probability-based ratio) are developed in the third section. In the fourth section, "descriptive" discriminant-analysis models (as opposed to "predictive" ones) establish that the FDIC's "net capital ratio" is as a matter of practice the most important variable separating "problem banks" from "nonproblem banks." The effectiveness of NCR in anticipating bank failures is analyzed in the fifth section, while the sixth section looks at how the state of the economy affects the incidence of problem banks. The chapter ends with a summary-and-conclusions section.

## 3.2 WHAT IS A PROBLEM BANK?

As indicated in Chapter 2, Federal banking agencies have interpreted their "safety-and-soundness" mandate as assigning them the task of failure prevention. By identifying banks with the highest failure risks as so-called problem banks, Federal banking agencies hope to achieve this goal. The FDIC's Division of Bank Supervision identifies three classes of problem banks, separated according to examiners' perceptions of the bank's failure (or insolvency) risk. The three classes are:[1]

1. Serious Problem—Potential Payoff (PPO): An advanced, serious problem bank presenting at least a 50 percent chance of requiring FDIC financial assistance in the near future.
2. Serious Problem (SP): A banking situation that threatens ultimately to involve the FDIC in a financial outlay unless drastic changes occur.
3. Other Problem (OP): A banking situation involving a significant weakness with a lesser degree of vulnerability than (1) or (2) and calling for aggressive supervision, and more than ordinary concern by the FDIC.

The FDIC's problem-bank list includes all banks assigned to any of these three risk classes. Informational input for determining whether or not a bank should be classified as a problem institution is collected via on-site bank inspections.[2] These examinations determine, among other things, whether a bank has violated laws or regulations; engaged in unsafe-and-unsound banking practices; or neglected the qualitative aspects of its loan portfolio. While many distressed banks show problems on several dimensions, the most common problem description, based upon an analysis of a January 1973 FDIC problem-bank list [see Sinkey and Walker (1975)], was "poor asset condition due to present and/or past management." For example, of the 318 problem areas described for the 210 banks on the list, poor asset condition was mentioned 206 times (64.8 percent). Poor asset condition (as shown below) basically means that a bank has a large volume of "substandard" loans relative to its capital and reserves. The second most common problem description was "prior and/or present self-serving management," which was mentioned 69 times (21.7 percent).

Since the banking reforms of the 1930s, even in the worst years both problem banks and failed banks represent relatively small percentages of the population of insured commercial banks. To use Benston's (1973) analogy, they represent only the tip of the iceberg. Moreover, the percentage of problem banks that eventually collapse has been small. Between the years 1959 and 1973, only 66 insured commercial banks failed.

In contrast, over this same period, hundreds of banks passed onto the FDIC's problem-bank list and lived to tell about it. Of the 66 bank closings during this period, 38 banks had been identified as problems before they failed; the remaining 28 banks failed without prior listing because of such concealed irregularities as embezzlement, fraud, or misapplication of funds.

Financial difficulties identified in so-called problem banks mainly reflect "poor asset condition," which usually can be attributed to weak or self-serving managers and/or directors. Moreover, except for "depression" failures, most bank failures have shown similar characteristics. However, fraudulent-type behavior has been more prevalent in failed banks than in so-called problem banks. Irregularities such as fraud, embezzlement, or misapplication of funds tend to be deliberately masked and therefore more difficult for bank examiners to uncover.[3] However, once such irregularities have been uncovered, they frequently have been so pervasive that failure was iminent and immediate. On balance, dishonest managerial behavior has not been as apparent in problem banks as it has been in failed banks.

To further clarify the concepts of a problem bank and a problem-bank list, let us examine the composition of the FDIC's December 31, 1975, problem-bank list. This list, which is maintained with the cooperation of the Comptroller of the Currency and the Board of Governors of the Federal Reserve System, included 347 commercial banks with total deposits of $20.4 billion. The insured deposits of these 347 banks were estimated to be $9.9 billion or 48.5 percent of their total deposits, an aggregate loss exposure of about $3.5 billion more than the deposit-insurance fund (as of June 30, 1975). Sixty-nine of the 347 banks (19.9 percent) were members of the Federal Reserve System (52 of the 69 were national banks). These 69 banks, however, accounted for 65 percent of total problem-bank deposits and for 45 percent of estimated insured problem-bank deposits.

According to degree of problem status (see Table 3.1) the list consisted of 27 PPO banks (7.7 percent), 88 SP banks (25.4 percent), and 232 OP banks (66.9 percent). The average OP bank had total deposits of $65 million with $28 million (43.1 percent) estimated to be insured. The average SP bank had total deposits of $54 million with $33 million (61.1 percent) estimated to be insured. And, finally, the average PPO bank had total deposits of $20 million with $15 million (75 percent) estimated to be insured. From these data, it is clear that the "riskiest" banks on the FDIC's problem list tend to be the smallest ones. More specifically, if all 27 PPO banks were to fail at once, insured depositors would require about $405 million for deposit payoffs, most of which, because of the "clean" assets in the failed banks, would be recouped via the liquidation

*Table 3.1*

Problem Banks: Risk Classifications and Deposits
(December 31, 1975)

| Risk Class | Number of Banks | Average Total Deposits ($millions) | Average Estimated Insured Deposits ($millions) |
|---|---|---|---|
| PPO | 27 | 20 | 15 |
| SP | 88 | 54 | 33 |
| OP | 232 | 65 | 28 |
| Total/Average | 347 | 59 | 28 |

*Source:* Problem-Bank List, Division of Bank Supervision, FDIC.

process. Moreover, if in addition to the 27 PPO banks the 88 SP banks also failed, the claim on the insurance fund only would be $3.3 billion or about one-half of the total fund. And, of course, with "clean" assets and purchase premiums from deposit assumptions, the actual loss to the fund would be expected to be relatively small.

Since the holding-company form of organization now dominates the commercial-banking industry, it is important and interesting to look for holding-company affiliations at problem banks. [As of year-end 1974, bank holdings companies controlled 3,462 commercial banks with $509 billion in deposits, accounting for 68.1 percent of commercial bank deposits, see Holland (1975).] Only 53 of the 347 problem banks (15.3 percent) were affiliated with multibank holding companies. Sixteen of the 53 affiliated banks were lead banks of multibank holding companies, while 37 banks simply were affiliates of multibank holding companies. Lead banks accounted for 9.8 percent ($2 billion) of the total problem-bank deposits and 14.2 percent ($1.4 billion) of the estimated insured problem-bank deposits; the corresponding figures for affiliated nonlead banks were 7.6 percent ($1.6 billion) and 12.3 percent ($1.2 billion). The average lead problem bank had total deposits of $450 million (the median deposit size was only $84 million and the average with one multibillion-dollar outlier excluded was $134 million). Estimated insured deposits at the average lead problem bank were $87 million (the median was $57 million). The average affiliated nonlead problem bank had total deposits of $42 million and estimated insured deposits of $33 million. Finally, the average problem bank affiliated with a one-bank holding company had total deposits of $57 million and estimated insured deposits of $25 million. On balance, distressing banks affiliated with holding companies tend to be larger than nonaffiliated problem banks. This is not unusual, however, since in general holding-company banks are larger than nonholding-company banks.

To summarize, the typical problem bank tends to be relatively small (i.e., total deposits less than $50 million), nonaffiliated, and a non-member unit bank, a description which fits the typical U.S. commercial bank. While the banking authorities do not take the failure of such institutions lightly (13 of the 16 failures of 1976 fit this mold), the collapse of such institutions on a limited basis does not present a threat to the deposit-insurance fund or to the "safety and soundness" of the banking industry. In fact, since the majority of past failures have been traced to incompetent and/or dishonest bank managers and/or directors, such closings are a desirable form of survival of the fittest. Let us now turn to the process by which the banking authorities identify so-called problem banks.

## 3.3 BANK CAPITAL AND THE LOAN-EVALUATION PROCESS

The FDIC's *Manual of Examination Policies* (1976) states:

> The primary purpose of bank examination and supervision is the protection of creditors, particularly depositors. Some qualifications are necessary, but in general, the degree of protection afforded depositors is closely related to *the strength of a bank's capital position.* For this reason many important phases of bank examination procedure have as their purpose *the determination and analysis of a bank's capital* [Section D, p. 2, emphasis added].

Although not an accounting audit, a bank examination is a detailed analysis of a bank's "safety and soundness." Restating from Chapter 2, the purposes of a bank examination are:[4]

1. To determine asset quality,
2. To determine the nature of liabilities,
3. To ascertain compliance with laws and regulations,
4. To evaluate controls, procedures, accounting practices, and insurance,
5. To evaluate management and its policies, and
6. To determine capital adequacy.

Presently, examiners' reports are confidential and not available to the public, or even to Congress, which recently requested access to the examination reports of disclosed "problem banks."

Traditionally, bank regulators have employed various "capital-adequacy" ratios as first approximations of a bank's risk exposure. The FDIC's *Manual* states that capital ratios are ". . . a first approximation of a bank's ability to withstand adversity" (Section D, p. 2). The *Manual* further explains, "In the average bank, with average management, the capital-asset ratio or the risk-asset ratio, when they go beyond reasonable bounds, may be of importance in deciding that additional capital is necessary (ibid.). However, the *Manual* also states that ". . . [capital] ratios alone are not conclusive, and they must be integrated with all other pertinent factors" (ibid.).

Although the banking agencies' manuals refer to benchmark measures of capital adequacy and the incorporation of other factors, in practice, the most important indicator of a bank's "safety and soundness" is the one that flows from the loan-evaluation process, that is, the ratio that relates a bank's adversely classified assets to its capital and reserves. Regarding loan evaluations, the FDIC's *Manual* states:

> One of the most important aspects of the examination process is the evaluation of loans, for, in large measure, it is the quality of a bank's loans which determines the risk to depositors. To a great extent, conclusions regarding the condition of the bank, the quality of its management, and its service to the community are weighted heavily by the examination's findings with regard to loans [Section H, p. 1].

Adversely classified assets (mainly low-quality loans) are listed as "loss," "doubtful," or "substandard" based upon examiners' estimation of probable default. The classification of assets is an "art" and not a "science," that is, an examiner's judgment is the primary determining factor.[5] According to the FDIC's *Manual,* the primary measure of a loan's riskiness is ". . . the willingness and ability of a debtor to perform as agreed . . ." (Section H, p. 1). The *Manual* interprets this to mean that the borrower has the financial resources to meet his or her interest and principal payments as contracted.[6]

Regarding the identification of loan problems, the *Manual* (Section H, pp. 1–3) lists the following items as often basic to the development of loan troubles:

1. Poor selection of risks,
2. Overlending,
3. Failure to establish or enforce liquidation agreements,
4. Incomplete credit information,
5. Overemphasis on income,
6. Self-dealing,
7. Technical incompetence,
8. Lack of supervision, and
9. Competition.[7]

In addition to evaluating individual loans, examiners are responsible for appraising a bank's loan-portfolio management. That is, they are supposed to look for prudent management and administration of the overall loan portfolio, including the establishment of sound lending and collection policies.

The end result of an examiner's loan evaluations is a list of loans that is subject to criticism and/or comment in the report of examination.[8] Ranked according to increasing risk of nonpayment, adversely classified loans are assigned to "substandard," "doubtful," or "loss" categories.[9] Since (as we document subsequently) a bank's volume of "substandard" loans relative to its capital and reserves is the banking agencies' most important indicator of a problem situation, it is useful to analyze this category in some detail.[10]

Regarding substandard classifications, the FDIC's *Manual* states:

> The Substandard category includes loans which have *positive* and *well defined weaknesses* which jeopardize the orderly liquidation of the debt. Such loans are inadequately protected by the current sound worth and paying capacity of the obligor, or pledged collateral, if any. They are characterized by a degree of risk which poses the distinct possibility that the bank will likely sustain some loss if the deficiencies are not corrected [Section H, p. 5].

The important words in this passage are the last thirteen. They clearly indicate that only a portion of a bank's "substandard" loans are relevant for estimating its true risk exposure. Moreover, if bank examiners do their job (i.e., see to it that the loan deficiencies are corrected), the implication is that losses from the "substandard" category will be quite small. However, on the same page as the above passage, the FDIC's *Manual* also states:

> It will be apparent that there is a close relationship between the several classifications, and no classification category should be viewed as more important than another. The uncollectibility aspect of Doubtful and Loss classifications make their segregation of obvious importance. On the other hand, it is the function of the Substandard classification to indicate those loans which are unduly risky and which may be a future hazard to the bank's solvency. No bank can safely hold a large amount of low quality loans, even though they are not presently subject to either a Doubtful or Loss classification [Section H, p. 5].

This passage, which suggests a more conservative treatment of "substandard" loans, accurately describes the way the banking agencies treat such loans in determining their lists of "problem banks." If "substandard" loans were weighted probabilistically to account for the fact that not all of these loans eventually are charged off against a bank's capital, the banking agencies would have (in a theory at least) a more relevant measure.

## 3.4 ALTERNATIVE WEIGHTED CAPITAL RATIOS

The FDIC's Form 96 provides a statistical summary of a bank examiner's report. The information on this form is further condensed into a ratings vector that consists of two capital-adequacy ratios, an earnings ratio, and a managerial rating.[11]

### 1. The FDIC's Adjusted Capital Ratio

The adjusted capital ratio (ACR) is defined as:

$$ACR = [K + R + N - L - .5D]/A, \qquad (3.1)$$

where   K = total capital accounts,
          R = valuation reserves,
          N = nonbook sound banking values,
          L = "loss" classifications,
          A = quarterly average of gross assets for the calendar year, where gross assets are defined as total balance-sheet assets including reserves but excluding expense accounts and cash-shortage accounts.

Equation (1) compares a bank's 'loss" and 50 percent of its "doubtful" classifications to its capital and reserves (N is relatively small and can be ignored in this discussion).[12] Equation (3.1) assigns a *zero* weight to the "substandard" classification.

### 2. The FDIC's Net Capital Ratio

The net capital ratio (NCR) is defined as:

$$NCR = [K + R + N - L - D - S]/A, \qquad (3.2)$$

where  S = "substandard" classifications. In equation (3.2), all three adverse-classification categories are assigned a weight of *one,* that is, equation (3.2) relates a bank's total classified assets to its capital and reserves. Ignoring N, equation (3.2) can be written as:

$$NCR = [K + R - C]/A, \qquad (3.3)$$

where

$$C = L + D + S.$$

The FDIC's "justification" for its conservative treatment of the "substandard" category was noted above (see the second quote from Section H (p. 5) of the *Manual*). In our statistical analysis, NCR proves to be the most important discriminator between problem and nonproblem banks. This means that, in practice, a bank's volume of "substandard" assets relative to its capital and reserves is the most important factor in identifying a problem situation.

### 3. A Probability-Weighted Capital Ratio

Because of inappropriate and arbitrary weighting schemes, equations (3.1) and (3.2) either understate or overstate, respectively, a bank's risk exposure to adversely classified assets. The following probability-weighted capital ratio (WCR) theoretically is more appealing:

$$\text{WCR} = [K + R + N - \gamma_L L - \gamma_D D - \gamma_S S]/A, \qquad (3.4)$$

where the $\gamma$ coefficients are "prospective probabilities" $(1 \geq \gamma_L > \gamma_D > \gamma_S \geq 0)$. One way to estimate these "prospective probabilities" would be to examine historical charge-off rates for each of the classified-asset categories, That is,

$$\hat{\gamma}_L = L^*/L,$$
$$\hat{\gamma}_D = D^*/D, \text{ and} \qquad (3.5)$$
$$\hat{\gamma}_S = S^*/S.$$

The starred (*) variables indicate the dollar amount of the particular classified-asset category that actually was written off against bank capital; they are *ex post* measures. In contrast, the nonstarred variables (L, D, S) are examiners' *ex ante* assessments of loan quality. To estimate the $\gamma$ coefficients would involve an extensive and detailed follow-up of individual classified assets.[13] Moreover, since the coefficients may differ for banks of different size and for different stages of the business cycle, these factors (and other ones deemed to be relevant) should be controlled when estimating the $\gamma$ coefficients. Given the resources available to the banking agencies and the need for a more relevant measure of a bank's risk exposure, such a study would be a valuable addition to banking research.[14]

### 4. An illustration

Consider two banks identical in all respects except name and composition of their classified assets. Both banks have a billion dollars in assets (and say $600 million in loans) equal to $920 million in deposits plus total capital of $80 million. Names for the banks and the hypothetical compo-

*Table 3.2*

Alternative Hypothetical Classified-Asset Structures
($millions)

| Classified Assets | First National Bank | Last National Bank |
|---|---|---|
| "Loss" | 10 | 50 |
| "Doubtful" | 20 | 20 |
| "Substandard" | 50 | 10 |
| Total | 80 | 80 |

sition of their classified assets appear in Table 3.2. Both banks have total classified assets equal to their capital stock. However, it is clear that the Last National Bank is more "risky" than the First, even though the NCR in this example is the same for both banks. In contrast, the ACR is lower for the Last National Bank, indicating that it is the "riskier" institution. The ACR, however, ignores the "substandard" classifications, which in First National's case are substantial. Assuming that $\gamma_L = .95$, $\gamma_D = .75$, and $\gamma_S = .50$, a WCR still indicates that First National is the "safer" institution, similar to the ACR rating. However, unlike the ACR, the WCR does not ignore the risk presented by the "substandard" category. In addition, the WCR recognizes that even though a loan may be classified "loss" there always is a chance for some recovery.

## 3.5 EMPIRICAL FINDINGS

Discriminant-analysis tests presented in this section show that the NCR is the most important variable separating "problem banks" from "nonproblem banks." These tests are "descriptive" and not "predictive." The analysis uses examiner-determined categories of problem and nonproblem banks, which are reclassified statistically to clarify how examiners distinguish between such banks.

The problem banks analyzed were the 143 commercial banks on the FDIC's March 31, 1974 problem-bank list.[15] These banks were compared with a random sample of 163 nonproblem banks, drawn from the 9,060 banks (about 65 percent of the population) with examination reports for the year 1973 on file with the FDIC as of December 31, 1973. If a bank had more than one report on file for the year, the latest one was used. Although no deliberate pairing was performed, no statistically significant differences emerged between the two groups either in average size or in average number of banking offices.[16]

Table 3.3

Discriminant-Analysis Tests: 143 Problem Versus 163 Nonproblem Banks Using 1973 Examination Data

| Test | | Mean (%) (Standard Deviation) | | Test of Equality | Test of Dispersion Matrix | Misclass.** Rate (%) | Type-I Error | Type-II Error |
|---|---|---|---|---|---|---|---|---|
| 1 | ACR | 6.4 (2.6) | 8.8 (2.5) | Reject (F = 68.6) | Reject (F = 55.2) | 26.8 | 35.0 | 19.6 |
| 2 | NCR | -2.3 (5.2) | 7.6 (3.0) | Reject (F = 428.8) | Reject (F = 42.6) | 4.6 | 4.9 | 4.3 |
| 3 | NIA* | 0.16 (1.21) | 0.85 (0.53) | Reject (F = 43.0) | Reject (F = 97.8) | 34.3 | 66.4 | 6.1 |
| 4*** | NCR NIA | (see above) | | Reject (F = 233.6) | Reject (F = 47.8) | 5.5 | 7.0 | 4.3 |
| 5 | SUB* | 11.6 (7.2) | 1.9 (2.2) | Reject (F = 268.9) | Reject (F = 182.1) | 12.4 | 19.6 | 6.1 |
| 6 | TCL* | 14.6 (8.2) | 2.3 (2.5) | Reject (F = 331.9) | Reject (F = 182.1) | 11.1 | 16.1 | 6.7 |
| 7 | TCA* | 10.1 (5.5) | 1.4 (1.5) | Reject (F = 370.4) | Reject (F = 218.5) | 9.8 | 14.0 | 6.1 |

*NIA = Net income (after taxes and securities gains or losses) as a percentage of total assets. SUB = Substandard loans as a percentage of total loans. TCL = Total classified loans (i.e., substandard + doubtful + loss) as a percentage of total loans. TCA = Total classified assets (loans and securities) as a percentage of total assets. ACR and NCR, components of the ratings vector, were defined in the text.

**Classifications were performed using (1) the Eisenbeis and Avery [1972] computer program MULDIS, (2) a quadratic discriminant function, since the null hypothesis of dispersion matrix equality between groups was rejected, (3) the Lachenbruch "holdout" classification technique, and (4) the sample proportions as a priori probabilities of group membership.

***Additional multivariate tests, not reported here, could not improve upon the classification accuracy of NCR, even if NCR was included in the set.

54

The purposes of discriminant analysis are to test for group mean and dispersion-matrix differences, to describe the overlap between groups, and to construct rules to classify observations into "appropriate" groups.[17] Using 1973 examination data, these tests are reported in Table 3.3. A total of 21 examination variables were tested. The results for six of these variables and a bivariate combination are presented in Table 3.3. The six variables are the components of the ratings vector, except for the managerial rating, which is a qualitative measure, and three ratios of classified loans (assets) to total loans (assets).[18]

For all six variables, tests of equality of group means and equality of group dispersion matrices were rejected. The tests included a bivariate test of NCR and NIA (net income, after taxes and securities gains and losses, as a percentage of total assets).[19] The most significant variable and the most important discriminator between the groups (on either a univariate or multivariate basis) was the net capital ratio [NCR, see equation (3.2) above]. The NCR for the average problem bank was −2.3 (5.2) compared to 7.6 (3.0) for the average nonproblem bank. (Figures in parentheses are standard deviations.) The NCR F-statistics were 428.8 for the group means (significant at the 0.29282 E-12 percent level) and 42.6 for the dispersion matrices (significant at the 0.67734 E-08 percent level). Using the Lachenbruch "holdout" classification technique, 95.4 percent of the 306 banks were reclassified correctly.[20] The Type-I error was 4.9 percent (7 banks) while the Type -II error was 4.3 percent (7 banks). The classification rule used for reclassifying the 306 banks was:[21]

**Rule:** Classify as a problem bank if NCR ≤ 2.74 percent.

To summarize, based upon either univariate or multivariate discriminant-analysis tests, NCR had the most accurate reclassification rate of any variable or set of variables. Recalling the construction of ACR and NCR [see equations (3.1) and (3.2) above], it is clear that a bank's volume of "substandard" loans is the kicker in the NCR formula. On average, substandard loans account for about 80 percent of a problem bank's classified loans (see tests 5 and 6 in Table 3.3). Thus, the present procedure for identifying problem banks depends largely on the amount of loans designated substandard. Moreover, examiners' record in determining whether a substandard loan actually is "substandard" is subject to question (see footnote 12).

## 3.6 THE NET CAPITAL RATIO AND RECENT BANK FAILURES

This section focuses upon whether or not the FDIC's net capital ratio has been a "predictor" of bank failures.

### 1. *Large Banks and the Predictability of NCR*

Since most failed banks were considered "problem banks" before they failed and since, as has been shown above, a large volume of "substandard" loans (i.e., a low net capital ratio) is the main criterion for classifying problem banks, the net capital ratio perforce (on an *ex post* basis) has been a predictor of most bank failures. To support this, consider NCR's record with respect to the financial difficulties of the following large banks: (1) the three largest bank failures (Franklin National of New York, USNB of San Diego, and Hamilton National of Chattanooga), (2) the emergency merger of Security National of Long Island, and (3) the distressed Bank of the Commonwealth of Detroit. All five of these banks had net capital ratios low enough to warrant classification as FDIC problem banks *prior* to their collapse. The relevant NCR information is contained in Table 3.4.

The FDIC had, on average, approximately 16 months lead time in these five cases. The Franklin case (see Chapter 6), which turned out to be the most complicated because of the bank's size and extensive international operations, had an eleven-month lead time. Security's lead time (see Chapter 7) was the shortest (six months), while Commonwealth's was the longest (34 months). Commonwealth, which first received FDIC financial assistance on January 18, 1972, received additional financial

*Table 3.4*

Large Banks and the Predictability of NCR

| Bank | Date of Exam that led to FDIC Problem Classification | NCR (1) / (2)* | Date of Failure, Merger, or Bailout | NCR Lead Time (months) |
|---|---|---|---|---|
| 1. USNB | 6-26-72 | -16/-12 | 10-18-73 | 16 |
| 2. Franklin | 11-14-73 | 2/0 | 10- 8-74 | 11 |
| 3. Hamilton | 9-30-74 | -3/-8 | 2-16-76 | 16 |
| 4. Security | 6-24-74 | 0 / 0** | 1-19-75 | 6 |
| 5. Commonwealth | 3- 7-69 | 2/-2 | 1-18-72† | 34 |

*As of (1) exam date that led to FDIC problem classification and (2) last exam before closing or financial aid.
**Indicates same exam date for both NCRs. As of January 1, 1973 and October 23, 1973, Security NCRs were 2.0 and 0.0, respectively; however, the bank was not listed by the FDIC as a "problem" bank during 1973.
†Commonwealth's second bailout occurred on May 5, 1976. As of June 30, 1975, Commonwealth's NCR was -1.0.

aid on May 22, 1976.[22] During the interval between its two financial infusions, Commonwealth continued to be classified as an FDIC "problem bank."

To summarize, the FDIC's NCR has been an accurate predictor of the financial difficulties of large banks. The banking authorities are, of course, most concerned about Type-I errors (i.e., classifying a failed bank, especially a large one, as nonfailed or nonproblem). Regarding the recent financial difficulties of billion-dollar banks, the FDIC has had a Type-I error of zero.

Regarding future forecasts, as of December 31, 1975, there were two billion-dollar banks on the FDIC's problem-bank list. These banks first were examined as problems on October 4, 1974, and May 9, 1975. Thus, their NCR lead times already have been 26 and 19 months, respectively. Perforce, both of these banks have low net capital ratios (i.e., 0.0 and −1.0) and large volumes of "substandard" loans. Of course, given their goal of failure prevention, the banking authorities try to correct a bank's financial difficulties and thus NCR predictions will be biased towards becoming Type-II errors (i.e., problem banks that do not fail or require financial assistance).

### 2. Small Banks and the Predictability of NCR

During 1975 and the first five months of 1976, eighteen commercial banks were declared insolvent (thirteen in 1975). Excluding Hamilton National, which was discussed above, the remaining seventeen banks (each with total deposits less than $100 million) had an average NCR (or problem-bank list) lead time of approximately 22 months (the median lead time was 20 months). The range of lead times ran from two weeks to 70 months. The $16-million Bank of Picayune (Mississippi) with a lead time of two weeks was the only "surprise" failure. The cause of Picayune's closing was "irregularities" (e.g., among other things the chief executive officer of the bank withheld about $600,000 in cash). During 1975, the FDIC's problem-bank list contained, on average, 283 banks. To summarize, most "problem" banks do not fail and most failed banks are classified as "problem" banks prior to their closings.

## 3.7 THE RELATIONSHIP BETWEEN PROBLEM BANKS AND THE ECONOMY

As indicated in Chapter 1, a bank-failure model should specify both internal and external factors to explain bank performance. In general, internal factors are those which the bank controls, such as the quality of management and its attitude toward risk-taking; the external factors are those which the bank does not control but must react to, such as the state of the economy. This methodological framework can, of course, be applied to problem and nonproblem banks as well as failed banks. This section relates the number of problem banks to the state of the economy.

Using PB to denote the number of problem banks, MGM to denote the overall quality of bank management, ECY to denote the state of the economy (e.g., recession or nonrecession), and RD to denote random disturbances, the general functional form of a problem-bank model can be expressed as:

$$\overset{\textstyle -\quad\ -\quad +/-}{PB = f(MGM, ECY, RD).} \tag{3.6}$$

The number of problem banks is expected to be inversely related to both the quality of management and the state of the economy. The effect of random disturbances is, of course, unknown. Since MGM cannot be measured directly, let us ignore it (a deliberate misspecification) and concentrate on the relationship between PB and ECY. Three alternative specifications of the dependent variable PB are employed: (1) PB = SP, where SP is the number of "potential-payoff" *and* "serious-problem" banks on the FDIC's problem-bank list (PPO banks are a subset of the FDIC's serious-problem category); PB = OP, where OP is the number of "other-problem" banks on the FDIC's problem-bank list; and (3) PB = TP, where TP is the total number of banks on the FDIC's problem-bank list, TP = SP + OP. The alternative forms of PB aggregate different levels of risk: SP includes the most-risky problem banks; OP the least risky problem banks; and TP combines the two risk classes to capture the average-risk problem bank. Since the most risky or vulnerable problem banks should be more sensitive to economic fluctuations than the least risky ones, SP should have a stronger relationship with ECY than OP does; TP should capture the average relationship.

Quarterly data (1968 IV–1976 II) for SP, OP, and TP are presented in Table 3.5. The mean values and standard deviations for SP, OP, and TP are 55 (28), 171 (38), and 226 (59), respectively. The coefficients of variation (standard deviation as a percentage of the mean) for the three variables are 50.9 percent, 22.2 percent, and 26.1 percent, respectively. These measures of relative dispersion indicate that SP has shown considerably more variation than either OP or TP.

The independent variable ECY was tested using three alternative forms: (1) a simple binary recession-nonrecession variable; (2) the dollar magnitude of the change in real gross national product (GNP in constant 1972 dollars); and (3) the percentage change in real GNP. Since commercial banks usually are not exmained more frequently than once a

*Table 3.5*

Problem Banks, 1968 IV – 1976 II

|        |     | Serious Problems | Other Problems | Total |
|--------|-----|------------------|----------------|-------|
| 1968   | IV  | 35  | 205 | 240 |
| 1969   | I   | 32  | 190 | 222 |
|        | II  | 30  | 181 | 211 |
|        | III | 39  | 175 | 214 |
|        | IV  | 39  | 177 | 216 |
| 1970   | I   | 45  | 181 | 226 |
|        | II  | 53  | 190 | 243 |
|        | III | 57  | 189 | 246 |
|        | IV  | 57  | 194 | 251 |
| 1971   | I   | 60  | 185 | 245 |
|        | II  | 60  | 182 | 242 |
|        | III | 58  | 185 | 243 |
|        | IV  | 53  | 186 | 239 |
| 1972   | I   | 47  | 179 | 226 |
|        | II  | 42  | 175 | 217 |
|        | III | 35  | 178 | 213 |
|        | IV  | 28  | 162 | 190 |
| 1973   | I   | 30  | 133 | 163 |
|        | II  | 29  | 129 | 158 |
|        | III | 33  | 115 | 148 |
|        | IV  | 36  | 119 | 155 |
| 1974   | I   | 42  | 102 | 144 |
|        | II  | 47  | 103 | 150 |
|        | III | 49  | 113 | 162 |
|        | IV  | 52  | 129 | 181 |
| 1975   | I   | 61  | 144 | 205 |
|        | II  | 95  | 176 | 271 |
|        | III | 109 | 201 | 310 |
|        | IV  | 115 | 232 | 347 |
| 1976   | I   | 124 | 235 | 359 |
|        | II  | 121 | 244 | 365 |
| Mean   |     | 55  | 171 | 226 |
| (Sd)   |     | (28) | (38) | (59) |

*Source:* Problem-Bank Lists, Division of Bank Supervision, FDIC.

year and since bank examiners are not likely to be oblivious to economic and financial developments and forecasts, the relationship between PB and ECY is expected to be a lagged one. For example, relating the number of problem banks in period t with the state of the economy in period t would be an inappropriate specification, since problem-bank lists are not contemporaneous reflections of the current effect of the economy but of past economic developments. This problem-bank lag has two components: (1) the bank-examination component and (2) the bureaucratic component. The examination component refers to the fact that examinations take time. In the smallest banks the time involved may be only a week or so, but in the largest banks examinations usually take several months. The bureaucratic component refers to the lag between the end of the examination (or the point in the examination at which it is determined that the bank may have financial weaknesses) and the date on which the bank is added to the problem-bank list. In the banking bureaucracy, examination reports go from the head or chief examiner to the regional director and then to the Washington office, all of which takes time. In addition to the time lag, the actual problem-bank lists may be subject to examiner identification error. As was noted above, the loan-evaluation process, the heart of a bank examination, is a very subjective technique. Thus, depending upon an examiner's zeal (or lack of it) and external stimuli such as economic forecasts (e.g., "the recession is expected to continue and bank loan losses are expected to be high") and adverse publicity about problem and failed banks, examiners' judgments and perceptions of banking weaknesses may be biased. Thus, the number of problem banks, in addition to reflecting past economic developments, should reflect examiners' attitudes and skills as shaped by bureaucratic and other pressures. Finally, as a technical point, although the FDIC's problem-bank list is updated continuously, the "official" list is only a quarterly one. Thus, the quarterly lists themselves are "outdated."

To determine the relationship between PB and ECY the following regression equation was estimated (using the ordinary least-squares technique):

$$PB_t = \beta_0 + \beta_1 ECY_{t-k} + U_t, \tag{3.7}$$

where t is a time subscript with $k = 0, 1, 2, \ldots 6$; U is a stochastic error term; and PB and ECY are as defined above. $\beta_0$ and $\beta_1$ are the regression coefficients with $\beta_0$ expected to be greater than zero and $\beta_1$ expected to be less than zero. The "best" regression results for SP (number of "serious-problem" banks), and OP (number of "other-problem" banks), and TP $=$ SP $+$ OP are presented in Table 3.6. "Best" was determined on the basis of the best overall regression results as measured by $R^2$, F, and DW. The appropriate lag structure was found to be 5 quarters or

*Table 3.6*

Estimated Relationship between the Number of Problem
Banks and the Economy, 1968 IV — 1976 II

| Dependent Variable* | Independent Variable | $\hat{\beta}_0$ | $\hat{\beta}_1$ | $R^2$ | F | DW | Sample Size |
|---|---|---|---|---|---|---|---|
| SP | $\triangle$ GNP ( -5) | 64 (3) | -1.66 (.23) | .6370 | 50.90 | 1.26 | 31 |
| OP | $\triangle$ GNP ( -5) | 181 (5) | -1.94 (.38) | .4770 | 26.45 | 0.73 | 31 |
| TP | $\triangle$ GNP ( -5) | 245 (7) | -3.61 (.47) | .6685 | 58.47 | 1.44 | 31 |

*The dependent variables (defined in the text) are measured as number of banks; the independent variable as quarterly change in real GNP lagged five quarters. $\beta_0$ is the estimated intercept to be interpreted as number of problem banks when $\triangle$ GNP = 0. $\beta_1$ is the estimated slope coefficient to be interpreted as the change in the number of problem banks given a $1 billion change in GNP five quarters ago. The figures in parentheses below the estimated coefficients are standard errors. $R^2$ is the coefficient of determination; F the regression F-statistic; and DW the Durbin-Watson statistic.

*Data Sources:* Problem Banks 1968 IV - 1976 II, Problem-Bank Lists, Division of Bank Supervision; FDIC, GNP (1972 dollars) 1967 II - 1976 II, Federal Reserve Bank of St. Louis.

fifteen months, that is, for shorter or longer lags the components of the vector [$R^2$, F, DW] each had smaller values. The choice between $\triangle$GNP and $\triangle$GNP/GNP was a toss-up; however, both of these variables outperformed the simple binary recession-nonrecession variable.

Interpreting the regression findings, the SP equation, which was superior to the OP equation as expected, indicated that a $10 billion quarterly decline in real GNP five quarters ago results in the addition of about 17 ( = 10 × 1.66) "serious problem" banks to the FDIC's problem-bank list [for a total SP of 81 = 64 (the intercept) + 17]. Conversely, a $10 billion increase in real GNP results in a reduction of SP by 17 banks. The maximum quarterly decline in real GNP over the sample period was $30.6 billion, implying an increase in SP of about 50 banks. Regarding the OP equation, the results suggest that a $10 billion decline in real GNP implies an increase (five quarters later) in OP banks of about 19 to a total of 200. The combined results for the SP and OP equations are identical to the TP equation, that is, a $10 billion change in real GNP leads to change in TP, in the opposite direction and five months later, of about 36 banks, consisting of 17 SP banks and 19 OP banks.

The weaker relationship for the OP equation (relative to the SP equation) suggests that other factors besides the state of the economy are more important in determining the number of OP banks. Given that the volume of substandard loans is the most important discriminator between problem and nonproblem banks, examiners' attitudes towards substandard classifications may be the missing link. Recall that the substandard category is the least risky and most subjective of examiners' classifications. For example, when the economy is in a recession (or a period of adverse banking publicity), examiners may be overscrupulous in their substandard classifications. In contrast, during periods of prosperity, examiners may tend to relax the intensity of their loan evaluations. In this regard, former FDIC Chairman Barnett (May 3, 1976) recently stated ". . . our examiners are not apt to be completely insensitive to recent economic and financial developments" (p. 12). The net effect of examiner overzealousness during recessionary periods would be to deepen the trough of the problem-bank cycle while underzealousness during nonrecessionary periods would tend to cut off the peak. On balance, since the banking authorities want to avoid making embarrassing Type-I errors (i.e., calling problem or failed banks nonproblem banks), they probably do not discourage examiners' overzealousness, especially during periods of economic recession and adverse banking publicity. As we have consistently argued, their goal is to prevent failures *and* to keep the Congressional "watchdogs" off their backs.

## 3.8 SUMMARY AND CONCLUSIONS

The primary supervisory technique employed by the banking authorities for identifying problem banks is the on-site bank examination. The banking agencies recognize (in words at least) that identification of banks experiencing financial difficulty is a multidimensional problem. However, in practice, bank capital and examiners' "substandard" loan classifications (as manifested in the FDIC's net capital ratio) are the important variables. Despite its theoretical shortcomings, the FDIC's net capital ratio does appear to have predictive content. Based upon analysis of recent problem and failed banks, this indicator has provided, on average, 16 months lead time in predicting the demise of large banks and 22 months lead time with respect to smaller banks. While it is tempting to conclude that with such lead times these banks failu. es should have been prevented, it is important to remember that the bar..ing authorities really do not have the power to prevent such failures, unless they want to run the banks themselves. Short of avoiding a full-scale financial panic, there is near-unanimous agreement that the banking authorities should not be running the banks. Moreover, the failure of such institutions usually means the elimination of incompetent and/or dishonest bank managers and/or directors, a desirable social goal.

This chapter also has shown that there is a significant relationship between the state of the economy and the number of problem banks. The effect of the business cycle is not manifested immediately in the number of problem banks but only after about a fifteen-month lag. This lag can be traced to three factors: (1) the existence of supervisory lags and discontinuities in the bank-examination process; (2) the de facto definition of a problem bank as one with a large volume of "bad" loans; and (3) the fact that "bad" loans are most prevalent after an economic recession. The estimated relationship between the economy and the number of problem banks was stronger for the highest-risk distressed banks, suggesting that other factors are important in determining the number of lower-risk problem banks.

# APPENDIX A
# 1975 BANK EXAMINATION CAPITAL RATIOS

The data in this appendix update the bank examination capital ratios (ACR and NCR) presented in Table 3.3 of this Chapter. Note that (1) for the 1973 nonproblem-bank group (presented in the text) a random sample of nonproblem banks was used, all other figures were for existing *populations* and (2) because of the 1974-1975 recession, lower capital ratios (i.e., larger volumes of classified assets) were excepted in 1975. The 1975 data are:

*Table 3.7*

1975 Bank Examination Capital Ratios
(Means and Standard Deviations)

| Ratio | Problem (347)* (%) | Nonproblem (14,524)* (%) |
|---|---|---|
| ACR | 6.14 (2.95) | 9.38 (4.48) |
| NCR | -3.77 (6.44) | 7.94 (3.25) |

*Indicates number of banks in the group. For comparative purposes, the 1973 ACR and NCR (from Table 3.3) are reproduced in Table 3.8.

*Table 3.8*

1973 Bank Examination Capital Ratios
(Means and Standard Deviations)

| Ratio | Problem (143)*<br>(%) | Nonproblem (163)*<br>(%) |
|---|---|---|
| ACR | 6.4<br>(2.6) | 8.8<br>(2.5) |
| NCR | -2.3<br>(5.2) | 7.6<br>(3.0) |

*Indicates number of banks in the group.

# NOTES

1. Mimeographed notes, Problem-Bank Section, Division of Supervision, FDIC (1973). Since all three banking agencies have basically the same approach to assessing risk, only one agency's concepts and measurements are needed to understand the process.

2. For national and state member banks the FDIC uses examination reports supplied by the Comptroller and the Federal Reserve, respectively.

3. A bank examination, although not an accounting audit, is a detailed analysis of a bank's operation. The reports generated by examinations are confidential and currently not available to the public.

4. Bank Examiner's Orientation Course, mimeographed notes (FDIC, 1973).

5. The FDIC's *Manual* states:

> Loan evaluation is not an exact science. The broad scope of the lending function and changing patterns in banking preclude the use of a single formula in the appraisal of loans. Much depends on the Examiner's knowledge, judgment, perception, analytical technique, and the ability to reach sound conclusions; attributes which are developed through training and experience. (Section H, p. 1.)

See Chapter 9 regarding bankers' opinions of examiners' training and experience.

6. The *Manual* adds, "[This] does not mean, however, that borrowers must at all times be in position to liquidate their loans for that would defeat the original purpose of extending credit" (ibid.).

7. Regarding the "competition" item, the *Manual* states:

> Competition between banks for size, profitability, and community influence sometimes results in compromise of sound credit principles and acquisition of unsound loans. The ultimate cost of unsound loans outweighs temporary gains in growth, income, and influence. (Section H. p. 3.)

8. Because of the sheer volume of loans, only a bank's larger lines of credit are evaluated. A bank's loan cutoff point will depend upon the individual characteristics of that bank. The FDIC's *Manual* states ". . . there should be direct correlation between the cutoff point utilized, the percentage of loans lined, and the management rating assigned after consideration of the bank's overall conditions as shown in prior examination reports" (Section H, p. 9).

9. Other loans of questionable quality, but involving insufficient risk to warrant an adverse classification, are listed as "Special Mention Loans." In addition, loans that are undue concentration of credit, technically deficient in documentation, or overdue are reported.

10. Loans deemed "uncollectable and worthless" are classified "loss," while those with "extremely high" risk of default but still a chance for partial collection are classified "doubtful." Examiners are cautioned to "make sparing use of the doubtful classification" (Section H, p. 5).

11. These capital ratios are derived from examination data and they differ substantially from the simple capital ratios (e.g., capital to assets (or risk assets)) derived from ordinary balance-sheet data.

12. Nonbook sound banking values include ". . . all nonbook assets of *determinable sound banking* value as well as *sound* and *bankable* book assets, the fair appraised value of which is in excess of book value" (Section L, p. 19).

13. Since examiners' criticisms may reduce the chances of a default (i.e., bank managers are expected to take remedial action on criticized loans), the $\gamma$'s may underestimate the accuracy of examiners' classifications. However, since the objective is to estimate a bank's risk exposure and not to determine the accuracy of examiners' classifications, the $\gamma$ technique is appropriate. To determine the accuracy of examiners' classifications, a bank's actual charge-offs should be retraced, as Wu (1969) did in his study of bank loan quality. See also Wojnilower (1962), Benston (1967), and Benston and Marlin (1974).

14. Before leaving the FDIC, I recommended that such a project be developed. Of course, it would be best for the banking agencies to develop a coordinated effort in this regard. Regarding the relevancy of the banking authorities' risk measures, the recent unauthorized disclosures of "problem-bank lists" led the banking agencies to say that some of their problem banks were not really problems. This suggests that the way the banking authorities identify so-called problem banks could be improved. The parade of disclosures began with the frontpage headlines "Citibank, Chase Manhattan on U.S. 'Problem' List," *The Washington Post* (January 11, 1976). In the *Post* article, James E. Smith, the U.S. Comptroller of the Currency, was quoted as saying, "They [Chase and Citibank] are strong, well-managed banks."

15. The list consisted of 113 insured nonmember banks, 11 state-member banks, and 19 national banks.

16. The typical problem bank was a unit bank with total deposits of $9.4 million. Five of the problem banks had total deposits greater than $100 million but less than $1 billion. Originally, 175 banks were selected for the nonproblem group, however, 12 banks were eliminated because of incomplete data.

17. See Eisenbeis and Avery (1972) for the foundations of discriminant analysis and Sinkey (1975) for an application of the technique.

18. The FDIC managerial ratings are GOOD, SATISFACTORY, FAIR, UN-SATISFACTORY, and POOR. The most common rating for the problem-bank was UNSATISFACTORY (65 percent of the banks), while for the nonproblem-bank group it was SATISFACTORY (71 percent).

19. The test of dispersion-matrix equality is important because if this hypothesis is rejected, a quadratic classification equation, rather than a linear one, should be used. See Eisenbeis and Avery (1972), especially pp. 37–52.

20. The Lachenbruch technique withholds the observation to be classified and computes the classification equation using N-1 observations. The withheld observation then is classified. This procedure is repeated until all observations have been classified.

21. This rule was derived from the following quadratic equation:

$$1.8195 \ (NCR) - 0.071387 \ (NCR)^2 - 4.4503 \leq 0.$$

If the value of the left-hand side of this equation is equal or less than zero, the bank is classified as a "problem bank."

22. Section 13(c) of the FDI Act permits the FDIC to deal with distressed banks short of actual failure. See Chapter 2.

Chapter 4

# Early-Warning Systems: Concepts and Procedures

Probably enough has been done, however, to indicate the promise of an analysis of this type, if applied not only to balance-sheet, but also to income and profit-and-loss data. A continuing study of this sort is badly needed. The necessary data are to be found in the office of the Comptroller of the Currency. Why cannot they be used? If they were, it appears certain that the misleading and often false standards which are held to distinguish sound from unsound banking would seen be dispelled.

Horace Secrist
*National Bank Failures*
*and Nonfailures* (1938), p. 300.

## 4.1 INTRODUCTION

Horace Secrist's dream of an "early-warning" or "surveillance" system for identifying "problem" or failing commercial banks soon may be realized. Since approximately four decades have elapsed since Secrist suggested that the banking agencies undertake such a project, he may have given up hope. It is to be hoped that he had a firm understanding of the bureaucratic lags that apply in a "jurisdictional tangle." Four decades may represent a bureaucratic speed record for reacting to such a proposal.

This chapter deals with early-warning or surveillance systems for identifying commercial banks with financial difficulties. It focuses on the concepts and procedures related to the origins, goals, alternative statistical techniques and approaches of such systems. The financial characteristics of problem and failed banks and alternative early-warning models are presented in the next chapter.

JAWS (*Just A* Warning System)

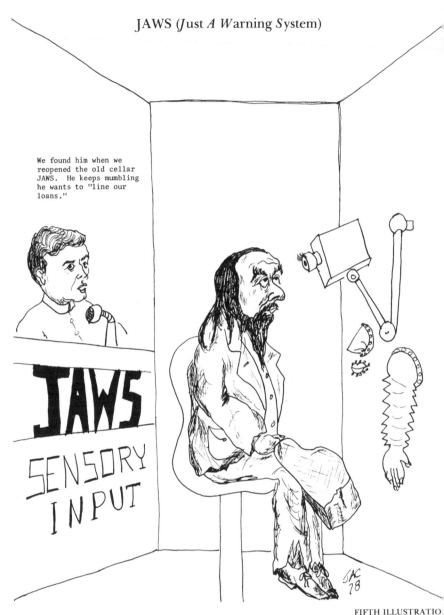

We found him when we
reopened the old cellar
JAWS. He keeps mumbling
he wants to "line our
loans."

FIFTH ILLUSTRATIO

## 4.2 THE ORIGINS AND DEFINITION OF EARLY-WARNING SYSTEM

The term "early-warning system" probably first was made popular by the British during World War II. On August 12, 1940, the Luftwaffe launched "Operation Adlerangriff" (Eagle Attack) against the British in a massive effort to destroy the Royal Air Force. However, the Luftwaffe was pitted against, among other things, a radar early-warning system. According to Addington (1971), "The RAF was braced for an attack, and the early-warning system gave adequate notice as the first German fighters swept over the Channel" (p. 133).

Throughout the Cold War period, the term early-warning system remained in military and civil-defense usage. However, during the Vietnam War, the technology made much greater use of such things as sorties, napalm, and saturation bombing. On balance, given the arms race and the threat of nuclear holocaust, "early-warning system" probably always will be a popular term, at least in the military environment.

The origin of the term's initial application to banking is not clear. However, in Secrist's (1938) research on failed and nonfailed banks, this concept appears to be the final goal of his analysis. I began using the term at the FDIC in 1972, when I first studied the financial characteristics of problem and nonproblem banks for the Division of Research. The project began with a request from the FDIC's Office of Management Systems (OMS) for some balance-sheet and income-expense characteristics and cutoff points relevant for distinguishing between problem and nonproblem banks. OMS had in mind a project in which Report of Condition and Report of Income data would be massaged and packaged so as to be more useful to the Division of Bank Supervision (DBS). It was logical that Research should provide some analytical input to the project. From the beginning, some sort of early-warning system seemed the logical outcome of the project. The first steps in the research would be to obtain DBS's list of problem banks, to find out what a problem bank is, and how DBS separated problem from nonproblem banks (see Chapter 3). It should be noted that the FDIC's problem-bank or early-warning research started prior to USNB's failure on October 18, 1973, which marked the start of the banking difficulties of the 1970s. Thus, the project was not initiated in response to a crisis, although it was given noticeable boosts by the events that followed.

Webster defines *early* as near the beginning of a process or series; *warning* as an alarm or signal; and *system* as a regularly interacting or interdependent group of items forming a unified whole. More specifically and appropriately for this context, *system* also connotes an organized or established procedure or a manner of classifying. Collecting definitions and applying them in a problem-bank context, *an early-warning system for identifying problem commercial banks* refers to an organized procedure (usually statistical) for identifying financial weaknesses early in the process of a bank's deterioration to warn or serve as signal to banking authorities, uninsured depositors, stockholders, and/or other interested parties.

## 4.3 THE PURPOSES AND POTENTIAL ADVANTAGES OF AN EARLY-WARNING SYSTEM

The basic concept (or null hypothesis) of any early-warning system focuses upon the information content of the data to be analyzed. In this particular case, the null hypothesis concerns the information content of balance-sheet and income-expense data relevant for identifying future "problem banks." Having analyzed these data, I am confident, as was Secrist, that the information content is there. Information relevant for scheduling bank examinations and even for excluding certain banks from the traditional bank-examination process is available. Of course, this does *not* mean that on-the-spot bank inspections would be eliminated entirely or that 100 percent accuracy in identifying problem banks would be achieved. On the contrary, all banks should be inspected at least once a year to check for the irregularities (e.g.,, insider transactions, brokered deposits, fraud, embezzlement, etc.) that have been the major causes of bank failures. However, these mandatory inspections would tend to be shorter and less costly than the traditional bank examination. Known "problem banks" and banks identified by the surveillance mechanism as either actually or potentially in need of special supervision should be given more detailed and thorough bank inspections. Just as traditional bank examinations, these inspections must be designed to pinpoint causes of financial difficulty and to suggest potential remedies.

Early-warning systems are not proposed as complete substitutes for existing bank-examination procedures and personnel, nor are they intended to replace the human skills and judgment needed to confront problems of bank supervision.[1] The realistic and limited objective of such systems is to improve the scheduling of bank examinations. Potential problem banks should be examined more frequently and more intensely than nonproblem banks.

The major potential advantages of an effective early-warning system are:

1. *Prevention of bank failures.* The "safety-and-soundness" mandate of bank regulation has focused upon the prevention of bank failure. Early identification of problem banks may result in fewer bank failures and smaller losses for the FDIC's deposit-insurance fund. Moreover, large losses, such as the $150 million loss the FDIC incurred in USNB's failure, reduce the percentage rebate of the net insurance-assessment income by the FDIC to insured banks. Clearly, an effective early-warning system promises monetary benefits for bankers.

2. *More efficient allocation of banking-agency resources.* Advance information regarding the condition of a bank should be an important fac-

tor in determining the order, scope, intensity, and frequency of a bank's examination. Such information should enable the banking agencies to allocate resources more efficiently among problem and nonproblem banks.

3. *Increasing the usefulness of balance-sheet and income data.* All three Federal banking agencies regularly collect useful data from the banks they supervise. These data are the primary inputs of the early-warning system. The value of these preexamination data would be enhanced greatly by an effective problem-bank-detection mechanism.

4. *Making the identification of problem banks more objective.* Relative to a bank's capital position, "substandard" loans are the most important variable separating problem from nonproblem banks. Regulatory authorities admit that the procedure for uncovering these "risky" loans is an "art" and not a "science." A more objective appraisal of a bank's potential riskiness would strengthen bank-examination procedures.

5. *Supplying the banking agencies with data to evaluate their examination and supervisory performances and the effectiveness of the early-warning system.* Given a "prediction" of a bank's "safety and soundness," the agencies would be able to evaluate bank examiners' ratings and vice versa. Moreover, an early-warning system should be an important pedagogical device for bank examiners and banking schools.

6. *Input for a variable deposit-insurance premium.* Since its inception deposit insurance has been criticized for not really being "insurance," since the assessment rate is the same for all banks, instead of varying with the bank's degree of "riskines" [see Bremer (1935), p. 135)]. In addition, the assessment is not paid directly by the beneficiary, the depositor. (The depositor pays indirectly through inefficiencies caused by regulation but benefits by a lower failure rate.) An early-warning system could provide an important input for the calculation of a variable-rate structure [see Mayer (1965)].

Regarding implementation of an early-warning system, two critical problems remain. First, the information must be extracted in a timely and efficient manner. And, second, supervisory and examination personnel must be convinced that the information is useful. The first problem can be resolved by having on-the-spot examinations begin after the data have been analyzed. For example, what is so sacred about starting the cycle of examinations in January of each year? Why not start each year's cycle of on-site examinations *after* year-end data have been analyzed? Based upon past experience, such examinations (for the entire population of insured banks) could begin in early May. In addition, since large banks present the greatest potential risk exposure to the FDIC insurance fund and the economy, they should be analyzed separately and with increased timeliness. Moreover, with income-expense data now being collected quarterly for the largest banks and semiannually for other banks, additional information is available for monitoring banks on a year-round basis.

## 4.4 SOME FUNDAMENTAL QUESTIONS ABOUT THE CONCEPT OF AN EARLY-WARNING SYSTEM

A number of interesting questions about the whole concept of an early-warning model can be considered.[1a] First, can a "usable" early-warning model be developed? The key to answering this question depends upon the *purpose* of the early-warning system. If the purpose of the system is to *predict* future bank failures, then, given the dishonesty factor and its importance in past bank failures, one would indeed be skeptical of achieving success. However, if the purpose of the system is to aid in the scheduling of bank examinations and the reallocation of scarce examiners' resources, then a successful surveillance or monitoring program probably can be developed. Except to look for embezzlement, fraud, and other irregularities, it is probably not necessary to examine (in the traditional way) every bank in every single year. How should the banking authorities determine the allocation of their scarce examination resources? Documented scientific evidence regarding the information content of balance-sheet and income-expense data suggests that the estimated relationships are accurate enough and stable enough for the second-best goal of scheduling bank examinations (as opposed to predicting bank failures). (The particular variables used for such purposes are described in the next chapter.)

Second, assuming that an early-warning model exists what sort of lead time will it provide and will this lead time be greater than that provided by present examination procedures? Since most early-warning research (as described in the next chapter) has shown that balance-sheet and income-expense differences have existed between problem (failed) and nonproblem (nonfailed) banks prior to their identification as financially troubled institutions by the banking agencies, one has to be optimistic regarding the lead time for such systems. Given the limited objective of using an early-warning mechanism as a device for scheduling bank examinations, the lead time should be greater under a combined surveillance and examination system.

Third, what does an early-warning model have to say about policy measures designed to prevent bank failures? Early warning is part of the identification problem of bank supervision; prevention is an enforcement problem. These two aspects of bank supervision are not completely divorced; however, an early-warning model would appear to have only limited usefulness in the *policy-enforcement* area.

Fourth, can an early-warning model shed any light on the issue of disclosure by banks and bank holding companies? Given that an early-warning model basically tests the information content of financial statements, such a model might be able to shed some light on the disclosure issue. Existing evidence seems to suggest that publicly available balance-sheet and income-expense data contain as much useful information as confidential examination data [see Herzig-Marz (1977)].

Fifth, could an early-warning mechanism lead to new sources of instability in the banking system because of misapplication of the predictions by the banking authorities? That is, in implementing an early-warning system would the banking authorities be acquiring a mechanism that generates self-fulfilling predictions and results in more rather than fewer bank failures? This scenario suggests that after a bank is predicted to be a "problem" that the banking authorities will misapply their remedial powers (to a greater extent than they have in the past) resulting in more rather than fewer bank failures. An early-warning system might result in more bank failures because of misidentification (i.e., Type-I errors) and hence a delayed on-site examination, but, other things equal, not because of greater misenforcement. A bank's estimated probability of failure *could* influence its treatment by examiners, the Federal Reserve discount window, etc., but that is highly unlikely, since most computer printouts of problem banks, especially those generated by research, are tolerated but not taken *that* seriously by the other members of the banking bureaucracy.

Except for the Comptroller's NBSS, early-warning research has been based upon esoteric techniques such as MDA, arctangent regression, and logit regression, techniques that are not easily understood by the layperson. Thus, the choice of techniques, while justified on academic grounds, has stifled the acceptance of early-warning models by supervisors and examiners. It is important that both the designers *and* the users of early-earning models understand how they work and the strengths and shortcomings of the models.

## 4.5 THE MULTIPLE DISCRIMINANT-ANALYSIS APPROACH

The basic statistical technique used in early-warning research at the FDIC was multiple discriminant analysis (MDA).[2] The critical feature of this technique is that it enables simultaneous consideration of many factors bearing on problem-bank status. Two approaches were employed. The first approach was the standard two-group MDA, which focused comparatively on groups of *examiner-determined* problem and nonproblem banks. In this approach, the goal is to distinguish between and reclassify problem and nonproblem banks on the basis of a model that provides maximum separation between groups of problem-nonproblem banks in past observations. In this context, the method asks whether a bank has financial characteristics more similar to the average problem bank than to the average nonproblem bank. The second approach (labeled the "outlier" technique) is a "bastard" form of MDA which employs only one group. This approach abandons the problem-nonproblem examiner dichotomy and hence the controvery about examiner identification error. The technique seeks to determine, from groups of banks with similar structural characteristics, which banks are outliers or atypical. Both approaches are discussed in detail in this chapter.

### a. The Standard Two-Group MDA Approach

MDA is basically an extension of univariate analysis of variance.[3] In this generalized context, vectors and dispersion (variance-covariance) matrices replace their univariate counterparts. The purposes of discriminant analysis are: to test for group mean and dispersion-matrix differences; to describe the overlap between groups; and to construct rules to classify observations (e.g., banks) into "appropriate" groups (e.g., problem-bank or nonproblem-bank groups).

The assumptions of discriminant analysis are: (1) the groups being analyzed are discrete and identifiable; (2) each observation in each group can be represented by a vector of variables (e.g., financial characteristics); and (3) the aforementioned variables are assumed to be continuous and multivariate normal in each group.

Regarding the first assumption, problem and nonproblem banks are "identifiable" in that the banking agencies have lists of banks they consider to need special supervision. Thus, by process of elimination, banks that are not on such lists are nonproblem banks. However, these banking groups may overlap to the extent that "examiner error" exists. That is, bank examiners may have been overscrupulous or lax in their examination procedures (or deceived by dishonest bankers), so that some banks listed as nonproblem institutions may in fact be problem banks and vice versa.

Regarding the second assumption, each bank in each group can be described by various financial characteristics measuring such things as profitability, liquidity, capital adequacy, sources and uses of revenue, etc. And finally, regarding the third assumption, most data sets are *not* likely to be multivariate normally distributed. Moreover, since most available normality tests are limited to one variable, multivariate normality is difficult to test. Furthermore, even if the assumption is violated, little can be done about it unless the joint probability density functions can be derived. On balance, most applied researchers have ignored the distribution problem and assumed that, if the assumption was violated, standard MDA procedures still would produce reasonable approximations.[4]

MDA should begin with the test of dispersion-matrix equality, since this test determines whether a linear or quadratic discriminant function should be used. If the equality hypothesis is rejected, a quadratic function should be employed; otherwise, a linear function is appropriate. Analyses of balance-sheet and income-expense data of problem and nonproblem banks rarely have found equal dispersion matrices across these groups. Consequently, the discriminant functions used almost always have been quadratic ones.

The significance of discriminant analysis is that it can, in the two-group case, reduce an m-dimensional problem to a one-dimensional level. That is, a multivariate test can be transformed to a univariate one via a linear or quadratic discriminant function, depending upon the test of dispersion-matrix equality. For simplicity, consider the linear discriminant function:

$$Z = X'B = b_1x_1 + b_2x_2 + \ldots + b_mx_m, \qquad (4.1)$$

where Z = the transformed one-dimensional discriminant variable (frequently referred to as the "Z-score" or discriminant score),

X = vector of *m* variables or characteristics (e.g., an operations and performance profile for a bank), and

B = vector of coefficients (to be determined).

The elements of the vector B, the b's, *can* be chosen to maximize the ratio of the weighted between-groups variance to the pooled within-groups variance of Z. [In nontechnical language, the purpose is to find the set of coefficients such that the differences between the two groups (e.g., problem and nonproblem banks) are maximized.] In the two-group case, the variance ratio maximized is

$$E = \frac{\dfrac{N_1N_2}{N_1 + N_2} \cdot B'dd'B}{B'S_WB}, \qquad (4.2)$$

where $N_1$ and $N_2$ are sample sizes, $\overline{X}_1$ and $\overline{X}_2$ are corresponding group mean vectors, $d = \overline{X}_1 - \overline{X}_2$, and $S_W$ is the pooled within-groups dispersion matrix.[5] Note that if there are no differences between the two groups (i.e., d = 0), then the variance ratio has a value of zero. In addition, note that if the group dispersion matrices (call them $S_1$ and $S_2$) are not equal, then it is not appropriate to pool $S_1$ and $S_2$ to form $S_w$.

Equation (4.2), after a slight adjustment, can be used to test for the significance of group mean differences (i.e., the significance of the distance (d = $\overline{X}_1 - \overline{X}_2$) between the two groups.[6] The assumptions of multivariate normality and dispersion-matrix equality are required for this test.[7] The adjusted E ratio has an F distribution with (m = number of variables) and ($N_1 + N_2 - m - 1$) degrees of freedom. As usual, if the test statistic is greater than the critical F-value, the null hypothesis of equality is rejected.

MDA is an important statistical technique for investigating group differences as measured by means and dispersion matrices. However, its main potential contribution to an early-warning system lies in its ability to classify observations into appropriate groups. Classifications are derived from a discriminant function such as equation (4.1) as follows. There is a cutoff Z-score, call it $Z_c$, associated with the estimated discriminant coefficients, the b's. Each observation to be classified will generate its own Z-score, call it $Z_i$. The relationship between $Z_i$ and $Z_c$ determines an observation's classification. For example, assuming a two-group model (e.g., problem-nonproblem) if $Z_i > Z_c$, assign to the nonproblem-bank group; if $Z_i \leq Z_c$, assign to the problem-bank group. If the estimated model can be shown to have predictive ability and other nice properties (e.g., stationarity over time), then it can be used to forecast banks that have characteristics *more similar* to problem banks than nonproblem banks. Such banks should, of course, be given priority supervisory attention.

The problems of classification focus upon the specification and choice of a criterion for "good classification" while the interpretation of this criterion depends upon the a priori probabilities of group membership and the costs of misclassification.[8] Discriminant-function coefficients are derived to minimize either (1) the expected overall classification error rate (R) or (2) the overall costs of misclassification (C).[9] Using Altman-Eisenbeis (1976) notation and a failure-prediction context, classification rules (for the two-group case) are derived by minimizing functions of the form:

$$R = q_1 p(1:2) + q_2 p(2:1) \text{ or} \tag{4.3}$$

$$C = q_1 p(1:2)C_{12} + q_2 p(2:1)C_{21}, \tag{4.4}$$

where

$q_1$ = prior probability of being classified as failed,

$q_2$ = prior probability of being classified as nonfailed,

$p(1:2)$ = conditional probability of being classified as nonfailed when in fact the bank is failed (Type-I error),

$p(2:1)$ = conditional probability of being classified as failed when in fact the bank is nonfailed (Type-II error),

$C_{12}$ = cost of Type-I error, and

$C_{21}$ = cost of Type-II error.

In some cases, one's assessment of classification efficiency may focus more upon one of the conditional-efficiency measures (i.e., a Type-I error or a Type-II error) rather than the overall error rate (R). For example, in terms of an early-warning system, the banking authorities, given their goal of failure prevention, would be most concerned about the size of the Type-I error and would be willing to accept a higher Type-II error for a lower Type-I error. However, as Joy and Tollefson (1975) point out, the total error rate (R) is the most complete measure of classification efficiency. In addition, Eisenbeis and Altman (1976) note that separate levels of acceptability for either of the conditional measures of efficiency introduce additional constraints not considered in the standard MDA classification model.

To qualify as a "predictive" classification, a priori probabilities of group membership and costs of classification must be treated explicitly. A priori probabilities or population priors are probabilities of group membership in the population. These probabilities are important because they determine: (1) the chance null hypothesis and (2) the MDA cutoff score (see equations (4.3) and (4.4) above). It is rather common practice for MDA researchers to set the a priori probabilities equal to their sample proportions. However, if the sample group frequencies are not equal to the a priori probabilities of group membership, then predictive inferences based upon such classifications may be seriously misleading. MDA classifications that do not incorporate a priori probabilities and, if relevant, costs of misclassification, are not "predictive" but only "descriptive" classifications, i.e., they describe the overlap between groups).

For illustrative purposes, consider a failure-prediction model based upon a paired sample of failed and nonfailed banks. In this case, using the sample proportions as a priori probabilities implies that $q_1 = q_2 = .5$. However, using the calendar year as a base to define populations, 1976 has produced the largest number of bank failures (sixteen) since 1942 (twenty). Thus, using 1976 as the relevant base year, $q_1 = 16/14,000 = .001$ or 0.1 percent. Alternatively, over the years 1964–1976, 88 insured commercial banks failed. On this basis, which would be more appropriate for a time-series study, $q_1 = 88/14,000 = .006$ or 0.6 percent. Clearly, $q_1 = .5$ would appear to be a much too generous estimate of the *a priori* probability of bank failure.[10]

The important point is that when sample proportions are employed as a priori probabilities, classification results tend to be more "descriptive" than "predictive." Moreover, without parametric adjustments, a "descriptive" model should not be applied to the population for "predictive" purposes.

One of the problem-bank models used in my early-warning research at the FDIC was presented in the *Journal of Finance* (March 1975). The classifications, based upon a ten-variable model, were considered to be "descriptive" ones. Let us examine the efficiency of these classifications using criteria proposed by Joy and Tollefson (1975). The classification results for the year 1972 for the 206 banks (a paired sample of 103 "new" problem banks and 103 nonproblem banks) are presented in Table 4.1.

Using the Type-I and Type-II errors from Table 4.1 *and* assuming that the sample proportions were equal to the a priori probability of problem status, the overall error (R) was (see equation 4.3)

$$R = .5 (.2815) + .5(.2136)$$

$$= .2476$$

Alternatively, the overall accuracy rate (1-R) was .7524. How "good" is this observed total efficiency? Joy and Tollefson (1975) have suggested that, in the absence of other criteria, alternative chance-classification schemes are an appropriate standard of comparison. They considered a naive maximum-chance model, which assigns all observations to the largest group, and a proportional chance model, which randomly assigns observations to groups with probabilities equal to group frequencies. In

*Table 4.1*

Classification Results for Problem and Nonproblem Banks

| Actual Membership | Total | Predicted Membership* | |
|---|---|---|---|
| | | Problem | Nonproblem |
| Problem | 103 | 74 | 29 |
| | | (71.85) | (28.15) |
| Nonproblem | 103 | 22 | 81 |
| | | (21.36) | (78.64) |
| Total | 206 | 96 | 110 |

*Predictions were made using a quadratic equation and the Lachenbauch holdout technique
Figures in parentheses are percentages.

this case, since the sample sizes or group frequencies are equal, the expected probability of correct classification under either chance model is .5, that is,

$$103/206 = (103/206)(103/206) + (103/206)(103/206) = .5$$

The performance of the problem-bank model (.75) was significantly better at the 5 percent level (Z = 7.4).[11]

As mentioned above, the banking authorities should be most concerned about the Type-I error in an early-warning system. Accordingly, the relative accuracy of the conditional efficiencies should be evaluated also. In this case, the relevant concern is with the probability of classifying a bank as a problem, given that it is a nonproblem. This probability is .7185 (= 1 minus the Type-I error of .2815). For the proportional-chance model, the conditional probability is .5, which is significantly lower than .7185 at the five percent level (Z = 6.4). Thus, the problem banks were classified significantly better than chance. Finally, note that the nonproblem banks also were classified significantly better than chance (i.e., .7864 versus .5 with Z = 8.4).

The problem banks analyzed in this model were identified as financially troubled institutions during 1972 and the first few months of 1973. In addition to the classifications based upon year-end 1972 data, classifications also were made using year-end 1971, 1970, and 1969 data. Although the efficiency of the classifications declined going back in time, only the 1969 problem-bank classifications did not significantly improve upon the chance models described above (i.e., .5364 versus .5 with Z = 1.1).[12]

To summarize, these problem-bank classifications, which are *representative* of the "best" error rates that I was able to achieve in the FDIC project, performed significantly better than alternative chance models. However, since the population a priori probability for a commercial bank to become a problem is not as high as .5 and since the costs of misclassification were ignored (whereas these costs are likely to be very important to the banking authorities, especially the costs of Type-I error), these classifications must be regarded as merely "descriptive" and not "predictive."[13] Thus, these results do not show that problem-bank models contain a substantial element of predictability. What they demonstrate is that problem and nonproblem banks have significantly different mean profiles and significantly different variance-covariance matrices. In addition, the classification results describe groups that appeared to have a substantial degree of group overlap.

As indicated in Chapter 3, the number of problem banks tends to vary with the state of the economy. Thus, based upon past history, about 3 percent of the population of banks tend to be considered problem institutions after recessionary periods and about 1 percent after nonrecessionary periods. On average, 2 percent is a reasonable estimate of the a priori probability of a commercial bank becoming a problem institution. Clearly, using $q_1 = .02$ and $q_2 = .98$ (as opposed to $q_1 = q_2 = .5$) will alter both the chance null hypotheses and the classification error rates and hence the results of the efficiency analysis conducted above. Applying the null hypothesis to the proportional-chance model, the expected total accuracy would be $(.02)(.02) + (.98)(.98) = .96$. Obviously, the MDA classification error rates will have to improve to outperform the proportional-chance model. While $q_2 = .98$ will result in an improvement in the Type-II error, $q_1 = .02$ will result in a deterioration of the Type-I error. These movements are just the opposite of the trade-off that the banking authorities would be willing to make. It is clear that the costs of misclassification need to be treated explicitly in this case.

From 1934 to 1975, 519 insured banks have failed with total losses to the FDIC of approximately \$237 million.[14] Thus, the average bank failure has cost the FDIC approximately \$457,000. In contrast, during 1975, the FDIC incurred *total* administrative and operating expenses of approximately \$68 million. Given the 8,595 insured nonmember banks in existence as of December 31, 1975, the FDIC spent approximately \$7,900 per bank. Alternatively, given the 28,254 field examinations and investigations conducted by the FDIC during 1975, the average cost of such a field operation was approximately \$2,400. Note that both of these figures reflect average costs and not the more relevant marginal costs. In addition, both of the figures could be viewed as overestimates, since supervisory costs were lumped together with other FDIC costs. Alternatively, if the activities of the FDIC's Division of Supervision are viewed as not being independent of the activities of other divisions (e.g., legal, research, etc.), the degree of overestimation would be much smaller. Whatever the proper nominal costs are, the important point is that a bank's failure would appear to be more costly than trying to prevent (over some reasonable period of time) the bank's collapse.[15]

Setting the average cost of a bank failure at \$457,000 and the "supervisory" expense-per-bank figure at \$7,900 produces a conservative estimate of the cost ratio of approximately 58-to-1. Weighting this ratio by the ratio of a priori probabilities of problem status ($.02/.98$), a weighted cost ratio is 1.18-to-1. That is, from equation (4.4), $(q_1/q_2)(C_{12}/C_{21}) = (.02/.98)(58) = 1.18$. Rewriting the ratio as $q_1C_{12}/q_2C_{21}$, it is clear that although $q_1$ is relatively small $C_{12}$ is relatively large and vice versa for $q_2$ and $C_{21}$. Thus, the net effect is a weighted cost ratio of approximately one, which is equal to $q_1/q_2$ when $q_1 = q_2$ (i.e., in paired-sample tests where sample proportions are used as the a priori probabilities).

The important point is that explicit treatment of the a priori probabilities of problem status *and* of the costs of misclassification suggests that for a (problem-bank) classification loss function these effects tend to be offsetting. Thus, this further analysis suggests that the classifications described above also can be interpreted as "predictive" ones.

An alternative way of approximating the ratio of misclassification costs in MDA analysis is to use the Bayesian approach suggested by Joy and Tollefson (1975), pp. 735–737. This approach focuses upon the expected costs of alternative decision-making processes, that is, on the costs of MDA relative to alternative models (e.g., chance models). Equation (4.4) represents the overall expected costs of misclassification for MDA, call it C (MDA). The expected costs of the proportional- and maximum-chance model are, respectively,

$$C(PROP) = q_1q_2C_{12} + q_1q_2C_{21} = q_1q_2(C_{12} + C_{21})$$

and

$$C(MAX) = q_1C_{12}.$$

The expected costs are, of course, determined by the prior probabilities ($q_i$) and the cost of misclassification ($C_{ij}$). In addition to the chance alternatives, nonchance alternatives may exist. For example, the bank-examination process could be viewed as alternative to an early-warning system and the costs of the two compared. However, since early-warning systems are not proposed as substitutes for the bank-examination process but as complements, they are not truly alternatives.

Since the $C_{ij}$ may be difficult to estimate in some cases, Joy and Tollefson have proposed the Bayesian approach as a way of evaluating alternative classification models when the $C_{ij}$ are unknown. Since the $C_{ij}$ have been estimated for this problem-bank framework (i.e., $C_{12}/C_{21} = 58$), this approach can be used to cross-check cost estimates. Using $q_1 = .02$ and $q_2 = .98$ and the Type-I and Type-II errors of .2815 and .2136, respectively, the expected cost of MDA is:[16]

$$C(MDA) = .0056C_{12} + .2093C_{21}.$$

Using the proportional-chance model, either classification error would occur with probability $q_1q_2 = (.02)(.98) = .0196$ and the expected cost is:

$$C(PROP) = .0196C_{12} + .0196C_{21}.$$

For the maximum-chance model, the expected cost is:[17]

$$C(MAX) = .02C_{12}.$$

To determine the least costly classification model, C(MDA) is compared to C(PROP) and C(MAX). The MDA aproach will be less costly than the proportional-chance model if and only if $C_{12} > 13.5C_{21}$; for the maximum-chance model, the requirement is $C_{12} > 14.5C_{21}$. Given the crude approximation $C_{12} = 58C_{12}$, it is clear that the MDA approach is "superior" to each of the alternative chance models.

It is important to note that the Bayesian approach suggested by Joy and Tollefson only attempts to determine a cost-cutoff point relevant for choosing one model over another. Since the only information required to make this decision is the ratio of costs relative to some critical value, knowledge of the actual misclassification costs is not needed. Thus, the critical range of 13.5 to 14.5 merely sets the minimum value (or "floor") above which the MDA model is deemed to be superior. In contrast, the estimated cost ratio of 58 was derived from the historical costs of bank failures and bank supervision. Finally, note that if the error rates were reestimated using $q_1 = .02$ and $q_2 = .98$ (see note 16) and if, for illustrative purposes, the Type-I error was .40 (up from .28) and the Type-II error was .05 (down from .21),[18] the relevant cost ratios would be 2.5 for the proportional-chance model and 4.1 for the maximum-chance model. Under these circumstances, it is even easier to chose the MDA approach over the alternative chance models.

The relative ease with which the MDA approach has been deemed to be "superior" to the alternative chance models suggests perhaps that chance models may be inappropriate alternatives in this context and/or that a cost ratio of 58 is an overestimate. Regarding the first point, it is naive to expect that the banking authorities realistically would consider using a chance model as a relevant decision-making alternative, especially given their Congressional mandate of failure prevention. But while the comparisons presented above may not be very realistic, they do indicate, on a mechanistic level, that the MDA approach is to be preferred. Regarding the second point, while the level of the estimated cost ratio (58) does appear to be "high," the conservative approach of the banking authorities since the 1930s suggests that the ratio should be high. Moreover, given the cost to the FDIC of USNB's failure ($150 million) and the banking difficulties of the 1970s, the banking authorities may figure that the cost ratio is getting even higher.

In addition to the efficiency and costs-of-misclassification aspects of an MDA prediction model, another aspect of predictability is the extent to which the sample banks are representative of the population of insured banks. An individual problem or failed bank is, of course, an atypical institution. Moreover, until recently, both typical problem and failed banks have been relatively small unit banks located in rural areas. But year in and year out, problem banks do tend to be more representative of the banking population than failed banks. Accordingly, a paired-sample technique treats a more representative sample of banks when problem banks (rather than failed ones) comprise the test group.

The more representative of the population the sample banks are, the more easily population inferences can be made. Thus, for predictive purposes, a random sample representative of the population is most appropriate. Research at the FDIC used *both* the paired- and random-sample techniques. Additional arguments in favor of a random sample for a control group are: (1) that a random sample is less time-consuming to generate and therefore less costly than a paired sample, and (2) since the matching or pairing process is never exact, arbitrary rules-of-thumb must be employed in the matching process.

### b. The Outlier Technique (Peer-Group Analysis)

The so-called outlier technique developed as an outgrowth of three factors. First, the results of the MDA approach showed a substantial degree of group overlap between examiner-determined problem and nonproblem banks in terms of balance-sheet and income-expense characteristics. Since it was impossible to determine the exact cause of the overlap (it was due to either examiner-identification error and/or incomplete MDA model development), an alternative approach to identifying potential problem banks was needed. Second, since large banks present the greatest degree of risk exposure to the FDIC's deposit-insurance fund, the FDIC sought a technique for evaluating the "safety and soundness" of such banks. Since (at that time) large problem banks were rare, a two-group problem-nonproblem approach was not feasible. Finally, my interest in analyzing the failures of USNB, Franklin, and other large billion-dollar banks required an alternative to the problem-nonproblem approach. An outlier or peer-group analysis seemed to meet these three requirements. It did not depend on examiners' identification or problem-nonproblem status; it could be used for evaluating the riskiness of large banks; and it could be used for case studies.

The basic premise of the outlier technique is to determine those banks that have balance-sheet and income-expense characteristics that are atypical or "outliers" relative to a control group of peer banks. Since the technique is not constrained by examiners' definitions of problem-nonproblem status, it is a very flexible one. For example, in addition to being used by the banking authorities, the technique can be employed by anyone (e.g., uninsured depositors, bank analysts, stockholders, academic researchers, etc.) interested in analyzing the performance or safety and soundness of any bank or group of banks. The technique, however, does present some problems in application. First, is the problem of determining the cutoff point for identifying outliers. Purely from a statistical-significance point of view, the standard 5 percent level of significance or a standard-deviation criterion presents an appealing framework. For example, the banking authorities, who are concerned about making Type-I errors (i.e., not identifying adverse outliers as outliers), could schedule bank examinations by moving from "adverse" outliers to "good" outliers, with the degree of examination intensity varying directly with the bank's degree of atypicalness. Moreover, at some point in the outlier spectrum, a critical "no-examination" point could be established beyond which banks only would be inspected for the things that have been the major causes of bank failures (e.g., fraud, embezzlement, insider transactions, etc.), factors likely to be deliberately concealed from balance-sheet and income-expense data. In addition, a bank's degree of examination intensity and its examination findings could be used to determine its assessment and examination fees and its deposit-insurance premium.

A second problem that arises in applying the outlier technique is to select appropriate variables. My personal preference is to begin with a "bottom-line" or profitability ratio to measure a bank's overall performance. Then, depending upon the purpose of the investigation, measures of liquidity, capital adequacy, loan quality and volume, sources and uses of revenue, etc., can be added.[19] These variables may be examined one at a time or as a set. If a set of variables is analyzed simultaneously, the only real constraint on the size of the set is the invertibility of the related variance-covariance matrix. In general, since banking variables are so closely related, it is difficult to obtain independent pieces of information. The more variables are included in a set, the greater are the chances that the matrix will be singular or noninvertible. This problem, of course, only arises when the data are analyzed simultaneously as in MDA or regression analysis. Alternatively, a set of variables can be analyzed individually and then combined using a weighting scheme based upon the research's judgment and knowledge of the task at hand; such an approach, however, is subject to the criticism of being arbitrary.

A third problem in using the outlier technique is to select an appropriate peer group. Stratification on the basis of factors such as asset or deposit size, location, structure, and type of business (e.g., retail vs. wholesale) is a common approach in the selection of a peer group. For example, in my analysis of USBN's collapse, the control or peer group consisted of the thirty largest branch banks in California, excluding such outliers as Bank of America and foreign-controlled banks. Thus, size, structure, and location were the control factors for determining the peer group.

The concept of outlier or peer-group analysis is the cornerstone of the Comptroller's National Bank Surveillance System (NBSS) that was proposed by Haskins and Sells (1975), pp. 59–78. Haskins and Sells recommended that NBSS consist of four basic components:

1. A data-collection system;
2. A computer-based monitoring system that would detect unusual or significantly changed circumstances within a bank and within the national banking system;
3. An evaluation by experienced personnel of the impact of such changes on bank soundness; and
4. A review procedure that would provide administrative controls over all proposed OCC remedial actions, including those of Washington personnel (p. 60).

The second component is, of course, the outlier or peer-group part of NBSS. According to Haskins and Sells, key-indicator ratios for each national bank would be compared with: (1) the bank's own past performance and (2) the current and past performance of the bank's peer group. On the basis of this analysis, early-warning action ". . . would be initiated for banks whose statistics either fall outside acceptable ranges or vary significantly within acceptable ranges" (p. 60).

The important components of the NBSS outlier analysis are the key indicators and the peer groups. Haskins and Sells (pp. 62–64) recommend 22 primary indicators (18 for banking departments and four for trust departments) and 17 additional key indicators for large banks (15 for banking departments and two for trust departments).[20] Some of the factors considered in selecting the peer groups for banks were (p. 65):

1. Competition,
2. Branching status,
3. Types of services offered,
4. Types of lending performed (wholesale banking, retail banking, consumer credit, etc.)
5. Geographic distribution, and
6. Size.

However, the peer groups that Haskins and Sells considered most meaningful for surveillance analysis were stratified only on the basis of asset size, branching status, and location [SMSA vs. non-SMSA, where Standard Metropolitan Statistical Area (SMSA) was defined as a county or contiguous counties containing a city of 50,000 population or more]. These suggested peer groups are presented in Table 4.2.

Haskins and Sells (p. 63) recommended that banks with assets in excess of $500 million be given the closest attention by NBSS, since the collapse of such an institution can have a significant effect on the public's confidence in the banking system. Table 4.2 shows that about 115 (2.5 percent) of these large banks have national charters. This is about two

*Table 4.2*

National-Bank Peer Groups Recommended by Haskins and Sells

| Asset Size and other Characteristics | Approximate Number of Banks | (%) |
|---|---|---|
| 1. Greater than $1 billion | 55 | (1.2) |
| 2. $500 million to $1 billion | 60 | (1.3) |
| 3. $100 million to $500 million | | |
|    a. Branching states | 200 | (4.3) |
|    b. Nonbranching states | 150 | (3.2) |
| 4. $25 million to $100 million | | |
|    a. Principal offices in an SMSA | | |
|       i. Branching states | 200 | (4.3) |
|       ii. Nonbranching states | 400 | (8.6) |
|    b. Principal offices not in an SMSA | | |
|       i. Branching states | 200 | (4.3) |
|       ii. Nonbranching states | 500 | (10.7) |
| 5. Less than $35 million | | |
|    a. Principal offices in an SMSA | | |
|       i. Branching states | 200 | (4.3) |
|       ii. Nonbranching states | 400 | (8.6) |
|    b. Principal offices not in an SMSA | | |
|       i. Branching states | 300 | (6.4) |
|       ii. Nonbranching states | 2,000 | (42.8) |
| Total | 4,665 | (100.0) |

*Source:* Haskins and Sells (1975), p. 66.

out of every third large commercial bank.[21] As such, the national bank-ing system presents the greatest threat to the safety and soundness of the banking industry. In contrast, about three out of every fifth nationally chartered bank (2,900, 2,000 of which are unit banks located in non-SMSA areas) has total assets of less than $25 million. While the custom-ers of these small institutions are no less deserving of government pro-tection than those of large institutions, de facto their banks receive less surveillance and therefore less protection because the risk to the system of the failure of a small bank is relatively small.

The NBSS recommended by Haskins and Sells was couched in a flexi-ble framework. Thus, the key indicators, peer groups, and other aspects of the system were designed such that changes in the individual components supposedly would not disrupt the system's overall effectiveness.

## 4.6 ALTERNATIVE SYSTEMS AND RESEARCH

Early-warning research at the Federal Reserve Bank of New York (Banking Studies Department) by Stuhr and Van Wicklen (1974), Korobow and Stuhr (1975), Korobow, Stuhr, and Martin (1976 and 1977), and Martin (1978) has been quite similar to the MDA analyses described above. Although the research at the New York Fed virtually parallels research at the FDIC, the efforts were developed independently, except for the exchange of ideas and papers at several seminars and meetings. Because of the similarity of research designs, the New York Fed studies will not be reviewed in detail.[22] There are, however, some characteristics of the New York Fed's research that should be emphasized. First, the research was of an "academic" nature and developed in-house, as opposed to the efforts of Haskins and Sells, who were hired as consultants by the Comptroller of the Currency. Second, the differences in the research efforts were of a relatively subtle nature and not differences of substance. For example, while my research used mainly MDA models, recent efforts by the New York Fed have focused upon arctangent and logit probability models. And third, the New York Fed's research has dealt mainly with member banks located in the Second Federal Reserve District. Thus, strictly speaking, their findings only are applicable to member banks in that District. The latest research output by the New York Fed has been a nationwide test of the early-warning concepts and procedures developed for member banks in its District. The models tested were regional and size-class early-warning functions for the years 1969–1975 (see Korobow et al., 1977).

To summarize, the purpose, foundations, and findings of the FDIC's and New York Fed's early-warning research have been quite similar. The main differences have been of an academic nature focusing upon such things as statistical models and theoretical issues. Thus, only in the narrowest sense of the term, can the two approaches be considered alternatives.

The Board of Governors of the Federal Reserve System was the last of the Federal banking agencies to hop on the early-warning bandwagon. As such, they should benefit from the research that has been completed at their sister agencies. Hanweck (1976) has reported that the Fed's early-warning research is part of a broader study designed to develop decision rules for classifying potentially failing banks and bank holding companies. The Fed's early-warning research is going to focus upon developing a failure-prediction model as opposed to a problem-prediction one and thus it can be regarded as an alternative to the FDIC's and the New York Fed's research. However, the proposed methodology of the research is quite similar to previous early-warning studies. For example, MDA is to be used to develop classification rules and to reduce the dimensionality of the variable space. But to test for the significance of exogenous variables and to estimate alternative classifications rules, multivariate probit analysis is planned.

The development of a failure-prediction model has an important potential advantage over the development of a problem-prediction one. Because of potential examiner-identification error, problem banks may not be as *distinct* from nonproblem banks, as failed banks are from nonfailed banks. (Recall that one of the assumptions of MDA is that the groups are discrete and identifiable.) Thus, other things being equal, failed-nonfailed groups would be expected to have less group overlap than problem-nonproblem groups. While some form of managerial dishonesty has been the number-one cause of most bank failures, a large volume of substandard loans relative to a bank's capital and reserves has been the most important variable separating problem and nonproblem banks. Thus, the other-things-equal constraint does not hold. Accordingly, since managerial dishonesty is likely to be deliberately concealed from balance-sheet and income-expense data, failed and nonfailed banks may exhibit more overlap than originally expected and thus their potential advantages over the problem-nonproblem approach may be eliminated. Because of the dishonesty factor, a failure-prediction model based upon financial data will be subject to a powerful test.

In addition to the early-warning research being conducted by the Federal banking agencies, a number of other groups, both private (i.e., nongovernment) and public, are or have been engaged in analyzing the "safety and soundness" of commercial banks und other financial institutions. While some of these groups have done research, most of the private groups have been engaged in the business of massaging data and selling the repackaged information (presumably at a profit) as some form of bank-performance or bank-quality analysis. To conclude this section, let us briefly mention some of these alternative systems and research.

The California and Illinois state banking commissions have done some work in the early-warning and surveillance area. The efforts of the California agency have been directed toward monitoring the operations and performance of both commercial banks and savings and loan associations. The Illinois program, which was started by former Commissioner Bob Bartell (currently President of the Federal Home Loan Bank of Chicago), focused upon commercial banks only. The Bartell-directed system attempted to combine computer-analyzed financial data with examiners' knowledge and experience.

Altman (1975, 1976), noted for his corporate bankruptcy models, has developed early-warning systems for savings and loan associations (SLAs) and over-the-counter broker-dealers. As in his analyses of corporate bankruptcy, Altman employed MDA to develop his prediction models. In his SLA study for the Federal Home Loan Bank Board, Altman (1975) employed a three-group classification based upon non-problem, temporary-problem, and serious-problem SLAs. Financial ratios and operational trends were used to develop a 12-variable performance-predictor system. In contrast, in his broker-dealer study, Altman (1976) used failed and nonfailed firms to develop an early-warning system. The MDA model developed in this case was a six-variable one. Finally, both the SLA and broker-dealer models employed quadratic classification equations.

In the private sector, three types of bank analysis are produced. First, large corporations conduct internal analyses designed to identify banks or bank holding companies with financial weaknesses. Financial managers of these corporations do not want to be embarrassed by having their liquid funds temporarily frozen or subject to loss because of a bank failure. As a result, corporations such as General Motors and Exxon use computers to monitor the financial performance of the banks they do business with. In addition to developing their own early-warning systems, these corporations may provide funding for research to be conducted by outside interest. For example, Gulf Oil Corporation Foundation provided partial funding for a commercial-bank failure-prediction study by Rose and Scott (1978).

The second type of bank (or bank holding company) analysis is being conducted by bank analysts or investment bankers and even by some large banks themselves. These analyses, which mainly focus upon large banks with actively traded issues, are designed for use by actual or would-be bank stockholders or debtholders. Individuals or businesses then can purchase comparative performance analyses of major bank and bank holding companies from these companies.

Finally, the third type of bank analysis focuses upon the performance of a bank or group of banks by geographic area such as state, SMSA, or county. Some of the more flexible programs permit the customer to select the members of the control group, while others are fixed and simply generate lists of banks in an area by deposit size, earnings, or some other variable. Such analyses are sold mainly to state banking associations and their member banks. For example, if a small-town banker wants to know how his or her bank is doing relative to the other banks in the town, county, or state such reports can be obtained. Most of these reports, however, do not supply analysis, only numbers.

## 4.7 SUMMARY AND CONCLUSIONS

The reader who expected to find in this chapter "the" early-warning system or "the" statistical model for identifying banks with financial difficulties probably was disappointed. The truth of the matter is that, in terms of a compact statistical model, an *operational* early-warning system currently does not exist. The New York Fed's models, which apparently are being applied to the entire Federal Reserve System's supervisory activities, come the closest to meeting this requirement. The FDIC's fast start in early-warning research appeared to be bogged down by uncertainty regarding the role of research in the agency and by changes in personnel. However, the FDIC recently instituted a computerized financial data analysis system, called Integrated Monitoring System (IMS), to oversee bank performance between examinations. Thus, in spite of the unsettled circumstances at the FDIC, some progress has been made. However, the FDIC's IMS is closer to an NBSS-type system than a statistical model. The Comptroller's NBSS is operational, but it does not meet the requirements of being a statistical model. However, in terms of an operational mechanism, an NBSS-type system may be the compromise result (between research and examination) of early-warning research.

## NOTES

1. Sinkey (1975), Guttentag (1975), Haskings and Sells (1975), Korobow and Stuhr (1975), and Stuhr and Van Wicklen (1974) have proposed that "early-warning" or "bank surveillance" systems be used to complement the traditional on-site, bank-examination process.

1a. Some of these questions were raised in an earlier version of Martin's (1978) paper.

2. The foundations of MDA are described in Eisenbeis and Avery (1972).

3. The description of MDA given in this section draws heavily on Eisenbeis and Avery (1972) and Eisenbeis (1977). The reader without a strong statistical background may want to skip this section.

4. Violation of this assumption is probably the least-worried-about problem in applications of discriminant anlaysis. See Eisenbeis (1977) for a discussion of this problem and of available normality tests.

5. There are several alternative methods of calculating a discriminant function. Since the ratio E is homogenous of degree zero, only the ratios of the coefficients can be determined uniquely (i.e., the coefficients are not unique.) See Eisenbeis and Avery (1972), p. 4–5.

6. The adjustment procedure is described by Eisenbeis and Avery (1972), p. 8.

7. If the dispersion matrices are not equal, the appropriate test (due to Anderson) is described in Eisenbeis and Avery (1972), p. 25.

8. See Eisenbeis and Avery (1972), Eisenbeis (1977), Sinkey (1975), Joy and Tollefson (1975), Altman (1976), and Altman and Eisenbeis (1976).

9. This statement is simply an alternative way of saying that the coefficients are derived to achieve maximum separation between the groups.

10. Regarding the a priori probabilities of corporate bankruptcy, Altman and Eisenbeis (1976), p. 12, have stated ". . . to the extent that failure is a dynamic process and is affected by exogenous forces which may vary systematically over time with the state of the economy, it may very well be that a priori probabilities themselves are random variables."

11. The test statistic, according to Joy and Tollefson(1975), p. 732, is:
$$Z = (\bar{y} - p)/(p(1 - p)/N)^{1/2},$$
where $\bar{y}$ is the proportion of observations correctly classified by the discriminant function; p is the probability of classification by chance; and N is the total sample size. Note that this Z is a test statistic and not a discriminant-function Z-score.

12. The sample sizes for 1969–1979 were 110 and 110 for a total of 220.

13. "Descriptive" classifications are useful for determining to what extent the groups overlap [see Sinkey (March 1975), pp. 31–33]. Highly accurate reclassifications imply little group overlap while highly inaccurate ones suggest a substantial degree of group overlap.

14. Includes estimated losses in 61 cases that still are active. Losses are calculated as disbursements minus recoveries minus estimated additional recoveries *(FDIC Annual Report 1975)*. As of March 15, 1975, the FDIC's revised estimate of its eventual loss in USNB's receivership was $150 million, the original estimate was $48.3 million. Thus, the FDIC could lose more money because of USNB's failure than it has on all previous bank closings.

15. In the case of a large problem bank, such as Franklin, the lender of last resort, the Fed, may be reluctant to subsidize it for very long—Franklin got about six months, see Chapter 6.

16. This is only an approximation since the error rates were estimated using $q_1 = q_2 = .5$. Ideally the discrimination function should be reestimated with $q_1 = .02$ and $q_2 = .98$ and the new error rates observed. However, the data needed for such a test are no longer available to me.

17. Note that this naive model assigns all banks to the nonproblem group and the only error observed is the Type-I misclassification.

18. The error rates would be expected to move in these directions, if $q_1 = .02$ and $q_2 = .98$ were substituted for $q_1 = q_2 = .5$. The arbitrarily-chosen error rates of .40 and .05 simply are used to indicate the direction the critical value is expected to move.

19. Chapter 5 of this book deals with ratio analysis for banks and discusses in detail various ratios and sets of ratios that can be used to measure a bank's performance.

20. These variables will be described in Chapter 5. "Large" applies to banks with assets of $500 million or more.

21. As of December 31, 1975, there were 187 large commercial banks with 124 supervised by the OCC, 41 by the Fed, and 22 by the FDIC. The figures for deposits greater than $1 billion were 60, 22, and 3, respectively.

22. See Altman et al. (1979) for a review of these studies and others.

# Financial Characteristics of Problem and Failed Banks

## 5.1 INTRODUCTION

This chapter focuses upon the financial characteristics of problem and failed banks based upon balance-sheet and income-expense data. Comparative ratio analysis is employed to analyze groups of (1) failed and nonfailed banks and (2) problem and nonproblem banks. Since most of my analyses of problem and nonproblem banks have been disseminated in other publications [Sinkey (1974–1978)], the emphasis is upon the financial characteristics of (1) failed and nonfailed banks and (2) unpublished problem and nonproblem banks results. Other researchers have found variables quite similar to those presented in this chapter to be important in their studies of distressed financial institutions. Thus, a growing body of evidence identifies variables that are important in analyzing the performance and "safety and soundness" of commercial banks. Consequently, individuals who want to undertake such analyses will find a solid foundation for "early-warning" or "surveillance" research in this chapter.

## 5.2 FINANCIAL RATIOS AND RATIO ANALYSIS

Ratio analysis is a technique or tool for evaluating the financial condition of a firm. The basic component of ratio analysis is a single ratio, constructed by dividing one balance-sheet and/or income-expense item by another. The denominator of such ratios may be conceived as a "base" or scale factor. For example, a profitability ratio would relate a firm's profits to its asset or equity-capital base to provide a return-on-assets or return-on-equity measure of a firm's overall or "bottom-line" perfor-

## Take Me To Your Ledger

SIXTH ILLUSTRATION

mance. Suppose that the return-on-equity is .10 or 10 percent. By itself, this piece of information does not tell us much about the financial condition of the firm. It does tell us that the firm's profits were positive. While this is better than negative profits (i.e., losses), we need a standard or norm against which to evaluate it. To provide a meaningful basis for evaluating a firm's financial condition, comparisons with other firms and/or with own performance at other times are required. The important point is that by themselves ratios are relatively useless. To be useful, ratios must be (1) analyzed over time (trend analysis) and/or (2) compared with a control group of *similar* firms (cross-section or peer-group analysis).

To illustrate, suppose that the firm with a 10 percent return-on-equity (ROE) had the following returns over the previous four periods:

| Period | ROE |
|--------|-----|
| t-1    | 8%  |
| t-2    | 6%  |
| t-3    | 4%  |
| t-4    | 2%  |

Suppose further that in period *t* a ROE distribution for a control group of similar firms is normally distributed with a mean of 6 percent and a standard deviation of 1.5 percent. A systematic analysis of this firm's performance indicates that it has improved significantly over the past five years (trend analysis) and that it is currently one of the top performers compared to its peers (cross-section or peer-group analysis).

One of the most important tasks for any financial manager (and particularly for a banker) is to evaluate a firm's past performance and its present strengths and weaknesses. Ratio analysis can provide an analyst with a fairly good picture of a firm's past and present financial condition. Regarding remedial action for observed malperformance, it is important to recognize that ratio analysis focuses only on *symptoms* not on *causes* of financial difficulty. The driving force behind an enterprise's performance is its management: financial planning, policies, and controls ultimately determine a firm's performance. Management is the major cause of business failure, either through inefficiencies or (especially in banking) some form of misconduct.

Most corporation-finance textbooks [e.g., Weston and Brigham (1975)] develop financial ratios for four aspects of a firm's financial condition: (1) liquidity, (2) debt or leverage, (3) activity, and (4) profitability. Liquidity ratios measure a firm's ability to meet its maturing current or short-term obligations. Debt or leverage ratios measure a firm's financial risk and ability to meet its long-term obligations (i.e., long-term liquidity or solvency). Activity ratios measure how efficiently or effectively a firm utilizes its resources. And finally, profitability ratios measure a firm's overall efficiency or "bottom-line" performance. Examples of these four different types of ratios are presented below.

### 1. Liquidity Ratios

A liquid asset is one that is readily converted into cash with little or no price depreciation (capital loss). Liquidity is a characteristic an asset may or may not possess and which a collection of assets (i.e., a firm) may or may not possess. Liquidity ratios basically compare short-term assets (STA) to short-term liabilities (STL), where short term usually means one year or less to maturity. In general, the larger STA is relative to STL, the greater is a firm's liquidity. However, if a firm has too many liquid assets, it can reduce its profitability because short-term or liquid assets usually have lower rates of return. Most liquidity ratios are special cases of the following general liquidity ratio:

$$\frac{\sum_{i=1}^{n} \gamma_i \, (STA)_i}{\sum_{i=1}^{m} \delta_i \, (STL)_i} , \qquad (5.1)$$

where $\gamma_i$ $(1 \geq \gamma_i \geq 0)$ is the liquidity coefficient attached to the ith short-term asset and $\delta_i$ $(1 \geq \delta_i \geq 0)$ is the maturity coefficient attached to the ith short-term liability. If $\gamma = 1$, the asset is considered to be perfectly liquid (i.e., easily and quickly converted into cash without price depreciation or capital loss, e.g., cash), while $\gamma = 0$ implies that the asset is perfectly illiquid (i.e., not convertible into cash or convertible into cash only with substantial price depreciation or capital loss). If $\delta = 1$, the liability is due (or past due), while $\delta = 0$ implies that the obligation is relatively small and/or not due for 12 months. Although $\delta$ so far has been treated as a maturity coefficient, it is a function of both the size and maturity of the short-term obligation, that is,

$$\delta_i = \delta \, (\overset{-}{\text{maturity}}, \overset{+}{\text{size}}). \qquad (5.2)$$

One of the most general and most frequently used liquidity ratios is the current ratio, that is,

$$\frac{\text{Current Assets}}{\text{Current Liabilities}} = \frac{\sum_{i=1}^{n} STA_i}{\sum_{i=1}^{m} STL_i} . \qquad (5.3)$$

Equation (5.3) is simply equation (5.1) with $\gamma = \delta = 1$ for included items and zero for excluded ones. The quick or acid-test ratio has $\gamma = \delta = 1$ except for $\gamma_j = 0$, where $\gamma_j =$ the coefficient for inventories, that is,

$$\frac{\text{Current Assets-Inventory}}{\text{Current Liabilities}} = \frac{\sum_{i=1}^{n} STA_i - STA_j}{\sum_{i=1}^{m} STL_i} , \qquad (5.4)$$

where the jth short-term asset is inventory. Thus, equation (5.4) is the same as (5.3), except that inventories, usually regarded as the least-liquid current asset, are excluded from the numerator. Accordingly, the quick ratio is regarded as a more stringent measure of liquidity than the current ratio.

The most stringent (or conservative) of the liquidity ratios derived from equation (5.1) is the cash ratio, that is,

$$\frac{\text{Cash} + \text{Marketable Securities}}{\text{Current Liabilities}} = \frac{\gamma_1 \, STA_1 + \gamma_2 \, STA_2}{\sum\limits_{i=1}^{m} STL_i} \qquad (5.5)$$

where $\gamma_1 = \gamma_2 = 1 = \delta_i$ and $STA_1$ = cash and $STA_2$ = marketable securities.

Liquidity ratios present a static picture of a firm's performance. Such a picture is only a first approximation because liquidity is a dynamic process that involves balancing cash inflows with cash outflows and stand-by commitments from lenders. If these flows are perfectly synchronized, a firm can meet its obligations without holding any liquid assets. However, in the real world imperfect synchronization tends to be the rule rather than the exception. Thus, firms need liquid assets to serve as a buffer or cushion for meeting excess cash outflows. Most liquidity ratios attempt to measure the size of this buffer or cushion, ignoring the quality of a firm's effort to balance its cash flows. In a dynamic context, liquidity ratios only provide a first approximation for assessing a firm's debt-paying ability.

### 2. Leverage Ratios

Financial leverage refers to the use of debt and/or preferred stock, instead of common stock, in a firm's capital structure. The concept is also referred to as "trading on equity." (The British call it "gearing.") Leverage is a central feature of corporate balance sheets. Commercial banks, in particular, are highly levered corporations, which helps explain why the banking authorities watch the risk structure of bank investments closely. A highly levered firm can be wiped out by unfavorable developments in only a fraction of the markets in which they invest. In contrast, favorable developments magnify earnings per share. Given a firm's operating results, financial leverage measures the responsiveness or elasticity of the rate of return on common equity to changes in earnings (before interest and taxes). The responsiveness is created by the debt or preferred-stock financing (leverage). For example, the typical commercial bank earns roughly 1.0 percent on its borrowings (assets). However, with a ratio of total assets to net worth of 12 to 1, this translates into a rate of return on bank capital of 12 percent. In contrast, a 1.0 percent *loss* on assets translates into a 12 percent loss on equity capital.

The magnifying effect of leverage works on either profits or losses. Thus, leverage increases the variability of shareholders' uncertain income. For this reason, leverage is regarded as a measure of a firm's riskiness. An unlevered firm will have relatively *stable* and relatively *low* earnings per share, other things equal, than a levered firm. The use of leverage amplifies the inherent variability of a firm's net operating earnings and increases the variability of shareholders' income. The degree by which the return on common equity increases measures the efficiency of debt management or leverage.

Leverage ratios reflect the extent of a firm's total indebtedness and its ability to meet its short- and long-term debt obligations. A firm's debt-paying ability depends upon both the size of its debt *and* the burden of its interest expense. A firm with high debt and low interest isn't any worse off than a firm with low debt and high interest.

The size of a firm's debt is usually measured on a relative basis with the scale factor (or denominator) expressed as total assets, total capitalization (i.e., long-term debt plus equity or net worth), or total equity capital. Debt (the numerator) usually is measured either as total debt (including current liabilities) or as long-term debt only. Three commonly used leverage ratios (derived from a firm's balance sheet) are: (1) total debt to total assets, (2) total debt to total equity (hence the familiar term debt-equity ratio), and (3) long-term debt to total capitalization. In general, the higher these ratios, the greater is the risk of insolvency or long-term illiquidity.

The interest-expense component of debt or leverage can be measured using income-statement data relative to earnings. Income-statement leverage ratios are often called coverage or "times-interest" ratios. Some of the commonly used coverage ratios are: (1) earnings before interest and taxes (EBIT) to total interest charges, referred to as the interest-coverage ratio; (2) earnings before interest but after taxes (EBIAT) to total interest *and* preferred-dividend payments, referred to as the preferred-dividend coverage ratio; and (3) EBIT plus other income (e.g., office rent) to total fixed charges (e.g., lease payments), referred to as the fixed-charge coverage ratio. Obviously, the higher these coverage ratios, the greater is a firm's ability to pay its interest and other fixed expenses.

### 3. Activity Ratios

These ratios measure a firm's ability to utilize its resources effectively. Both balance-sheet and income-statement data are used in constructing activity ratios. "Turnover" ratios are examples of commonly used activity ratios. A turnover ratio expresses the "flow" variable, usually sales, to alternative "stock" variables such as total assets or inventory, hence the terms asset turnover and inventory turnover. Some commonly used activity ratios are: (1) sales to total assets, (2) sales to inventory, and (3) sales to fixed assets. In general, the higher the value of this type of activity ratio, the more efficiently a firm is operating.

Operating-expense ratios are another example of frequently used activity ratios. This type of ratio relates an expense item to a balance-sheet item or to total operating income. For example, focusing upon labor efficiency, a firm's total wage bill can be compared to its asset base or its total operating income. A firm's overall cost efficiency can be judged by its ratio of total operating expense to total assets or to total operating income. In general, operating-expense ratios should be minimized subject to employee morale and input-quality constraints (e.g., noncompetitive wages may adversely affect a firm's ability to attract qualified employees and the morale of existing employees).

### 4. Profitability Ratios

These ratios measure a firm's overall efficiency or "bottom-line" performance. The numerator of a profitability ratio employs the profits figure (e.g., before *or* after taxes), while the denominator incorporates the relevant base such as sales, total assets, or equity capital. Although no single ratio provides enough information to judge the financial condition and performance of a firm, a profitability ratio is perhaps, because of its comprehensiveness, the "best" indicator of a firm's overall performance or efficiency. For example, consider a return-on-equity (ROE) decomposition model [see Cole (1974)] as a measure of a firm's overall performance or efficiency. Let

$$\text{ROE} = \frac{\text{Net Income or Profits (after taxes) (NI)}}{\text{Average Total Equity Capital (E)}},$$

$$\text{PM} = \text{After-tax Profit Margin}$$
$$= \frac{\text{Net Income}}{\text{Operating Revenue or Sales (OR)}},$$

$$\text{AU} = \text{Asset Utilization}$$
$$= \frac{\text{Operating Revenues}}{\text{Average Assets (A)}}, \text{ and}$$

$$\text{EM} = \text{Equity Multiplier or Leverage}$$
$$= \frac{\text{Average Assets}}{\text{Average Equity}}.^1$$

Then,

$$\text{ROE} = \frac{\text{NI}}{\text{E}} = \frac{\text{NI}}{\text{OR}} \times \frac{\text{OR}}{\text{A}} \times \frac{\text{A}}{\text{E}} = \text{PM} \times \text{AU} \times \text{EM}. \qquad (5.6)$$

Or in words, return-on-equity is equal to the product of after-tax profit margin times asset utilization times leverage. This decomposition analysis indicates how comprehensive a ROE profitability ratio is (i.e., it incorporates profit margin, NI/OR; an activity ratio, OR/A; and a leverage ratio, A/E). Note that the first two terms on the RHS of equation (5.6) can be combined to form a return-on-assets (ROA) model, that is,

$$ROA = \frac{NI}{A} = \frac{NI}{OR} \times \frac{OR}{A} = PM \times AU. \tag{5.7}$$

Thus, equation (5.6) can be viewed as the product of ROA (sometimes called "earning power") and the equity multiplier, that is,

$$ROE = ROA \times EM = \frac{NI}{A} \times \frac{A}{E} = \frac{NI}{E}. \tag{5.8}$$

ROE and ROA are two commonly used measures of a firm's current profitability. A firm's cumulative or long-term profitability can be measured by the ratio of retained earnings (from the balance sheet) to total assets. In addition, the gross and net profit margins on sales frequently are employed as profitability measures. Note that the net profit margin on sales is simply the after-tax profit margin factor (NI/OR) from the ROE model. Finally, gross profit margin is simply sales less costs of goods sold divided by sales.

The impact of financial leverage upon ROE can be seen differently. Equation (5.8) can be rearranged to yield:

$$ROE = \frac{NI/A}{1 - D/A} \tag{5.9}$$

where D/A is the total debt-to-total asset measure of financial leverage. Other things equal, ROE varies directly with the amount of debt in the capital structure and liability accounts of the firm. Leverage, both financial and operating, is of course a "double-edged sword."[2] That is, increasing the amount of financial leverage magnifies potential gains *and* potential losses. This occurs because leverage involves the use of assets and/or liabilities (including preferred stock), which have fixed costs associated with their use, to produce a higher rate of return (or rate of loss) on sales or investment than otherwise would be possible. The specific ratios that an analyst examines depend upon the purpose and intended use of the analysis. For example, a commercial banker evaluating a business' creditworthiness for a short-term loan should focus especially closely upon the firm's ability to meet its short-term obligations (i.e., its liquidity). In contrast, long-term creditors must concentrate on a firm's staying power: its earning potential and operating efficiency. Before becoming stockholders, risk-averse investors should focus upon the firm's earnings stability and its leverage position, etc. However, in each case, a group or profile of ratios should be analyzed on a comparative basis against either a relevant peer group or industry norms.

Altman, Haldeman, and Narayanan (1977) have recently developed a bankruptcy-prediction model (called ZETA) for manufacturing and retail firms.[3] Using a paired-sample of bankrupt (consisting of 29 manufacturing firms and 24 retail firms) and nonbankrupt (32 and 26, respectively) firms and MDA, they found that a seven-variable model was ". . . quite accurate up to five years prior to failure with successful classification of well over 90 percent of our sample one-year prior and 70 percent accuracy up to five years" (p. 3). The seven variables are:

1. *Return on Assets.* Ratio of earnings before interest and taxes to total assets.
2. *Stability of Earnings.* The inverse of the standard error of estimate around a ten-year trend in return on assets.
3. *Debt Service.* Ratio of earnings before interest and taxes to total interest payments (including the amount inputed from capitalized-lease liabilities). This is the familiar interest-coverage ratio.
4. *Cumulative Profitability.* Ratio of retained earnings (balance sheet) to total assets.
5. *Liquidity.* Ratio of current assets to current liabilities, the current ratio.
6. *Capitalization.* Ratio of the five-year average market value of common stock to total long-term capital.
7. *Size.* Measured by total assets.

The group means and univariate F-tests for these seven variables one year prior to bankruptcy are presented in Table 5-1. The analyst interested in assessing a firm's potential bankruptcy might consider this seven-variable profile. Finally, note that since Altman et al. did not present the weights used in their ZETA models (linear and quadratic), they are not presented here.[4]

### 5. Ratio-Analysis Summary

This section has focused upon ratio analysis from the corporation-finance viewpoint. Comparative ratio analysis is a convenient and useful *tool* for identifying *symptoms* of financial strength *and* weakness in business firms. Four aspects of a firm's financial condition are emphasized: (1) liquidity, (2) leverage, (3) activity, and (4) profitability. While the

*Table 5.1*

Seven-Variable Failure-Prediction Model
(One Year Prior to Failure)

|  | Variable | Group Mean | | Univariate F-Test |
|---|---|---|---|---|
|  |  | Failed | Nonfailed |  |
| 1. | Return on Assets | -0.56 | 11.18 | 54.3 |
| 2. | Stability of Earnings | 168.70 | 578.40 | 33.8 |
| 3. | Debt Service (log)* | 96.25 | 116.20 | 26.1 |
| 4. | Cumulative profitability | -0.07 | 29.35 | 114.6 |
| 5. | Liquidity | 1.56 | 2.60 | 38.2 |
| 6. | Capitalization | 40.63 | 62.10 | 31.0 |
| 7. | Size (log)* | 198.50 | 222.20 | 5.5 |

*Indicates that the variable was log (10) transformed.
*Source:* Altman, *et al.* (1977), Appendix B. p. 40.

specific ratios that an analyst examines depend upon the purpose and intended use of the analysis, a *complete* investigation must focus upon a group or profile of ratios. No single ratio provides enough information to judge the financial condition and performance of a firm. A convenient starting point for evaluating a firm's performance is to conduct a ROE decomposition analysis.

# 5.3 FINANCIAL CHARACTERISTICS OF PROBLEM AND FAILED BANKS

This section focuses upon ratios that can be used to evaluate the strengths and weaknesses of commercial banks. The ratios presented are illustrated using data from recent bank failures and recent FDIC problem-bank lists. Since the methods of problem-bank analysis were discussed in the previous chapter, let us focus upon the failed-bank data and methods for analyzing these figures.

## 1. Failed Banks: Data and Methods

Over the six-year period 1970–1975, thirty-seven insured commercial banks failed (see Table 5.2). These 37 failed banks and a paired sample of 37 nonfailed banks are analyzed in this chapter. The nonfailed banks were matched or paired on the basis of (1) deposit size, (2) number of

Table 5-2

Failed Banks, 1970-1975

| Bank | Location | Date |
|------|----------|------|
| 1. State Bank of Prairie City (P)[*] | Prairie City, Iowa | 2/22/70 |
| 2. Peoples State Savings Bank (P) | Auburn, Michigan | 4/18/40 |
| 3. Farmers Bank of Petersburg (P) | Petersburg, Kentucky | 6/25/70 |
| 4. Eatontown National BAnk (P) | Eatontown, New Jersey | 8/7/70 |
| 5. First State Bank of Bonne Terre (A) | Bonne Terre, Missouri | 8/24/70 |
| 6. City Bank of Philadelphia (A) | Philadelphia, Pennsylvania | 9/3/70 |
| 7. Berea Bank and Trust (A) | Berea, Kentucky | 10/8/70 |
| 8. Sharpstown State Bank (P) | Houston, Texas | 1/25/71 |
| 9. Farmers State Bank of Carlock (P) | Carlock, Illinois | 2/17/71 |
| 10. Bank of Salem (P) | Salem, Nebraska | 4/5/71 |
| 11. The First Nat. Bank of Cripple Creek (P) | Cripple Creek, Colorado | 11/30/71 |
| 12. First Community State Bank of Savannah (P) | Savannah, Missouri | 12/30/71 |
| 13. Birmingham-Bloomfield Bank (A) | Birmingham, Michigan | 2/16/71 |
| 14. Surety Bank and Trust Colmpany (P) | Wakefield, Massachusetts | 5/19/72 |
| 15. Delta Security Bank and Trust Co. (P) | Ferriday, Louisiana | 1/19/73 |
| 16. Elm Creek State Bank (P) | Elm Creek, Nebraska | 5/7/73 |
| 17. The First State Bank (P) | Vernon, Texas | 7/16/73 |
| 18. Skyline National (A) | Denver, Colorado | 3/26/73 |
| 19. First National Bank of Eldora (A) | Eldora, Iowa | 10/5/73 |
| 20. United States National Bank (A) | San Diego, California | 10/18/73 |
| 21. American Bank and Trust Co. (A) | Orangeburg, South Carolina | 9/20/74 |
| 22. Tri-City Bank (A) | Warren, Michigan | 9/27/74 |
| 23. Franklin National Bank (A) | New York, New YOrk | 10/8/74 |
| 24. Cromwell State Savings Bank (A) | Cromwell, Iowa | 10/9/74 |
| 25. Swope Parkway National Bank (DINB) | Kansas City, Missouri | 1/3/75 |
| 26. Northern Ohio Bank (A) | Cleveland, Ohio | 2/14/75 |
| 27. Franklin Bank (P) | Houston, Texas | 3/24/75 |
| 28. Chicopee Bank and Trust (A) | Chicopee, Massachusetts | 5/9/75 |
| 29. Algoma Bank (A) | Algoma, Wisconsin | 5/30/75 |
| 30. Bank of Picayune (A) | Picayune, Mississippi | 6/18/75 |
| 31. Bank of Chidester (A) | Chidester, Arkansas | 7/1/75 |
| 32. State Bank of Clearing (A) | Chicago, Illinois | 7/12/75 |
| 33. Astro Bank (A) | Houston, Texas | 10/16/75 |
| 34. American City Bank and Trust (A) | Milwaukee, Wisconsin | 10/21/75 |
| 35. Peoples Bank of the Virgin Islands (DINB) | Charlotte Amalie, Virgin Islands | 10/24/75 |
| 36. Peoples Bank (A) | Wilcox, Arizona | 12/19/75 |
| 37. First State Bank (A) | Jennings, Kansas | 12/27/75 |

[*]Letters in parentheses indicate the FDIC'S disposition of the failed bank, that is, a deposit payoff (P), a deposit assumption by another insured bank (A), or the establishment of a Deposit Insurance National Bank (DINB).

The 37 failed banks consisted of 27 insured nonmember banks, 8 national banks, and 2 state member banks. Four of the 37 failed banks (Skyline National, Northern Ohio, Astro Bank, and Peoples Bank of the Virgin Islands) were not established until 1971.

branches, and (3) location (SMSA or county). The matching process, which focused on conditions one year prior to failure, was an iterative one. That is, if on the first iteration a bank was not paired "exactly," a second iteration was conducted, etc. The matching technique succeeded at least to this extent: (1) no statistically significant differences exist between the failed and nonfailed *groups* on the basis of size or number of offices and (2) each nonfailed bank was located in the same SMSA or county (or contiguous county in the case of an isolated rural bank) as its failed counterpart. The average total-asset size and average number of offices of the failed and nonfailed groups *one-year prior to failure* are presented in Table 5.3

Year-end consolidated Report of Condition (i.e., balance-sheet) and Report of Income (i.e., income-expense) data were collected from one year prior to failure up to six years prior to failure. The sample period was 1969 to 1974. Thus, for banks that failed in 1970, only data from one year prior are analyzed; for banks that failed 1971, data from one *and* two years prior are analyzed; etc. The sample sizes for the various years prior to failure are presented in Table 5.4. In Table 5.4, the "ad-

*Table 5.3*

Failed and Nonfailed Banks: Asset Size
and Number of Offices One Year Prior to Failure

| (1) | (2) | (3) | (4) | (5) | (6) | (7) |
|---|---|---|---|---|---|---|
| | | | Coeffi- | | | |
| | | Standard | cient of | Max | Min | F- |
| Group Variable | Mean | Deviation | Variation (3/2) | Value | Value | statistic* |
| Failed Banks (37) | | | | | | |
| Total Assets** | 156.8 | 638.1 | 4.07 | 3,804.9 | 597.0 | 0.12 |
| Number of Offices | 6.8 | 19.8 | 2.91 | 104 | 1 | 0.03 |
| Nonfailed Banks (37) | | | | | | |
| Total Assets** | 113.2 | 428.9 | 3.79 | 2,606.7 | 937.0 | 0.12 |
| Number of Offices | 6.0 | 20.0 | 3.33 | 121 | 1 | 0.03 |

* Tests for the equality of group means between the two groups for the particular variable.
** Total assets are in millions of dollars.
*Source:* Reports of Condition and Income, 1969-1974, Federal Deposit Insurance Corporation.

*Table 5.4*

Failed Banks 1970-1975: Sample Sizes Various
Years Prior to Failure

| | Sample Size | | | |
|---|---|---|---|---|
| | Failed or Nonfailed | | Total | |
| Year Prior to Failure* | Original | Adjusted | Original | Adjusted |
| 1 | 37 | 33 | 74 | 66 |
| 2 | 30 | 26 | 60 | 52 |
| 3 | 24 | 20 | 48 | 40 |
| 4 | 23 | 19 | 46 | 38 |
| 5 | 17 | 14 | 34 | 28 |
| 6 | 13 | 10 | 26 | 20 |

*On average, the actual years prior to failure are .5, 1.5, 2.5, 3.5, 4.5, and 5.5 respectively.
*Source: Annual Report* (various issues), Federal Deposit Insurance Corporation.

justed" sample allows for start-up experience (i.e., newly chartered banks are deleted), while the original sample does not. Stated years prior to failure are on average six months less than the actual time. For example, on January 3, 1975, Swope Parkway National Bank failed and on December 27, 1975, First State Bank failed. Using December 31, 1974, data, the data for the latter bank was one-year prior; however, for the former bank the lead time was effectively zero. Thus, the average time before failure was six months. The distribution of the 37 failed banks with respect to the month of failure is presented in Table 5.5. Prior to December 31, 1975, the banking agencies only collected income-expense data annually at year's end. Now it is being collected semi-annually for all banks and quarterly for the largest banks. Thus, only one income-expense statement per bank per year was available during the 1969–1974 sample period. While using the last income-expense statement prior to failure for all banks that failed in the next year produces a heterogeneous group with respect to time before failure, it is impossible to homogenize the group in the time domain. Using the next-to-last statement prior to failure for the banks that failed in the first or second quarter of the year would provide a longer lead time and make the aver-

*Table 5.5*

Thirty-Seven Failed Banks: Month of Failure

(1970 - 1975)

| Month | Number of Failures |
|---|---|
| January | 3 |
| February | 4 |
| March (1st Quarter) | 2 (9) |
| April | 2 |
| May | 4 |
| June (2nd Quarter) | 2 (8) |
| July | 3 |
| August | 2 |
| September (3rd Quarter) | 3 (8) |
| October | 8 |
| November | 1 |
| December (4th Quarter) | 3 (12) |
| Total | 37 |

*Source: Annual Report* (various issues), Federal Deposit Insurance Corporation.

age lead time about twelve months. However, since the actual data collection was easier using the last available income statement for all banks regardless of when they failed during the next year, it was used. All the reader has to remember is that *on average* 1, 2, 3, 4, 5, and 6 years prior actually means .5, 1.5, 2.5, 3.5, 4.5, and 5.5 years prior.

In addition to the 37 banks that failed between 1970 and 1975, the 16 banks that failed during 1976 are analyzed as a holdout sample. (These sixteen failures in 1976 constituted the largest number of closings in a single year since 1942 when 20 banks failed.) The insured commercial banks that failed during 1976 are listed in Table 5.6. The mean deposit size for these sixteen failures was $56.1 million; however, the median deposit size was only $14 million. Only three of the 1976 failures had total deposits greater than $55 million, while only one of the failures had deposits greater than $200 million. The largest failure, the $336 million Hamilton National Bank of Chattanooga, had serious problems in its real estate loan portfolio which led to its downfall (see Chapter 7).

Table 5.6

1976 Bank Failures

| Bank | Date | Approximate Deposit Size (millions) |
|---|---|---|
| 1. Bank of Bloomfield, New Jersey (A)* | 1/10 | 25.9 |
| 2. Bank of Woodmoor, Colorado (A) | 1/16 | 3.6 |
| 3. Hamilton National Bank, Chattanooga (A) | 2/16 | 336.0 |
| 4. South Texas Bank, Houston (A) | 2/26 | 8.4 |
| 5. First State Bank of Northern California, San Leandro (A) | 5/21 | 54.3 |
| 6. Northeast Bank, Houston (A) | 6/3 | 17.5 |
| 7. First State Bank of Hudson County, Jersey City, NJ (A) | 6/14 | 13.2 |
| 8. Mt. Zion Deposit Bank, Mt. Zion, Kentucky (P) | 6/25 | 0.5 |
| 9. Coronado National Bank, Denver (P) | 6/25 | 2.5 |
| 10. Citizens State Bank, Carrizo Springs, Texas (P) | 6/28 | 14.7 |
| 11. New Boston Bank and Trust, Boston (A) | 9/14 | 6.0 |
| 12. American Bank and Trust, New York City (A) | 9/15 | 199.0 |
| 13 Hamilton Bank and Trust, Atlanta (A) | 10/8 | 32.0 |
| 14. Centennial Bank, Philadelphia (A) | 10/20 | 12.4 |
| 15. First State Bank and Trust, Rio Grande City, Texas (A) | 11/19 | 12.2 |
| 16. International City BAnk and Trust, New Orleans (A) | 12/3 | 160.0 |

Notes: *Letter in parentheses indicates FDIC action (see notes to Table 5.2 for explanation). The 1976 bank failures had a mean deposit size of 56.1 million; however, the median size was only $14 million.

Source: FDIC News Release (various issues), 1976, Federal Deposit Insurance Corporation.

## 2. Some "Bottom-Line" Measures of Bank Performance

When analyzing a bank's performance or "safety and soundness," I prefer to begin at the bottom line and work up. That is, I focus upon the bank's overall performance as measured by the following seven profitability variables:

1.  OIA = Total operating income as a percentage of total assets (this measures asset utilization or revenue generation per dollar of assets).

2.  OEA = Total operating expense as a percentage of total assets (this measures cost-control effectiveness or expense per dollar of assets).

3.  NOA = OIA − OEA = Net operating income (before taxes or securities gains or losses) as a percentage of total assets (this measures operating performance).

4.  NIA = Net income (after taxes and securities gains or losses) as a percentage of total assets (this measures overall performance relative to total assets).

5.  NIO = Net income as a percentage of total operating income (this measures net profit margin).

6.  NIE = Net income as a percentage of total equity capital or ROE (this measures net profitability from the stockholders' point of view).

7.  OEOI = OEA/OIA = Total operating expense as a percentage of total operating income (this measures operating performance).

To eliminate any possible confusion about the definitions of these variables, their construction in terms of Report of Condition (RC, see Table 5.7) and Report of Income (RI, see Table 5.8) items numbers are:

1. OIA = RI1(h)/RC14
2. OEA = RI2(k)/RC14
3. NOA = RI3/RC14
4. NIA = RI10/RC14
5. NIOI = RI10/RI1(h)
6. NIE = RI10/RC35
7. OEOI = RI2(k)/RI1(h).

# Table 5.7

## CONSOLIDATED REPORT OF CONDITION OF BANK AND DOMESTIC SUBSIDIARIES

FDIC Form 64 (12-74)

### at the close of business on _____

Name and Address of Bank

**RETURN ORIGINAL AND ONE COPY TO FDIC, WASHINGTON, D. C. 20429**

PLEASE READ CAREFULLY "INSTRUCTIONS FOR THE PREPARATION OF REPORT OF CONDITION."
Every item and schedule must be filled in. Printed items must not be amended. Amounts which cannot properly be included in the printed items must be entered under "Other assets" or "Other liabilities."

| ASSETS | Dollars | | | Cts. | |
|---|---|---|---|---|---|
| 1. Cash and due from banks (including $_____ unposted debits)(Schedule D, item 7) | | | | | 1 |
| 2. (a) U.S. Treasury securities _____ $_____ (Total items | xxx | xxx | xxx | xx | |
| (b) Obligations of Federal Financing Bank _____ $_____ { 2(a) & (b)) = | | | | | 2 |
| 3. Obligations of other U. S. Government agencies and corporations | | | | | 3 |
| 4. Obligations of States and political subdivisions | | | | | 4 |
| 5. Other securities (including $_____ corporate stocks) | | | | | 5 |
| 6. Trading account securities | | | | | 6 |
| 7. Federal funds sold and securities purchased under agreements to resell | | | | | 7 |
| 8. Other loans (Schedule A, item 8) | | | | | 8 |
| 9. Bank premises, furniture and fixtures, and other assets representing bank premises | | | | | 9 |
| 10. Real estate owned other than bank premises | | | | | 10 |
| 11. Investments in subsidiaries not consolidated | | | | | 11 |
| 12. Customers' liability to this bank on acceptances outstanding | | | | | 12 |
| 13. Other assets (item 6 of "Other Assets")(including $_____ direct lease financing) | | | | | 13 |
| 14. TOTAL ASSETS | | | | | 14 |
| **LIABILITIES** | | | | | |
| 15. Demand deposits of individuals, partnerships, and corporations (Schedule E, item 3) | | | | | 15 |
| 16. Time and savings deposits of individuals, partnerships, and corporations (Schedule F, item 5) | | | | | 16 |
| 17. Deposits of United States Government (Schedule E, item 4 and Schedule F, item 6) | | | | | 17 |
| 18. Deposits of States and political subdivisions (Schedule E, item 5 and Schedule F, item 7) | | | | | 18 |
| 19. Deposits of foreign governments and official institutions (Schedule E, item 6 and Schedule F, item 8) | | | | | 19 |
| 20. Deposits of commercial banks (Schedule E, items 7 and 8 and Schedule F, items 9 and 10) | | | | | 20 |
| 21. Certified and officers' checks, etc. (Schedule E, item 9) | | | | | 21 |
| 22. TOTAL DEPOSITS _____ $_____ | xxx | xxx | xxx | xx | 22 |
| (a) Total demand deposits (Schedule E, item 10) _____ $_____ | xxx | xxx | xxx | xx | (a) |
| (b) Total time and savings deposits (Schedule F, item 11) _____ $_____ | xxx | xxx | xxx | xx | (b) |
| 23. Federal funds purchased and securities sold under agreements to repurchase | | | | | 23 |
| 24. Other liabilities for borrowed money | | | | | 24 |
| 25. Mortgage indebtedness | | | | | 25 |
| 26. Acceptances executed by or for account of this bank and outstanding | | | | | 26 |
| 27. Other liabilities (item 7 of "Other Liabilities" schedule) | | | | | 27 |
| 28. TOTAL LIABILITIES | | | | | 28 |
| 29. MINORITY INTEREST IN CONSOLIDATED SUBSIDIARIES | | | | | 29 |
| **RESERVES ON LOANS AND SECURITIES** | | | | | |
| 30. Reserve for bad debt losses on loans (set up pursuant to Internal Revenue Service rulings) | | | | | 30 |
| 31. Other reserves on loans | | | | | 31 |
| 32. Reserves on securities | | | | | 32 |
| 33. TOTAL RESERVES ON LOANS AND SECURITIES | | | | | 33 |
| **CAPITAL ACCOUNTS** | | | | | |
| 34. Capital notes and debentures | | | | | 34 |
| 35. Equity capital, total (items 36 to 40 below) | | | | | 35 |
| 36. Preferred stock-total par value | | | | | 36 |
| (No. shares outstanding _____ ) | | | | | |
| 37. Common stock-total par value | | | | | 37 |
| (No. shares authorized _____ ) (No. shares outstanding _____ ) | | | | | |
| 38. Surplus | | | | | 38 |
| 39. Undivided profits | | | | | 39 |
| 40. Reserve for contingencies and other capital reserves | | | | | 40 |
| 41. TOTAL CAPITAL ACCOUNTS (items 34 and 35 above) | | | | | 41 |
| 42. TOTAL LIABILITIES, RESERVES, AND CAPITAL ACCOUNTS (items 28, 29, 33, and 41 above) | | | | | 42 |
| **MEMORANDA** | | | | | |
| 1. Average of total deposits for the 15 calendar days ending with call date | | | | | 1 |
| 2. Average of total loans for the 15 calendar days ending with call date | | | | | 2 |
| 3. Unearned discount on instalment loans included in total capital accounts | | | | | 3 |
| 4. Standby letters of credit | | | | | 4 |

I,_____ of the above named bank do hereby declare that this report of condition
(Name and title of officer authorized to sign report)

(including the information on the reverse side hereof) is true and correct, to the best of my knowledge and belief.

_____
(Signature of officer authorized to sign report)

We, the undersigned directors attest the correctness of this report of condition (including the information on the reverse side hereof) and declare that it has been examined by us and to the best of our knowledge and belief is true and correct.

NOTE—This report must be signed by an authorized officer, attested by not less than three directors (or by at least two if there are not more than three directors) other than the officer signing the report, and forwarded within 10 days after receipt of request. (See Section 7 of the Federal Deposit Insurance Act.)

_____
_____  } Directors
_____

## Table 5.7 (Cont.)

**SCHEDULE A—LOANS AND DISCOUNTS (including rediscounts and overdrafts)**

| | Dollars | | | Cts. | |
|---|---|---|---|---|---|
| 1. Real estate loans (include only loans secured primarily by real estate): | xxx | xxx | xxx | xx | 1 |
| (a) Secured by farm land (including improvements) | | | | | (a) |
| (b) Secured by 1-to 4-family residential properties (other than farm): | xxx | xxx | xxx | xx | (b) |
| (1) Insured by the Federal Housing Administration | | | | | (b-1) |
| (2) Guaranteed by the Veterans Administration | | | | | (b-2) |
| (3) Not insured or guaranteed by FHA or VA (conventionally financed) | | | | | (b-3) |
| (c) Secured by multifamily (5-or-more) residential properties: | xxx | xxx | xxx | xx | (c) |
| (1) Insured by the Federal Housing Administration | | | | | (c-1) |
| (2) Not insured by FHA (conventionally financed) | | | | | (c-2) |
| (d) Secured by non-farm non-residential properties (e. g., business, industrial, hotels, office buildings, churches) | xxx | xxx | xxx | xx | (d) |
| 2. Loans to financial institutions: | | | | | 2 |
| (a) To domestic commercial and foreign banks | | | | | (a) |
| (b) To other financial institutions (include loans to sales finance, personal finance, insurance and mortgage cos, factors, mutual savings banks, savings and loan assns, Federal lending agencies, and all other business and personal credit agencies) | xxx | xxx | xxx | xx | (b) |
| 3. Loans for purchasing or carrying securities (secured or unsecured): | | | | | 3 |
| (a) To brokers and dealers in securities | | | | | (a) |
| (b) Other loans for the purpose of purchasing or carrying stocks, bonds, and other securities | | | | | (b) |
| 4. Loans to farmers (secured and unsec. except loans sec. by real estate—include loans for household and personal expenditures) | | | | | 4 |
| 5. Commercial and industrial loans (include all loans for commercial and industrial purposes, secured or unsecured, except those secured by real estate above) | | | | | 5 |
| 6. Loans to individuals for household, family, and other personal expenditures (exclude business loans, loans to farmers, and loans secured by real estate above; include purchased paper): | xxx | xxx | xxx | xx | 6 |
| (a) To purchase private passenger automobiles on instalment basis | | | | | (a) |
| (b) Credit cards and related plans: (1) Retail (charge account) credit card plans | | | | | (b-1) |
| (2) Check credit and revolving credit plans | | | | | (b-2) |
| (c) To purchase other retail consumer goods on instalment basis:(1) Mobile homes, not including travel trailers | | | | | (c-1) |
| (2) Other retail consumer goods | | | | | (c-2) |
| (d) Instalment loans to repair and modernize residential property | | | | | (d) |
| (e) Other instalment loans for household, family, and other personal expenditures | | | | | (e) |
| (f) Single payment loans for household, family, and other personal expenditures | | | | | (f) |
| 7. All other loans (incl. overdrafts) (to churches, hospitals, charitable or educational institutions, etc., not secured by real estate above) | | | | | 7 |
| 8. TOTAL LOANS AND DISCOUNTS (items 1 to 7) (must agree with item 8 of "Assets") | | | | | 8 |

**SCHEDULE D—CASH, BALANCES WITH OTHER BANKS, AND CASH ITEMS IN PROCESS OF COLLECTION**

| | Dollars | | | Cts. | |
|---|---|---|---|---|---|
| 1. Cash items in process of collection and unposted debits drawn on the reporting bank-total | | | | | 1 |
| (Banks electing to report subitems (a) and (b), or (a) and (c)—see Instructions) | | | | | |
| (a) Cash items in process of collection including exchanges for clearing house (item 1 less subitem (b) or (c)) | $ xxx | xxx | xxx | xx | (a) |
| (b) Actual amount of all unposted debits or single factor_____% of item 22 | $ xxx | xxx | xxx | xx | (b) |
| (c) Separate amount of unposted debits or separate factors: | | | | | |
| (1) Actual amount for Demand Deposits or_____% of item 10, Schedule E | $ xxx | xxx | xxx | xx | (c-1) |
| (2) Actual amount for Time and Savings Deposits or____% of item 11, Sch. F | $ xxx | xxx | xxx | xx | (c-2) |
| 2. Demand balances with banks in the U.S. | | | | | 2 |
| 3. Other balances with banks in the United States (including all balances with American branches of foreign banks) | | | | | 3 |
| 4. Balances with banks in foreign countries (including balances with foreign branches of other American banks) | | | | | 4 |
| 5. Currency and coin | | | | | 5 |
| 6. Reserve with Federal Reserve Bank (banks members F. R. System only) | | | | | 6 |
| 7. TOTAL of items 1 to 6 (must agree with item 1 of "Assets") | | | | | 7 |

**SCHEDULE E—DEMAND DEPOSITS**

| | | | |
|---|---|---|---|
| 1. Deposits of mutual savings banks | | | 1 |
| 2. Deposits of other individuals, partnerships, and corporations | | | 2 |
| 3. Total of items 1 and 2 (must agree with item 15 of "Liabilities") | | | 3 |
| 4. Deposits of United States Government | | | 4 |
| 5. Deposits of States and political subdivisions | | | 5 |
| 6. Deposits of foreign governments and official institutions, central banks and international institutions | | | 6 |
| 7. Deposits of commercial banks in the U.S. | | | 7 |
| 8. Deposits of banks in foreign countries (including balances of foreign branches of other American banks) | | | 8 |
| 9. Certified and officers checks, travelers' checks, letters of credit, etc. (must agree with item 21 of "Liabilities") | | | 9 |
| 10. TOTAL DEMAND DEPOSITS (items 3 to 9) (must agree with item 22(a) of "Liabilities") | | | 10 |

**SCHEDULE F—TIME AND SAVINGS DEPOSITS**

| | | | |
|---|---|---|---|
| 1. Savings deposits | | | 1 |
| 2. Deposits accumulated for payment of personal loans | | | 2 |
| 3. Deposits of mutual savings banks | | | 3 |
| 4. Other time deposits of individuals, partnerships, and corporations | | | 4 |
| 5. Total of items 1 to 4 (must agree with item 16 of "Liabilities") | | | 5 |
| 6. Deposits of United States Government | | | 6 |
| 7. Deposits of States and political subdivisions | | | 7 |
| 8. Deposits of foreign governments and official institutions, central banks and international institutions | | | 8 |
| 9. Deposits of commercial banks in the United States | | | 9 |
| 10. Deposits of banks in foreign countries (including balances of foreign branches of other American banks) | | | 10 |
| 11. TOTAL TIME AND SAVINGS DEPOSITS (items 5 to 10) (must agree with item 22(b) of "Liabilities") | | | 11 |

**SCHEDULE OF OTHER ASSETS** | | | **SCHEDULE OF OTHER LIABILITIES** | | | |
|---|---|---|---|---|---|---|
| 1. Securities borrowed | $ | | 1. Securities borrowed | $ | | 1 |
| 2. Income earned or accrued but not collected | | | 2. Dividends declared but not yet payable | | | 2 |
| 3. Insurance and other expenses prepaid | | | 3. Income collected but not earned | | | 3 |
| 4. Cash items not in process of collection | | | 4. Expenses accrued and unpaid | | | 4 |
| 5. All other (itemize): | | | 5. Amounts due F. R. bank or other banks (transit account) | | | 5 |
| | | | 6. All other (itemize): | | | 6 |
| 6. TOTAL (must agree with item 13 of "Assets") | | | 7. TOTAL(must agree with item 27 of "Liabs.") | | | 7 |

**SCHEDULE FDI—OTHER DATA FOR DEPOSIT INSURANCE ASSESSMENTS**

| | Dollars | | | Cts. | |
|---|---|---|---|---|---|
| 1. Uninvested trust funds (cash) held in bank's own trust department | | | | | 1 |
| 2. Unposted credits (see Instructions): | xxx | xxx | xxx | xx | 2 |
| (a) Actual amount of all unposted credits or single factor _____% of item 22 | | | | | (a) |
| OR | | | | | |
| (b) Separate amount of unposted credits or separate factors: | | | | | |
| (1) Actual amount for Demand Deposits or _____% of item 10, Schedule E | | | | | (b-1) |
| (2) Actual amount for Time and Savings Deposits or_____% of item 11, Schedule F | | | | | (b-2) |

108

Table 5.8

FDIC Form 73 (12-69)

## CONSOLIDATED REPORT OF INCOME—CALENDAR YEAR 1974
### (Including Domestic Subsidiaries)

Name and Address of Bank

**RETURN ORIGINAL AND ONE COPY TO FDIC, WASHINGTON, D.C. 20429**

PLEASE READ CAREFULLY "INSTRUCTIONS FOR THE PREPARATION OF REPORT OF INCOME."
Every item and section must be FILLED in.
Printed items must not be amended.

| SECTION A – SOURCES AND DISPOSITION OF INCOME | Dollars | Cts. | |
|---|---|---|---|
| **1. OPERATING INCOME:** | | | 1 |
| (a) Interest and fees on loans | | | (a) |
| (b) Income on Federal funds sold and securities purchased under agreements to resell | | | (b) |
| (c) Interest and dividends on investments (exclude trading account income): | | | (c) |
| 1. U. S. Treasury securities | | | 1 |
| 2. Securities of other U. S. Government agencies and corporations | | | 2 |
| 3. Obligations of States and political subdivisions | | | 3 |
| 4. Other securities | | | 4 |
| (d) Trust department income | | | (d) |
| (e) Service charges on deposit accounts | | | (e) |
| (f) Other service charges, collection and exchange charges, commissions, and fees | | | (f) |
| (g) Other operating income (itemize net income on trading account, net earnings from foreign branches and other amounts over 25% of total) | | | (g) |
| (h) Total operating income | | | (h) |
| **2. OPERATING EXPENSE:** | | | 2 |
| (a) Salaries and wages of officers and employees (**Number on payroll at the end of period** _____) | | | (a) |
| (b) Pensions and other employee benefits | | | (b) |
| (c) Interest on deposits | | | (c) |
| (d) Expense of Federal funds purchased and securities sold under agreements to repurchase | | | (d) |
| (e) Interest on other borrowed money | | | (e) |
| (f) Interest on capital notes and debentures | | | (f) |
| (g) Occupancy expense of bank premises, net | | | (g) |
| Gross occupancy expense _____ $_____ | | | |
| Less rental income _____ $_____ | | | |
| (h) Furniture and equipment, depreciation, rental costs, servicing, etc. | | | (h) |
| (i) Provision for loan losses (or actual net loan losses) | | | (i) |
| (j) Other operating expenses (itemize amounts over 25% of total) | | | (j) |
| (k) Total operating expense | | | (k) |
| **3. INCOME BEFORE INCOME TAXES AND SECURITIES GAINS OR LOSSES** (Item 1(h) minus 2 (k))[1] | | | 3 |
| **4. APPLICABLE INCOME TAXES** | | | 4 |
| **5. INCOME BEFORE SECURITIES GAINS OR LOSSES** (Item 3 minus 4)[1] | | | 5 |

| | (1) Gross | | (2) Net of Tax Effect | | |
|---|---|---|---|---|---|
| | Dollars | Cts. | Dollars | Cts. | |
| **6. NET SECURITIES GAINS OR LOSSES** (show net loss as minus or in parentheses) | | | | | 6 |
| **7. NET INCOME BEFORE EXTRAORDINARY ITEMS** (Item 5 plus or minus 6)[1] | XXX | XXX | XXX | XX | 7 |
| **8. EXTRAORDINARY CHARGES OR CREDITS** (show net charges as minus or in parentheses and itemize each charge and credit) | | | | | 8 |
| **9. LESS MINORITY INTEREST IN CONSOLIDATED SUBSIDIARIES** | | | | | 9 |
| **10. NET INCOME** (Item 7 plus or minus 8, minus 9)[1] | | | | | 10 |

[1] If a loss, indicate by a minus sign or in parentheses.

I, _____ of the above-named bank, hereby certify that the foregoing statement
(Name of officer authorized to sign report) (Title)
(including the information on the back) is true, to the best of my knowledge and belief.

_____
(Date)

_____
(Signature of officer authorized to sign report)

Table 5.8 (Cont.)

| SECTION B - CHANGES IN CAPITAL ACCOUNTS DURING CALENDAR YEAR | Dollars | Cts | |
|---|---|---|---|
| 1. NET INCOME TRANSFERRED TO UNDIVIDED PROFITS (Item 10 from face side) | | | 1 |
| 2. OTHER INCREASES IN CAPITAL ACCOUNTS: | | | 2 |
| (a) Common stock (par value) sold (excluding $_____ common stock dividends issued) | | | (a) |
| (b) Common stock (par value) issued incident to mergers, etc. | | | (b) |
| (c) Preferred stock or capital notes and debentures sold (par or face value) | | | (c) |
| (d) Premium on new capital stock sold | | | (d) |
| (e) Addition to surplus, undivided profits and reserves incident to mergers, etc. | | | (e) |
| (f) 1. Transfer from reserve for bad debt losses on loans setup pursuant to IRS rulings (must agree with Section D, Column 1, Item 7) | | | (f) 1 |
| 2. Transfer from other reserves on loans (must agree with Section D, Column 2, Item 7) | | | (f) 2 |
| (g) Transfer from reserves on securities (must agree with Section D, Column 3, Item 7) | | | (g) |
| (h) All other increases in capital accounts (itemize) | | | (h) |
| (i) Total other increases in capital accounts | | | (i) |
| 3. OTHER DECREASES IN CAPITAL ACCOUNTS: | | | 3 |
| (a) Cash dividends declared on common stock | | | (a) |
| (b) Cash dividends declared on preferred stock | | | (b) |
| (c) Preferred stock or capital notes and debentures retired (par or face value) | | | (c) |
| (d) Premium paid on preferred stock retired | | | (d) |
| (e) Reduction in surplus, undivided profits and reserves incident to mergers, etc. | | | (e) |
| (f) 1. Transfer from undivided profits to reserve for bad debt losses on loans (must agree with Section D, Column 1, Item 4 less Item 2 (i) of Section A) $_____ Less: Amount of income tax effect $_____ | | | (f) 1 |
| 2. Transfer to other reserves on loans (must agree with Section D, Column 2, Item 4) | | | (f) 2 |
| (g) Transfer to reserves on securities (must agree with Section D, Column 3, Item 4) | | | (g) |
| (h) All other decreases in capital accounts (itemize) | | | (h) |
| (i) Total other decreases in capital accounts | | | (i) |
| 4. NET CHANGE IN TOTAL CAPITAL ACCOUNTS (Item 1 plus 2(i) minus 3(i); indicate net decrease by minus sign or in parentheses. Must agree with the net change at Item 7 of Section C). | | | 4 |

**SECTION C -- CAPITAL ACCOUNTS AT END OF PRECEDING AND CURRENT YEAR**

The items in this Section must agree with the corresponding items in the Condition Reports rendered as of the same dates. The items in the first column must agree with the corresponding items for the same date in the preceding Report of Income.

| | December 31, 1973 | December 31, 1974 | |
|---|---|---|---|
| 1. Capital notes and debentures | | | 1 |
| 2. Preferred stock | | | 2 |
| 3. Common stock | | | 3 |
| 4. Surplus | | | 4 |
| 5. Undivided profits | | | 5 |
| 6. Reserve for contingencies and other capital reserves | | | 6 |
| 7. Total capital accounts (net change of $_____ during the period must agree with Item 4 of Section B) | | | 7 |

**SECTION D -- RESERVE FOR BAD DEBTS AND OTHER RESERVES**

| | Reserve for bad debt losses and other reserves on loans | | Reserves on securities | |
|---|---|---|---|---|
| | Reserve set up pursuant to Internal Revenue Service rulings | Other reserves on loans | | |
| 1. Balance preceding December 31, | | | | 1 |
| 2. Additions due to mergers and absorptions | | | | 2 |
| 3. Recoveries credited to these reserves | | | | 3 |
| 4. Transfers to these reserves (included in Item 2(i) of Section A and 3(f)1, 3(f)2 or 3(g) of Section B) | | | | 4 |
| 5. Total (sum of Items 1, 2, 3, and 4) | | | | 5 |
| 6. Losses charged to these reserves | | | | 6 |
| 7. Transfers from these reserves (included in Item 2(f)1, 2(f)2, or 2 (g) of Section B) | | | | 7 |
| 8. Balance current December 31, (Must agree with corresponding items in Condition Report if rendered as of the same date) | | | | 8 |

**MEMORANDA**

| | | |
|---|---|---|
| 1. Total provision for Federal, State and local income taxes for current year (Must agree with Item 4 of Section A plus or minus the difference between Columns 1 and 2 at Items 6 and 8 of Section A and the tax effect inset to Item 3(f)1 of Section B) | | 1 |
| (a) Provision for Federal income taxes $_____ | | (a) |
| (b) Provision for State and local income taxes $_____ | | (b) |
| 2. Recoveries of previous years' income taxes reflected in Item 2(h) of Section B | | 2 |
| 3. Payments reflecting adjustments to previous years' income taxes included in Item 3(h) of Section B | | 3 |
| 4. Minority interest in Item 5 of Section A, income before securities gains or losses. | | 4 |
| 5. Total amount of accretion of discount on securities reflected in income Items 1(c)1 to 1(c)4 of Section A | | 5 |
| 6. If this bank merged or consolidated with any banks during this period, list the banks (Figures should reflect full year operations for these banks) | | 6 |

110

Since I prefer to work with these variables in percentage form rather than ratio form, the ratios then are multiplied by 100.

The application of these seven ratios is illustrated in Tables 5.9–5.14 for the failed and nonfailed banks described above. The tables correspond to the one-through-six years prior to failure, respectively. In each of the tables, the group means, group standard deviations, and univariate F-statistics are presented.

A number of important conclusions can be drawn from Tables 5.9–

*Table 5.9*

Overall Performance Measures: One Year Prior to Failure
(33 failed bank and 33 nonfailed banks, 1970 - 1975)

Group Means (s.d.) %

| Variable | Failed | Nonfailed | F-statistic |
|---|---|---|---|
| 1. OIA | 6.90 (1.12)* | 6.51 (1.24) | 1.81 |
| 2. OEA | 7.14 (2.32) | 5.16 (1.31) | 18.28 |
| 3. NOA | -0.23 (1.76) | 1.36 (0.60) | 24.16 |
| 4. NIA | -0.35 (1.73) | 1.02 (0.44) | 19.36 |
| 5. NIOI | -4.00 (22.90) | 16.36 (8.31) | 23.05 |
| 6. NIE | -6.42 (27.87) | 14.15 (6.91) | 20.57 |
| 7. OEOI | 102.40 (23.21) | 78.57 (9.47) | 29.85 |

*Figures in parentheses are standard deviations. For NIE, the failed-bank group had only 32 members and the corresponding test statistic is a "t" and not an "F." $F(1,33)$ at the 5 percent level of significance equals 4.17.

*Source:* Reports of Condition and Income, 1969 - 1974, Federal Deposit Insurance Corporation.

*Table 5.10*

Overall Performance Measures: Two Years Prior to Failure
(26 failed banks and 26 nonfailed banks, 1971 - 1975)

| Variable | Group Means (s.d.) % | | F-statistic |
| --- | --- | --- | --- |
| | Failed | Nonfailed | |
| 1. OIA | 6.56 (1.29)* | 6.21 (0.77) | 1.40 |
| 2. OEA | 5.81 (1.42) | 5.11 (0.96) | 4.28 |
| 3. NOA | 0.75 (1.07) | 1.10 (0.57) | 2.11 |
| 4. NIA | 0.60 (0.86) | 0.81 (0.41) | 1.15 |
| 5. NIOI | 9.57 (13.35) | 13.27 (6.57) | 1.60 |
| 6. NIE | 6.65 (19.39) | 11.82 (6.60) | 1.66 |
| 7. OEOI | 88.52 (14.97) | 82.04 (9.08) | 3.56 |

*Figures in parentheses are standard deviations. $F_{(1,26)}$ at the 5 percent level of significance equals 4.22.
*Source:* Reports of Condition and Income 1969 - 1973, Federal Deposit Insurance Corporation.

5.14. First, up to four years prior to failure, the average failed bank's overall performance was significantly worse than the average nonfailed bank. The second year prior to failure, however, is an exception and appears to be a statistical anomaly relative to the other three years. That is, the only significant variable in the second year prior was OEA, while in the first and fourth years prior all of the variables except OIA were significant. In the third year prior, all seven of the variables were statistically significant. It is possible that the changing size of the sample (33 to

*Table 5.11*

Overall Performance Measures:  Three Years Prior to Failure
(20 failed banks and 20 nonfailed banks,  1972 - 1975)

Group Means (s.d.) %

| Variable | Failed | Nonfailed | F-statistic |
|----------|--------|-----------|-------------|
| 1.  OIA | 6.52 (0.89)* | 5.92 (0.59) | 6.20 |
| 2.  OEA | 6.01 (1.18) | 4.70 (0.77) | 17.37 |
| 3.  NOA | 0.51 (0.71) | 1.23 (0.58) | 12.19 |
| 4.  NIA | 0.17 (1.04) | 0.89 (0.36) | 8.34 |
| 5.  NIOI | 2.89 (16.05) | 15.04 (6.19) | 9.97 |
| 6.  NIE | 2.34 (14.73) | 13.41 (6.57) | 9.42 |
| 7.  OEOI | 91.96 (10.61) | 79.26 (9.85) | 15.39 |

*Figures in parentheses are standard deviations. $F_{(1,20)}$ at the 5 percent level of signifi-
cance equals 4.35.
*Source:* Reports of Condition and Income, 1969 - 1972, Federal Deposit Insurance Corporation.

26) and different data periods (1969–1974 vs. 1969–1973) produce this
aberration in the second year prior.

In general, poor profitability can be traced to inadequate revenue
flows (OIA) and/or lack of expense controls (OEA). Thus, the second
major conclusion is that the significantly lower profitability of the average failed bank was due to significantly higher operating expenses
rather than lack of operating revenue. In fact, except for year six, the
average failed bank generated more operating revenue per dollar of as-

*Table 5.12*

Overall Performance Measures: Four Years Prior to Failure
(19 failed banks and 19 nonfailed banks, 1973 - 1975)

Group Means (s.d.) %

| Variable | Failed | Nonfailed | F-statistic |
|----------|--------|-----------|-------------|
| 1. OIA | 6.31 (0.97)* | 5.98 (0.82) | 1.23 |
| 2. OEA | 5.81 (1.38) | 4.75 (0.87) | 7.94 |
| 3. NOA | 0.50 (0.84) | 1.23 (0.65) | 8.99 |
| 4. NIA | 0.37 (0.77) | 0.88 (0.36) | 6.85 |
| 5. NIOI | 6.33 (12.21) | 14.87 (6.13) | 7.40 |
| 6. NIE | 4.56 (14.57) | 12.20 (4.78) | 4.72 |
| 7. OEOI | 91.72 (13.38) | 79.47 (10.65) | 9.75 |

*Figures in parentheses are standard deviations. $F(1,19)$ at the 5 percent level of signifi-
cance equals 4.38.
*Source:* Reports of Condition and Income, 1969 - 1971, Federal Deposit Insurance Corporation.

sets than the average nonfailed bank; however, the difference was statistically significant only in the third year prior.

Third, although the average failed bank's profitability declined
dramatically from the third year prior to the first year prior (from the
second year prior to the first year prior the drop-off was even more
substantial because of the second year's apparent data abnormality),
there was a clear deterioration in the performance of the average failed
bank over the six-year period. For example, in year six NOA was 0.96
percent; in year three it was 0.51 percent; and in year one it was −0.23

*Table 5.13*

Overall Performance Measures: Five Years Prior to Failure
(14 failed banks and 14 nonfailed banks, 1974 - 1975)

Group Means (s.d.) %

| Variable | Failed | Nonfailed | F-statistic |
|---|---|---|---|
| 1. OIA | 6.27 (1.25)* | 6.06 (0.66) | 0.31 |
| 2. OEA | 5.50 (1.58) | 4.78 (0.66) | 2.50 |
| 3. NOA | 0.77 (0.87) | 1.29 (0.58) | 3.39 |
| 4. NIA | 0.49 (0.68) | 0.88 (0.39) | 3.64 |
| 5. NIOI | 7.93 (10.51) | 14.58 (6.39) | 4.08 |
| 6. NIE | 7.05 (7.30) | 11.62 (4.84) | 3.80 |
| 7. OEOI | 87.24 (13.77) | 78.96 (9.09) | 3.53 |

*Figures in parentheses are standard deviations. $F_{(1.14)}$ at the 5 percent level of significance equals 4.60.
*Source:* Reports of Condition and Income, 1969 - 1970, Federal Deposit Insurance Corporation.

percent. In contrast, the figures for the average nonfailed bank were 1.24, 1.23, and 1.36 percent, respectively. The reason for the average failed bank's deterioration can be traced to OEA which went from 5.10 percent to 6.01 percent to 7.14 percent over the sixth, third, and first years prior to failure.[5]

The test of the equality of group means is only one aspect of group structure. A complete analysis requires two additional tests. First, the equality of group dispersions (variance-covarience matrices) should be tested. For a single variable, this is simply a test of equality of group

*Table 5.14*

Overall Performance Measures:  Six Years Prior to Failure
(10 failed banks and 10 nonfailed banks, 1975)

Group Means (s.d.) %

| Variable | Failed | Nonfailed | F-statistic |
|---|---|---|---|
| 1.  OIA | 6.06 (0.52)* | 6.23 (0.78) | 0.32 |
| 2.  OEA | 5.10 (0.90) | 4.98 (0.77) | 0.09 |
| 3.  NOA | 0.96 (0.87) | 1.24 (0.45) | 0.84 |
| 4.  NIA | 0.71 (0.57) | 0.86 (0.21) | 0.64 |
| 5.  NIOI | 11.53 (9.15) | 13.97 (3.30) | 0.61 |
| 6.  NIE | 7.65 (5.67) | 11.65 (3.30) | 3.72 |
| 7.  OEOI | 84.30 (13.81) | 80.01 (6.79) | 0.78 |

*Figures in parentheses are standard deviations. $F(1,10)$ at the 5 percent level of significance equals 4.96.
*Source:* Reports of Condition and Income, 1969, Federal Deposit Insurance Corporation.

variances. Second, the extent to which the distributions overlap should be tested. In general, for the seven performance measures presented in Tables 5.9–5.14, the closer to the failure date, the more unequal were the group variances and the less was the degree of group overlap. Conversely, the more distant the failure date, the more similar the underlying distributions appeared to be.

Visual inspection of the standard deviations in Tables 5.9–5.14 provides a preliminary indication of the equality of group variances and the extent of group overlap. To illustrate a more scientific approach to these tests, consider the equality-of-group variance tests for OEA and OEOI presented in Table 5.15. For OEA, the group variances were significantly different in the first five years prior to failure, but not in the sixth year prior. For OEOI, the hypothesis of equality was rejected only in the first, second, and sixth years prior. Thus, the fourth major conclusion is that failed and nonfailed banks tend to have significantly different group dispersions, which tend to become more unequal as the date of failure becomes more imminent.

Mean profiles and group dispersions reflect only two aspects of group structure. The question remains as to what extent the groups overlap. Two statistical techniques are used to examine the relative positions and shapes of the distributions. First, Cooley and Lohnes (1971) have developed a chi-square measure of group overlap which provides information about the location of variables (or vectors of variables relative to the group means (or group mean vectors). Chi-square measures of group overlap for OEA and OEOI are presented in Table 5.16. The significance level of the chi-square score provides an approximation of the percentage of the *population* of failed banks (nonfailed banks) that can be expected to lie farther from the failed-bank group's center (nonfailed-bank group's center) than the mean or mean vector of the nonfailed group (failed group). Thus, for example, for OEA one year prior to failure, the percentages were 39.27 for the failed-bank group and 12.98 for the nonfailed-bank group. These percentages are interpreted as follows: (1) for the failed-bank group. 39.27 percent of the population of failed banks (approximately 13 of the 33 sample failed banks) are expected to lie farther from mean of the failed group ($\overline{OEA}_F = 7.14$ percent) than the mean of the nonfailed group ($\overline{OEA}_{NF} = 5.16$ percent) and (2) for the failed group, 12.98 percent of the *population* of nonfailed banks (about four of the 33 sample nonfailed banks) are expected to lie

Table 5.15

Failed and Nonfailed Banks: Equality of

Group Variances

| | Variance of OEA | | | | Variance of OEOI | | | |
|---|---|---|---|---|---|---|---|---|
| Year Prior to Failure | Failed (%) | Nonfailed (%) | F-statistic | Signif-icance level (%) | Failed (%) | Nonfailed (%) | F-statistic | Signif-icance level (%) |
| 1 | 5.37 | 1.71 | 9.81 | 0.17 | 538 | 90 | 22.56 | 0.00[*] |
| 2 | 2.01 | 0.91 | 3.68 | 5.51 | 224 | 82 | 5.89 | 1.52 |
| 3 | 1.39 | 0.60 | 3.22 | 7.26 | 113 | 97 | 0.10 | 74.86 |
| 4 | 1.91 | 0.75 | 3.66 | 5.57 | 179 | 113 | 0.91 | 34.11 |
| 5 | 2.51 | 0.43 | 8.70 | 0.31 | 190 | 83 | 2.10 | 14.70 |
| 6 | 0.81 | 0.59 | 0.21 | 64.33 | 191 | 46 | 3.99 | 4.58 |

Notes:  [*]Indicates a very small positive number.

Data Source: Reports of Condition and Income, 1969-1974, Federal Deposit Insurance Corporation.

Table 5.16

Failed and Nonfailed Banks:  Chi-Square Measures

of Group Overlap

Significance Level of the Chi-Square Score

| Year Prior to Failure | Total Sample Size | OEA | | OEOI | |
|---|---|---|---|---|---|
| | | Failed/Nonfailed | Nonfailed/Failed | Failed/Nonfailed | Nonfailed/Failed |
| 1 | 66 | 39.27 | 12.98 | 30.43 | 1.18 |
| 2 | 52 | 62.45 | 46.88 | 66.52 | 47.57 |
| 3 | 40 | 26.53 | 8.89 | 21.48* | 21.48* |
| 4 | 38 | 44.52 | 22.42 | 36.00 | 25.00 |
| 5 | 28 | 64.70 | 26.91 | 54.76 | 36.22 |
| 6 | 20 | 89.10* | 89.10* | 75.61 | 52.77 |

Notes:   *Indicates that the test of group overlap was based upon equal group dispersions. The significance level is stated as a percentage and is interpreted as follows: X percent of the population of Y banks (for Y/Z) are expected to lie farther from the mean for the Y banks than the mean for the Z banks.

Data Source:  Reports of Condition and Income 1969-1974 Federal Deposit Insurance Corporation.

farther from mean of the nonfailed group (5.16 percent) than the mean of the failed group (7.14 percent). In other words, 39.27 percent of the *population* of failed banks are expected to have OEA values that are *either* less than 1.98 percent *or* greater than 12.30 percent, while 12.98 of the *population* of nonfailed banks are expected to have OEA values *either* less than −1.98 (which is impossible) *or* greater than 12.30 percent. With the exception of the second year prior, there was a fairly steady decrease in the degree of group overlap as failure became more imminent.

An alternative way of examining group overlap is to employ discriminant-analysis classification procedures. Classification results using OEOI and OEA (separately) are presented in Table 5.17. The classifications were performed using the Lachenbruch holdout technique, a method which almost eliminates sample bias because the classified observation is not used in the calculation of the classification rule. Thus, a different classification rule is computed for each observation (bank) that is classified. Depending upon the test of the equality of variances, either a quadratic or linear function was employed. The sample proportions .5 and .5 were used as the a priori probabilities of failure and nonfailure, respectively. Since the sample proportions and population priors (say .01 and .99) are not equal, the classifications in Table 5.17 normally would be regarded as being only "descriptive" and not "predictive." However, as was shown in the previous chapter, when the bank regulators' costs of misclassification are considered explicitly, the sample-proportions method provides a reasonable estimate of the population priors adjusted for misclassification costs. Thus, the classifications in Table 5.17 (and in the remainder of this book) are considered to be both descriptive and predictive.

Table 5.17

Failed and Nonfailed Banks: Classification Results

| Variable/Year Prior | | Total Banks Reclassified (Paired Sample) | Type-I Error | | Type-II Error | | Total Error | |
|---|---|---|---|---|---|---|---|---|
| OEOI | 1 | 66 | 13 | (39.39) | 3 | (9.09) | 16 | (24.24) |
| | 2 | 52 | 10 | (38.46) | 5 | (19.23) | 15 | (28.85) |
| | 3 | 40 | 5 | (25.00) | 7 | (35.00) | 12 | (30.00 |
| | 4* | 38 | 6 | (31.58) | 6 | (31.58) | 12 | (31.58) |
| | 5* | 28 | 5 | (35.71) | 4 | (28.57) | 9 | (32.14) |
| | 6 | 20 | 6 | (60.00) | 1 | (10.00) | 7 | (35.00) |
| OEA | 1 | 66 | 16 | (48.48) | 4 | (12.12) | 20 | (30.30) |
| | 2 | 52 | 14 | (53.85) | 4 | (15.38) | 18 | (34.61) |
| | 3 | 40 | 8 | (40.00) | 2 | (10.00) | 10 | (25.00) |
| | 4 | 38 | 10 | (52.63) | 3 | (31.58) | 13 | (34.21) |
| | 5 | 28 | 10 | (71.43) | 2 | (14.29) | 12 | (42.86) |
| | 6* | 20 | 5 | (50.00) | 4 | (40.00) | 9 | (45.00) |

Notes: *Indicates linear classification, others are quadratic. All classifications were performed using the Lachenbruch holdout technique and a priori probabilities were set equal to the sample proportions (.5, .5). Figures in parentheses are percentages.

Data Source: Reports of Condition and Income, 1969-1974, Federal Deposit Insurance Corporation.

The predictive content of a classification is determined by its accuracy. Overall accuracy is judged by the total error rate (or by its converse one minus the total classification error rate). The type-I error measures the misclassification rate for the failed-bank group while the type-II error measures the misclassification rate for the nonfailed-bank group. Given their safety-and-soundness mandate, the banking authorities are most concerned about failed banks classified as nonfailed banks (type-I errors).

In terms of group overlap, the classifications for OEOI and for OEA in Table 5.17 *describe* groups with a considerable degree of overlap. However, they also *describe* groups that were relatively distinct even four or five years prior to failure. The type-I and type-II errors indicate that in most cases it is easier to identify nonfailed banks correctly than failed ones when using "bottom-line" measures of performance.

Of the "bottom-line" measures of bank performance discussed above, OEOI is the best discriminator between the failed and non-failed banks with an overall accuracy between 66–75 percent. NOA is a very close second. On balance, the differences between the various measures are not great. However, none of the single variables is as accurate as the many-variable tests of bank soundness, to be discussed later.

### 3. Roe Decomposition Analysis

The components of the ROE model (ROE = PM X AU X EM = ROA X EM) for the failed and nonfailed banks are presented in Table 5.18. Except for the second year prior, the average failed bank's ROE (or ROA) deteriorates steadily over the six years prior to failure.[6] In addition, the dispersion about the mean increases as failure approaches. Compared to the average nonfailed bank, the average failed bank has (again except for the second year prior) a significantly lower ROE.[7] For example, six years prior to failure the average 1975 failed bank returned only $7.65 per $100 of equity capital compared to $11.65 per $100 of equity for the average nonfailed bank. These means, based upon 1969 data, are different at the 6.98 percent level of significance. Since the sample size becomes larger as failure approaches, some of the observed differences may be due to the resulting increase in statistical precision.

The major difference in the average failed bank's ROE and the average nonfailed bank's ROE can be traced to the profit-margin variable (PM), which is significantly lower (at the 5 percent level) in the first, third, and fourth years prior. The equity multiplier (EM) is not significantly different in any of the prior periods while the asset utilization (AU) is significantly higher for the average failed bank in the third year prior only. Since ROA = PM X AU, the combined effect of PM and AU is manifested in ROA. Except for the second and sixth years prior, ROA is significantly different between the two groups. For example, in the third year prior to failure, the average failed bank earned seventeen cents per $100 of assets compared to eighty-nine cents per $100 of assets for the average nonfailed bank.

The reason for the relatively poor profit performance of recent failed banks (whether measured by ROE or ROA) can be traced to poor spread management. Moreover, the culprit in the spread deficiency is the cost or expense component. Three expense items that reduce the cost efficiency of failed banks are presented in Table 5.19. These items, expressed as a percentage of operating income, are (1) provision for loan losses (an indicator of loan quality); (2) expenditures for federal funds (an indicator of the aggressiveness of liability management); and (3) other operating expenses (an indicator of the effectiveness of expense controls). Regarding the last item, an example of what a small ($10 million in assets) bank's schedule of "other expenses" might include is presented in Table 5.20. This particular example describes a bank that has had some financial difficulties and, typical of such banks, its ratio of other expenses to operating income is a high 19.25 percent.

The financial drain that the three expense items in Table 5.19 placed on the average failed bank's operating income is illustrated more vividly

## Table 5.18

### Return-on-Equity Analysis: Failed and Nonfailed Banks 1970 - 1975

| Year Prior to Failure | Failed Banks | | | | | Nonfailed Banks | | | | | Number of Banks in Each Group |
|---|---|---|---|---|---|---|---|---|---|---|---|
| | ROE (%) | ROA (%) | PM (%) | AU (%) | EM (Ratio) | ROE (%) | ROA (%) | PM (%) | AU (%) | EM (Ratio) | |
| 1 | -6.42 (27.87)* | -0.35 (1.73) | -4.00 (22.90) | 6.90 (1.12) | 13.39 (13.70) | 14.15 (6.91) | 1.02 (0.44) | 16.36 (8.31) | 6.51 (1.24) | 14.28 (4.29) | 33 |
| 2 | 6.65 (19.39) | 0.60 (0.86) | 9.57 (13.35) | 6.56 (1.29) | 15.50 (7.32) | 11.82 (6.60) | 0.81 (0.41) | 13.27 (6.57) | 6.21 (0.77) | 14.98 (4.83) | 26 |
| 3 | 2.34 (14.73) | 0.17 (1.04) | 2.89 (16.05) | 6.52 (0.89) | 15.05 (5.67) | 13.41 (6.57) | 0.89 (0.36) | 15.04 (6.19) | 5.92 (0.59) | 15.67 (5.50) | 20 |
| 4 | 4.56 (14.57) | 0.37 (0.77) | 6.33 (12.21) | 6.31 (0.97) | 14.41 (4.74) | 12.20 (4.78) | 0.88 (0.36) | 14.87 (6.13) | 5.98 (0.82) | 14.96 (4.64) | 19 |
| 5 | 7.05 (7.30) | 0.49 (0.68) | 7.93 (10.51) | 6.27 (1.25) | 12.17 (3.86) | 11.61 (4.84) | 0.89 (0.36) | 14.58 (6.59) | 6.06 (0.66) | 14.47 (4.95) | 14 |
| 6 | 7.65 (5.67) | 0.71 (0.57) | 11.53 (9.15) | 6.06 (0.53) | 10.99 (3.36) | 11.65 (3.30) | 0.86 (0.21) | 13.97 (3.60) | 6.23 (0.78) | 14.20 (5.04) | 10 |

*Figures in parentheses are standard deviations. The variables are defined in the text. ROE in the first year prior was calculated using 32 banks in each group.
*Source:* Reports of Condition and Income, 1969 - 1974, Federal Deposit Insurance Corporation.

121

Table 5.19

Expenses of Failed and Nonfailed Banks 1970-1975
(as a percentage of total operating income)

| | Failed | | | Nonfailed | | |
|---|---|---|---|---|---|---|
| Year Prior to Failure | Provision for Loan Losses | Expenditures for Federal Funds | Other Expenses | Provision for Loan Losses | Expenditures for Federal Funds | Other Expenses |
| 1 | 10.80 (13.08) | 3.50 (8.21) | 19.19 (9.79) | 1.83 (2.45) | 1.36 (4.33) | 11.01 (3.87) |
| 2 | 3.28 (11.56) | 2.99 (6.22) | 17.26 (10.55) | 2.10 (3.00) | 0.94 (3.64) | 11.74 (4.63) |
| 3 | 5.84 (9.32) | 1.64 (3.63) | 16.82 (9.18) | 1.62 (2.10) | 0.38 (1.35) | 11.47 (5.07) |
| 4 | 4.86 (7.68) | 2.00 (5.02) | 17.92 (9.93) | 1.70 (1.62) | 0.48 (1.44) | 11.89 (5.02) |
| 5 | 3.08 (3.54) | 2.32 (6.16) | 17.22 (7.40) | 1.65 (1.81) | 0.43 (1.53) | 12.54 (4.78) |
| 6 | 5.09 (4.18) | 1.10 (3.29) | 16.65 (4.55) | 3.45 (3.49) | 0.79 (2.48) | 14.59 (5.40) |

Notes: Figures in parentheses are standard deviations. The number of banks in each group is 33, 26, 20, 19, 14, and 10 for the years one through six prior, respectively.

Data Source: Reports of Income 1969-1974, Federal Deposit Insurance Corporation.

when these three items are combined. For example, in the first year prior, the combined expenses for the average failed bank are 33.49 percent (18.19 percent) of operating income compared to only 14.21 percent (6.09 percent) for the average nonfailed bank.[8] This composite expense item is significantly different between the two groups in each prior year except the sixth. In the fifth year prior, the group means (standard deviations) are 22.63 percent (9.00) and 14.62 percent (5.21) with an F-statistic of 8.28 (significant at the 0.79 percent level).

Regarding the individual components of the composite expense item (see Table 5.19), "other" expenses is the most important variable; it is statistically significant in five of the first six years prior. Provision for loan losses is most important in the first year prior and to a lesser extent in the third and fourth years prior. Expenditures for Federal funds, which tends to be a better problem indicator for large banks rather than small ones, is not statistically significant in any of the years.

Comparing the ratio of the standard deviation to the mean (i.e., the coefficient of variation, a measure of relative dispersion) for the expense data in Table 5.19, it is clear that the failed-bank group is more dispersed than the nonfailed-bank group. Moreover, as indicated by the following classification-accuracy rates for the *composite expense item* for years 1–6, there also is considerable overlap between the two groups: 76 percent, 69 percent, 80 percent, 68 percent, 64 percent, and 55 percent. The corresponding type-I error percentages are 39, 54, 30, 47, 36, and 40.

*Table 5.20*

Schedule of Other Operating Expenses

|  | Monthly 1977 |
|---|---:|
| Advertising | $ 900.00 |
| Bank travel | 350.00 |
| Business development | 275.00 |
| Cost of insuring deposits – FDIC | 275.00 |
| Directors' fees | – 0 – |
| Equipment maintenance | 725.00 |
| Postage | 1,300.00 |
| Express and freight | 500.00 |
| General insurance | 1,100.00 |
| Int. payable on Fed. funds | – 0 – |
| Machine rentals | 700.00 |
| Legal service | 350.00 |
| Examinations | 700.00 |
| Credit report costs | -200.00 |
| Professional services – other | 400.00 |
| "The Club" expense | 1,000.00 |
| Stationary and supplies | 1,700.00 |
| Small fixtures | 150.00 |
| Dues – social clubs | 125.00 |
| Dues – business clubs | 150.00 |
| Publications and subscriptions | 75.00 |
| Telephone and telegraph | 1,300.00 |
| Cafeteria | 175.00 |
| Charitable contributions | 200.00 |
| Data processing | 2,500.00 |
| Miscellaneous expense | 400.00 |
| Other losses | 200.00 |
| Reserve for bond losses | – 0 – |
| Total other operating expense | $15,350.00 |
| Total operating income | $79,750.00 |
| Other/operating income | 19.25% |

### 4. The Capital Adequacy of Failed Banks

One of the ongoing controversies in commercial banking focuses upon the relationship between bank capital and bank soundness—the so-called capital-adequacy question. Studies of bank failures in the 1930s [e.g., Secrist (1938)] found little or no relationship between the incidence of failure and capital adequacy, as measured by various capital ratios. Is this conclusion still valid for the bank failures of the 1970s? Single- and multiple-variable tests are conducted to investigate this question. Of course, we already know (from Chapter 3) that failed banks have grossly inadequate capital when *examiners' perceptions* of asset quality are included in the capital ratio (i.e., the FDIC's net capital ratio).

The studies of bank failures in the 1930s compared *one variable at a time*. Recent studies, however, have employed multiple-variable techniques. For example, using a broad definition of bank failure to include emergency mergers, financial assistances, etc. (in addition to insolvencies) and *multiple-variable* logit analyses, Martin (1978) concludes that capital adequacy (as measured by the ratio of capital to risk assets) is an important explanatory variable in his failure model. In another recent bank-failure study, Santomero and Vinso (1977) conclude that the traditional capital-asset ratio, if combined with a measure of the variability of a bank's capital, is an effective problem-bank screen. Both the Martin and the Santomero and Vinso studies deal only with Federal Reserve member banks.[9] In addition, Santomero and Vinso's study uses an arbitrary definition of what constitutes a "problem bank." The analyses presented in this section apply to all declared commercial-bank insolvencies (i.e., *de jure* failures) for the 1970–1975 period.

For the purposes of this study, bank capital is defined as the financial cushion or buffer to absorb bank losses. It is measured narrowly as total capital and more broadly as equity *plus* reserves (for bad-debt losses) on loans and securities.[10] The "adequacy" of this capital is measured relative to total assets (A), total deposits (D), and total loans (L). The ratios are identified as KA or KRA, KD or KRD, and KL or KRL, where K indicates the equity definition and KR the equity-plus-reserves definition. The use of total assets and total deposits in the denominator of the ratio is based upon tradition, while total loans is employed because these assets represent a bank's riskiest class of assets. Thus, KL and KRL can be viewed as capital-to-risk assets ratios.[11] All of these capital ratios are, of course, only crude approximations of a bank's capital adequacy. More refined measures, such as ACR and NCR discussed in Chapter 3, make specific adjustments for a bank's classified or risky assets. Finally, the *variability* of a bank's capital adequacy, in addition to its level, as suggested by Santomero and Vinso, also should be considered.

The capital ratio that shows the most significant difference between the failed- and nonfailed-bank groups for each of the six years prior to failure is presented in Table 5.21. KRL is the most important discriminator for the first four years prior while KD and KA are the most important in the fifth and sixth years before failure, respectively. However, note that in the fifth and sixth years prior KD and KA are *higher* for the average failed bank than for the average nonfailed bank. In the first four years before failure both KD and KA are *lower* for the average failed bank than the average nonfailed bank, but in neither case are the differences statistically significant. Thus, the typical failed bank for the 1970–1975 period did *not* have less capital per dollars of assets (or deposits) compared to a group of control banks; however, it did have significantly less capital per dollar of loans (risk assets).[12]

The Comptroller of the Currency (in the past) has used a benchmark KRL of one dollar of capital for every seven dollars of loans (or KRL = 14.28 percent) for identifying potential "problem" banks. Using this as a cutoff value and the data one year prior to failure, twenty-two of the failed banks (66.67 percent) have less than one dollar of capital for every seven dollars of loans; however, thirteen of the nonfailed banks (39.39 percent) also have less than the one-to-seven capital requirement. For the second, third, and fourth years prior, the KRL type-I error rates (percent) are 23.08, 40.00, and 42.10.

Although the KRL one-to-seven cutoff value is based upon the experiences of the Comptroller's office, it still is an *arbitrary* figure. Cutoff values based upon *MDA models* produced about the same overall accuracy in reclassifying the sample banks, but they are more efficient in identifying failed banks. The type-I error rates (percent) associated with the quadratic MDA equations for the first four years before failure are 15.15, 15.38, 20.00, and 21.05, respectively. For the first year prior, the quadratic equation is

$$-.68933 - .13835(\text{KRL}) + .01148(\text{KRL})^2.$$

If the value of this equation for the ith bank is *less* than 0.61135, the bank is classified as a member of the failed-bank group, that is, the bank's KRL is more similar to the average failed bank's KRL than the average nonfailed bank's KRL. The cutoff value associated with the quadratic equation is KRL = 18.26. In other words, if a bank's KRL is less than 18.26, it was assigned to the failed group.[13] Compared to the Comptroller's bench-figure of 14.28, it is obvious that a higher KRL value would produce a lower type-I error—at the expense of a higher type-II error. This trade-off is achieved, however, without sacrificing overall accuracy.

*Table 5.21*

Capital Ratios for Failed and Nonfailed Banks, 1970 - 1975

| Year Prior to Failure | Number of Banks in Each Group | Ratio | Average Failed Bank (%) | Average Nonfailed Bank (%) | F-statistic | Level of Significance (%) |
|---|---|---|---|---|---|---|
| 1 | 33 | KRL | 13.25 (6.31)* | 19.35 (8.57) | 10.82 | 0.16 |
| 2 | 26 | KRL | 14.21 (5.88) | 13.44 (8.95) | 4.05 | 4.96 |
| 3 | 20 | KRL | 14.59 (4.16) | 18.64 (8.35) | 3.77 | 5.97 |
| 4 | 19 | KRL | 15.57 (5.92) | 19.25 (8.41) | 2.43 | 12.78 |
| 5 | 14 | KD | 10.67 (4.11) | 8.69 (3.02) | 2.11 | 15.83 |
| 6 | 10 | KA | 9.90 (3.15) | 7.89 (2.78) | 2.28 | 14.87 |

*Figures in parentheses are standard deviations.
*Data Source:* Reports of Condition, 1969 - 1974, Federal Deposit Insurance Corporation.

Two of the banks that failed in the 1970–1975 era are Franklin National Bank of New York and United States National Bank of San Diego.[14] On the list of largest U.S. bank failures, these banks rank first and second, respectively. Franklin's KRLs for the four years prior (1970–1973) to its failure in 1974 are (beginning with 1970) 12.71 percent, 11.67 percent, 10.60 percent, and 8.98 percent, respectively. Even for a bank its size, these KRL levels are below average. In addition, the downward trend is more severe than that experienced by other billion-dollar banks. For example, the KRLs for Franklin's control bank are 14.51, 15.03, 13.73, and 13.96. The corresponding data (1969–1972) for USNB, which failed in 1973, are 12.01, 11.08, 10.92, and 10.88 (percent); for USNB's control bank, the KRLs are 10.03, 10.30, 8.88, and 8.83 (percent). As a final illustration, consider the KRLs for Hamilton National Bank of Chattanooga, which closed on February 16, 1976 and currently ranks as the third-largest U.S. bank failure (also see Chapter 7). These data cover the years 1972–1976. Beginning with 1972, the data are 14.14, 11.86, 12.82, and 11.67 (percent). Thus, using the Comptroller's KRL benchmark of 14.28, of these five banks only Franklin's control bank in 1970 and 1971 is not in need of "supervisory attention."

To summarize, a bank's equity capital plus its reserves for loan losses (relative to its loans) has been a fairly good indicator of the incidence of bank failure for the 1970–1975 period. On a one-variable-at-a-time basis, this capital-adequacy measure has one of the best type-I error rates of any of the variables tested; however, its type-II error is quite high and hence its overall accuracy is not impressive (i.e., 58–65 percent).[15] Clearly, it cannot be concluded that bank capital and bank soundness were unrelated during the 1970–1975 era. The role of bank capital in a multiple-variable context is explored in the next section.

### 5. Multiple-Variable Tests of Bank Soundness: Failure-Prediction Models

Altman (1975) has suggested three alternative weighting schemes for failure-prediction models:

1. Models with *different* variables and *different* coefficients for each period prior to failure;
2. A model with the *same* variables but *different* coefficients for each period, with the data in each period determining the optimal coefficients; and
3. A model with the *same* variables and the *same* coefficients for each period.

Since the first strategy is the most general and flexible of the three, it is the one employed. The MDA models to be presented below are the "best" models (best in terms of overall classification accuracy) of those tested. The variables selected for testing are based upon the "theory" of ratio analysis and upon my experience in developing problem-prediction models. Since most of the banks included in the failed-bank group were identified as problem banks prior to their failure, banks approaching failure tend to have financial characteristics similar to problem institutions. Thus, failure-prediction models should not be markedly different from problem-prediction models.

**a. The "Best" Model One Year Prior to Failure.** The "best" model one year prior to failure is a two-variable one, consisting of the operating-efficiency variable (OEOI) and an investments-to-asset ratio (IA), where IA = RC (2+3+4+5+5+6+7)/RC-14 (see Table 5.7 for the RC items). IA, other things equal, is a measure of safety (or risk)—the higher the IA ratio the fewer loans made and hence the safer the bank. The group means (standard deviations) for the failed and nonfailed groups are OEOI = 102.04 percent (23.21 percent) and IA = 19.51 percent (10.27 percent) versus OEOI = 78.56 percent (9.47 percent) and IA = 39.68 percent (14.46 percent), respectively. The group means and group dispersion matrices are statistically different at a very high level of significance. The linear and quadratic classification-equation accuracies are quite comparable, with the quadratic only slightly more accurate (83.33 percent versus 81.82 percent). The type-I and type-II errors for the quadratic equation are 18.18 percent and 15.15 percent, respectively.

Using the sixteen banks that failed in 1976 as a holdout sample (see Table 5.6), the linear model correctly identifies fifteen of the banks (93.75 percent) as future failures, based upon data as of December 31, 1975. The quadratic equation correctly identifies only nine of the banks (56.25 percent), suggesting an "overfitting" of the sample.

The linear classification equation is

$$Z = -2.9403 + 0.073563(\text{OEOI}) - 0.12557(\text{IA}).$$

If the value of this equation (the Z score) is greater than zero, the bank is classified as having OEOI and IA characteristics more similar to the average failed bank (one year prior to failure) than the average nonfailed bank. The Z scores range from $-0.22$ for First Rio B&T (discussed below) to 13.2 for Centennial Bank of Philadelphia. The latter has data of OEOI = 279 percent and IA = 35 percent.

The quadratic classification equation is:

$$Z = -62.41 + 1.504(\text{OEOI}) + .22018(\text{IA} - .0095 \, (\text{OEOI})^2 \\ - .0025 \, (\text{IA})^2 + .0046(\text{OEOI})(\text{IA}).$$

If Z is less than $-1.1288$, the bank is assigned to the failed group. Note that in this quadratic formulation IA has the opposite (and a priori incorrect) sign from IA in the linear equation and that the economic meaning of the signs on the squared and cross-product terms are difficult to interpret.

The bank missed by the linear model is the First State Bank and Trust Company of Rio Grande City, Texas. As mentioned in Chapter 2, the FDIC considered this bank to be unsafe and unsound prior to its failure because of an excessive amount of loans to its controlling stockholder and persons associated with him. Two days after the FDIC terminated the bank's deposit insurance, it was closed. Given the nature of this bank's difficulties, a failure-prediction model based upon ordinary balance-sheet and income-expense data would not be expected to flag such a bank. (First Rio's data are OEOI = 66 percent and IA = 17 percent.) This type of case clearly illustrates the need for on-site bank inspections and the complementarity (as opposed to substitutability) of early-warning mechanisms to such inspections.

**b. The "Best" Model Two Years Prior to Failure.** The two-variable model consisting of OEOI and IA (described above) is the "best" model two years prior to failure. The group means (standard deviations) for this year are OEOI = 88.52 percent (14.97 percent and IA = 22.34 percent (7.16 percent) for the failed group and OEOI = 82.04 percent (9.08 percent) and IA = 38.28 percent (14.60 percent) for the nonfailed group. The group means and variance-covariance matrices are significantly different. The quadratic equation correctly classifies 82.69 percent of the 52 banks while the linear equation's accuracy rate is 75 percent. However, with the holdout sample of sixteen failed banks, the quadratic model does not predict any of the banks to be future failures while the linear model flags fourteen of the sixteen banks (87.5 percent). Overall, the linear model has to be judged superior. The linear classification equation is:

$$Z = -0.38483 + 0.048389(OEOI) - 0.12345(IA)$$

If Z is greater than zero, the bank is classified as a member of the failed group.

**c. The "Best" Model Three Years Prior to Failure.** This model consists of three variables: OEOI, SLA, and SFA. SLA (=RC4/RC14) measures a bank's investment in state and local debt obligations as a percentage of total assets. It is, in effect, a special case of IA and, like IA, it is a measure of safety. NFA (=(RC7-RC23)/RC14) measures a bank's net investment in Federal funds. The numerator of NFA is Federal funds sold minus Federal funds purchased. A negative Federal-funds position implies either liquidity needs or aggressive action to meet loan demand—in either case an indicator of potential financial difficulties.

The group means (standard deviations) are OEOI = 91.96 percent (10.61 percent), NFA = 1.81 percent (6.01 percent), and SLA = 5.26

percent (5.99 percent) for the twenty failed banks and OEOI = 79.26 (9.85 percent), NFA = 3.61 percent (5.74 percent), and SLA = 11.12 percent (5.69 percent) for the twenty nonfailed banks. While the group means are different at the .002 percent level of significance, the group dispersion matrices are not significantly different. The linear equation correctly classifies 87.5 percent of the forty banks; the quadratic equation correctly classifies 85 percent of the sample. With the holdout sample of fifteen failed banks (one less bank than the previous year because of lack of data), the accuracy rates are 53.33 percent (linear) and 100 percent (quadratic). However, since in the original-sample test the dispersion matrices are equal (i.e., there is no reason to use a quadratic equation) and since some of the quadratic results, while they are mathematically correct, do not make economic sense, the linear model must be judged as the "superior" one. The linear classification equation is:

$$Z = -7.3136 + .12112 \, (OEOI) - 0.025895(NFA) - 0.28788 \, (SLA).$$

If Z is greater than zero, the bank is classified as a future failure. Finally, note that all the coefficients have a priori correct signs.

   **d. The "Best" Model Four Years Prior to Failure.** This model is a three-variable one consisting of NOA, FPOI, and LD. The profitability (NOA) and expense (FPOI) variables are discussed above.[16] LD (=RC8/RC14) is the traditional loan-to-deposit ratio and a measure of riskiness or safety. Very high LDs indicate that deposits are being channeled into "riskier" loans, as opposed to "safer" security investments.

   The group means (standard deviations) are NOA = 0.50 percent (0.84 percent), FPOI = 24.78 percent (14.59 percent) and LD = 64.41 percent (12.45 percent) for the nineteen failed banks and NOA = 1.23 percent (0.65 percent), FPOI = 14.08 percent (5.55 percent), and LD = 52.22 percent (14.37 percent) for the paired nonfailed banks. The group dispersion matrices are different at the 2.36 percent level of significance while the group means are different at the 0.12 percent level. Both the linear and quadratic functions have the same overall classification accuracy (84.21 percent), but the linear function correctly classifies one more failed bank than the quadratic one (i.e., it had a lower type-I error). With respect to the holdout sample (now reduced to fourteen failed banks), the linear model's accuracy rate is 57.14 percent compared to 0.0 percent for the quadratic equation. The linear classification is:

$$Z = -4.3441 - 1.1289(NOA) + 0.042249(FPOI) + 0.077150(LD)$$

If Z is greater than zero, the bank is assigned to the failed group. Failed-group designation means that four years prior to historical failures, the assigned bank has characteristics more similar to the average failed bank than the average nonfailed bank.

**e. The "Best" Model Five Years Prior to Failure.** This model consists of four variables LRI, IVI, FPOI, and SLA. The last two variables are discussed above. LRI [=RI1(a)/RI1(h)] is a measure of loan-revenue concentration and IVI [=RI1C(1+2+3+4)/RI1(h)] is a measure of revenue derived from investments. Both of these variables are measured as a percentage of total operating income and they are, of course, negatively correlated (−.81).

The group means (standard deviations) are (14 banks in each group):

| Variable | Failed Group | Nonfailed Group |
|---|---|---|
| | (%) | (%) |
| LRI | 70.18  (9.53) | 60.63  (10.50) |
| IVI | 18.01  (10.13) | 24.15  (9.52) |
| FPOI | 22.63  (9.00) | 14.62  (5.21) |
| SLA | 4.72  (6.10) | 8.61  (4.87) |

The group means are signfiicantly different at the 0.07 percent level; however, the variance-covariance matrices are not significantly different.

The linear function correctly classifies 85.72 percent of the total sample of 28 banks (75 percent for the quadratic function) and 78.57 percent of the failed banks (71.43 percent of the quadratic function). Using the holdout sample of fourteen failed banks, the linear equation correctly classifies eight banks (57.14 percent) compared to only four banks (28.57 percent) for the quadratic model. The linear classification equation is:

$$Z = -28.736 + 0.30427 \, (LRI) + 0.24006 \, (IVI) + 0.28333 \, (FPOI) - 0.22548 \, (SLA).$$

If Z is greater than zero, the bank is assigned to the failed group. Note that the expected sign for IVI is negative, while the estimated one is positive. However, based upon either a forward or backward stepwise ranking of the four variables, IVI ranks least important.

**f. The "Best" Model Six Years Prior to Failure.** This model consists of two variables OEOI and LRI, both of which have been discussed previously. The group means (standard deviations) are OEOI = 84.30 percent (13.81 percent) and LRI = 71.67 percent (10.68 percent) for the failed group (10 banks) and OEOI = 80.01 percent (6.79 percent) and LRI = 58.60 percent (10.47 percent) for the paired nonfailed banks. The dispersion matrices are not significantly different while the group means are different at the 2.87 percent level. The linear MDA function correctly classifies 70 percent of the 20 banks compared to 85 percent for the quadratic method. Using the holdout sample (now reduced to 13 failed banks), the linear equation flags ten banks (76.92 percent) compared to only four banks (30.77 percent) for the quadratic mechanism.

Although an original-sample model for seven years prior to failure is not developed, the model for six years prior is applied to data (1969) for eleven of the holdout-sample banks that failed in 1976. The linear function correctly identifies six of the eleven banks (54.54 percent) as members of the failed group. The quadratic equation does not flag any of the eleven banks. The linear classification equation is:

$$Z = -12.598 + 0.054216(OEOI) + 0.12504(LRI)$$

If Z is greater than zero, the bank is assigned to the failed group.

The three largest bank failures in 1976 (see Table 5.6) were Hamilton National ($336 million), American B&T ($200 million), and International City B&T ($160 million). Based upon 1969 data, seven years prior to failure, all three of these banks are identified as future failures. Their 1969 data and Z-scores are:

| Bank | OEOI (%) | LRI (%) | Z-score |
|---|---|---|---|
| Hamilton | 78 | 71 | 0.51 |
| American | 90 | 75 | 1.66 |
| International | 98 | 59 | 0.09 |

Over the next six years and based upon the six *linear* models described above, Hamilton is flagged in three of the years (1970, 1974, 1975); American in four of the years (1971–1972, 1974–1975); and International in five of the years (1970, 1972–1975).

The linear models presented above are summarized in Table 5.22. While these models are described as the "best" ones for the respective years prior to failure, in many cases they are only marginally superior to alternative specifications. The common factors in most of the specifications are measures of risk (or safety) and return, with the risk variables being very simple measures of banking risk such as IA, LD, or LRI.

Compared to problem-bank models, these failure-prediction models are similar in the variables that act as effective discriminators. However, in terms of overall classification accuracy, failure-prediction models are slightly more accurate (5–10 percentage points) than problem-prediction models, indicating (not unexpectedly) a greater degree of separation between failed and nonfailed banks than between problem and nonproblem banks.

The models presented in Table 5.22 are based upon a flexible strategy

*Table 5.22*

Linear Failure -Prediction Models:
Classification Results, 1969 - 1976

| Model | Year Before Failure | Original Sample Overall Accuracy (%) | Type-I Error (%) | Size | Holdout Sample Accuracy (%) | Size |
|---|---|---|---|---|---|---|
| OEOI, IA | 1 | 81.82 | 18.18 | 66 | 93.75 | 16 |
| OEOI, IA | 2 | 75.00 | 11.54 | 52 | 87.50 | 16 |
| OEOI, SLA, NFA | 3 | 87.50 | 15.00 | 40 | 53.33 | 15 |
| NOA, FPOI, LD | 4 | 84.21 | 10.53 | 38 | 57.14 | 14 |
| LRI, IVI, FPOI, SLA | 5 | 85.72 | 21.43 | 24 | 57.14 | 14 |
| OEOI, LRI | 6 | 70.00 | 30.00 | 20 | 76.92 | 13 |
| OEOI, LRI | 7 | – | – | – | 54.54 | 11 |

The variables used in the alternative models are defined in the text. The original-sample classifications were performed using the Lachenbruch holdout technique and a priori probabilities equal to the sample proportions. Since data beyond 1969 were not employed, the original-sample size declines as the time before failure increases. The holdout sample consisted of the 16 banks that failed in 1976. The holdout sample size decreases because some of the failed banks were newly chartered ones and thus did not have data available for very many years before their failures.

of different variables and different coefficients for each period prior to failure. Comparing these results with the strategy of the same variables but different coefficients for each period, the completely flexible strategy is superior. For example, using (OEOI, IA) as the fixed set of variables, the overall accuracy rates for years 3–6 before failure (based upon different coefficients) are: 77.50 percent, 76.32 percent, 71.43 percent, and 65.00 percent. (The rates for one and two years prior are presented in Table 5.22.) The corresponding type-I errors are 20.00 percent. 21.05 percent, 28.57 percent, and 40.00 percent. Using the strategy of the same variables (OEOI, IA) and the same coefficients (from one year prior) applied to the holdout sample with data from *two* years prior, this strategy is inferior to the strategy of the same variables but with different coefficients (i.e., 75 percent accuracy versus 87.5 percent). On balance a strategy of different variables with different coefficients appears to be the best approach.

### 6. Problem Banks Revisited

As mentioned at the beginning of this chapter, analyses of problem-nonproblem banks have been published in a number of different places.

It is not my intention to rehash those findings here. The material presented in this section focuses upon several heretofore unpublished aspects of a seven-variable early-warning system (EWS). This model was first presented at the Conference on Financial Crises in May 1977 [see Sinkey (1977)].

The seven variables used in the model are:

1. LRI = interest and fees on loans as a percentage of total operating income (this measures revenue concentration).

2. OEOI = total operating expense as a percentage of total operating income (this measures operating efficiency).

3. USA = U.S. government securities as a percentage of total assets (this measures liquidity and asset composition).

4. SLA = state and local securities as a percentage of total assets (this measures asset composition).

5. LA = total loans as a percentage of total assets (this measures loan volume).

6. NFA = net federal funds (sales minus purchases) as a percentage of total assets (this measures Federal-funds activity and aggressiveness of liability management).

7. KRA = capital and reserves for bad debt losses on loans as a percentage of total assets (this measures capital adequacy).

Using this model, examiner-determined problem-nonproblem situations have been reclassified with about 75 percent accuracy using a quadratic equation. The coefficients or weights for the quadratic equation based upon 1974 and 1975 populations of problem-nonproblem banks are presented in Table 5.23. A simpler approach that is just about as efficient (the trade off is a higher type-I error) is to use only the first two variables LRI and OEOI (e.g., the failure model for *six* years prior presented above).

To illustrate this simpler approach, consider the linear and quadratic equations for the *one-year-prior failure model* for OEOI and LRI. The linear equation is:

$$Z = -13.406 + 0.0767(\text{OEOI}) + 0.0987 \,(\text{LRI}).$$

If Z is greater than zero, the bank is assigned to the *failed* group. The quadratic equation is:

$$Z = -10.539 + 1.2882 \,(\text{OEOI}) - 0.8587(\text{LRI}) - 0.0093 \,(\text{OEOI})^2 \\ + 0.0014(\text{LRI})^2 + 0.0040 \,(\text{OEOI}) \,(\text{LRI}).$$

*Table 5.23*

Coefficients (or Weights) for a Seven-Variable Problem-Bank EWS

The quadratic classification equation is the sum of the following 36 terms. Note that each term consists of a weight multiplied by a variable or product of variables.

| Variables | 1975 Population Weights | 1974 Population Weights |
|---|---|---|
| Constant term | -45.7930 | -55.4120 |
| LRI | .7371 | .7759 |
| OEOI | .5191 | .2582 |
| USA | .5788 | .4622 |
| SLA | 1.3081 | .9741 |
| LA | -.3096 | .1469 |
| NFA | 1.3074 | 1.2300 |
| KRA | -.7011 | 1.3801 |
| (LRI) (LRI) | -.0065 | -.0053 |
| (OEOI) (OEOI) | -.0036 | -.0016 |
| (USA) (USA) | .0011 | .0081 |
| (SLA) (SLA) | -.0028 | -.0015 |
| (LA) (LA) | -.0028 | -.0083 |
| (NFA) (NFA) | -.0035 | -.0059 |
| (KRA) (KRA) | .1463 | .0996 |
| (LRI) (OEOI) | -.0016 | -.0024 |
| (LRI) (USA) | -.0124 | -.0039 |
| (LRI) (SLA) | -.0070 | -.0082 |
| (LRI (LA) | .0082 | .0097 |
| (LRI) (NFA) | -.0103 | -.0049 |
| (LRI) (KRA) | .0030 | -.0355 |
| (OEOI) (USA) | -.0008 | -.0018 |
| (OEOI) (SLA) | -.0046 | -.0016 |
| (OEOI) (LA) | .0026 | .0021 |
| (OEOI) INFA) | -.0006 | -.0010 |
| (OEOI) (KRA) | .0106 | .0050 |
| (USA) (SLA) | -.0044 | .0036 |
| (USA) (LA) | .0093 | .0008 |
| (USA) (NFA) | -.0105 | -.0061 |
| (USA) (KRA) | -.0136 | -.0267 |
| (SLA) (LA) | .0024 | .0020 |
| (SLA) (NFA) | -.0136 | -.0071 |
| (SLA) (KRA) | -.0325 | -.0263 |
| (LA) (NFA) | -.0003 | .0065 |
| (LA) (KRA) | -.0368 | -.0042 |
| (NFA) (KRA) | -.0236 | -.0236 |

The quadratic classification-equation rules are: Assign to the problem group if the value of the quadratic equation is less than -7.4482 (1975) or less than -2,4391 (1974).

135

If Z is less than −1.2437, the bank is assigned to the failed group. The overall classification accuracy rates for these equations are 81.82 percent (linear) and 83.34 percent (quadratic); the type-I errors are 27.27 percent and 24.24 percent, respectively. Note that these type-I errors are higher than the one for the (OEOI, IA) model presented in the previous section; hence, the designation of the (OEOI,IA) model as the "best" one for one year prior.

Returning to problem banks and the seven-variable model, consider the regional data (as of December 31, 1974) presented in Table 5.24. The differences across the fourteen FDIC regions can be summarized by the following means taken from Table 5.24.

| Variables | Maximum | Minimum | Range |
|---|---|---|---|
| | (%) | (%) | (%) |
| 1. LRI | 68.79 | 53.27 | 15.52 |
| 2. OEOI | 89.03 | 76.24 | 12.79 |
| 3. USA | 24.58 | 8.68 | 15.90 |
| 4. SLA | 14.16 | 9.72 | 4.44 |
| 5. LA | 59.53 | 46.47 | 13.06 |
| 6. NFA | 7.02 | 3.22 | 3.80 |
| 7. KRA | 9.55 | 8.04 | 1.51 |

The findings suggest that a decentralized EWS may be more appropriate; however, based upon some limited testing, regional models have not been more efficient (accurate) than an aggregate national model. The potential advantage of a regional approach is getting regional personnel more involved (on the surface at least) in the EWS. Just as Sears, Roebuck and Co. uses a series of regional models in its credit-scoring analyses, regional EWS models should be explored by the banking authorities.

One practical problem that hampers the development of a regional EWS is the fact that some regions do not have enough problem or failed banks to develop statistically meaningful results. Research at the Federal Reserve Bank of New York has been hampered by this shortcoming. Of course, one can always argue that such regions do not need EWSs because they have so few banks with financial difficulties. However, this ignores the basic fact that the purpose of an EWS is to assist in a more efficient allocation of the banking authorities' scarce resources.

Another interesting way to look at this seven-variable model is to compare banks located in SMSAs with banks not located in SMSAs and then

*Table 5.24*

A Seven-Variable EWS: (December 31, 1974) Regional Data

| Variable | | Region or Group | | | |
|---|---|---|---|---|---|
| | Problem Group | Non-problem Group | Region 1 Boston | Region 2 New York | Region 3 Philadelphia | Region 4 Richmond |
| LRI | 68.44 | 58.61 | 68.79 | 62.62 | 63.51 | 63.34 |
| OEOI | 102.01 | 80.69 | 86.04 | 89.03 | 81.40 | 83.28 |
| USA | 12.57 | 17.18 | 17.11 | 8.68 | 8.90 | 8.14 |
| SLA | 6.72 | 12.57 | 9.72 | 12.77 | 14.16 | 14.19 |
| LA | 59.21 | 50.06 | 59.53 | 53.97 | 56.20 | 52.42 |
| NFA | 3.73 | 5.41 | 3.77 | 3.22 | 4.86 | 5.73 |
| KRA | 8.18 | 8.78 | 9.60 | 9.38 | 9.30 | 9.55 |

| | Region 5 Atlanta | Region 6 Columbus | Region 7 Memphis | Region 8 Madison | Region 9 Chicago | Region 10 Minneapolis |
|---|---|---|---|---|---|---|
| LRI | 59.86 | 59.43 | 59.07 | 64.70 | 53.27 | 55.40 |
| OEOI | 83.86 | 77.98 | 79.76 | 84.05 | 81.24 | 81.22 |
| USA | 13.83 | 16.70 | 15.01 | 15.10 | 22.83 | 24.58 |
| SLA | 14.17 | 12.76 | 14.12 | 11.66 | 12.15 | 10.50 |
| LA | 50.13 | 50.27 | 49.15 | 56.73 | 46.49 | 49.93 |
| NFA | 5.64 | 6.70 | 5.22 | 3.75 | 4.83 | 3.74 |
| KRA | 9.12 | 8.99 | 8.68 | 8.48 | 8.17 | 8.04 |

| | Region 11 St. Louis | Region 12 Omaha | Region 13 Dallas | Region 14 San Francisco |
|---|---|---|---|---|
| LRI | 54.49 | 56.77 | **59.52** | 62.25 |
| OEOI | 78.67 | 76.23 | 79.21 | 87.74 |
| USA | 20.46 | 20.78 | 13.24 | 12.35 |
| SLA | 12.72 | 10.63 | 13.81 | 10.65 |
| LA | 46.47 | 48.44 | 48.84 | 53.91 |
| NFA | 7.02 | 6.75 | 6.20 | 4.18 |
| KRA | 9.04 | 8.63 | 9.02 | 8.25 |

Data are regional or group means expressed as percentages.
*Source:* Reports of Condition and Income, FDIC.

to split the SMSA banks on the basis of deposit size. These data, for December 31, 1975, are presented in Table 5.25 and they suggest a number of conclusions. First, regardless of size or location, problem banks tend to make more loans (LA) and fewer investments (USA and SLA) than nonproblem banks; consequently, they are more dependent on loan revenue (LRI) for income. Since problem banks make more loans, it is tempting to conclude that they are serving their communities better. However, we will resist that temptation, since the historical record indicates that these additional loans frequently are channeled to "insiders" such as relatives, business associates, or friends rather than the general community.

Second, problem banks, regardless of size or location, are less efficient than nonproblem banks (i.e., they have higher operating expenses per dollar of operating income, OEOI). The most inefficient problem banks are those with total deposits less than $100 million dollars and located in an SMSA (OEOI = 112.19 percent); the most efficient problem banks are the rural or non-SMSA ones (OEOI = 97.63 percent). As mentioned before, the "cause" of this inefficiency can be traced to three expense items: (1) provision of loan losses, (2) expenditures for Federal funds, and (3) "other expenses." Most problem banks have poor loan quality and hence they have difficulties with loan losses. In contrast, smaller problem banks have difficulties controlling their "other expenses" (see Table 5.20), while larger problem banks tend to be net borrowers from the Federal-funds market (see NFA for SMSA banks with total deposits greater than $100 million in Table 5.25). Finally, note that non-SMSA nonproblem banks (OEOI = 81.58 percent) are "more efficient" than SMSA nonproblem banks (OEOI = 87.83 percent), which is probably due to their greater degree of monopoly power (i.e., less competition).

The last conclusion relates to the capital adequacy (or leverage) of problem banks. While problem banks tend to have lower capital ratios than nonproblem banks, these differences usually are not statistically significant on a univariate basis. Moreover, using various ranking techniques to determine the importance of individual variables, a capital ratio rarely emerges among the top three or four variables. Despite these negative findings, it cannot be concluded that capital ratios are unimportant. Frequently when five or more variables are considered in a model, a capital ratio proves important. In the previous section, the "best" failure-prediction models had four or fewer variables. This limitation was dictated in some cases by insufficient degrees of freedom caused by small sample size. For the data in Table 5.25, the greatest KRA difference is between problem (7.89 percent) and nonproblem (8.86 percent) banks not located in SMSAs. The average problem bank located in an SMSA tends to have the lowest KRA of all banks. Finally, the typical nonproblem bank located in an SMSA tends to have a lower capital ratio

## Table 5.25

### Problem-Nonproblem Bank Data

#### EWS SMSA
#### Group Means, December 31, 1975

|      | Problem Group | Nonproblem Group |
|------|---------------|------------------|
| LRI  | 69.10         | 61.45            |
| OEOI | 111.08        | 87.83            |
| USA  | 13.95         | 17.21            |
| SLA  | 7.13          | 12.03            |
| LA   | 56.61         | 50.55            |
| NFA  | 2.20          | 3.43             |
| KRA  | 8.12          | 8.79             |

#### EWS NON-SMSA
#### Group Means, December 31, 1975

|      | Problem Group | Nonproblem Group |
|------|---------------|------------------|
| LRI  | 73.46         | 59.59            |
| OEOI | 97.63         | 81.58            |
| USA  | 12.96         | 20.46            |
| SLA  | 8.20          | 12.58            |
| LA   | 59.87         | 49.24            |
| NFA  | 4.17          | 4.46             |
| KRA  | 7.89          | 8.86             |

#### EWS SMSA: Deposit Disaggregation

| Total Deposits: $> \$100$ | | | Total Deposits $< \$100$ | | |
| Group Means, December 31, 1975 | | | Group Means, December 31, 1975 | | |
|      | Problem Group | Non-problem Group |      | Problem Group | Non-problem Group |
|------|---------------|-------------------|------|---------------|-------------------|
| LRI  | 69.84         | 64.41             | LRI  | 68.95         | 60.96             |
| OEOI | 102.21        | 87.36             | OEOI | 112.19        | 87.90             |
| USA  | 8.79          | 12.71             | USA  | 14.64         | 17.94             |
| SLA  | 9.78          | 12.65             | SLA  | 6.79          | 11.93             |
| LA   | 58.23         | 51.43             | LA   | 56.38         | 50.41             |
| NFA  | -0.11         | 0.03              | NFA  | 2.48          | 3.99              |
| KRA  | 7.71          | 8.10              | KRA  | 8.18          | 8.90              |

Data are expressed as percentages and the number of banks in each group equals that population as of December 31, 1975.

*Source:* Reports of Condition and Income, FDIC.

than a rural nonproblem bank, which simply reflects the fact that larger banks tend to have lower capital ratios (i.e., they are more highly levered).

### 7. Identifying Large Problem Banks

This section focuses upon 892 insured commercial banks with total deposits equal to or greater than $100 million (as of December 31, 1975). Twenty-nine of these banks (consisting of fourteen insured-nonmember banks, twelve national banks, and three state-member banks) were listed by the FDIC's Division of Bank Supervision (DBS) as problem banks on December 31, 1975. Data for these problem-and nonproblem-bank groups, using the seven variables discussed in the previous section, are presented in Table 5.26.

Using these banks and the seven-variable EWS (with coefficients determined by the data, not the coefficients in Table 5.23), a quadratic MDA classification experiment is conducted.[17] The model identifies forty banks with characteristics more similar to the average large problem bank than the average large nonproblem bank. Sixteen of the flagged banks are on DBS's problem-bank list, an accuracy rate of 55.17 percent. In contrast, 839 of the 863 nonproblem banks (97.72 percent) are correctly identified. The overall accuracy rate is 95.85 percent (855 out of 892). With respect to PPO and SP banks, the reclassification rates are 100 percent (1 for 1) and 80 percent (8 out of 10), respectively. The high type-I error (44.83 percent) is due to the 7 out of 18 (38.9 percent) accuracy for the OP category.[18] Since OP banks constitute the "gray area" in the problem-bank spectrum, they are, of course, the most difficult ones to reclassify.

If the EWS was the only mechanism for identifying problem banks, the type-I error of 44.83 percent would be unacceptable. However, since such systems are designed to complement rather than replace the traditional on-site bank examination, their usefulness can be evaluated on a marginal basis. For example, the EWS indicated that there were 24 additional banks that should have been on the problem-bank list and thirteen banks on the list that should not have been on it. Is this information useful for supervisory purposes? The most important information regards the EWS-flagged banks not on the list. It is a simple matter for the banking authorities to run a check on these banks. If the follow-up supports (or cannot disprove) the EWS's findings, these banks are pushed to the front of the on-site examination queue. Thus, EWS can be used as an aid to scheduling on-site bank inspections. As one cynic remarked (I wish that I had said it first), "Any systematic method for arranging bank examinations would be better than scheduling them to minimize examiners' travel expenses."

*Table 5.26*

Seven-Variable EWS for Large Banks
(December 31, 1975)

| Variable | Problem-Bank Group (%) | Nonproblem-Bank Group (%) |
|---|---|---|
| LRI | 69.16 | 64.46 |
| | (9.61)* | (9.55) |
| | | |
| OEOI | 102.73 | 87.16 |
| | (17.44) | (7.30) |
| | | |
| USA | 9.96 | 12.90 |
| | (5.39) | (7.82) |
| | | |
| SLA | 9.14 | 12.90 |
| | (5.74) | (5.20) |
| | | |
| LA | 57.88 | 51.64 |
| | (7.81) | (9.35) |
| | | |
| NFA | -0.44 | 0.11 |
| | (4.66) | (6.22) |
| | | |
| KRA | 7.62 | 8.13 |
| | (1.76) | (1.58) |

*Figures in parentheses are standard deviation. There are 29 banks in the problem group and 863 banks in the nonproblem group. All banks have total deposits ≥ $100 million.

*Source:* Reports of Condtion and Income, FDIC.

It should be mentioned that this particular experiment took place during the first week of May 1976, four months after the collection date of the data. This lag is fairly representative of the time it takes the FDIC to compile an edited computer tape for the *population* of insured commercial banks. It is an enormous task to arrange hundreds of pieces of information for over 14,000 observations, especially when some of the data are obviously incorrect and need to be verified with the reporting bank. One way of reducing this lag would be to compile a tape consisting of only the 1000 largest banks, which present the greatest potential risk to the FDIC insurance fund and whose reports are less likely to contain errors. Eventually, one can foresee the day (perhaps in *1984*) when the

*Table 5.27*

OEOI for 53 "Problem" Banks

| Identifying Agent | OEOI (%) | | |
| --- | --- | --- | --- |
| | Mean | Maximum | Minimum |
| EWS (24)* | 101.1 | 122.3 | 67.6 |
| DBS and EWS (16) | 119.3 | 164.6 | 87.6 |
| DBS (13) | 95.3 | 103.0 | 78.4 |
| Total (53) | 105.2 | 164.6 | 67.6 |

*Figures in parentheses are number of banks in each group.

banking authorities will be able to monitor (via an elaborate computer network) the daily condition of the banking system or at least of the nation's largest banks.

Let us now focus upon the operating efficiency (OEOI) of the 53 banks that are flagged by either DBS or EWS. (Sixteen of the banks are identified by both DBS and EWS.) Stratified according to identifying agent, these data are presented in Table 5.27. Clearly, the average bank flagged by both DBS and EWS is the most inefficient. Seven of the 53 banks have OEOI ratios less than 90.0 percent; 14 banks have values between 90.0 and 100.0 percent; and 32 banks have ratios greater than 100.0 percent. The corresponding distribution for the 24 EWS banks is 3, 6, and 15. The distribution of these OEOI ratios by identifying agent is presented in Table 5.28.

*Table 5.28*

OEOI Distribution by Identifying Agent

| OEOI Values | Identifying Agent (number of banks) | | | |
| --- | --- | --- | --- | --- |
| | EWS (24) | DBS and EWS (16) | DBS (13) | Total |
| Less than 90.0% | 3 | 1 | 3 | 7 |
| $90.0 \leq OEOI < 95.0$ | 4 | 1 | 2 | 7 |
| $95.0 \leq OEOI < 100.0$ | 2 | 2 | 3 | 7 |
| $100.0 \leq OEOI < 105.0$ | 7 | 2 | 5 | 14 |
| $105.0 \leq OEOI < 120.0$ | 6 | 5 | 0 | 11 |
| Greater than 120.0 | 2 | 5 | 0 | 7 |
| Total | 24 | 16 | 13 | 53 |

Table 5.29

Seven-Variable Profile for Three EWS Banks

| Variable (%) | Bank 1 | Bank 2 | Bank 3 |
|---|---|---|---|
| LRI | 68.96 | 78.26 | 61.39 |
| OEOI | 122.28 | 102.52 | 67.55 |
| USA | 8.20 | 15.08 | 21.08 |
| SLA | 6.65 | 0.29 | 9.94 |
| LA | 60.26 | 72.03 | 55.16 |
| NFA | -1.18 | -7.17 | 0.36 |
| KRA | 4.86 | 9.62 | 9.53 |

Finally, consider the entire seven-variable profile for three anonymous banks presented in Table 5.29. The MDA probabilities associated with these three EWS banks being members of the problem group are 99.98 percent, 92.95 percent, and 56.90 percent, respectively. If a bank's probability of group membership is greater than 50 percent, it is assigned to the problem-bank group. Only four of the twenty-four EWS banks (including bank #3 in Table 5.29) have variable profiles that do not appear to warrant further investigation (i.e., they appear to be statistical anomalies). In addition, two other banks have data that are abnormal because they are relatively new institutions (i.e., classification should await additional start-up experience). On balance, then, eighteen of the twenty-four EWS banks appear in need of remedial attention.

## 5.4 SUMMARY AND CONCLUSIONS

This chapter focuses upon the financial characteristics of recent problem and failed banks. The analytical approach develops from ratio analysis, while the statistical implementation is conducted using multiple discriminant analysis. The chapter aims to establish a solid foundation for early-warning or bank-surveillance research. The major conclusions of this chapter are: (1) problem and failed banks have similar financial characteristics; (2) failed banks (problem banks) have significantly different financial profiles compared to nonfailed banks (nonproblem banks); (3) distributions of variables for failed banks have less overlap with nonfailed banks than the distributions of problem banks with nonproblem banks; (4) reclassifications and predictions of financially-troubled banks are accurate enough to justify developing an operational early-warning or surveillance mechanism to complement the traditional, on-site bank examination; and (5) once dimensions such as profitability, uses of revenue (costs), asset composition, and capital adequacy are captured, the specification of the individual variables (e.g., OEOI vs. NOA) is relatively unimportant.

The remaining chapters of this book focus upon (1) the decline and fall of several large commercial banks during the 1970's (Chapters 6 and 7); (2) the commercial bank-REIT debacle of the 1970s (Chapter 8); and the attitudes of bankers toward the major issues in banking (Chapter 9). The last chapter attempts to summarize the book and indicate future directions for research into problem and failed banks.

## NOTES

1. Average balance-sheet items are used to make the "stock" and "flow" variables more compatible. The ROE equation is, of course, only an identity.

2. Operating leverage refers to the use of fixed-cost operating assets to increase a firm's operating income by a greater percentage than sales increase. Breakeven analysis measures the extent to which operating leverage is employed.

3. Altman (1968) is of course famous for an earlier failure-prediction model. The 1977 model incorporates a number of improvements and extensions over the 1968 version.

4. Keeping such information secret substantially increases the probability of obtaining consulting contracts. The weights used in Altman's 1968 linear model were, to his financial regret, publicized widely. The investment firm of Wood, Struthers & Winthrop, which partially supported the 1977 research, has obtained a trademark for ZETA.

5. The expense categories that contributed to this deterioration are discussed below.

6. The anomalies associated with the data for the second year prior are discussed above.

7. The group variances are significantly different in each of the first four years prior.

8. Figures in parentheses are standard deviations. The F-statistic for the group means is 33.33, indicating a highly significant difference.

9. For additional comments on both of these studies see Altman et al.

10. In terms of the Report of Condition presented in Table 5.7, equity capital is item 35 and the reserves category is item 33. Notes and debentures (item 34), sometimes referred to as debt capital, are not included in our definition of capital.

11. Prior to NBSS, the Office of the Comptroller of the Currency used the reciprocal of these ratios as benchmark measures of a national bank's capital adequacy [see Sinkey and Walker (1975), pp. 214–215].

12. Sinkey and Walker (1975) arrive at a similar conclusion in their analyses of the "capital adequacy" of problem-nonproblem banks.

13. The *linear* equation for the first year prior is: 1.7543 − .10763 KRL. If the value of this equation for the ith bank is greater than zero, the bank is classified as a failure. The associated cutoff value is KRL = 16.30. The KRL group vari-

ances are different at the 8.86 percent level of significance. The overall accuracy of the linear and quadratic equations is the same (65.15 percent); however, the quadratic equation has a lower type-I error (by two banks).

14. The downfalls of these two banks are analyzed in detail in Chapters 6 and 7, respectively.

15. For example, compare KRL's classification accuracy (especially with respect to the failed-bank group) with the results for OEOI in Table 5.17.

16. The correlation coefficient between NOA and FPOI is $-.68$. For the most part, multicollinearity is an irrelevant concern in MDA, unless it produces singular dispersion matrices. In fact, high negative correlations have been shown to be desirable properties for MDA variables to have.

17. The "adjusted" prior probabilities employed are 15 percent (problem) and 85 percent (nonproblem). Based upon recent "worst-case" experience, a bank has about a 3 percent chance of making the FDIC's problem-bank list. Adjusting for costs of misclassification using a trial-and-error process produced the 15/85 priors. The important factor in selecting the cutoff point was the accuracy of the replications.

18. The problem-bank categories PPO (potential payoff), SP (serious problem), and OP (other problem) are defined at the end of Chapter 1.

Chapter 6

# Franklin National Bank of New York: The Largest Bank Failure in U.S. History

On Franklin National
"People who can read a balance sheet were out of there long ago."
—Harry Keefe

## 6.1 INTRODUCTION

This chapter analyzes in detail the collapse of Franklin National Bank of New York. The first part of the chapter focuses upon four pre-collapse events: (1) the identification of Franklin as a "problem" bank by the banking authorities; (2) the deposit assumption arranged by the Federal Deposit Insurance Corporation; (3) the timing of Franklin's closing; and (4) the subsidy, at taxpayers' expense, provided by the Federal Reserve System.

In the next section, a brief sketch of Franklin's prior development is presented. The third and fourth parts of the chapter present postmortem analyses of Franklin's decline, using financial-statement information and capital-market information, respectively. If the "smart money" was out of Franklin before its financial difficulties became public knowledge, what information did sagacious analysts read and why didn't the banking authorities react to this same information? The purpose of these *ex post* exercises is to determine what information, if any, might have been arrayed in an early-warning system to identify Franklin's impending financial difficulties. The chapter ends with summary-and-conclusions section.

The overall purpose of this chapter is to show that existing, routinely collected banking data, if properly analyzed, should be useful in identifying potential problem banks. By developing and using screening models

National Bank Soothsayer (NBSS)

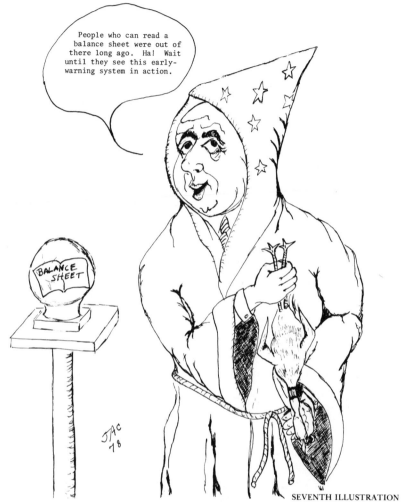

SEVENTH ILLUSTRATION

such as those described in this chapter, the banking authorities should be able to allocate their scarce resources more efficiently and thus be able to concentrate on those banks that really need close supervision.

## 6.2 PRE-FAILURE EVENTS

### *1. The Identification of Franklin as a Problem Bank*

On October 8, 1974, Franklin National Bank of New York (Franklin) became the largest bank failure in U.S. history.[1] Nine months before its downfall Franklin was the nation's twentieth-largest bank with total deposits of $3.7 billion. Franklin's collapse came exactly 355 days after what most observers thought would be the all-time, largest bank failure, U.S. National Bank of San Diego.

As a nationally chartered bank, Franklin was subject to the examination and supervision of the Office of the Comptroller of the Currency. By statute, national banks are to be examined four times during each two-year period, but the Comptroller has the authority to waive one of the examinations. The ultimate purpose of such examinations (as explained in Chapter 2) is to prevent bank failures. Moreover, the major causes of bank failures and problem banks have been dishonest and/or inept managers. In general, it appears that Franklin's failure was caused by inept management; in contrast, USNB's collapse (see Chapter 7) appeared to be due to self-serving managerial practices.

Based upon a four-month-long examination that began on November 13, 1973, and ended on March 8, 1974, the Comptroller's office became aware that Franklin had serious financial difficulties. Franklin was, among other things, borrowing short and lending long, which all banks do; however, the problem was the degree to which Franklin was playing the game. For example, approximately one-sixth of Franklin's liabilities were obtained at very high interest rates from the Federal-funds market (see Table 6.2). This meant that Franklin's leverage was based upon a volatile and short-term foundation. In addition, Franklin was lending these rate-sensitive funds to high-risk businesses.[2] On balance, Franklin was operating precariously on a razor's edge. The Comptroller's office recommended that Franklin begin a $1 billion retrenchment program.

At this point in time, apparently the public had little knowledge about Franklin's financial mismanagement. However, on May 1, the Federal Reserve Board denied a bid by Franklin New York Corporation (FNYC), Franklin's parent, to acquire Talcott National Corporation, a financial concern located in New York. The basis for the Fed's denial was that the acquisition would only be "a complicating and diversionary factor" in Franklin's effort to retrench [see Brimmer (1976)]. The Talcott decision, which was opposed by the Comptroller's office because of concern about adverse publicity, triggered rumors about Franklin's viability. As a result, Franklin's liquidity became impaired and on May 8 it was forced to borrow $110 million from the Federal Reserve Bank of New York (see Table 6.1).

On May 10, 1974, FNYC announced that it would not pay its regular quarterly dividend and that Franklin had sizable foreign exchange losses (announced on May 13 to be $14 million). The passing of a regular quarterly dividend by a large bank was unprecedented and was viewed by many analysts as an indicator of the seriousness of Franklin's financial

*Table 6.1*

Franklin National Bank
Daily Borrowing from Federal Reserve
($ millions)

| | May | June | July | August | September | October |
|---|---|---|---|---|---|---|
| 1 | | 1,170 | 1,255 | 1,400 | 1,470 | 1,738 |
| 2 | | 1,170 | 1,295 | 1,430 | 1,470 | 1,767 |
| 3 | | 1,215 | 1,320 | 1,430 | 1,490 | 1,703 |
| 4 | | 1,215 | 1,320 | 1,430 | 1,465 | 1,723 |
| 5 | | 1,255 | 1,310 | 1,430 | 1,495 | 1,723 |
| 6 | | 1,230 | 1,310 | 1,400 | 1,481 | 1,723 |
| 7 | | 1,260 | 1,310 | 1,420 | 1,481 | 1,723 |
| 8 | 110 | 1,260 | 1,320 | 1,400 | 1,481 | |
| 9 | 125 | 1,260 | 1,355 | 1,420 | 1,500 | |
| 10 | 135 | 1,270 | 1,345 | 1,420 | 1,516 | |
| 11 | 135 | 1,070 | 1,345 | 1,420 | 1,482 | |
| 12 | 135 | 1,060 | 1,400 | 1,415 | 1,482 | |
| 13 | 550 | 1,120 | 1,400 | 1,395 | 1,477 | |
| 14 | 690 | 1,135 | 1,400 | 1,420 | 1,477 | |
| 15 | 780 | 1,135 | 1,380 | 1,410 | 1,477 | |
| 16 | 880 | 1,135 | 1,375 | 1,475 | 1,465 | |
| 17 | 960 | 1,155 | 1,410 | 1,475 | 1,485 | |
| 18 | 960 | 1,130 | 1,390 | 1,475 | 1,473 | |
| 19 | 960 | 1,100 | 1,410 | 1,415 | 1,512 | |
| 20 | 980 | 1,160 | 1,410 | 1,435 | 1,527 | |
| 21 | 1,060 | 1,190 | 1,410 | 1,445 | 1,527 | |
| 22 | 1,130 | 1,190 | 1,390 | 1,440 | 1,527 | |
| 23 | 1,120 | 1,190 | 1,390 | 1,445 | 1,480 | |
| 24 | 1,130 | 1,200 | 1,410 | 1,445 | 1,468 | |
| 25 | 1,130 | 1,180 | 1,400 | 1,445 | 1,443 | |
| 26 | 1,130 | 1,215 | 1,410 | 1,445 | 1,693 | |
| 27 | 1,130 | 1,195 | 1,410 | 1,460 | 1,735 | |
| 28 | 1,115 | 1,235 | 1,410 | 1,490 | 1,735 | |
| 29 | 1,140 | 1,235 | 1,415 | 1,470 | 1,735 | |
| 30 | 1,115 | 1,235 | 1,430 | 1,470 | 1,717 | |
| 31 | 1,170 | | 1,390 | 1,470 | | |

*Source:* U.S. Congress (1975), p. 243.

*Table 6.2*

Franklin's Domestic Liability Structure
($ millions)

| Liabilities | December 31, 1973 | June 30, 1974 | Dollar Flow Dec.-June | Percentage Change |
|---|---|---|---|---|
| Total Deposits | 2,600 | 1,577 | -1,023 | -39.3 |
| IPC Demand | 981 | 575 | -406 | -41.3 |
| IPC Savings | 445 | 385 | - 60 | -13.5 |
| IPC Time | 539 | 285 | -254 | -47.3 |
| State & Political | 308 | 200 | -108 | -35.1 |
| Commercial Bank | 223 | 53 | -170 | -76.2 |
| Other | 104 | 79 | - 25 | -24.0 |
| Federal Funds Purchased | 796 | 394 | -402 | -50.5 |
| Other Liabilities | 408 | 1,619 | 1,211 | 296.8 |
| Total | 3,804 | 3,590 | -214 | -5.6 |

Except for the deposits of foreign governments, included in the "other" deposit category, the data exclude foreign deposits. As of November 14, 1973, deposits in Franklin's foreign offices totalled $1,141 million; by May 14, 1974, these deposits were down to $514 million. Three months later, they were $341 million.

The June 30th "other liabilities" figure mainly consists of Franklin's borrowings from the Federal Reserve Bank of New York. At the time Franklin was closed on October 8, 1974, its indebtedness to the Federal Reserve was $1,732 million.

*Source:* Report of Condition, Federal Deposit Insurance Corporation.

difficulties. On May 14, the directors of FNYC disclosed a shake-up of Franklin's top management, including the removal of the president. The managerial changes were a further indication that Franklin's problems were more severe than "unauthorized foreign exchange transactions." As of May 14, 1974, Franklin was listed as a "potential payoff" by the FDIC's Division of Bank Supervision. This meant that Franklin presented a 50 percent chance of requiring FDIC financial assistance in the near future.

The banking agencies feared that Franklin's unfavorable public announcements might precipitate a crisis of confidence in the bank. As of the close of business May 15, 1974, less than four working days after the first of these announcements, Franklin's loan at the New York Federal Reserve Bank's discount window was $780 million, an increase of $645 million (see Table 6.1). As documented in Table 6.2, Franklin was forced to the discount window because of deposit withdrawls and its inability to continue borrowing large amounts in the Federal-funds market. The structure of Franklin's *domestic* liabilities as of December 31, 1973, and June 30, 1974, are presented in Table 6.2 (see also Tables 6.3 and 6.4).

*Table 6.3*

Franklin National Bank
Funds Flow: May 8, 1974 through October 7, 1974
($ millions)

| Outflows: Decreases in<br>Liabilities and Capital | 5/8/74<br>through<br>10/7/74 | 5/8/74<br>through<br>6/30/74 | 7/1/74<br>through<br>10/7/74 |
|---|---|---|---|
| Federal Funds | $535 | $346 | $189 |
| Repurchase Agreements | 175 | 175 | – – |
| Money Market Certificates of Deposit | 411 | 323 | 88 |
| Time Savings Deposits of Individuals,<br>Partnerships and Corporations | 128 | 52 | 76 |
| Other Domestic Time Deposits | 108 | 105 | 3 |
| Domestic Demand Deposits | 741 | 504 | 237 |
| Foreign Branch Deposits | 679 | 392 | 287 |
| Foreign Exchange Transactions | 23 | 15 | 8 |
| Capital Funds* | 22 | 22 | – – |
| Total Outflows | $2,822 | $1,934 | $888 |
| Inflows: Reductions in Assets | | | |
| Loans | $227 | $ 93 | $134 |
| Investments | 113 | 75 | 38 |
| Foreign Branch Investments | 198 | 108 | 90 |
| Cash | 561 | 452 | 109 |
| Total Inflows | $1,099 | $728 | $371 |
| Net Outflow (Increase in Federal<br>    Reserve Borrowings) | $1,723 | $1,206 | $517 |

*Decrease caused by operating losses and realized losses on securities, loans and foreign exchange transactions.
*Source:* Franklin National Bank International Reports, reprinted in U.S. Congress (1975), pp. 218, 224 - 225.

*Table 6.4*

Franklin National Bank
Federal Funds Purchases, Certificates of Deposit, and Foreign Branch Time Deposit
($ millions)

| Date | Federal Funds | Certificates of Deposit Over $100,00 | Total | Foreign Branch Time Deposits Outstanding | As a percent of Total Deposits |
|------|------|------|------|------|------|
| December 31, 1973 | $797* | $451** | NA | $1,136 | 30 |
| May 3, 1974 | 601 | 473 | $680 | 926 | 27 |
| June 30, 1974 | 224+ | 151 | 255 | 508 | 24 |
| October 1, 1974 | 8 | 72 | 197 | 241 | 17 |

\* Includes repurchase agreements.
\*\* As of December 26, 1973.
+ Includes $200 million of secured Federal Funds purchases from the other members of the New York Clearing House Association.
*Source:* Franklin National Internal Reports, reprinted in U.S. Congress, (1975); pp. 221 - 223.

### 2. The Deposit Assumption

When an insured bank is closed by its chartering authority, the two basic ways that the FDIC can fulfill its insurance obligations are: (1) a deposit payoff or (2) a deposit assumption.[3] In making this choice, the FDIC has interpreted Section 13(e) of the Federal Deposit Insurance Act (". . ..reduce the risk or avert a threatened loss to the Corporation . . .") to mean choose between a payoff or an assumption on the basis of minimum cost to the deposit-insurance fund. In addition, the FDIC, as receiver of a closed bnak, has a fiduciary obligation tò the owners and creditors of a failed institution to realize the maximum value for the bank's business. To extract this value, the FDIC tries to establish a uniform basis for competitive bidding by more than one bank. Regarding the choice between a payoff or an assumption, an important FDIC policy consideration is not to contribute more cash toward a deposit assumption than would be necessary to pay off all insured depositors up to the statutory limit. In Franklin's case, the FDIC's cash-outlay cutoff point, based upon the $20,000 deposit-insurance ceiling then in force, was estimated to be $750 million. With respect to the competitive bidding, there were sixteen banking organizations that expressed a preliminary interest in acquiring Franklin.[4] Of these sixteen, only four organizations eventually submitted bids to the FDIC. The highest bid was $125 million by European-American Bank and Trust Company (EAB&T), an insured-nonmember bank jointly owned by six of the largest banks in Europe. (These European banks had combined assets of more than $90 billion in October 1974.) The other three bids, two of which would have been acceptable to the FDIC in the absence of EAB&T's higher bid, were submitted by Manufacturers Hanover Trust Company, Chemical Bank, and First National City Bank.

The purchase-and-assumption agreement between the FDIC and EAB&T is depicted by the T-accounts presented in Table 6.5.[5] EAB&T

*Table 6.5*

T-Accounts for Franklin's Deposit Assumption

Franklin National Bank of New York
($ millions, as of October 8, 1974)

| Assets | $3,658 | Deposits | $1,369 |
|---|---|---|---|
| EAB&T required to accept | (1,487) | Federal Reserve Bank of New York Discount-Window Loan | 1,732 |
| EAB&T required to reject | (2,171) | Capital and other liabilities | 557 |
| | $3,658 | | $3,658 |

European-American Bank and Trust Company
(marginal T-account, millions of dollars)

| Assets selected from Franklin | $1,487 | Deposits assumed from Franklin | $1,369 |
|---|---|---|---|
| Premium paid to FDIC | 125 | Other liabilities assumed from Franklin | 243 |
| | $1,612 | | $1,612 |

Federal Deposit Insurance Corporation
(marginal T-account, $ millions)

| Franklin's assets rejected by EAB&T | $2,171 | Federal Reserve Bank of New York Discount-Window Loan | $1,732 |
|---|---|---|---|
| Less EAB&T premium paid to FDIC | -125 | Other liabilities | 314 |
| | $2,046 | | $2,046 |

was required to select $1,487 million of Franklin's $3,658 million in assets, an amount equal to Franklin's deposits ($1,369) and certain other liabilities ($243 million) assumed by EAB&T, less EAB&T's purchase premium ($125 million). Franklin's other liabilities ($2,046 million), mainly consisting of its New York Fed loan of $1,732 million, were assumed by the FDIC. The FDIC has since repaid Franklin's discount-window loan with interest. The rate of interest on the FDIC's note to the Fed, which matured on October 8, 1977, was 7.52 percent.[6] The deposit-assumption agreement depicted in Table 6.5 was the culmination of five months of activity in which five Federal agencies (FDIC, Comptroller of the Currency, Federal Reserve, Treasury Department, and SEC), the New York State Banking Department, the New York Clearing House Association, some twenty banking institutions, and even Franklin itself participated.[7]

### 3. How to Handle a Large Problem Bank

The handling of Franklin's demise was a controversial matter.[8] The major criticism focused upon (1) the timing of Franklin's closing, (2) the subsidy provided by the Federal Reserve, and (3) the length of time it took the FDIC to arrange a deposit assumption. Although only the Comptroller's office could declare Franklin insolvent, criticism concerning the timing of Franklin's closing must be borne by all three of the banking agencies. Apparently Franklin could have been declared insolvent any time after May 12, 1974 [see Rose (1974), p. 226]. However, the bank was not closed until October 8, 1974. If Franklin had been closed immediately, the need for a $1.7 billion loan from the Federal Reserve would have been avoided. However, the important question is whether or not the shock effect of such a sudden closing would have produced a domestic and/or international monetary crisis. Given the circumstances, this should have been (and apparently was) the major concern of the banking agencies.[9] For example, according to Brimmer (1976), the Fed's major purposes were to minimize attrition in the CD market for large regional banks and to minimize the danger to the international money market.

Regarding the possibility of a financial panic, some members of the New York financial community supposedly were aware of Franklin's problems before the information became public. For example, Morgan Guaranty (then Franklin's major correspondent bank) stopped selling Federal funds to Franklin in the fall of 1973.[10] Thus, some of the announcement effect of a swift closing of Franklin probably had already been discounted at least in New York City. However, there still was a considerable amount of uncertainty regarding the regional and international effects and it is difficult to fault the banking agencies for being cautious.

An alternative plan of action would have been to close Franklin in late May after the initial announcement effect had dissipated. This plan would have given the domestic and international markets a chance to discount the possibility of Franklin's insolvency and would have reduced the size and duration of Franklin's interest-rate subsidy from the Federal Reserve. However, this arrangement would have put pressure upon the FDIC to arrange an emergency deposit assumption. Former FDIC Chairman Frank Wille (1974), p. 44, stated than an earlier resolution of Franklin ". . . would have been a financial disaster for the trust fund FDIC administers."

It is important to understand the nature of the subsidy involved in the Fed's loan to Franklin. For 153 days, from May 8 to October 7, Franklin was borrowing continuously, at below-market rates from the New York Fed (see Table 6.1). Until September 25, Franklin was paying only 8 percent (the discount rate on "eligible" collateral) or 8.5 percent (the rate on "other" collateral) for this money.[11] However, beginning September 25, the Fed established a new special discount rate for "member banks requiring exceptionally large assistance over a prolonged period of time."[12] This rate, which may not exceed the rate established for emergency loans to nonmember banks, was set at 10 percent. During Franklin's period of Fed indebtedness, it is highly unlikely that it could have borrowed anywhere except from the Fed; if it could have, the risk premium probably would have been prohibitive.

Regarding discount-window loans, Kane (1974), p. 849, contends that a troubled bank, to compensate for its riskiness, should pay at least a one-percent premium over the Federal-funds rate. Using this rule, the interest-rate subsidy that Franklin received from the Fed (for the major portion of its indebtedness) was in the 450–500 basis-points range. During the last twelve days, the subsidy was approximately 300 basis points (3 percentage points). Given that Franklin's average indebtedness to the Fed was $1,298 million, the dollar amount of the Fed's interest-rate subsidy to Franklin was approximately $25 million over the five-month borrowing period.[13]

It is important to distinguish between the benefits that accrued because of: (1) the Fed's *loan* to Franklin (on average $1.3 billion for five months) and (2) the Fed's *subsidy* to Franklin ($21 million to $25 million or more depending on the risk premium). The two major beneficiaries of the Fed's *loan* were (1) Franklin's uninsured depositors and (2) the FDIC and FDIC-insured bankers. Franklin's big lenders benefited because they were given time to withdraw their unprotected funds, especially holders of three-to-six-months CDs and term Federal funds. For example, from June 7 to August 30, approximately $550 million of uninsured deposits were withdrawn from Franklin (see Table 6.6). The FDIC benefited because it was given time to arrange a deposit assumption that placed a less severe financial strain on its trust fund. Consequently, percentage rebates of net insurance-assessment income by the FDIC to insured banks were not reduced by Franklin's collapse.[14] Bank-

*Table 6.6*

Franklin National Bank: Uninsured Deposits and Collateral Pledged
for Advance
($ millions)

| | Uninsured Deposits | | | |
| | Demand Deposits (Domestic Offices) | Time Deposits (Domestic Offices) | Demand (Foreign Branches) | Time (Foreign Branches) | Total |
|---|---|---|---|---|---|
| June 7, 1974 | 494 | 388 | .4 | 616 | 1,498.4 |
| July 5, 1974 | 480 | 261 | .3 | 478 | 1,291.3 |
| August 30, 1974 | 473 | 219 | .2 | 306 | 998.2 |

Collateral Pledged for Advance, October 8, 1974

| | Face Value |
|---|---|
| Commercial Loans | $1,182 |
| Foreign Branch Loans | 515 |
| Consumer Loans | 134 |
| Mortgage and Construction Loans | 350 |
| Broker Loans | 7 |
| U.S. Government Agency Bond Coupons | 13 |
| Public Housing Authority Bonds | 6 |
| Municipal Bonds | 198 |
| Corporate Debentures | 11 |
| Bankers' Acceptances | -4 |
| Term Federal Funds | 5 |
| Certificates of Deposit | 1 |
| Foreign Branch Placements | 102 |
| Due from Banks | 27 |
| Total | $2,555 |

*Source:* U.S. Congress (1975, pp. 223 and 231).

ers also gained because the FDIC's reputation for insulating uninsured depositors was maintained.

The *subsidy* to Franklin was tied to the differential between the "market rate for troubled-bank loans" and the Fed's discount rate. A discount rate at below-market (above-market) rates means an outright subsidy (tax) to the borrowing bank. Certainly, as Kane (1974), p. 849, has proposed, a problem bank should pay a premium (i.e., be taxed) to compensate for its above-average riskiness. In the absence of the Fed's subsidy, Franklin's earnings (or capital) would have been depleted by an additional $25 million and the bank probably would have been closed sooner than it was. However, if without the subsidy Franklin had been closed sooner, the full benefits of the Fed's loan might not have been realized. That is, since the benefits of the loan were not independent of the subsidy, the beneficiaries of the loan would have had less time to protect their own interests. How long Franklin could have stayed in business without the Fed's subsidy and what differential benefits might have occurred are interesting counterfactual propositions that I will not attempt to untangle.

Finally, and perhaps most importantly, the Fed's subsidy to Franklin was at taxpayers' expense. When the Fed makes loans to troubled banks at bargain rates, it channels less money into the U.S. Treasury. In Franklin's case, the estimated cost to taxpayers was $25 million. In a quasi-regulated industry, someone has to pay for the "panic-prevention subsidies" [Kane's terminology (1974), p. 846] that replace market forces.

Although the Fed did not have the de jure power to close Franklin, it did have the de facto power, via its discount window. If Franklin had received traditional discount-window surveillance, it would not have been permitted to borrow over $1 billion in less than one month (May). Instead, the Fed chose to treat the loan as an exercise (in a very broad sense) of its lender-of-last-resort function, that is, as having fundamental responsibility for the viability of the financial system as a *whole*. However, once Franklin's difficulties were disclosed and the chances of a financial panic diminished, the Fed (having fulfilled its lender-of-last-resort functions) would have been justified in denying Franklin further discount-window assistance. Assuming that subsidizing a mismanaged bank (once the chances of a financial panic have been reduced) is not a legitimate lender-of-last-resort function, this action would have forced the Comptroller to declare Franklin insolvent. The main reason the Fed continued to subsidize Franklin was to give the FDIC time to ". . . achieve a more permanent solution to the bank's difficulties" [*Annual Report* (1974), p. 21]. The length of time (July 2 to October 8) that the FDIC took to arrange Franklin's take-over became a source of irritation to the Fed.[15]    However, because bank regulation is indeed "a jurisdictional tangle that boggles the mind," once the Fed committed itself to giving the FDIC time, it could not undercut its sister agency. Moreover, it is difficult to support the claims, as some Fed officials have argued, that the longer Franklin's problems remained unresolved that (1) the more difficult finding an equitable solution would become and (2) the greater were the dangers to the banking system.[16] Why more difficult and an equitable solution for whom? It would seem that the longer Franklin remained in the news the less harm it could do to the banking system. After five months of headlines, Franklin's closing was anticlimactic; the event already had been discounted.

To summarize, although the banking authorities identified Franklin National Bank of New York as a "problem" institution seven months before its collapse, they could not (or perhaps would not) prevent it from going belly-up. Thus, on October 8, 1974, Franklin became the largest bank failure in U.S. history. Because the deposit assumption arranged by the FDIC was a long (five months) and complicated one, the Fed was "forced" to keep Franklin afloat via its discount window. On average for the five-month period, Franklin borrowed $1.3 billion at a below-market rate of 8.0 percent. The Fed's bargain rate, not the loan itself, resulted in a $25 million subsidy to Franklin at taxpayers' expense. The major beneficiaries of the Fed's loan were Franklin's uninsured depositors, the FDIC and FDIC-insured bankers, and, assuming the chances for a financial panic had not been averted, the U.S. economy and the world economy.[17]

## 6.3 FRANKLIN'S FORTY YEARS 1934–1974: A BRIEF NARRATION

This section focuses upon the evolution of Franklin from a small, depression-era bank in 1934 to its tripartite banking business of 1974 (retail-wholesale-international).[18]

### 1. Retail Banking and Arthur Roth

When Arthur Roth took over Franklin on April 30, 1934, the bank barely had $500,000 in deposits; when he was removed by the directors as chairman and chief executive officer of the bank in 1968, the bank had about $2 billion in deposits. This is a growth factor of 4,000 for the 34-year period. Roth was an aggressive and innovative person. He pioneered such things as (1) the use of the name "savings account" for commercial banks' consumer time deposits (which at the time was forbidden by New York State law—Roth eventually won in the U.S. Supreme Court); (2) the first bank charge card—the Franklin Charge Plan;

and (3) in an attempt to create a wider market for Franklin's stock, the first detailed annual report ever published by a commercial bank.

The backbone of Franklin's phenomenal growth was its retail banking business based on Long Island. The direct stimulus for the early growth was the expanding housing market on Long Island (especially Nassau County) following the Second World War. In addition, Roth was influential in transforming Nassau County from a bedroom community for the "Big Apple" into an industrial community in its own right.

By December 31, 1973, Franklin had an extensive branching network consisting of 104 locations in three areas—Nassau County (49), New York City (31), and Suffolk County (24). Franklin's competitive position in these three banking markets is presented in Tables 6.7 and 6.8. Clearly, Franklin had a competitive advantage in Nassau and Suffolk Counties in 1973; it controlled 34.0 percent of the offices and 50.7 of the total deposits in Nassau and 23.5 percent of the offices and 36.9 percent of the total deposits in Suffolk. In contrast, in New York City, Franklin

*Table 6.7*

Franklin's Market Share: Number of Offices
(December 31, 1973)

| Banking Organization | Market | | | | |
| | NYC | Nassau | Suffolk | Other | Total |
|---|---|---|---|---|---|
| Chase Manhattan | 176 | 17 | 4 | 17 | 214 |
| Citicorp | 176 | 26 | 3 | 22 | 227 |
| Manufacturers Hanover | 160 | 9 | 9 | 11 | 189 |
| Chemical | 124 | 15 | 11 | 16 | 166 |
| Bankers Trust | 87 | 11 | 13 | 21 | 132 |
| J.P. Morgan | 6 | – | – | – | 6 |
| Marine Midland | 18 | 6 | 25 | 21 | 70 |
| Charter New York | 16 | – | 1 | 17 | 34 |
| Bank of New York | 9 | 11 | 12 | 60 | 92 |
| Franklin | 31 | 49 | 24 | – | 104 |
| Total | 803 | 144 | 102 | 185 | 1,234 |
| Franklin's Percentage | 3.9 | 34.0 | 23.5 | – | 8.4 |

*Source:* Brimmer (1976), Table 1. "Other" market includes Westchester, Rockland, and Putnam.

*Table 6.8*

Franklin's Market Share: Total Deposits
($ millions, June 30, 1973)

| Banking Organization | | | Market | | |
|---|---|---|---|---|---|
| | NYC | Nassau | Suffolk | Other | Total |
| Chase Manhattan | 16,112.1 | 133.6 | 25.0 | 98.5 | 16,369.2 |
| Citicorp | 14,937.7 | 256.9 | 18.4 | 207.8 | 15,420.8 |
| Manufacturers Hanover | 10,302.1 | 35.2 | 76.5 | 31.4 | 10,455.2 |
| Chemical | 9,116.3 | 149.3 | 78.7 | 205.6 | 9,549.9 |
| Bankers Trust | 8,104.2 | 96.9 | 83.1 | 143.8 | 8,428.0 |
| J.P. Morgan | 7,424.2 | – | – | – | 7,424.2 |
| Marine Midland | 2,861.0 | 48.3 | 182.7 | 113.9 | 3,205.9 |
| Charter New York | 4,575.3 | – | – | 179.6 | 4,575.3 |
| Bank of New York | 1,391.2 | 109.9 | 73.2 | 917.1 | 2,491.4 |
| Franklin | 1,361.2 | 853.4 | 314.8 | – | 2,529.7 |
| Total | 76,185.6 | 1,683.5 | 852.4 | 1,897.7 | 80,619.2 |
| Franklin's Percentage | 1.8 | 50.7 | 36.9 | – | 3.1 |

*Source:* Brimmer (1976), Table 2. "Other" market includes Westchester, Rockland and Putnam.

was at a competitive disadvantage; it had only 3.9 percent of the offices and only 1.8 percent of the total deposits. After only a decade of being allowed to branch in New York City, Franklin had established 31 offices (29.8 percent) there, where it generated 53.8 percent of its total deposits. However, this was not where Franklin had its market power; its market power was on Long Island.

## 2. Wholesale Banking and the Move into New York City: Franklin's Achilles Heel

In retrospect, Roth's decision to move into New York City was a fatal one. Or, if you believe in a paternalistic approach to bank regulation, former Comptroller Saxon's decision to permit Franklin to branch into New York City was a bad one.[19] The Fed ("I told you so") had opposed the granting of the application. According to Brimmer (1976), p. 9, the consensus at the Fed was that the maximum public benefit would derive from Franklin concentrating its efforts in the retail banking market on

Long Island. The irony of Roth's decision to move into New York City was that in his younger days Roth was "bashful" about branching.

Franklin's move into the "Big Apple" came in 1964. As a result, Franklin was in direct competition with some of the giants of the banking industry for both retail (consumer) and wholesale (business) accounts. The competition in wholesale banking, where Franklin had hoped to make inroads, was particularly fierce. Unfortunately, the prime-rate customers were not flocking to Franklin's doors while the high-risk companies were, which was not unusual since Franklin was the new bank in the market. What was unusual, however, was the fact that most of these high-credit-risk companies were accommodated by Franklin at prime or near-prime terms (i.e., at interest rates and compensating-balance requirements which did not adequately reflect the risks involved; see note 2).

A fundamental principle of banking and finance is that the interest rate that determines the value of a risky asset (e.g., a loan) depends upon the general level of interest rates (measured by a relevant risk-free opportunity cost. e.g., the interest rate on a U.S. government security) plus a premium that depends upon the riskiness of the income from the asset. The greater the perceived risk there is, the higher the risk premium should be. The variables involved here are, of course, *expected* risk and *expected* return. The expectational aspects allow for different risk-return judgments to exist. The bench mark for evaluating these risk-return perceptions is called the security market line (SML), which reflects the rate of return required by the average investor (or the market) to compensate for bearing risk. The SML, which is an *optimal* concept, is a locus of points indicating the maximum return for a given level of risk or the minimum risk for a given return. Points below the SML are suboptimal, while points above it are highly desirable and would be competed away.

Using the concept of the SML, Franklin's suboptimal wholesale banking activities are depicted in Figure 6.1. The vertical intercept of the SML is the risk-free rate of return, R. The point on the SML is an optimal one and indicates the risk-return combination associated with a prime-rate business loan. The point F is a suboptimal one—to depict Franklin's inefficient business-loan management. To compensate for the level of risk associated with the business loans that Franklin was making, the effective rate of interest should have been $R_F*$. Think of the rates of return indicated by the SML as interest rates which have been adjusted for risk. In this illustration, their values are determined in the business-loan market by the activities of the bankers in the market, reflecting their attitudes toward bearing risk.

Commercial banks traditionally have been described as "conservative" lending institutions, a conservatism that no doubt has been reinforced by

Figure 6.1

Franklin's Business Loans and the Security Market Line

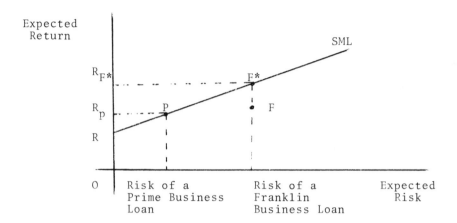

the banking authorities' surveillance of the quality of banks' loan portfolios. The fact that high-risk borrowers usually obtain financing from nonbank commercial lenders such as factors and finance companies indicates that the conservative label (i.e., the regulatory-induced, low-risk preference label) is not unwarranted. Franklin's willingness to supply funds to high-risk borrowers was not a bad strategy—its mistake was not receiving adequate compensation for the risks that it bore.

The risks that Franklin took on the asset side of its balance sheet over the years 1964–1970 led to rapid growth. To finance this expansion, Franklin had to rely heavily on purchased money such as CDs and Federal funds, which at times (e.g., 1966 and 1969–1970) proved to be a very expensive proposition. As we see later in this chapter, the overall impact of this growth strategy on Franklin's performance was generally adverse.

To summarize, on a less-grandiose scale and at a less-rapid pace, Franklin's bite into the Big Apple might have been successful. However, the bites were too big, too numerous, and confined to the bruised and maggoty parts of the apple. Franklin, like Hawwāh (Eve), discovered that the apple can indeed be a forbidden fruit.

### 3. International Banking

Until 1969 Franklin's international department was only a token banking operation. However, in 1969, when competition in international money and capital markets increased significantly, Franklin opened its

London branch. Similar to its move into New York City and wholesale banking, Franklin moved into London and international banking willing to take risks, to pay a premium for deposits, and to shave the size of its spread to attract business. While these policies were not very profitable ones, they did attract business. By year-end 1973, Franklin had amassed about 1-billion in deposits at its London branch (about 20 percent of its total assets). These London deposits were allocated between foreign loans (about 60 percent) and extensions of credit to other financial institutions in the London interbank market (about 40 percent).[20]

### 4. Summary and Conclusions

By December 31, 1973, Franklin's banking business had evolved to its tripartite structure of retail, wholesale, and international elements. The retail segment, with its 73 branches on Long Island, was the only strong and viable part of the business. The wholesale and international segments were weak links characterized by undue risk taking and inadequate spread management.

## 6.4 POSTMORTEM ANALYSIS I: EARLY WARNING BASED UPON BALANCE-SHEET AND INCOME-EXPENSE INFORMATION

### 1. Methodology and Data

Early-warning systems designed to predict troubled or failed banks can be viewed as a new twist on an old theme. That is, credit-scoring models have been developed [by Orgler (1970) and others] to evaluate the creditworthiness of banks' customers. The failures of Franklin and United States National Bank of San Diego, the emergency merger of Security National Bank of Long Island, the REIT and New York City crises, and 29 bank failures in 1975 and 1976 (16 in 1976) have generated concern about the "creditworthiness" or "safety and soundness" of banks and the banking industry. By the principle of symmetry, credit-scoring techniques can be adapted by depositors, investors, regulators, and other interested parties to evaluate the creditworthiness of banks.

Developing a unique application of discriminant analysis, this section presents a "credit-scoring" or "early-warning-system" analysis of Franklin's collapse. The application is "unique" because only *one* group is employed; ordinarily, two or more groups are used in discriminant analysis. Since the number of Franklin-size problem and/or failed banks is not large enough to permit two-group tests of failed/problem versus nonfailed/nonproblem, one-group discriminant analysis is used. The statistical adaptation is referred to as an "outlier" or "peer-group" model (see Chapter 4).

It is hypothesized that the major causes of bank failures and problem banks are dishonest and/or inept bank managers. Over a period of time, such factors should be reflected in a bank's balance-sheet and income-expense data. However, lack of integrity in management is apt to be deliberately masked and therefore harder to uncover (as the USNB case proved; see Chapter 7). Many of the variables examined in this section are, in essence, proxies for the managerial performance of the sample banks. These variables (ratios and growth rates), while not directly measuring managerial ability, do nevertheless capture the *ex post* consequences of management's decisions. The ratios are designed to measure Franklin's operations and performance in such areas as liquidity, loan operations, asset and deposit compositions, operating efficiency, profitability, capital adequacy, and sources and uses of revenue; the growth rates are designed to measure Franklin's rate of expansion of assets, deposits, and capital.

Both single-variable and multivariable tests are employed to identify the financial characteristics which distinguish Franklin from a control group of the fifty largest U.S. banks (in terms of total domestic deposits as of December 31, 1973).[21] These focal characteristics, mainly in the form of financial ratios, are derived from year-end balance sheets and income statements for the period 1969 to 1973 and from balance sheets only from June 30, 1974. The data are "domestic only" and only partially take account of foreign operations. That is, the balance sheets do not include foreign items and foreign income and expense items are reported as "net remittable income" and included in "other" income. Given the sizes of the sample banks, and hence the extent of their foreign operations, this is a shortcoming of the analysis. Suffice it to say that analyses employing consolidated domestic and foreign data may produce different findings.[22]

The statistic used in the outlier tests is a chi-square score which indicates the degree of similarity between Franklin's variable profile and the control group's mean vector.[23] That is, a high chi-square score indicates that Franklin was not similar to the average control bank while a low chi-square score implies that Franklin was similar to the average control bank. However, the chi-square score is only an absolute measure and does not indicate the direction of atypicalness (i.e., "safe and sound" vs. problem). The level of significance of Franklin's chi-square score (expressed as a percentage) gives the approximate percentage of observations whose variable profiles would be expected to be more dissimilar than Franklin's variable profile compared to the group mean vector. A significance level of five percent (approximately two standard deviations from the control group's mean in the univariate case) is used to define an "outlier."

To summarize, the statistical tests are designed to determine if Franklin was an outlier (or atypical) compared to the 50 largest U.S. banks over the test period. Franklin was identified as a financially troubled institution by the Comptroller of the Currency based upon an examination that began on November 15, 1973. Thus, four of the six financial statements to be analyzed are preproblem observations. The purpose of these tests is not to second-guess any of the banking agencies regarding the identification of Franklin's problems, but to emphasize that existing, routinely collected data, if properly used, can be a valuable adjunct to existing bank-examination policies and procedures.

## 2. Empirical Findings

Results and analyses in this section are presented in the following order:

1. Single-variable tests of bank soundness and performance;
2. A simple risk-return analysis; and
3. A seven-variable test based upon the EWS discussed in the previous two chapters.

**a. Single-Variable Tests.** The first set of empirical results presented are single-variable outlier tests for the following six measures of a bank's overall performance:

1. OIA = Total operating income as a percentage of total assets,

2. OEA = Total operating expense as a percentage of total assets,

3. NOA = Net operating income as a percentage of total assets,

4. NIA = Net income as a percentage of total assets,

5. NIK = Net income as a percentage of total capital, and

6. OEOI = Total operating expense as a percentage of total operating income.

The first four variables measure revenue generation, expense control, operating performance, and overall (or "bottom-line") performance, respectively, relative to total assets. The next variable measures profitability from the point of view of the stockholders, while the last variable measures operating efficiency. Data for these six variables are presented in Table 6.9, while univariate outlier tests for the six variables are presented in Table 6.10. (Note that NIK differs slightly from the NIE or ROE of Chapter 5 because the denominator of NIK includes capital note and debentures, RC34 from Table 5.7.)

## Table 6.9

### Six Measures of Overall Banking Performance
### (percentages)

| Variable | 1969 Franklin | 1969 Average Control Bank | 1970 Franklin | 1970 Average Control Bank | 1971 Franklin | 1971 Average Control Bank | 1972 Franklin | 1972 Average Control Bank | 1973 Franklin | 1973 Average Control Bank |
|---|---|---|---|---|---|---|---|---|---|---|
| OIA | 6.17 | 5.88 (0.71) | 5.86 | 6.06 (0.74) | 5.49 | 5.51 (0.70) | 4.90 | 5.19 (0.71) | 6.91 | 6.38 (0.57) |
| OEA | 5.19 | 4.62 (0.72) | 5.05 | 4.83 (0.74) | 5.01 | 4.48 (0.73) | 4.59 | 4.27 (0.74) | 6.60 | 5.43 (0.64) |
| NOA | 0.98 | 1.27 (0.29) | 0.81 | 1.23 (0.32) | 0.48 | 1.03 (0.29) | 0.31 | 0.92 (0.29) | 0.30 | 0.96 (0.32) |
| NIA | 0.76 | 0.76 (0.16) | 0.69 | 0.80 (0.19) | 0.57 | 0.78 (0.20) | 0.40 | 0.71 (0.17) | 0.36 | 0.71 (0.21) |
| NIK | 12.03 | 10.48 (1.93) | 12.08 | 10.96 (1.97) | 8.41 | 10.74 (1.85) | 6.40 | 10.10 (1.84) | 6.08 | 10.75 (2.08) |
| OEOI | 84.06 | 78.27 (5.40) | 86.14 | 79.54 (5.30) | 91.19 | 81.04 (5.80) | 93.77 | 82.08 (6.10) | 95.60 | 84.90 (5.16) |

Data are as of December 31 of the year indicated. Figures in parentheses are standard deviations.
*Sources:* Reports of Income and Condition, FDIC.

## Table 6.10

### Franklin National Bank

Univariate Outlier Tests for Six Measures of Overall Banking Performance

| Variable | 1969 Chi-Square Score | 1969 Signif-icance Level(%) | 1970 Chi-Square Score | 1970 Signif-icance Level(%) | 1971 Chi-Square Score | 1971 Signif-icance Level(%) | 1972 Chi-Square Score | 1972 Signif-icance Level(%) | 1973 Chi-Square Score | 1973 Signif-icance Level(%) |
|---|---|---|---|---|---|---|---|---|---|---|
| OIA | 0.16 | 68.84 | 0.08 | 78.02 | 0.00 | 98.33 | 0.16 | 68.43 | 0.86 | 35.44 |
| OEA | 0.64 | 42.47 | 0.08 | 77.31 | 0.54 | 46.31 | 0.19 | 66.44 | 3.40 | 6.53 |
| NOA | 0.92 | 33.81 | 1.75 | 18.63 | 3.62 | 5.70 | 4.43 | 3.53 | 4.12 | 4.24 |
| NIA | 0.00 | 97.30 | 0.31 | 57.44 | 1.14 | 28.59 | 3.15 | 7.59 | 2.83 | 9.26 |
| NIK | 0.64 | 42.15 | 0.32 | 57.04 | 1.58 | 20.84 | 4.06 | 4.40 | 5.02 | 2.50 |
| OEOI | 1.15 | 28.38 | 1.55 | 21.32 | 3.06 | 8.00 | 3.67 | 5.55 | 4.30 | 3.80 |

The "outlier" statistic is a chi-square score which indicates the degree f similarity between Franklin's variable profile and the control group's mean vector (see Appendix A and footnote 23. A high chi-square score, for example NOA in 1971, indicates that Franklin was not similar to the average control bank while a low chi-square score, for example NOA in 1969, implies that Franklin was similar to the average control bank. Finally, the significance level gives the approximate percentage of observations whose variable profiles would be expected to be more dissimilar than Franklin's variable profile compared to the group mean vector. For example, the significance level of NOA's 1969 chi-square score (5.70 percent) implies that approximately three other banks had NOA values that were further from the group mean (in either direction) than Franklin, where 3 = .057(50) = 2.85 and 50 = number of observations in the control group.

The results for NOA or OEOI indicate that as early as 1971 Franklin's operating performance was significantly worse than the average control bank. Looking at NOA for 1971, Franklin was earning, before taxes and securities gains and losses, 48 cents per $100 of assets compared to 103 cents per $100 of assets for the average control bank. Over the next two years, Franklin's NOA averaged 30 cents per $100 of assets compared to 94 cents per $100 of assets for the average control bank. From 1969 to 1973, Franklin's NOA declined by 69.4 percent (from 98 cents to 30 cents) compared to only a 24.4 percent decline (from 127 cents to 96 cents) for the average control bank. A similar picture of Franklin's operating inefficiency is depicted by OEOI. For example, in 1972, Franklin's ratio of operating expenses to operating income (OEOI) was 0.9377285 while the average control bank's was 0.8208432 with a variance of 0.003725947. Thus, in 1972, Franklin's chi-square score for OEOI was (see Appendix A)

$$\hat{\chi}^2_{1,cf} = (0.9377285 - 0.8208432)^2/0.003725947$$
$$= 3.666762.$$

This score was significant at the 5.5508 level. Only three banks had values of OEOI that were farther from the control group's mean of 82.1 percent than Franklin's OEOI of 93.8 percent. The values of OEOI for these three more-distant outliers were 62.1 percent, 68.5 percent, and 94.4 percent. Thus, only one member of the control group was more inefficient than Franklin during 1972.

In terms of after-tax returns (NIA and NIK), Franklin was not a significant outlier until 1972. In 1973, Franklin again was an outlier on the basis of these rates of return. Over the years 1969 to 1973, Franklin's NIA and NIK both declined by approximately 50 percent. In contrast, for the average control bank NIA declined by only 6.6 percent while NIK increased by 2.6 percent. The significant drop in Franklin's earnings over this period was reflected in the price of its parent holding company's stock which was selling for $35-5/8 a share on December 31, 1969, and $17-5/8 a share on December 31, 1973.[24] By comparison, Moody's index of New York City Bank Stocks was quoted at $171.02 in December of 1969 and at $263.65 in December of 1973. Since the price of a stock is closely related to a company's earnings record, it is not surprising that the 50 percent decline in Franklin's net profitability was matched by a 50 percent fall in the parent company's stock price. The strongest form of the efficient-market hypothesis insists that all relevant information on the future performance of any asset is included and properly discounted in its current price. While this hypothesis is anathematized by those employed in brokerage houses, it should not be denounced by the banking authorities. Thus, in addition to banks' earnings, the banking agencies should consider monitoring the bank stock prices (of actively traded issues) as a potential indicator of banks' future financial difficulties.

Although Franklin had made substantial improvement in reducing its expenditures per dollar of assets over the years 1969–1972, three of its expense items still were significantly different from the average control bank's items. The three variables are:

1. EFFI = expenditures on Federal funds as a percentage of total operating income,

2. PLLI = provision for loan losses as a percentage of total operating income, and

3. NOCI = net occupancy expense of bank premises as a percentage of total operating income.

The data for these three variables are presented in Table 6.11. Except for the year 1971, Franklin spent (as a percentage of total operating income) approximately twice as much on these three items as the average control bank. The most significant relative drain upon Franklin's operating revenue was its substantial expenditures in the Federal-funds market. Franklin's higher occupancy costs primarily reflected the fact that Franklin came to New York City "building monuments—impressive and very costly structures" [Rose, (1974), p. 121]. Finally, Franklin's relatively higher provision for loan losses mainly reflected the bank's inferior loan quality.

Part of the reason for Franklin's poor earnings record was its loan portfolio. Price, quantity, and quality measures of Franklin's loan portfolio are depicted in Table 6.12. Price (GLR for gross loan rate) is measured by interest and fees on loans as a pecentage of total loans; quantity (LA) is measured by total loans as a percentage of total assets; and quality (NLLL) is measured by net loan losses (charge-offs minus recoveries) as a percentage of total loans.

The data in Table 6.12 reveal that, on average, Franklin made fewer loans, charged higher prices, and had larger loan losses than the average control bank. The most significant differences were in 1969 for GLR and in 1971 and 1973 for NLLL. The higher loan rates and higher loan losses depicted in Table 6.12 tend to reflect the nonprimeness of Franklin's customers.

An alternative and superior measure of the quality of Franklin's loan portfolio is presented in Table 6.13. These data are based upon examin-

## Table 6.11

### Selected Expense Items as a Percentage of Total Operating Income

| Variable | 1969 Franklin | 1969 Average Control Bank | 1970 Franklin | 1970 Average Control Bank | 1971 Franklin | 1971 Average Control Bank | 1972 Franklin | 1972 Average Control Bank | 1973 Franklin | 1973 Average Control Bank |
|---|---|---|---|---|---|---|---|---|---|---|
| EFFI | 22.2 | 7.0 (4.2) | 20.8 | 7.6 (4.4) | 9.1 | 6.2 (3.6) | 12.8 | 7.2 (4.1) | 27.3 | 12.8 (6.3) |
| PLLI | 0.2 | 1.3 (0.6) | 1.6 | 1.6 (0.7) | 4.0 | 2.2 (1.1) | 4.6 | 2.4 (1.2) | 4.7 | 2.3 (1.1) |
| NOCI | 4.3 | 3.4 (1.3) | 4.4 | 3.7 (1.4) | 5.8 | 4.0 (1.7) | 7.7 | 4.2 (1.8) | 5.4 | 3.5 (1.6) |
| Total | 26.7 | 11.7 | 26.8 | 12.9 | 18.9 | 12.4 | 25.1 | 13.8 | 37.4 | 18.6 |

Data are as of December 31 of the year indicated. Figures in parentheses are standard deviations.
*Source:* Reports of Income, FDIC.

Table 6.12

Franklin's Loan-Portfolio Characteristics

| Year | Price (GLR) | | Quantity (LA) | | Quality (NLLL) | |
|------|-----------|---------|-----------|---------|-----------|---------|
|      | Franklin  | Control | Franklin  | Control | Franklin  | Control |
| 1969 | 8.68      | 7.41    | 50.8      | 56.7    | 0.02      | 0.13    |
|      |           | (0.63)  |           | (5.0)   |           | (0.08)  |
| 1970 | 8.14      | 7.89    | 45.2      | 53.3    | 0.40      | 0.31    |
|      |           | (0.75)  |           | (5.5)   |           | (0.17)  |
| 1971 | 6.81      | 6.75    | 50.4      | 52.6    | 0.83      | 0.34    |
|      |           | (0.73)  |           | (5.9)   |           | (0.23)  |
| 1972 | 6.28      | 6.14    | 50.7      | 54.7    | 0.48      | 0.21    |
|      |           | (0.79)  |           | (6.2)   |           | (0.17)  |
| 1973 | 8.32      | 7.79    | 57.1      | 57.2    | 0.71      | 0.25    |
|      |           | (0.54)  |           | (6.0)   |           | (0.22)  |

Data are as of December 31 of the year indicated. Figures in parentheses are standard deviations.
*Sources:* Reports of Income and Condition, FDIC.

ers' judgments regarding the quality of Franklin's loans. The classified categories loss, doubtful, substandard, and special mention were defined in Chapter 3. [See Tables 3.3 and 3.4 in Chapter 3 for comparisons between Franklin's classifications (in Table 6.13) and those for the average problem bank and the average nonproblem bank.] Franklin's classified loans (excluding special mention) as a percentage of its total loans were 5.9 percent, 6.5 percent, and 7.7 percent as of December 1972, December 1973, and June 1974, respectively. In contrast, using 1973 examination data, the average nonproblem bank's corresponding percentage was 2.3 with a standard deviation of 2.5 percent. Thus, by June 1974, Franklin's classified loans as a percentage of its total loans were more than two standard deviations away from the mean for the typical nonproblem bank.

The only significant difference in the composition of Franklin's loan portfolio relative to the control group was in the relatively minor loan category, loans to financial institutions. This category is further divided into loans "to domestic commercial and foreign banks" and "to other financial institutions." Data for these two loan categories, as a percentage of total loans, are presented in Table 6.14.

*Table 6.13*

Examiners' Judgments of the Quality of Franklin's Loan Portfolio

| Category | December, 1972 | | December, 1973 | | June, 1974 | |
|---|---|---|---|---|---|---|
| | Amount* | Percent | Amount* | Percent | Amount* | Percent |
| Nonclassified | 1,627.9 | 89.4 | 1,880.9 | 86.6 | 1,742.6 | 87.3 |
| Classified | | | | | | |
| Loss | 7.0 | 0.4 | 12.0 | 0.5 | 13.5 | 0.7 |
| Doubtful | 22.0 | 1.2 | 40.0 | 1.8 | 40.0 | 2.0 |
| Substandard | 80.0 | 4.4 | 90.0 | 4.1 | 100.0 | 5.0 |
| Special Mention | 84.0 | 4.6 | 149.0 | 6.9 | 100.0 | 5.0 |
| Total Classified | 193.0 | 10.6 | 291.0 | 13.3 | 253.5 | 12.7 |
| Total Loans | 1,820.9 | 100.0 | 2,171.9 | 100.0 | 1,996.1 | 100.0 |
| Equity Capital | 162.9 | – | 167.8 | – | 142.9 | – |
| Classified Loans (excluding Special Mention) as a Percentage of Equity | – | 67.0 | – | 84.6 | – | 107.4 |
| Total Classified Loans as a Percentage of Equity | – | 118.7 | – | 173.4 | – | 177.4 |

* Amounts in $ millions.
*Source:* Brimmer (1976), Table 4.

The asset compositions of the sample banks are presented in Table 6.15. As a percentage of total assets, the following assets categories are measured:

1. Cash and Due from Banks,
2. Federal Funds Sold and REPOS,
3. U.S. Treasury Securities,
4. Other U.S. Government Securities,
5. Obligations of States and Political Subdivisions.
6. Loans, and
7. Other Assets

A bank's asset portfolio basically consists of its liquidity (or reserve) account, its investment account, and its loan account. Alternative measures of Franklin's liquidity can be obtained by summing the following items from Table 6.15:

*Table 6.14*

Loans to Financial Institutions
(as a percentage of total loans)

| Year | To Domestic Commercial and Foreign Banks | | Other Financial Institutions | |
|------|-----------|-----------------|-----------|-----------------|
| | | Average Control | | Average Control |
| | Franklin | Bank | Franklin | Bank |
| 1969 | 4.7 | 1.2 | 14.7 | 8.2 |
| | | (1.3) | | (4.7) |
| 1970 | 3.7 | 1.2 | 14.4 | 9.1 |
| | | (1.4) | | (5.3) |
| 1971 | 7.2 | 2.3 | 16.4 | 8.6 |
| | | (1.9) | | (5.3) |
| 1972 | 7.5 | 2.8 | 14.8 | 10.0 |
| | | (2.8) | | (5.9) |
| 1973 | 10.9 | 3.6 | 13.5 | 10.8 |
| | | (2.9) | | (6.2) |
| 1974 | 10.6 | 4.0 | 11.9 | 10.9 |
| | | (3.4) | | (6.1) |

Data are as of December 31 of the year indicated, except the date for 1974 which are as of June 30. Figures in parentheses are standard deviations.
*Sources:* Reports of Condition, FDIC.

1. Items (1 + 2),
2. Items (1 + 2 + 3),
3. Items (1 + 2 + 3 + 4), or
4. Items (1 + 3 + 4).

If liquidity is measured by items (1 + 2), then Franklin's investment portfolio would be measured by items (3 + 4 + 5). From 1969 to 1972, based upon any of the four alternative liquidity measures, Franklin's liquidity appeared to be quite similar to the average control bank. How-

## Table 6.15

### Asset Composition

| As a Percentage of Total Assets: | 1969 Franklin | 1969 Control | 1970 Franklin | 1970 Control | 1971 Franklin | 1971 Control | 1972 Franklin | 1972 Control | 1973 Franklin | 1973 Control | 1974 Franklin | 1974 Control |
|---|---|---|---|---|---|---|---|---|---|---|---|---|
| 1. Cash | 13.9 | 19.2 (6.1) | 11.0 | 18.7 (6.1) | 15.9 | 18.6 (6.4) | 18.6 | 18.3 (5.8) | 16.2 | 16.9 (4.9) | 7.9 | 17.1 (7.5) |
| 2. Federal Funds Sold | 4.0 | 1.1 (1.2) | 9.8 | 2.1 (2.9) | 5.6 | 2.7 (3.5) | 7.6 | 3.1 (3.5) | 2.9 | 3.5 (4.0) | 1.2 | 3.6 (3.7) |
| 3. U.S. Treasuries | 7.5 | 6.5 (2.2) | 4.8 | 6.9 (2.7) | 3.3 | 6.5 (2.8) | 0.2 | 5.8 (2.7) | 2.5 | 4.1 (2.1) | 3.4 | 3.5 (1.9) |
| 4. U.S. Governments | 1.4 | 0.5 (0.8) | 4.5 | 0.9 (1.3) | 4.1 | 1.0 (1.2) | 2.6 | 1.1 (1.1) | 3.8 | 1.5 (1.6) | 5.5 | 1.6 (1.5) |
| 5. Municipals | 14.8 | 10.2 (3.2) | 14.5 | 11.5 (4.2) | 12.1 | 11.9 (3.9) | 8.7 | 10.9 (3.5) | 7.4 | 9.6 (3.5) | 8.9 | 9.4 (3.8) |
| 6. Loans | 50.8 | 56.7 (5.0) | 45.2 | 53.3 (5.5) | 50.4 | 52.6 (5.9) | 50.7 | 54.7 (6.2) | 57.1 | 57.2 (6.0) | 55.6 | 57.8 (6.6) |
| 7. Other Assets | 7.6 | 5.8 (2.2) | 10.2 | 6.6 (2.7) | 8.6 | 6.7 (3.1) | 11.6 | 6.1 (2.1) | 10.1 | 7.2 (2.4) | 17.5 | 7.0 (2.5) |
| Total | 100.0 | 100.0 | 100.0 | 100.0 | 100.0 | 100.0 | 100.0 | 100.0 | 100.0 | 100.0 | 100.0 | 100.0 |

Data are as of December 31 of the year indicated, except the data for 1974 which are as of June 30. Figures in parentheses are standard deviations.
Source: Reports of Condition, FDIC.

ever, as depicted in Table 6.16 over the next eighteen months, Franklin's liquidity showed substantial deterioration relative to the control group.

Let us now consider the growth rates presented in Table 6.17. These percentage changes, calculated on an annual basis (December–December) except for 1974 (June–December), are for the following balance-sheet items:

1. Total Assets,
2. Total Loans,
3. IPC Demand Deposits,
4. Savings Deposits,
5. IPC Time Deposits,
6. Total Deposits, and
7. Total Capital.

After substantial deposit growth during 1970 (27.3 percent), Franklin grew at much slower rates during 1971 and 1972. (Recall that Franklin grew rapidly from 1964 to 1969.) During 1973, Franklin's total deposits contracted by 3.3 percent. Over the first six months of 1974 as Franklin's problems were made public, its total deposits declined by 39.3 percent. This substantial runoff consisted mainly of a 41.3 percent drop in IPC demand deposits and a 47.3 percent decline in IPC time deposits. In addition, of course, Franklin's Federal-funds spigot was shut off. (See

*Table 6.16*

Liquidity Measures

| Liquidity Definition | Dec 1972 _ | Dec 1973 | Dec 1973 _ | June 1974 | Dec 1972 _ | June 1974 |
|---|---|---|---|---|---|---|
| | Franklin | Control | Franklin | Control | Franklin | Control |
| Items (1+2) | -27.1 | -4.7 | -52.4 | +1.5 | -65.3 | -3.3 |
| Items (1+2+3) | -18.2 | -9.9 | -42.1 | -1.2 | -52.6 | -11.0 |
| Items (1+2+3+4) | -12.4 | -8.1 | -29.1 | -0.8 | -37.9 | -8.8 |
| Items (1+3+4) | +5.1 | -10.7 | -25.3 | -1.3 | -21.5 | -11.9 |

*Source:* Derived from Table 6.15.

## Table 6.17

### Rates of Growth
#### (percent)

| Variable | 1970 Franklin | 1970 Control | 1971 Franklin | 1971 Control | 1972 Franklin | 1972 Control | 1973 Franklin | 1973 Control | 1974 Franklin | 1974 Control |
|---|---|---|---|---|---|---|---|---|---|---|
| Assets | 16.4 | 8.4 (7.6) | 0.0 | 10.8 (9.8) | 10.0 | 16.0 (9.4) | 6.0 | 14.3 (9.6) | -5.6 | 5.8 (9.5) |
| Loans | 3.7 | 1.9 (8.4) | 11.3 | 9.2 (9.1) | 10.8 | 20.7 (11.8) | 19.3 | 19.7 (9.6) | -8.1 | 6.5 (6.2) |
| Demand Deposits (IPC) | 3.5 | 1.0 (6.9) | 7.5 | 4.6 (8.4) | 15.2 | 15.4 (8.8) | -7.6 | 3.0 (8.4) | -41.3 | -8.5 (6.9) |
| Savings Deposit | 3.9 | 5.8 (7.5) | 12.2 | 18.3 (24.2) | 3.6 | 9.9 (18.1) | -9.5 | -3.9 (19.8) | -13.3 | 0.4 (9.0) |
| Time Deposits (IPC) | 20.3 | 56.5 (65.4) | -8.3 | 17.0 (19.4) | 37.1 | 23.5 (24.3) | 2.7 | 30.9 (31.8) | -47.3 | 19.2 (17.0) |
| Total Deposits | 27.3 | 11.3 (6.4) | 6.7 | 11.2 (7.7) | 4.1 | 14.1 (8.5) | -3.3 | 9.5 (9.4) | -39.3 | 4.4 (10.8) |
| Capital | 5.7 | 7.4 (7.0) | 18.3 | 10.3 (8.6) | 0.9 | 12.2 (11.7) | 1.6 | 6.7 (5.3) | -24.2 | 4.3 (4.9) |

Rates of growth were computed on an annual basis (December-December), except the rates for 1974 which were on a seminannual basis (December-June). Figures in parentheses are standard deviations.
*Source:* Reports of Condition, FDIC.

Tables 6.1–6.4 and 6.6 above for additional liability flows.) Finally, note that during both 1972 and 1973 Franklin's capital grew at rates significantly below those of the control group. In fact, during those years, only two members of the control group had lower rates of capital growth.

To summarize, these single-variable tests for the period December 1969 to June 1974 do not present Franklin's performance in a very favorable light. The picture is one of a bank with poor loan quality, aggressive liability management, and burdensome fixed expenses due to a rapid and extravagant expansion program. The combined effect of these factors led to a poor bottom-line performance as early as 1971 and continuing until October 8, 1974, when Franklin was closed.

**b. A Simple Two-Variable Test.** The outlier tests presented in this section are based upon a simple "risk-return" framework. The results are presented in Table 6.18 and summarized in the risk-return diagram depicted in Figure 6.2.

The variables employed in these tests are not the traditional *expectational* ones suggested by portfolio theory or capital-asset pricing models, but rather proxies for expected return and risk, as measured by NOA and NLLL, respectively. NOA and NLLL were defined above. NOA measures actual return and NLLL measures loan quality or the riskiness of a bank's loan portfolio. While actual return is a rather common proxy for expected return, loan quality is not typically used as a proxy for expected risk. However, in banking, loan quality, is considered to be an important element of a bank's risk exposure. Thus, NLLL can be viewed as a partial first approximation of a bank's actual risk and hence a proxy for expected risk. In Table 6.18 and Figure 6.2, outlier tests also are presented for Security National Bank of Long Island, Morgan Guaranty Trust Company, and First National City Bank. On January 19, 1975, Security National was acquired by Chemical Bank of New York in an emergency merger, the largest consolidation in U.S. banking history.

Franklin's risk-return data indicate that in 1971, 1972, and 1973 it was an outlier compared to the control group. The results for Security National indicate that it was an outlier in 1973 and 1974. During these years, both Franklin and Security were characterized as low-return high-risk banking institutions. In contrast, Morgan also was an outlier in 1971, 1972, and 1973. However, it was a "safe-and-sound" outlier, characterized by high return and low risk. As mentioned above, Morgan (then Franklin's major correspondent bank) stopped selling Federal funds to Fanklin in the fall of 1973.

The risk-return grid in Figure 6.2 was constructed using the grand means for the control group listed at the bottom of Table 6.18. Over the years 1969–1974, the average control bank earned, before taxes and security gains or losses, $1.07 per $100 of assets and charged off only 26

*Table 6.18*

Risk-Return Data and Outlier Tests
1969 - 1974

| Bank/Year | NOA | NLLL | Chi-Square Score | Significance Level (%) |
|---|---|---|---|---|
| Franklin | | | | |
| 1969 | 0.98 | 0.02 | 2.70 | 25.89 |
| 1970 | 0.81 | 0.40 | 1.84 | 39.80 |
| 1971 | 0.48 | 0.83 | 6.50 | 3.87 |
| 1972 | 0.30 | 0.48 | 7.65 | 2.18 |
| 1973 | 0.30 | 0.71 | 8.86 | 1.19 |
| | | | | |
| Security | | | | |
| 1969 | 1.14 | 0.14 | 0.19 | 90.83 |
| 1970 | 1.03 | 0.56 | 2.51 | 28.44 |
| 1971 | 0.85 | 0.30 | 0.51 | 77.45 |
| 1972 | 0.70 | 0.31 | 0.98 | 61.13 |
| 1973 | 0.51 | 0.94 | 16.71 | 0.02 |
| 1974 | -2.65 | 3.73 | 155.58 | 0.00* |
| | | | | |
| Morgan | | | | |
| 1969 | 1.55 | 0.04 | 2.12 | 34.53 |
| 1970 | 1.71 | 0.35 | 2.45 | 29.41 |
| 1971 | 1.75 | 0.07 | 6.74 | 3.44 |
| 1972 | 1.68 | 0.08 | 8.11 | 1.73 |
| 1973 | 1.69 | 0.03 | 6.26 | 4.38 |
| 1974 | 1.61 | 0.27 | 3.07 | 21.48 |
| | | | | |
| FNC | | | | |
| 1969 | 1.14 | 0.11 | 0.22 | 89.36 |
| 1970 | 1.24 | 0.52 | 1.53 | 46.39 |
| 1971 | 1.21 | 0.41 | 0.61 | 73.46 |
| 1972 | 1.41 | 0.29 | 2.99 | 22.44 |
| 1973 | 1.45 | 0.47 | 3.40 | 18.22 |
| 1974 | 1.58 | 0.45 | 3.66 | 16.02 |
| | | | | |
| Average Control Bank** | | | | |
| 1969 | 1.28 | 0.12 | — | — |
| 1970 | 1.24 | 0.30 | — | — |

*Table 6.18* (Cont.)

Risk-Return Data and Outlier Tests
1969 - 1974

| Bank/Year | NOA | NLLL | Chi-Square Score | Significance Level (%) |
|---|---|---|---|---|
| Average Control Bank** | | | | |
| 1971 | 1.04 | 0.33 | — | — |
| 1972 | 0.93 | 0.21 | — | — |
| 1973 | 0.98 | 0.22 | — | — |
| 1974 | 0.95 | 0.38 | — | — |
| Average | 1.07 | 0.26 | | |

*Indicates a very small positive number.
**The control group consisted of the 50 largest banks (as of December 31, 1973). NOA = net operating income (before taxes and security gains and losses) as a percentage of total assets and NLLL = net loan losses as a percentage of total loans.
*Source:* Reports of Income and Condition, December 31, 1969-1974, FDIC.

cents per $100 of loans. (The averages for the 1969–1973 period were 1.09 and 0.24.) The extreme lower-righthand area of Figure 6.2 (i.e., the very high-risk and very low-return area) is the "red-flag" section. By year-end 1970, both Franklin and Security appeared in the above-average risk and below-average return quadrant. At this time, however, they were not significantly different from the center of the control group. By year-end 1971, Franklin was a significant outlier and, by year-end 1973, Security was a significant outlier. Both Franklin and Security failed to return to the center of the control group once they had gone astray.[25]

It is interesting to contrast and compare the movements of Franklin, Security, and Citibank in Figure 6.2. As of year-end 1969, these three banks were bunched relatively close together, both to each other and to the center of the control group. However, from 1970 to 1974, Franklin and Security moved southeast while FNC moved northeast. A northeasterly movement indicates that higher loan losses are compensated for by higher operating income, as governed by the so-called risk-return trade-off. In contrast, Franklin and Security were not compensated (at least *ex post*) for their increased "riskiness." They incurred both higher loan losses *and* received lower operating income over the years 1970–1974.

Figure 6.2

Risk-Return Diagram
1969-1974

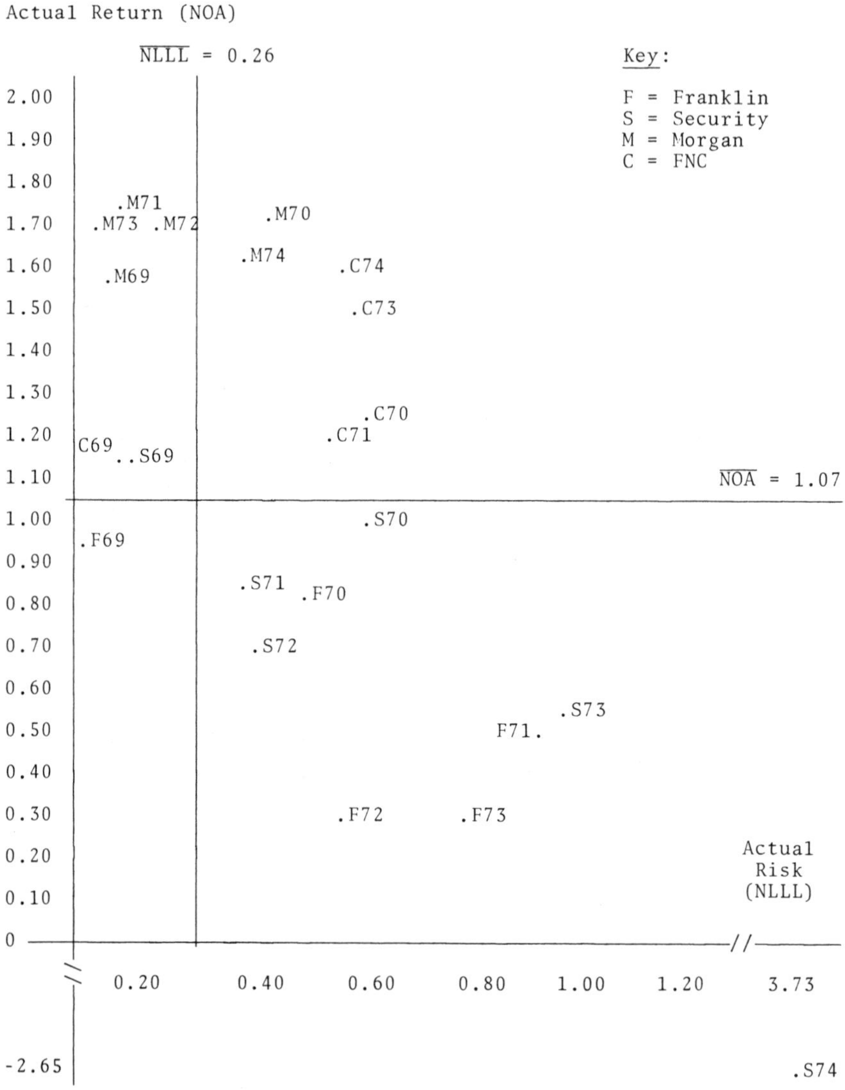

Actual Return (NOA)

$\overline{\text{NLLL}}$ = 0.26

Key:

F = Franklin
S = Security
M = Morgan
C = FNC

```
2.00 |
     |
1.90 |
     |
1.80 |
     |     .M71
1.70 | .M73 .M72    .M70
     |
1.60 |  .M69        .M74    .C74
     |
1.50 |                 .C73
     |
1.40 |
     |
1.30 |
     |                     .C70
1.20 | C69              .C71
     |    ..S69
1.10 |                                      NOA = 1.07
     |
1.00 |                      .S70
     | .F69
0.90 |
     |
0.80 |             .S71  .F70
     |
0.70 |             .S72
     |
0.60 |
     |                              .S73
0.50 |                         F71.
     |
0.40 |
     |
0.30 |             .F72    .F73
     |
0.20 |                               Actual
     |                               Risk
0.10 |                               (NLLL)
     |
   0 |_____//_____
     |
     ~|
      | 0.20   0.40   0.60   0.80   1.00   1.20   3.73
      |
-2.65 |                                          .S74
```

Let us examine the risk-return performance of four additional low-level outliers. Since at the time one of these banks was considered to be a "problem" bank and two of the other three banks had been receiving adverse publicity due to poor performance, the power of the risk-return analysis tends to be enhanced by these findings. The four banks are referred to as outliers 1, 2, 3, and 4. The average NOA and average NLLL for these four banks for the 1969 to 1974 period were:

| Bank | $\overline{\text{NOA}}$ | $\overline{\text{NLLL}}$ |
|------|------|------|
| Outlier 1 | 0.67 | 0.44 |
| Outlier 2 | 0.76 | 0.58 |
| Outlier 3 | 1.19 | 0.80 |
| Outlier 4 | 0.43 | 0.37 |

The corresponding figures for the average control bank were $\overline{\text{NOA}}$ = 1.07 and $\overline{\text{NLLL}}$ = 0.26. The average NOA and average NLLL for Franklin for the 1969 to 1973 period were 0.57 and 0.49, respectively (see Table 6.18). Outliers 1, 2, and 4 have data similar to Franklin's. Outlier 1 is the problem bank. Outlier 3 has shown the most-rapid and serious deterioration as exhibited by the following data:

| Year | NOA | NLLL |
|------|------|------|
| 1972 | 1.52 | 0.48 |
| 1973 | 0.91 | 0.83 |
| 1974 | −0.09 | 1.90 |
| Average | 0.78 | 1.07 |

The corresponding chi-square scores and significant levels (%) for Outlier 3 are 5.87 (5.31 percent), 9.77 (0.76 percent), and 26.97 (0.0001 percent). In each of the years the bank was a statistically significant outlier.

Finally, note that for the year 1973 a simple univariate ranking of outlier 3 based upon NOA would not have been as meaningful as the combined [NOA, NLLL] analysis.

**c. A Seven-Variable Test.** The final set of outlier tests are presented in Tables 6.19 and 6.20 and based upon the seven-variable EWS discussed in Chapters 4 and 5. The seven variables are:

1.  LRI = interest and fees on loans as a percentage of total operating income (measures revenue concentration).

2. OEOI = total operating expense as a percentage of total operating income (measures operating efficiency).

3.  USA = U.S. government securities as a percentage of total assets (measures liquidity and asset composition).

4. SLA = state and local securities as a percentage of total assets (measures asset composition).

5. LA = total loans as a percentage of total assets (measures loan volume).

6. NFA = net federal funds (sales minus purchases) as a percentage of total assets (measures Federal-funds activity and aggressiveness of liability management).

7. KRA = capital and reserves for bad debt losses on loans as a percentage of total assets (measures capital adequacy).

The data for these seven variables for the years 1969–1973 for Franklin and the average control bank are presented in Table 6.19. The chi-square scores to determine if Franklin was an outlier in those years are presented in Table 6.20.

Except for 1971, Franklin's chi-square scores indicate that it was a statistically significant outlier compared to the average control bank. These multivariate outlier tests pinpoint Franklin's atypicalness with respect to: (1) its inefficient operating performance (OEOI); (2) its below-average capital adequacy (KRA); (3) its heavy indebtedness to the Federal-funds market in 1969 and 1973 (NFA); and (4) its portfolio composition (USA, SLA, LA) and loan-revenue generation (LRI). To conclude from this atypicalness that Franklin was a problem bank prior to 1971 is not obvious. The interpretation of Franklin's heavy Federal-funds indebtedness in 1969 is ambiguous. For example, no conceptual distinction can be made between offensive use of Federal funds (i.e., to finance loan expansion) and defensive borrowing (i.e., to meet liquidity requirements). While an offensive policy involves risk, defensive borrowing is an indication of actual difficulty.[26] By 1970, however, Franklin's Federal-funds position was reversed and not atypical again until 1973. In addition, by year-end 1970, Franklin's capital ratio indicates a high risk exposure, but by 1971 this position was not significantly different from the average control bank. The most revealing indicator of Franklin's impending doom was its operating inefficiency. By 1971, the level of deterioration (from 1969) of this variable made Franklin look significantly different from the average control bank. Moreover, during 1972 and 1973, Franklin's operating efficiency continued to deteriorate relative to the average control bank.

Checking the chi-square score of other banks in the control group, the seven-variable model, like the risk-return model, was successful in isolating several banks that then had financial difficulties. For example, the chi-square scores and significance levels for Outlier 3 (discussed above) for the 1972 to 1974 period were 8.73 (27.28 percent), 10.35 (16.95 per-

Table 6.19

Data for Seven-Variable Outlier Test
(percentages)

| Variable | 1969 Franklin | 1969 Average Control Bank | 1970 Franklin | 1970 Average Control Bank | 1971 Franklin | 1971 Average Control Bank | 1972 Franklin | 1972 Average Control Bank | 1973 Franklin | 1973 Average Control Bank |
|---|---|---|---|---|---|---|---|---|---|---|
| LRI | 71.4 | 71.6 (4.8) | 62.9 | 69.5 (5.6) | 62.5 | 64.5 (6.2) | 65.1 | 64.8 (7.2) | 68.7 | 69.8 (6.3) |
| OEOI | 84.1 | 78.3 (5.4) | 86.1 | 79.5 (5.3) | 91.2 | 81.0 (5.8) | 93.8 | 82.1 (6.1) | 95.6 | 84.9 (5.2) |
| USA | 8.9 | 7.0 (2.2) | 9.3 | 7.9 (3.0) | 7.4 | 7.5 (3.1) | 2.8 | 6.9 (3.1) | 6.3 | 5.7 (2.6) |
| SLA | 14.8 | 10.1 (3.3) | 14.5 | 11.5 (4.2) | 12.1 | 11.9 (3.9) | 8.7 | 10.9 (3.5) | 7.4 | 9.6 (3.5) |
| LA | 50.8 | 56.7 (5.1) | 45.2 | 53.3 (5.5) | 50.4 | 52.6 (5.9) | 50.7 | 54.7 (6.2) | 57.1 | 57.2 (6.0) |
| NFA | -13.9 | -3.8 (2.9) | 8.8 | -3.4 (3.2) | -2.1 | -4.4 (3.5) | -5.3 | -5.0 (3.9) | -18.0 | -7.4 (5.0) |
| KRA | 7.4 | 8.6 (1.3) | 6.7 | 8.5 (1.4) | 7.7 | 8.4 (1.6) | 7.0 | 8.0 (1.3) | 6.7 | 7.6 (1.4) |

Notes: Data are as of December 31 of the year indicated. Figures in parentheses are standard deviations. Note that a negative value for NFA means a net indebtedness (sales minus purchases) to the federal-funds market.
Source: Reports of Income and Condition, FDIC.

183

*Table 6.20*

Seven-Variable Outlier Test

| Year | Franklins' Chi-Square Score | Level of Significance (percent) |
|------|------------------------------|----------------------------------|
| 1969 | 16.77 | 1.89 |
| 1970 | 18.39 | 1.03 |
| 1971 | 6.34 | 50.03 |
| 1972 | 15.47 | 3.04 |
| 1973 | 17.63 | 1.37 |

cent), and 21.34 (0.33 percent), respectively. These results suggest that the bank was not as significant an outlier as the "risk-return" model indicated. However, the models are different and therefore the results are not directly comparable. The major reason for the bank's more favorable rating by the seven-variable model appeared to be due to its "capital adequacy" as measured by KRA. For the 1972 to 1974 period, the bank's KRAs were 9.67, 8.71, and 9.11, respectively. The average control bank's KRA for 1974 was 7.43 with a standard deviation of 1.26 (see Table 6.19 for 1972 and 1973 data). In contrast to its "adequate" capital, the bank was relatively illiquid as measured by USA with percentages of 0.82, 0.51, and 0.50 for the years 1972, 1973, and 1974, respectively. For 1974, the average control bank's liquidity was 5.21 with a standard deviation of 2.31 (see Table 6.19 for 1972 and 1973 data). Outlier 3, like other banks in the sample, tended to use liability management to meet its liquidity needs and/or loan demand. The bank's high loan volume as measured by LA (roughly 64 percent for the 1972 to 1974 period compared to 56 percent for the average control bank) indicated that it was "accommodating" its loan customers. Of course, making more and more loans usually increases the riskiness of a bank's loan portfolio, resulting in higher loan losses.

On balance, the seven-variable model paints a more detailed picture of a bank's overall peformance. Consequently, it should (in theory at least) be a more reliable indicator of a bank's true atypicalness and potential problem status.

**d. Summary Inference and Comparisons.** By year-end 1971, or year-end 1972 at the latest, Franklin's atypicalness was beginning to suggest that it was a troubled bank. The importance of this *ex post* observation is that routinely collected banking data, if properly analyzed, can be useful in evaluating the creditworthiness of banks. Comparing the univariate, bivariate, and seven-variable tests, the univariate and bivariate tests tended to outperform the seven-variable tests in terms of consistently indicating Franklin's atypicalness. In addition, the bivariate tests, because of its added risk dimension, outperformed the univariate tests. Moreover, the power of the risk-return analysis was enhanced because it identified several "problem" banks as low-level outliers. The seven-variable models, as well as the univariate ones, also were successful in flagging low-level outliers that eventually encountered financial difficulties; however, they were not as consistent as the risk-return model. These outlier tests were conducted using ordinary balance-sheet and income-expense data and not bank-examination data which focus upon detailed loan evaluations. Recall that early-warning systems are designed to complement traditional on-site bank inspections by providing interexamination information about banks' safety and soundness and signaling the need for closer and more frequent examination.

**4. Summary and Conclusions.** Using a unique adaptation of discriminant analysis, this section has presented an outlier or peer-group model of our largest bank failure. The purpose of the tests was to determine what balance-sheet and income-statement figures could have been arrayed in an early-warning system to spot Franklin's developing problems. The methodological approach amounted to a new twist on an old theme, that is, "credit-scoring" techniques applied to banks rather than to bank's customers.

Harry Keefe, a noted bank analyst, has said that "People who can read a balance sheet [and presumably an income statement] were out of there [Franklin] long ago" (inserts mine). The univariate, bivariate, and multivariate outlier tests conducted in this chapter all indicate that by year-end 1972 suspicious evidence on Franklin had accumulated. Moreover, as early as year-end 1971, univariate income measures and risk-return analysis indicated that Franklin was a significant outlier. Morgan Guaranty evidently was aware of Franklin's outlier characteristics. It was out of Franklin by the fall of 1973.

The major contribution of this analysis has been to show that existing, routinely-collected banking data, if properly analyzed, should be useful in identifying potential problem banks. The banking agencies collect a wealth of data; the information content of these data should be fully utilized. By developing *and* using screening models such as those described in this section, the banking authorities should be able to allocate their scarce resources more efficiently and thus be able to concentrate on those banks that really need close supervision.

## 6.5 POSTMORTEM ANALYSIS II: EARLY WARNING BASED UPON MARKET INFORMATION

### 1. Beta

The most celebrated measure of a security's *systematic* risk (i.e., risk that cannot be diversified away) is known as "Beta."[27] The concept of Beta focuses upon the systematic risk an individual security adds to a well-diversified portfolio. It abstracts from additional risk associated with placing one's wealth entirely in that security. The fully diversified portfolio is referred to as the "market portfolio." It represents the total bundle of securities that must be traded in equilibrium and usually is proxied by some market index such as the Dow-Jones Industrial Average or Standard & Poor's Stock Index. Beta measures systematic risk as the relative volatility between a security's *expected* rate of return $R_j$ (its yield over the planned *holding period*) and the *expected* rate of return on the market portfolio, $R_M$. It summarizes the effects of common forces (such as those associated with the business cycle) that impact systematically and simultaneously, but in different degrees, on equilibrium $R_j$. In this model, $R_j$ is viewed as the sum of the systematic element $E(R_j | R_M)$, and a random or unsystematic element, $u_j$, with zero mean and finite variance. In capital-market *equilibrium,* the conditional expectation should be a linear function of the expected return on the market portfolio:

$$E(R_j | R_M) = \alpha_j + \beta_j R_M \tag{6.1}$$

where $\alpha_j = (1 - \beta_j)R_F$ and $R_F$ is the risk-free rate of interest. The correspondence between $\alpha_j$ and $(1 = \beta_j)R_F$ establishes that in equilibrium the expected return on any security (or portfolio) is a linear combination of the risk-free rate and the expected return on the market portfolio. That is,

$$\begin{aligned} E(R_j | R_M) &= (1 - \beta_j)R_F + \beta_j R_F \\ &= R_F + (\beta_j(R_M - R_F)). \end{aligned} \tag{6.1'}$$

Equation (6.1') means that the risk-free asset and market portfolios span the investors opportunity set.

Sharpe (1964) refers to equation (6.1) as asset j's "security-market line" (see Figure 6.1) or in general the "Capital Asset Pricing Model" (CAPM).[28] It is a mechanism for determining equilibrium prices. Given the expected return on the market portfolio, each security's return is a linear function of its systematic risk.

Because it is an index, Beta has a major selling point: it is easy to interpret. As a measure of risk, the values $\beta_j = 0$ and $\beta_j = 1$ are important (see equation 6.1'). If $\beta_j = 0$, $E(R_j | R_M)$ equals the risk-free rate, $R_F$. If $\beta_j = 1$, $E(R_j | R_M)$ equals the return on the market portfolio, $R_M$. A security whose Beta is unity is as risky (volatile) as the market portfolio. A security whose $\beta_j$ is less than unity (a "defensive" security) is less risky (volatile) than the market portfolio while a security whose $\beta_j$ exceeds unity (an "aggressive" security) is more risky (volatile) than the market portfolio.[29]

### 2. The Market Model

Since Betas and expected returns are not directly observable, empirical tests of the asset-pricing model require the development of assumptions so that reasonable "proxies" can bridge the gap between the observable and unobservable variables. The modus operandi is to combine the pricing model with three further restrictions on the random-error term imposed by the classical linear regression model. The combined "pricing-regression" model is what the literature calls the "market model." In the pricing model, the random-error term, $u_j$, which captures diversifiable (or residual) risk, is assumed to have zero expectation and finite variance. The so-called ordinary least-squares (OLS) assumptions further restrict the random error-term such that

1. $E(u_j | R_M) = 0$,
2. $Cov(u_j, u_k) = 0$ for $j \neq k$, and
3. $V(u_j) = \sigma^2$ for all $j$.

In words, (1) $u_j$ is distributed independently of $R_M$; (2) $u_j$ is distributed independently of the error term for any other asset; and (3) the variance of $u_j$ is contant (homoskedasticity). If these additional restrictions are not violated, regressions of $R_j$ on $R_M$ produce best linear unbiased estimates of $\alpha_j$ and $\beta_j$. The reliability of these estimates depends upon the "goodness of fit" as measured by the coefficient of determination, $R^2 = 1 - \Sigma(R_j - \hat{R}_j)^2 / \Sigma(R_j - \bar{R})^2$. The higher the $R^2$, the better the fit and the more reliable are the estimated parameters. In contrast, the lower the $R^2$, the wider the scatter and the less reliable are the estimated parameters.

To summarize, in the market model, the total risk of any security consists of its systematic (nondiversifiable) risk plus its residual (diversifiable) risk. The smaller the residual risk, the more diversifiable it is.

### 3. Estimating Beta and Its Meaningfulness

Statistically, Beta equals the covariance between the jth security's return and the return on the market portfolio, Cov ($R_j$, $R_M$), divided by the variance of the return on the market portfolio, $V(R_M)$. It is the slope of the linear conditional expectation, $E(R_j | R_M)$, and has the same formula as the slope of the regression of $R_j$ on $R_M$:

$$\beta_j = \frac{Cov(R_j, R_M)}{V(R_M)} = \frac{\rho_{jM}\sigma_j\sigma_M}{\sigma^2_M} . \tag{6.2}$$

In practice, the population variance and covariance terms are unknown and are estimated using observations on *ex post* $R_j$ and $R_M$ (not *ex ante* observations as the theory requires) to generate sample variance and covariance terms.

Since it is easy to estimate Beta mechanically from historical data, there is an overabundance of computer-generated Betas. However, it is far more difficult to establish that these measurements are *meaningful*. This difficulty arises because of problems associated with (1) defining the relevant holding period (e.g., monthly, quarterly, or annually) and determining whether or not the risk rankings are sensitive to this definition; (2) finding the proper index to represent the market portfolio; (3) establishing that the estimated Betas are stationary over time; and (4) developing a proxy for the risk-free rate (which is difficult because of uncertain inflation) to test the restriction that $\alpha_j = (1 - \beta_j)R_F$.

### 4. The CAPM and the Market Model Applied to Franklin New York Corporation 1965–1973

The purpose of this section is to analyze the rate of return on the common stock of Franklin New York Corporation, the holding company for Franklin National Bank of New York, to determine (1) the riskiness of the stock as measured by its Beta and (2) whether or not the market was emitting any early-warning signals about Franklin's impending collapse. Our analyses use the models discussed in the previous sections.

   **a. Estimating Franklin's Beta.** The most common method for estimating a stock's Beta is simply to regress over time the stock's rate of return against an appropriate market index. That is, estimate the so-called market model:

$$R_{j,t} = \alpha_j + \beta_j R_{M,t} + u_{j,t} \tag{6.3}$$

where t is a time subscript. This is the first step in a two-step procedure employed in most empirical tests of the market model. The second step uses the estimated Beta from the first step to generate (via the CAPM) the security's expected rate of return.

The market index used by Altman (1975) in estimating equation (6.3) is Standard & Poor's Index of New York City Banks. Monthly returns for $R_j$ and $R_M$ for five-year periods from 1965 to 1973 (60 observations for each period) are employed. Regression results are presented in Table 6.21.[30] They indicate that (1) Franklin's beta is stable and *low* over the entire period (i.e., Franklin's historical return is less volatile (risky) than the average large NYC bank's return and (2) the regression line is statistically significant in each of the five-year periods, except the last

*Table 6.21*

Franklin's Estimated Beta 1965 - 1973

Market Model: $R_{FNYC} = a + \beta R_{S+PNYCBANKS} + U$

| Period | Intercept $\hat{a}$ | Slope $\hat{\beta}$ | $\overline{R}^2$ | F |
|---|---|---|---|---|
| 1965 - 1969 | 0.38 (0.48) | 0.54* (2.85) | 0.11 | 8.15 |
| 1966 - 1970 | 0.83 (0.99) | 0.53* (2.90) | 0.11 | 8.43 |
| 1967 - 1971 | 0.44 (0.51) | 0.54* (2.64) | 0.09 | 6.97 |
| 1968 - 1972 | 0.20 (0.22) | 0.50* (2.37) | 0.07 | 5.63 |
| 1969 - 1973 | -1.18 (0.87) | 0.49 (1.86) | 0.05 | 3.46 |

*Indicates statistical significance (from zero) at the 5 percent level. These coefficients (*) are also significantly different from 1.0. Figures in parentheses are t-values for the zero test. Holding-period return does *not* include dividends.
*Source:* Altman (1975).

one, but the model explains only about ten percent of the variation in Franklin's return.

Given Franklin's estimated Beta, the second step is to compare forecasts of Franklin's expected return with the actual return. The expected returns, $\hat{R}_{FNB}$, are generated from the following CAPM equation:

$$\hat{R}_{FNB,t} = R_{TB,t} + \beta_{t-60,t-12}(R_{S\&P,t} - R_{TB,t}) \qquad (6.4)$$

where $t$ = 1970, 1971, 1972, 1973 and $R_{TB}$ = three-month Treasury bill. The interest rates are expressed on a monthly basis and the Betas used are those from Table 6.21. Thus, for the year 1970, the estimated Beta for the 1965 to 1969 period is used; for 1971, the 1966 to 1970 Beta is used; and so on. This is a moving-average approach designed to capture any change in Franklin's market sensitivity. The next step is to compare $\hat{R}_{FNB}$ with $R_{FNB}$ (i.e., to analyze the behavior of the monthly residuals, $e_t = R_{FNB,t} - \hat{R}_{FNB,t}$). In particular, Altman focuses upon the cumulative residual, $CR = \sum_{t=1}^{48} e_t$, which is plotted in Figure 6.3. If capital markets are inefficient, Franklin's $e_t$ should fluctuate around zero and its CR should be approximately zero over the sample period. This is the hypothesis Altman tests.

From January 1970 to September 1971 (except for May and July of 1970), the CR is positive. However, after September, the CR is never positive again, although there are eight months in which the individual residuals are positive. Note that a positive residual appears as an "uptick" in the CR graph and a negative residual as a "downtick." From January 1970 to June 1971, there are nine downticks; however, after that, there are twenty-one downticks and only eight upticks. For a bank approaching failure, if capital markets are inefficient, the residuals should fluctuate around zero. By December 1973, the CR is a −69 percent. It *appears* that the market is reacting to Franklin's deteriorating condition as early as late 1971, which is consistent with the early-warning signal given by the balance-sheet and income-expense data.[31]

The meaningfulness of Altman's findings hinges upon (1) the relevant holding period being one month and whether or not the findings are sensitive to this definition; (2) the choice of the bank index to proxy the market portfolio; (3) the choice of the three-month Treasury bill rate to proxy the risk-free rate; (4) the stationarity of the estimated Betas; (5) the low explanatory power of the estimated market model, 5% to 11% (i.e., the high "information risk" in using the $\alpha_j$ and $\beta_j$ estimates); and (6) the arbitrariness of the cumulative-residual test to deal with nonsta-

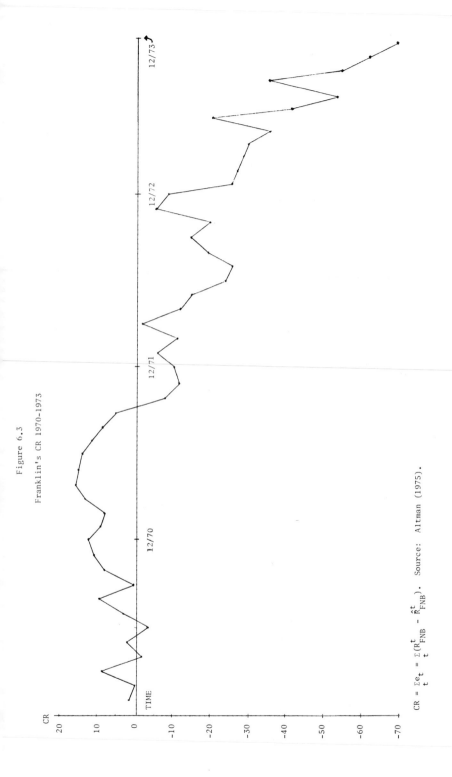

Figure 6.3

Franklin's CR 1970-1973

$CR = \sum_t e_t = \sum_t (R_{FNB}^t - \hat{R}_{FNB}^t)$. Source: Altman (1975).

tionarity. On balance, the conclusion that the market was aware of Franklin's financial difficulties is forced on a partly unwilling model.

### 5. Section Summary and Conclusion

In a recent study comparing market and regulatory assessments of bank condition, Herzig-Marx (1977) concludes that bank-examination ratings and market-risk premiums contain basically the same information. Thus, assessments about bank condition by regulators and market investors should be much the same. This section has focused upon the concept of Beta and the so-called market model to test the market's efficiency regarding Franklin's impending collapse. While the pattern of Franklin's cumulative residuals appears to indicate that the market was efficient and aware of Franklin's financial difficulties, it is hard to establish that these findings are meaningful because of numerous problems associated with estimating the asset-pricing model. The *nondiscounted* results suggest that the market and an early-warning system (using accounting data) came to the same conclusion about Franklin at roughly the same time (1971).

# 6.6 SUMMARY AND CONCLUSIONS

This chapter explores in detail the rise and fall of Franklin National Bank. In four decades, Franklin moves from a tiny Long Island bank to the twentieth largest bank in the U.S. (with $5 billion in total assets) to finally the largest bank failure in U.S. history. Important lessons can be learned from Franklin's dramatic experience. First, Franklin presents a near-perfect case study in both the dos and don'ts of bank management. Franklin's achievements in establishing a strong retail-banking network on Long Island are squandered on attempts to enter the highly competitive wholesale- and international-banking markets centered in New York City. Second, while rapid growth and aggressiveness work for Franklin in establishing its retail-banking market, in the wholesale and international arenas the same policies backfire. And third, the early-warning signals generated by ex-post analyses of Franklin's collapse underscore the potential usefulness of early-warning systems on an ex-ante basis. By developing and using screening models such as those described in this chapter, the banking authorities should be able to allocate their scarce resources more efficiently and thus be able to concentrate on those banks that really need close supervision.

# APPENDIX A: COMPUTATION OF CHI-SQUARE SCORES

The chi-square scores presented in this paper serve as a measure of resemblance between Franklin and the average control bank and provide an approximation of the percentage of the population of control banks that can be expected to lie farther from the control group's center (in either direction from the mean vector) than Franklin. Since the chi-square measures are in terms of absolute differences, the direction of the individual banks (i.e., "safe and sound" or "problem") must be determined from the original data. The types of outliers that the banking agencies are looking for are, of course, those in the "problem" direction. The chi-square score employed in this paper is computed as follows:

$$\hat{\chi}^2_{m,cf} = (\overline{X}_c - X_f)' S_c^{-1} (\overline{X}_c - X_f), \qquad (A.1)$$

where,

$\hat{\chi}^2$ = estimated chi-square score,
$m$ = number of variables,
$c$ = control group,
$f$ = Franklin,
$\overline{X}_c$ = control group's mean vector,
$X_f$ = Franklin's variable profile, and
$S_c^{-1}$ = inverse of control group's variance-covariance matrix.

For a univariate test, the chi-square score is simply

$$\hat{\chi}^2_{1,cf} = (\overline{X}_c - x_f)^2 / s_c^2. \qquad (A.2)$$

That is, the chi-square score is the square of the difference between the control group's mean ($\overline{x}_c$) and Franklin's value of x, divided by the control group's variance. For example, in 1972, Franklin's ratio of operating expenses to operating income (OEOI) was 0.9377285 while the average control bank's was 0.8208432 with a variance of 0.003725947. Thus, in 1972, Franklin's chi-square score for OEOI was

$$\hat{\chi}^2_{1,cf} = (0.9377285 - 0.8208432)^2 / 0.003725947$$
$$= 3.666762.$$

This score was significant at the 5.5508 level. Only three banks had values of OEOI that were farther from the control group's mean of 82.1 percent than Franklin's OEOI of 93.8 percent. The values of OEOI for these three more-distant outliers were 62.1 percent, 68.5 percent, and 94.4 percent. Thus, only one member of the control group was more inefficient than Franklin during 1972.

Appendix B

Table 6.22

Bank Stock Prices

| Date | Moody's Averages NYC | Moody's Averages Outside NYC | Moody's Averages Combined | USNB Low | USNB High | Franklin Low | Franklin High | Security Low | Security High |
|---|---|---|---|---|---|---|---|---|---|
| 1 71 | 171.640 | 107.240 | 135.520 | 26.000 | 29.000 | 38.500 | 39.000 | 39.500 | 40.250 |
| 2 71 | 175.160 | 108.950 | 137.940 | 26.500 | 27.500 | 37.375 | 37.875 | 38.250 | 39.000 |
| 3 71 | 194.160 | 118.190 | 149.310 | 24.000 | 24.500 | 41.250 | 41.750 | 42.000 | 42.750 |
| 4 71 | 184.340 | 115.700 | 145.690 | 27.500 | 28.500 | 44.750 | 45.750 | 41.500 | 42.000 |
| 5 71 | 170.880 | 108.290 | 135.640 | 26.000 | 27.000 | 43.000 | 43.500 | 41.000 | 41.750 |
| 6 71 | 165.770 | 104.630 | 131.340 | 26.250 | 27.250 | 42.250 | 42.750 | 37.500 | 38.250 |
| 7 71 | 165.270 | 106.570 | 130.490 | 26.250 | 29.000 | 38.625 | 39.125 | 37.500 | 38.250 |
| 8 71 | 167.670 | 104.410 | 133.280 | 28.250 | 29.000 | 36.000 | 36.250 | 37.000 | 37.750 |
| 9 71 | 169.020 | 104.080 | 131.910 | 28.250 | 27.750 | 35.750 | 36.250 | 36.250 | 37.000 |
| 10 71 | 173.950 | 106.380 | 134.760 | 27.000 | 28.500 | 31.750 | 32.250 | 34.000 | 34.000 |
| 11 71 | 183.950 | 114.220 | 140.260 | 28.000 | 28.000 | 29.750 | 30.250 | 31.250 | 34.250 |
| 12 71 | 190.430 | 112.860 | 147.660 | 27.500 | 28.000 | 33.125 | 32.750 | 33.250 | 35.000 |
| 1 72 | 188.390 | 114.040 | 146.020 | 25.500 | 27.375 | 31.125 | 31.625 | 33.500 | 34.500 |
| 2 72 | 187.170 | 133.440 | 146.140 | 26.875 | 24.750 | 34.875 | 35.375 | 33.250 | 35.750 |
| 3 72 | 204.480 | 138.540 | 162.440 | 24.000 | 25.750 | 32.250 | 32.750 | 33.250 | 34.000 |
| 4 72 | 203.700 | 131.190 | 169.770 | 25.000 | 26.750 | 31.375 | 31.875 | 33.250 | 34.000 |
| 5 72 | 207.060 | 136.590 | 165.720 | 26.000 | 27.750 | 28.375 | 28.875 | 30.250 | 30.750 |
| 6 72 | 222.610 | 142.320 | 167.580 | 27.000 | 29.000 | 28.000 | 28.500 | 30.250 | 31.250 |
| 7 72 | 237.250 | 150.190 | 177.540 | 28.000 | 29.250 | 31.000 | 31.750 | 35.250 | 35.750 |
| 8 72 | 241.670 | 152.260 | 188.380 | 28.250 | 28.000 | 33.000 | 33.500 | 35.000 | 35.500 |
| 9 72 | 239.740 | 153.210 | 191.660 | 28.250 | 28.750 | 31.250 | 31.750 | 31.250 | 31.750 |
| 10 72 | 230.820 | 150.190 | 191.340 | 27.750 | 29.950 | 29.405 | 34.595 | 30.125 | 33.250 |
| 11 72 | 241.160 | 151.420 | 185.930 | 28.000 | 28.750 | 34.105 | 34.595 | 30.125 | 33.250 |
| 12 72 | 240.950 | 140.470 | 191.030 | 26.750 | 27.000 | 27.500 | 29.500 | 29.000 | 30.625 |
| 1 73 | 226.450 | 135.620 | 184.880 | 25.750 | 22.000 | 27.625 | 28.000 | 25.250 | 25.750 |
| 2 73 | 226.150 | 128.920 | 175.590 | 26.000 | 24.500 | 26.625 | 28.125 | 21.750 | 22.250 |
| 3 73 | 218.050 | 131.980 | 176.450 | 20.000 | 23.750 | 24.250 | 27.125 | 17.750 | 18.250 |
| 4 73 | 235.670 | 127.610 | 167.430 | 23.500 | 21.750 | 28.000 | 24.750 | 17.750 | 18.500 |
| 5 73 | 235.440 | 142.530 | 167.530 | 22.750 | 23.500 | 28.000 | 28.500 | 17.125 | 17.625 |
| 6 73 | 266.590 | 135.780 | 177.750 | 21.500 | 23.750 | 23.500 | 24.750 | 16.375 | 16.875 |
| 7 73 | 279.450 | 146.170 | 194.110 | 20.750 | 21.750 | 21.250 | 24.000 | 16.375 | 19.750 |
| 8 73 | 279.450 | 153.030 | 193.490 | 0.0 | 0.0 | 25.875 | 21.750 | 19.250 | 17.500 |
| 9 73 | 250.090 | 137.860 | 202.470 | 0.0 | 0.0 | 21.500 | 26.375 | 17.500 | 17.675 |
| 10 73 | 263.650 | 141.040 | 208.820 | 0.0 | 0.0 | 19.000 | 22.000 | 14.875 | 15.000 |
| 11 73 | 245.500 | 145.710 | 187.390 | 0.0 | 0.0 | 17.250 | 18.750 | 14.500 | 14.875 |
| 12 73 | 252.060 | 147.520 | 195.590 | 0.0 | 0.0 | 18.270 | 20.500 | 14.500 | 18.000 |
| 1 74 | 246.470 | 142.360 | 189.730 | 0.0 | 0.0 | 19.750 | 20.500 | 15.000 | 15.000 |
| 2 74 | 240.110 | 143.960 | 196.380 | 0.0 | 0.0 | 17.250 | 17.500 | 14.375 | 14.750 |
| 3 74 | 216.200 | 118.130 | 188.130 | 0.0 | 0.0 | 15.750 | 16.500 | 14.250 | 14.750 |
| 4 74 | 188.790 | 98.670 | 166.690 | 0.0 | 0.0 | 15.750 | 16.500 | 9.750 | 10.750 |
| 5 74 | 182.750 | 89.100 | 161.690 | 0.0 | 0.0 | 0.0 | 0.0 | 10.250 | 10.750 |
| 6 74 | 162.430 | 79.430 | 138.740 | 0.0 | 0.0 | 0.0 | 0.0 | 12.250 | 12.750 |
| 7 74 | 148.640 | 72.130 | 130.750 | 0.0 | 0.0 | 0.0 | 0.0 | 9.500 | 10.000 |
| 8 74 | 185.250 | 106.200 | 106.200 | 0.0 | 0.0 | 0.0 | 0.0 | 9.500 | 10.000 |
| 9 74 | 182.690 | 91.820 | 106.020 | 0.0 | 0.0 | 0.0 | 0.0 | 7.500 | 9.500 |
| 10 74 | 170.860 | 91.930 | 133.220 | 0.0 | 0.0 | 0.0 | 0.0 | 7.500 | 8.250 |
| 11 74 | | 92.950 | 132.140 | 0.0 | 0.0 | 0.0 | 0.0 | 4.750 | 5.500 |
| 12 74 | | | 121.850 | 0.0 | 0.0 | 0.0 | 0.0 | | |

Sources: Bank and Quotation Record and Moody's Bank and Finance Manual.

# NOTES

1. Unless otherwise noted, many of the facts and figures in this section and the following one are derived from Wille (1974). See also U.S. Congress (1975).

2 According to Jerome Twomey, a former executive vice president at Franklin, "To be perfectly frank, in those years [the years after Franklin's expansion into New York City] nearly every company that was written up in the *Wall Street Journal* for unusual accounting practices became our customer" [Rose (1974), p. 220, insert mine].

3. A bank is declared insolvent either by the Comptroller of the Currency in the case of a nationally-chartered bank or by a state-banking commissioner in the case of a state-chartered bank. The Fed has the potential de facto power to close a troubled bank simply by denying it access to the discount window; the FDIC's de facto power is withdrawal of deposit insurance. See Chapter 2 for more detail.

4. The sixteen banking organizations were: First National City Bank, The Chase Manhattan Bank, N.A., Manufacturers Hanover Trust Company, Chemical Bank, Bankers Trust Company, Charter New York Corporation, Marine Midlands Banks, Inc., The Bank of New York, European-American Bank & Trust Company, Barclays Bank of New York, Algemena Bank Nederland, N.V., Royal Bank of Canada Trust Company, First Commercial Banks, Inc., United Bancorportation, Lincoln First Banks, Inc., and First Empire State Corporation.

5. Regarding Franklin's 109 domestic branch facilities, EAB&T eventually requested the transfer of leases on 100 of these offices. The nine rejected branches and 26 of the accepted branches are located in New York City. The remaining seventy-four branches are located on Long Island. Regarding Franklin's foreign offices, EAB&T is operating Franklin's London branch but has closed Franklin's three other foreign branches.

6. The rate of interest was determined to be the average rate of return on the Federal Reserve's open-market account on the day Franklin was closed. The relevant opportunity cost, of course, would have been the marginal rate of return.

7. For a detailed account of these events see Wille (1974).

8. See Welles (1974), and Kane (1974), pp. 848–850, and Brimmer (1976).

9. See *Annual Report* (1974) Federal Reserve Bank of New York, p. 23 and Brimmer (1976).

10. See Rose (1974), p. 225.

11. The face value of Franklin's collateral was $2,555 million, an "overcollateralization" of $832 million (see Table 6.6). However, since this collateral was both more risky and less liquid than the Fed's alternative investments, the real extent of the overcollateralization would depend upon the market value of the collateral.

12. Federal Reserve Bulletin (October 1974), p. 741.

13. Kaufman (1975), pp. 780–781, has estimated this subsidy to be about 4 percent (about $21 million). The difference between Kane's and Kaufman's estimates is the troubled-bank risk premium included in Kane's calculation but not in Kaufman's.

14. In the failure of the U.S. National Bank of San Diego, the FDIC set aside (as a reserve for loss) $198 million. The size of this reserve was almost entirely

responsible for the drop in the deposit-insurance assessment credit from 59.7 percent in 1972 to 48.6 percent in 1974 [see Wille (1974)]. If the FDIC had not been able to arrange a deposit assumption, its immediate deposit-payoff cash outlay in the Franklin case would have been approximately $750 million. This would have had a significant adverse effect, at least in the short run, on both the insurance fund and the assessment credit.

15. According to Welles (1974), the Fed was embarrassed and distressed because the FDIC took so long to arrange a deposit assumption. Welles reports one Fed official as saying, "If Arthur Burns had been running the show the thing could have been done in two weeks, maybe even over the weekend" (p. 720).

16. These officials also argued correctly that the longer Franklin was subsidized the higher the costs would be to the government. See Welles (1974), p. 42.

17. According to Brimmer (1976) p. 39, a former member of the Board of Governors of the Federal Revenue System, the Fed recognized a new dimension in its responsibility in its handling of the Franklin affair. "This was the clear and explicit acceptance of the use of central bank resources to help stabilize money markets beyond its own national boundaries."

18. See Brimmer (1976) and Mayer (1974) for additional details of this evolutionary process. Unless otherwise noted, many of the facts and figures in this section are derived from these two sources.

19. Comptroller Saxon believed in freedom of entry and consequently his decisions regarding charter and branch applications mainly were designed to promote competition. For an example of an exception see Mayer (1974), pp. 383–384.

20. The London interbank market consists of a network of foreign commercial banks with reciprocal arrangements for holding deposits and extending credits. Banks in London are the kernel of the interbank market, but the market itself is international in scope. Entry into the market is relatively unrestricted. See Brimmer and Dahl (1975) and Brimmer (1976). Also see note 17 above, regarding how Franklin's foreign footings affected the Fed's lender-of-last-resort thinking.

21. The largest bank in the control group had total deposits of $26.4 billion, while the smallest bank had deposits of $1.4 billion. The average sample bank had total deposits of $4.6 billion; the standard deviation of the group mean was $5.0 billion. As of December 31, 1973, Franklin's total *domestic* deposits were $2.6 billion.

22. My suspicion, based upon some limited testing using consolidated data (in an FDIC internal document), is that such data (i.e., foreign and domestic) would not produce significantly different results. However, the end result would depend upon the effect of changes in Franklin's data relative to the changes for individual banks in the control group. Also see Brimmer (1976), pp. 15–20, regarding the profitability of foreign branches.

23. The classification section of the Eisenbeis and Avery (1972) computer program (MULDIS) is used to perform these tests. Given a vector of variables to characterize the operation and performance of the sample banks (or simply a single variable for a univariate test), the computer program generates the group

mean vector (for the control banks) and then compares Franklin's variable pro-file to this group mean vector. The computation of the test statistic, a chi-square score, is presented in Appendix A of this chapter. Discriminant-analysis proce-dures for examining group overlap and the relative positions of individual ob-servations are described in Eisenbeis and Avery (1973).

24. Franklin's stock-price data for the period January 1971 to May 1974 are presented in Appendix B of this chapter. For comparison purposes, data for Moody's bank averages, USNB of San Diego (closed on October 18, 1973), and Security National Bank of Long Island (emergency merger on January 19, 1975) also are presented.

25. Visualizing a risk-return ellipse, centered at the intersection of the means and running northwest to southeast, Morgan forms the northwest border (indi-cating extreme "safety and soundness") while Franklin and Security form the southwest border, the extreme weakness frontier. Note the elliptical distortion caused by Security's 1974 data points (−2.65, 3.73).

26. Given the discussion earlier in this chapter, the offensive interpretation would appear to describe correctly Franklin's Federal-funds activity in 1969.

27. Professor Edward J. Kane's notes (Lecture 3, revised June 1977, pp. 48–56.) from his B.A. 920 course at the Ohio State University were helpful in pre-paring this section.

28. Roll (1977) contends that the two-parameter, asset-pricing theory is test-able in principle, but that ". . . no correct and ambiguous test of the theory has appeared in the literature and there is practically no possibility that such a test can be accomplished in the future" (pp. 129–130).

29. A security whose $\beta_j$ is negative (a rare occurrence) moves in the *opposite* direction of the market portfolio. Such a security would be valuable to offset the effects of the business cycle.

30. These tests were performed by Altman (1975) for his comments on my Franklin National paper presented at the Southern Finance Association's annual meeting in 1975. He has graciously made his findings available to me. Any errors of interpretation are, of course, my responsibility.

31. Pettway (1978) analyzed the average cumulative residuals for seven large failed banks (including Franklin) and came to a similar conclusion regarding the efficiency of capital markets for bank stocks.

# Chapter 7

# *The Demise of Other Large U.S. Banks*

## 7.1 Introduction

There have been relatively few large bank failures in U.S. history. However, nine of the ten largest failures (unadjusted for inflation and the increased use of banking services) have occurred since 1970 (see Table 7.1, a reproduction of Table 1.6). The largest bank failure, Franklin National, was studied in detail in the previous chapter. The purpose of this chapter is to examine: (1) the demise of the second and third largest de

*Table 7.1*

Ten Largest U.S. Bank Failures
(as of December 31, 1977)

| Bank | Year Closed | Total Deposits ($ millions) |
|---|---|---|
| 1. Franklin National Bank, New York | 1974 | $1,445 |
| 2. United States National Bank, San Diego | 1973 | 932 |
| 3. Hamilton National Bank, Chattanooga | 1976 | 336 |
| 4. American Bank & Trust, New York | 1976 | 199 |
| 5. International City B&T, New Orleans | 1976 | 160 |
| 6. American City Bank & Trust, Milwaukee | 1975 | 145 |
| 7. American Bank & Trust, Orangeburg, S.C. | 1974 | 113 |
| 8. Northern Ohio Bank, Cleveland | 1975 | 95 |
| 9. Public Bank, Detroit | 1966 | 93 |
| 10. Sharpstown State Bank, Texas* | 1971 | 67 |

*Indicates a deposit payoff, other are deposit assumptions. Total deposits are in nominal dollars.

*Sources: Annual Report of the FDIC* (various issues) and FDIC Press Releases (various issues).

198

jure bank failures, USNB of San Diego and Hamilton National Bank of Chattanooga, respectively, and (2) the emergency merger of Security National Bank of Long Island with Chemical Bank of New York. Although Security National was an economic failure, its demise did not enter the official failure record because the bank was not declared insolvent. Instead Security was purchased before it failed for $40 million by Chemical. Except for this technicality, Security, with $1.3 billion in deposits, is (unofficially) the second largest bank failure in U.S. history. In this chapter, Security is referred to as a bank failure (de facto), although it officially (de jure) is not one.

The collapse of these three financial institutions is reviewed chronologically beginning with the most recent one, Hamilton National (February 16, 1976). Next, the emergency merger of Security (January 19, 1975) is considered, and finally the C. Arnholt Smith/USNB disaster (October 18, 1973) is analyzed.

## 7.2 HAMILTON NATIONAL BANK OF CHATTANOOGA

On June 31, 1975, Hamilton National Bank is the 195th largest bank in the U.S. with total assets of $461.3 million. At 4:00 P.M. on February 16, 1976, a Monday, Hamilton became the third largest bank failure in U.S. history. Prior to its downfall, Hamilton was the largest, oldest, and most prestigious bank in Chattanooga and the lead bank of Hamilton Bancshares, Inc., a holding company with interests in Tennessee and Georgia. By the end of that third week in February, the holding company and three of its nonbank subsidiaries (Hamilton Mortgage Corp., Hamilton Financial Services, Inc., and Hamilton Factors, Inc.) filed voluntary petitions for court protection under Federal bankruptcy laws.

Hamilton National Bank was declared insolvent by the Comptroller of the Currency. According to his affidavit, "The poor condition of Hamilton National was directly attributable to the large number of real estate loans originated or acquired from Hamilton Mortgage Corporation." The extent of this involvement is indicated by the fact that 87 percent of the bank's questionable loans were acquired from the mortgage subsidiary. These real estate loans were the proximate cause of the bank's downfall. The loans mainly were speculative ones spread throughout the Southeast and especially in Atlanta. (Some fundamental changes in the bank's overall policies that occurred in the early 1970s and no doubt contributed to the bank's downfall are explored later in this chapter.)

The deposit liabilities of Hamilton National were assumed by First Tennessee National Bank (now First Tennessee Bank, N.A.), a newly chartered national bank affiliated with First Tennessee National Corporation, a billion-dollar-plus multibank holding company. First Tennessee was the highest bidder ($16,251,000) among three Tennessee holding companies interested in acquiring Hamilton. The sealed bids were submitted five mintues after the bank was closed, and by 6:30 P.M. of the same day the FDIC-arranged deposit assumption was approved by the Comptroller, the Fed, and the U.S. District Court. The T-accounts for this transaction are presented in Table 7.2. Note that the *market* value (not the book value) of the assets rejected by First Tennessee will deter-

*Table 7.2*

T-Accounts for Hamilton's Deposit Assumption

Hamilton National Bank
($ millions as of February 16, 1976)

| Assets | $412 | Deposits | $336 |
|---|---|---|---|
| | | Other liabilities | 49 |
| | | Capital | 27 |
| | $412 | | $412 |

First Tennessee National Bank
(millions of dollars)

| Cash | $ 24 | Deposits | $336 |
|---|---|---|---|
| Assumed Assets | 314 | Other liabilities | 49 |
| FDIC Gross | | Capital Notes* | 8 |
| Advance** | 71 | Equity Capital* | 16 |
| | $409 | | $409 |

FDIC
(marginal T-Accounts, millions of dollars)

| Rejected Assets | $ 98 | Owed to FDIC | |
|---|---|---|---|
| (Book Value) | | Ins. Fund (Gross | |
| | | Advance)** | $ 71 |
| | | Equity Claims | 27 |
| | $ 98 | | $ 98 |

\* Purchased by the FDIC from FTNB's holding company.
\*\* Net Advance = gross advance less purchase premium = $71M-$16M=$55M.
*Source: FDIC News Release*, PR-10-76 (Feb. 16, 1976)

mine whether or not the FDIC incurs a loss as a result of the bank failure.

Since the date of the original transaction, The FDIC has repurchased about $56 million in assets that were first accepted by the assuming bank. Thus, the total pool of liquidation assets was approximately $154 million. As of June 30, 1977, the FDIC has recovered (through the liquidation of assets and the collection of interest, rent, and other income) about 42 percent of the total amount ($105 million) advanced by the agency. As of mid-year 1977, the *book* value of the remaining assets held by the FDIC (including charged-off loans) was $113.8 million. The FDIC's claims based upon cash advances (with allowed interest at 6.5 percent per annum) and costs of liquidation have priority over the claims of shareholders and other interested parties.

### 1. The Roots of Hamilton's Collapse

Prior to its downfall, Hamilton's examination reports and financial statements (see Chapters 2 and 5) indicate that the bank has financial difficulties. These data are, of course, only symptoms or reflections of the policies instituted by the bank's managerial team and its board of directors. Significant policy changes had taken place in the bank in the early 1970s. This section focuses upon these changes and the effects they have on the bank's performance.

Hamilton National was established in 1889.[1] The bank was managed very conservatively and possibly for that reason it made it through the Depression. During the 1920s, the bank did not have a significant risk exposure in real estate. Ironically, it was an overexposure to speculative real estate ventures in the 1970s that precipitated the bank's demise—a fatalistic twist on Santayana's adage about learning from past mistakes.

During the 1970s, Hamilton shifted from "go-slow" banking to "go-go" banking. The name of the parent holding company was changed from Hamilton National Associates to the chic Hamilton Bancshares Inc. The goal of the new holding company was to become, through expansion and diversification, a state-wide banking system. A former general vice-president of Citizens and Southern National Bank in Atlanta (one who was by-passed for the C&S presidency), N. Rountree Youmans, was brought in to manage the new company. His chic name went well with the holding company's chic name. Youmans, who took over in 1972, generated the desired expansion and diversification. By 1975, the holding company had picked up eight banks (the base was ten) and had diversified into (among other things) factoring, financing sales of mobile homes, and, into what proved to be the Achilles' heel, the mortgage business. The latter, Hamilton Mortgage Corporation, was formed in 1972 and based in Atlanta, not in Chattanooga. The construction business was unwittingly booming in Atlanta in those days and that is where Youmans had his connections. In addition, since Tennessee had a state usury law and Georgia didn't, out-of-state loans appeared to be more profitable (unadjusted for risk).

By mid-year 1974, Hamilton Mortgage had generated more than $200 million in real estate loans, the bulk of which were in the Atlanta area. Based upon an inspection that began on September 30, 1974, bank examiners from the Comptroller's office uncovered about $100 million of those loans in Hamilton National Bank. In addition, they found about $30 million in loans from other Hamilton Bancshares' affiliates in the bank. The sale of these loans from Hamilton's subsidiaries back to Hamilton National were in violation of Section 23(a) of the Federal Reserve Act. The Comptroller ordered that such sales be stopped.

In March 1975, Youmans was removed and J. E. Whitaker, the former chairman, took over the sinking ship. Under Youmans' leadership the price of a share of Hamilton Bancshares went from $10 to $20; a few months later the stock was worthless. Needless to say, those stockholders who got caught holding empty bags were soured on "go-go" backing. In many corporate business failures, the owners file suits seeking to recover their losses. Frequently, a class-action suit is filed by one owner on behalf of all stockholders, as was done in the Hamilton case (see *The American Banker,* February 25, 1976).

### 2. A Look at Some Symptoms

A convenient starting point for analyzing a bank's performance is at the bottom-line and one of the best bottom-line measures is OEOI, which has been used extensively in this book. Hamilton's operating efficiency (OEOI) for the years 1969–1975 is presented in Table 7.3 (see Tables 5.09–5.14 for comparisons).

The impact of Hamilton's bad real estate loans on its operating efficiency in 1975 is illustrated by the following two facts: (1) provision for loan losses increased from $772,000 to $6,785,000 and (2) interest and fees on loans declined from $31,793,000 to $20,139,000. If these two items had remained at their 1974 levels, Hamilton's 1975 OEOI would have been 82.60 percent. Clearly, the poor quality of these loans was the direct cause of Hamilton's poor bottom-line performance. On a relative basis, very few banks could absorb such a disaster and still remain solvent.

Let us now focus upon some of the more subtle changes that occurred in Hamilton's financial statements as it shifted from go-slow to go-go banking. In 1969, Hamilton had total assets of $302 million; by year-end

*Table 7.3*

Hamilton's Operating Efficiency
(1969 - 1975)

| Year | OEOI (%) | Percentage Change |
|------|----------|-------------------|
| 1969 | 78.00 | – – – |
| 1970 | 78.55 | 0.01 |
| 1971 | 76.04 | -3.19 |
| 1972 | 82.28 | 8.21 |
| 1973 | 84.65 | 2.95 |
| 1974 | 90.61 | 7.04 |
| 1975 | 132.07 | 45.76 |

*Source: Reports of Income,* 1969-1975, FDIC.

1974, its assets were $577 million, an increase of 91.06 percent (18.21 percent per annum). This growth was financed mainly with purchased funds. For example, from year-end 1972 to year-end 1974, time deposits increased from $94 million to $222 million and during this period Hamilton was very active in the Federal-funds market.

The four expense items that changed most significantly for Hamilton over the years 1969 to 1975 are presented in Table 7.4. For the year 1969, these four items used up 38.30 percent of Hamilton's total operating income; during 1974, they used up 68.37 percent. Then, in 1975, with the increase in provision for loan losses and the decline in loan revenue, they drained off 106.22 percent of operating income. Over the years 1972 to 1975, Hamilton spent $15 million on the purchase of Federal funds (including REPOS).

A return-on-equity (ROE) decomposition analysis for Hamilton is presented in Table 7.5 (see Table 5.18 for comparisons). Hamilton managed to increase its ROE by 52.86 percent from 1969 to 1973 as it improved both its profit margin (PM) and asset utilization (AU) and by employing greater leverage via its equity multiplier (EM). Over the same time period, Hamilton's return-on-assets (ROA) increased by 40 percent. During 1974, Hamilton's ROE declined as its PM dropped by 34.01 percent due to higher operating and interest expenses (see Table 7.4).[2] In 1975, the impact of the recession in the construction and real estate industries clobbered Hamilton because of its overexposure in those areas.[3] The recession, of course, affected the performance of all banks; however, only banks that were severely overextended got burnt.

## Table 7.4

Selected Expense Items for Hamilton National Bank, 1969-1975
($ thousands)

| Year | Interest on Deposits | Federal Funds Expenses* | Provision for Loan Losses | Other Expenses | Total Operating Expenses | Total Operating Income | Cols. 1 - 4 Cols. 6 |
|------|---------------------|-------------------------|---------------------------|----------------|--------------------------|------------------------|---------------------|
| 1969 | $ 2,935 | $ 832 | $ 389 | $2,040 | $12,618 | $16,177 | 38.30% |
| 1970 | 4,144 | 817 | 685 | 2,289 | 14,788 | 18,827 | 42.15 |
| 1971 | 5,267 | 774 | 421 | 2,352 | 15,993 | 21,031 | 41.91 |
| 1972 | 6,349 | 1,580 | 478 | 2,894 | 18,997 | 23,089 | 48.94 |
| 1973 | 9,883 | 4,986 | 623 | 2,975 | 27,660 | 32,675 | 56.52 |
| 1974 | 18,689 | 5,404 | 772 | 4,639 | 39,104 | 43,155 | 68.37 |
| 1975 | 17,704 | 3,030 | 6,785 | 6,035 | 41,748 | 31,610 | 106.22 |

*Includes securities sold under agreement to repurchase (REPOS).
Source: Reports of Income, 1969-1975, FDIC.

*Table 7.5*

Hamilton National Bank: Return-on-Equity Analysis

| Year | ROE (%) | ROA (%) | PM (%) | AU (%) | EM (Ratio) |
|------|---------|---------|--------|--------|------------|
| 1975 | -30.70  | 1.71    | -25.80 | 6.63   | 17.94      |
| 1974 | 10.33   | 0.61    | 8.18   | 7.47   | 16.91      |
| 1973 | 13.88   | 0.84    | 12.44  | 6.72   | 16.59      |
| 1972 | 12.39   | 0.74    | 14.03  | 5.31   | 16.64      |
| 1971 | 12.18   | 0.75    | 13.72  | 5.47   | 16.23      |
| 1970 | 11.05   | 0.71    | 12.70  | 5.57   | 15.62      |
| 1969 | 9.08    | 0.60    | 11.24  | 5.34   | 15.12      |

ROE = PM x AU x EM and ROA = PM x AU for all figures stated in ratio form. See Table 5.18 for comparison with failed- and non-failed bank data.
*Source: Reports of Condition and Income,* 1969-1975, FDIC.

### 3. Summary and Conclusions

The failure of Hamilton National Bank of Chattanooga was due directly to the illegal channeling of speculative (risky) real estate loans from Hamilton Mortgage Corporation back to Hamilton National. The impact of these risky loans on the bank's loan portfolio was realized in 1975 following the 1974 recession. Heavy loan losses and nonaccruing loan revenues devastated the bank. In the Comptroller's judgment, the bank could not survive and it was declared insolvent. While the overextended real estate loan portfolio was the proximate cause of Hamilton's downfall, the fundamental cause of the bank's demise was a deliberate shift in bank policy from "go-slow" to "go-go" banking. Under the old "conservative" regime, Hamilton probably would not have been caught in such a risky position. The hard lesson of the 1970s is that go-go banking is not always leisure suits and windfall profits; sometimes it is losing your shareholders' quiana shirts and windfall losses—"bye-bye" banking.

## 7.3 SECURITY NATIONAL BANK OF LONG ISLAND: OUR NATION'S LARGEST EMERGENCY BANK CONSOLIDATION

On January 19, 1975, the financially troubled Security National Bank of Long Island (Security) was acquired by Chemical Bank of New York for $40 million. The Security-Chemical emergency merger has the distinction of being the biggest bank consolidation in U.S. history. As of December 31, 1974, Security was the 68th largest bank in the U.S. with total deposits of $1.3 billion. Bank regulators had been concerned that, if Security failed shortly after the closing of Franklin National Bank of New York (October 8, 1974), confidence in the banking system would have been impaired. Consequently, the banking authorities did not permit Security to fail with all the fanfare that a billion-dollar banking organization would normally generate. Security was, so to speak, swept under the failure rug.

This section focuses upon analyses of Security's stock-price movements and financial statements prior to its collapse. The major purpose is to determine what balance-sheet and income-statement figures, if any, could have been arrayed in an early-warning system to spot Security's financial difficulties. Potential indicators are formed from the bank's balance sheets and income statements for the period December 1969 to December 1974. These variables are compared with the average performance of a control group of 49 large U.S. banks. The comparisons are based upon both single-variable and multiple-variable tests.

### 1. Security: A Glamour Stock?

At one time, Security National Bank was considered to be "a glamour stock among investors and analysts."[4] During January of 1971, Security's stock was selling for about $40 per share; on January 13, 1975, six days before its emergency merger with Chemical National Bank, Security traded (over the counter) at $4 per share. In less than four years, its price had declined by ninety percent. On balance, this decline was a steady one and not a sudden drop off. For example, during January of 1972, Security sold for about $34 per share; during January of 1973, its price was $30 per share; and during January of 1974, the price was $14 per share.

For the period January 1971 to December 1974, Security's stock prices and, for comparison purposes, Moody's stock-price averages for (1) New York City banks, (2) Banks Outside New York City, and (3) Banks-Combined (NYC Banks and Out-of-Town Banks) are presented in Table 7.6. These data indicate that for the period January 1971 to January 1974 Security's stock price *declined* by about 55 percent while Moody's three averages *increased* in the 35–42 percent range. During 1974, with the impact of the USNB and Franklin failures and the REIT crisis providing significant adverse publicity for the banking industry, Security's stock price and Moody's averages declined by 71 percent and 30–43 percent, respectively. The largest decline in the price of Security's stock oc-

*Table 7.6*

Bank Stock Prices: Security and Moody's Averages

| Date | Security | | Moody's Averages | | |
| | | | New York | Outside | |
| | Low | High | City | NYC | Combined |
|---|---|---|---|---|---|
| January 1971 | 39.50 | 40.25 | 171.84 | 107.24 | 135.52 |
| July 1971 | 37.50 | 38.25 | 163.27 | 105.09 | 130.49 |
| January 1972 | 34.25 | 35.00 | 188.39 | 112.86 | 146.02 |
| July 1972 | 30.75 | 31.25 | 222.61 | 142.32 | 177.54 |
| January 1973 | 30.12 | 30.62 | 240.95 | 140.47 | 184.83 |
| July 1973 | 17.12 | 17.62 | 259.44 | 142.53 | 194.11 |
| January 1974 | 17.50 | 18.00 | 244.59 | 145.21 | 189.23 |
| July 1974 | 12.25 | 12.75 | 182.75 | 89.10 | 130.75 |
| December 1974 | 4.75 | 5.50 | 170.86 | 82.95 | 121.85 |
| Change: Jan. 1971-Dec. 1974 | -34.75 | -34.75 | -0.98 | -24.29 | -13.67 |
| Percent | -87.98 | -86.34 | -0.57 | -22.65 | -10.09 |
| Change: Jan. 1971-Jan. 1974 | -22.00 | -22.00 | 72.75 | 37.97 | 53.71 |
| Percent | -55.70 | -54.66 | 42.34 | 35.41 | 39.63 |
| Change: Jan. 1974-Dec. 1974 | -12.75 | -12.75 | -73.73 | -62.26 | -67.38 |
| Percent | -72.86 | -70.83 | -30.14 | -42.88 | -35.61 |

*Sources: Bank and Quotation Record* and *Moody's Bank and Finance Manual.*

curred over the six-month period January 1973 to July 1973 when its price dropped by 13 points (43.2 percent) from 30 to 17. In contrast, for the same period, Moody's averages increased by 2–19 points. On balance, for most of the period 1971–1974, Security's stock price was declining while Moody's averages were increasing.

The data in Tables 6.22 and 7.6 suggest that, in general, the market for large banks' equity securities is reasonably efficient and that, in particular, the market was emitting early-warning signals regarding Security's impending collapse. Pettway (1978) has conducted a much more rigorous test of the "efficient-market hypothesis" with respect to banks with actively-traded equity issues. Using a methodology similar to the one employed by Altman (1975) in his analysis of Franklin's residuals (described in Chapter 6), Pettway develops and tests a "market screen" as a potential early-warning mechanism. Six large commercial banks that have failed since 1972 or that have been reorganized to avoid failure since 1972 (e.g., Security) are analyzed. Using two heuristic filters (a runs test and a t-test), Pettway finds substantial lead times with respect to alternative critical dates (e.g., the date the banks were added to the FDIC's problem-bank list) for most of the six banks.[5] For Security, Pettway reports problem-bank-list lead time of 163 weeks using the runs test and 170 weeks using the t-test. Recall that Security was added to the FDIC's problem-bank list based upon the Comptroller's examination that began on June 24, 1974 (see Table 3.4) and that it was merged with Chemical on January 19, 1975. Pettway's findings suggest that the market was emitting early-warning signals as early as the summer of 1971, three and one-half years before Security's demise. Looking at the data in Table 7.6 (or in Table 6.22), the summer of 1971 appears to be a bit premature as an early-warning date. However, by July 1972 (compared to January 1971) Security's stock price has dropped by 25 percent from $40 per share to $30 per share. Over the same time period, Moody's "Combined" bank average increased by 31 percent. Thus, a crude analysis of Security's stock price data suggests an early-warning signal two and one-half years before the bank's collapse.

To summarize, there is evidence indicating that the market place was aware of Security's financial difficulties and that it transmitted this information into investors' perceptions of the bank's stock price and required rate of return. A scientific test of the efficient-market hypothesis suggests a three and one-half year early-warning signal for Security relative to its emergency merger.

## 2. Identification of Security as a "Problem Bank"

As a nationally chartered bank, Security was subject to the examination and supervision of the Office of the Comptroller of the Currency. To evaluate its insurance risk, the FDIC receives the examination reports of national and state-member banks from the Comptroller and the Federal Reserve, respectively. Based upon the Comptroller's examination of October 23, 1973, Security's management was rated "unsatisfactory" by the FDIC.[6] This meant that Security's management was of "generally inferior ability or character, or (one) which may be definitely losing ground." Despite this unsatisfactory managerial rating, Security was not listed as a problem bank by the FDIC's Division of Bank Supervision. However, based upon the Comptroller's examination of June 24, 1974, Security was classified by the FDIC as a "serious-problem" bank (i.e., a bank which threatens ultimately to involve the FDIC in a financial outlay unless drastic changes occur).

Interestingly, the FDIC's summary examination ratings for these October and June dates were almost identical.[7] At about the time Security was added to the FDIC's problem-bank list (recall that there is a lag between when an exam begins and when the bank is placed on the list), a noted bank analyst, Harry Keefe (speaking at an FDIC conference in November, 1974), indicated that Security had serious financial difficulties. Frank Wille, then Chairman of the FDIC, inquired if Security was on the FDIC's problem list. Security *may* have been added to the list at that moment.

As established in Chapter 3, a bank's volume of substandard loans relative to its capital and reserves is the most important *examination* variable separating problem banks from nonproblem banks. Security's volume of substandard loans increased from $27 million in September 1970 to $105 million by June 1974. The biggest jump was a $38 million increase that occurred between the January and October 1973 exams.

Security's problem loans (like Hamilton's) mainly were connected with its real estate loan portfolio. These loans were showing a high delinquency rate as a result of the recession in the construction industry and future loan losses were expected to be heavy. In addition, as indicated by the management ratings discussed above, Security had managerial problems. These two factors probably would have created a crisis of confidence in the bank.

The banking authorities decided to seek a merger partner for the ailing bank without financial assistance from the FDIC if possible. Chemical Bank (among others) was interested and a negotiated price for Security was reached the weekend prior to January 19, 1975. Since the banking authorities considered the situation to be an "emergency," the Fed ruled that the anticompetitive effects of the acquisition would be outweighed by the public benefits derived by eliminating the crisis.

Unlike the Franklin and USNB collapses, Security's weaknesses were not known publicly until about one week before its emergency consolidation. Prior to its crisis merger, Security's most potentially adverse publicity occurred in April of 1974 and focused upon its attempts to recover damages sustained in connection with some loans made by its April 7, 1972, acquisition, Royal National Bank of New York.[8] The basis of Security's claim was that Royal had exceeded its legal lending limit to several affiliated borrowers. Except for this report, Security's coverage in the financial press was either neutral or favorable, e.g., "Bank Sponsors Hockey and Basketball Clinic in New York," *The American Banker* (August 30, 1973).

### 3. New York City: A Nice Place to Visit but Don't Try to Branch There from Long Island

Before changes in New York state law permitted their entry into New York City, Franklin National Bank and Security National Bank were the two largest banks located on Long Island. Many analysts believe that Franklin's move into New York City was a fatal one. Mike Merkin, a former vice-chairman of Franklin, sarcastically stated, "What business had Roth [Arthur Roth, chairman of Franklin when it started branching into the city in 1964] coming to New York? He didn't even know the way to "21" [Rose (1974), p. 121]." Apparently Security's managers didn't know the way to "21" either.

On April 7, 1972, Security (then with $1.1 billion in deposits) acquired the $257.9 million-deposit Royal National Bank of New York. The Comptroller's approval stated that ". . . the resulting bank will emerge as a particularly *aggressive* competitor in the business of firms based in the metropolitan area with loan requirements up to $5 million whose executives perfer to deal with a bank's senior management" (emphasis mine).[9] Aggressive banks such as Security and Franklin have found the banking environment in the Big Apple to be laced with a deadly poison—known in the business world as insolvency.

### 4. Evidence of Security's Demise from Its Financial Statements

This section focuses upon Security's financial characteristics relative to a control group of 49 large U.S. banks. The control group is the same group employed in Chapter 6 for Franklin's outlier tests. When the control group for Franklin's analyses was selected, Security was one of the 50 largest banks in the U.S. Hence, it was included in the control group. It was a relatively easy task to delete Security from the control group and to compare its data with the 49-bank control group. Since Security failed on January 19, 1975, the year-end 1974 data do not provide enough lead time to justify early-warning consideration, even on an *ex post* basis. Accordingly, evidence from the years 1969–1973 will be emphasized. By year-end 1974, Security's data were so bad that it was trivial to conclude that the bank had financial difficulties.

Let us again begin with the operating efficiency measure, OEOI. These data are presented in Table 7.7. They indicate a steady deterioration in Security's OEOI since 1969. By 1973, Security's OEOI was significantly different from the control group's OEOI. Only one bank had a higher OEOI (95.28 percent). From year-end 1972 to year-end 1973, Security's total operating expenses (including interest) increased by $37 million, a 38 percent increase. Over the next year, the increase was $68 million, a 50 percent increase, with $54 million of the total increase ac-

Franklin's Arthur Roth Trying to Find '21'

EIGHTH ILLUSTRATION

counted for by provision for loan losses. During 1973, the bulk of the $37 million increase in expenses was related to the cost of money, that is, interest on deposits increased by about $16.5 million and expenditures on Federal funds increased by about $13 million. Over the years 1972– 1974, Security's total operating income was $113 million, $145 million,

*Table 7.7*

Security's Operating Efficiency, 1969-1974

| | | OEOI* (%) | |
|---|---|---|---|
| Year | Security | Average Control Bank Mean | Standard Deviation |
| 1969 | 81.68 | 78.20 | 5.43 |
| 1970 | 83.06 | 79.47 | 5.33 |
| 1971 | 84.54 | 80.97 | 5.83 |
| 1972 | 86.41 | 82.00 | 6.13 |
| 1973 | 93.52 | 84.73 | 5.05 |
| 1974 | 129.10 | 87.69 | 5.18 |

*OEOI = Total operating expense as a percentage of total operating income.
*Source: Reports of Income,* 1969-1974, FDIC.

and $156 million, respectively. The year before its collapse Security's loan revenue did not drop off substantially as Hamilton National's did. The impact of the recession, of course, had a greater effect upon Hamilton's loan portfolio than it did on Security's loan portfolio. Security's interest and fees on loans for the years 1972–1974 were $79 million, $114 million, and $129 million, respectively.

Five measures of Security's overall banking performance for the years 1969–1974 are presented in Table 7.8. The five variables, which were defined earlier, are OIA, OEA, NOA, NIA, and NIK. The outlier tests for these five variables indicate that Security was not adversely atypical until 1973. In that year, Security was an outlier with respect to OIA, OEA, and NIK. During 1973, Security earned $7.98 per $100 of assets, but spent $7.46 per $100 of assets. The comparable figures for the average control bank were $6.38 and $5.43, respectively. Regarding NIK, Security was returning $7.19 per $100 of capital (down) $7.05 from 1971) compared to $10.83 for the average control bank. By year-end 1974, Security was an outlier with respect to all five variables (individually).

The data for a multiple-variable outlier test of Security's financial soundness are presented in Table 7.9. The chi-square scores for the tests are presented in Table 7.10.[10] The model is the seven-variable one first discussed in Chapter 5.

Security was an outlier or close to being one in each of the six years. However, except for 1974, it is difficult to interpret Security's atypical-

## Table 7.8

### Security National Bank: Five Measures of Overall Banking Performance

| Variable | 1969 Security | 1969 Average Control Bank | 1970 Security | 1970 Average Control Bank | 1971 Security | 1971 Average Control Bank | 1972 Security | 1972 Average Control Bank | 1973 Security | 1973 Average Control Bank | 1974 Security | 1974 Average Control Bank |
|---|---|---|---|---|---|---|---|---|---|---|---|---|
| OIA | 6.22 | 5.88 (0.72) | 6.11 | 6.06 (0.75) | 5.52 | 5.51 (0.71) | 5.19 | 5.19 (0.72) | 7.98 | 6.35 (0.52) | 9.11 | 7.74 (0.77) |
| OEA | 5.08 | 4.61 (0.72) | 5.07 | 4.83 (0.74) | 4.67 | 4.47 (0.73) | 4.49 | 4.27 (0.75) | 7.46 | 5.38 (0.57) | 11.77 | 6.80 (0.92) |
| NOA | 1.14 | 1.27 (0.30) | 1.03 | 1.23 (0.32) | 0.85 | 1.03 (0.29) | 0.71 | 0.92 (0.29) | 0.52 | 0.97 (0.32) | -2.66 | 0.94 (0.39) |
| NIA | 0.84 | 0.76 (0.16) | 0.91 | 0.79 (0.19) | 0.84 | 0.78 (0.20) | 0.64 | 0.71 (0.18) | 0.51 | 0.72 (0.21) | -2.23 | 0.71 (0.24) |
| NIK | 11.93 | 10.45 (1.94) | 14.05 | 10.90 (1.94) | 14.24 | 10.67 (1.80) | 11.02 | 10.08 (1.85) | 7.19 | 10.83 (2.04) | -42.35 | 11.09 (2.89) |

Data (expressed as percentages are as of December 31 of the year indicated.
*Source: Reports of Income and Condition, 1969-1974,* FDIC.

*Table 7.9*

Security National Bank: Seven-Variable Profile for Outlier Test

| Variable | 1969 Security | 1969 Average Control Bank | 1970 Security | 1970 Average Control Bank | 1971 Security | 1971 Average Control Bank | 1972 Security | 1972 Average Control Bank | 1973 Security | 1973 Average Control Bank | 1974 Security | 1974 Average Control Bank |
|---|---|---|---|---|---|---|---|---|---|---|---|---|
| LRI | 73.1 | 71.5 (4.9) | 69.5 | 69.5 (5.6) | 62.3 | 64.6 (6.2) | 69.8 | 64.7 (7.2) | 78.7 | 69.7 (6.2) | 82.3 | 72.9 (5.8) |
| OEOI | 81.7 | 78.2 (5.4) | 83.1 | 79.5 (5.3) | 84.5 | 81.0 (5.8) | 86.4 | 82.0 (6.1) | 93.5 | 84.7 (5.1) | 129.1 | 87.7 (5.2) |
| USA | 10.9 | 7.0 (2.1) | 10.5 | 7.8 (3.0) | 11.1 | 7.5 (3.0) | 8.0 | 6.9 (3.1) | 7.8 | 5.6 (2.7) | 8.2 | 5.2 (2.3) |
| SLA | 18.7 | 10.0 (3.0) | 24.8 | 11.2 (3.8) | 22.8 | 11.7 (3.6) | 22.0 | 10.6 (3.1) | 7.3 | 9.7 (3.5) | 9.3 | 9.2 (3.8) |
| LA | 58.3 | 56.7 (5.1) | 50.3 | 53.4 (5.6) | 52.6 | 52.6 (6.0) | 54.8 | 54.7 (6.2) | 70.9 | 57.0 (5.8) | 65.9 | 57.1 (6.3) |
| NFA | -6.1 | -3.8 (2.9) | -5.4 | -3.3 (3.2) | -6.6 | -4.3 (3.5) | -11.5 | -4.8 (3.8) | -6.9 | -7.4 (5.1) | -11.1 | -5.9 (4.1) |
| KRA | 8.4 | 8.6 (1.3) | 7.6 | 8.5 (1.4) | 6.8 | 8.4 (1.6) | 6.7 | 8.0 (1.3) | 8.2 | 7.6 (1.4) | 8.2 | 7.4 (1.3) |

Data (expressed as percentages) are as of December 31 of the year indicated. Figures in parentheses are standard deviations. A negative value for NFA indicates a net indebtedness (sales minus purchases) the Federal-Funds market.

*Source: Reports of Income and Condition, 1969-1974, FDIC.*

*Table 7.10*

Security National Bank: Seven-Variable Outlier Tests

| Year | Chi-Square Score | Level of Significance (%) |
|---|---|---|
| 1969 | 14.00 | 5.12 |
| 1970 | 17.83 | 1.28 |
| 1971 | 12.65 | 8.10 |
| 1972 | 23.70 | 0.13 |
| 1973 | 9.69 | 20.66 |
| 1974 | 104.26 | 0.01 |

ness as an indicator of serious problem status. For example, in the years 1969 to 1972, Security's atypicalness was dominated by its substantial holding of municipal obligations (SLA), which were more than three standard deviations away from the control group's mean.[11] The financial profile also reveals at various times a heavy indebtedness to the Federal-funds market (NFA); a low capital ratio (KRA); heavy loan volume (LA) and loan-revenue concentration (LRI); and, as discussed above, poor operating efficiency (OEOI).

On balance, Security was a statistical outlier on the basis of this seven-variable model. However, *prior to 1974,* it is not obvious that Security should have been classified as a so-called problem bank. At best, the data indicate that Security was certainly atypical and that it had some adverse trends. While such a bank may not warrant classification as a problem institution, it should merit close attention as a *potential* problem bank.

Similar to the growth patterns exhibited by Franklin and Hamilton, Security expanded very rapidly prior to its downfall. Annual growth rates for Security's total assets, total loans, IPC demand deposits, IPC time deposits, total deposits, and total capital for the years 1970–1974 are presented in Table 7.11. For the first three years of this period, Security grew significantly faster than the average control bank. As of year-end 1969, Security's total assets and total deposits were $973 million and $788 million, respectively; by year-end 1972, the figures were $2,185 million and $1,713 million, respectively. The three-year growth rates were 124 percent and 117 percent, respectively. Such rapid expansion is difficult to manage efficiently even by top quality personnel. The problem becomes even more complicated when top management is rated "FAIR," as Security's executives were during these critical years.

Table 7.11

Security National Bank: Rates of Growth, 1970-1974

| Variable | 1970 Security | 1970 Average Control Bank | 1971 Security | 1971 Average Control Bank | 1972 Security | 1972 Average Control Bank | 1973 Security | 1973 Average Control Bank | 1974 Security | 1974 Average Control Bank |
|---|---|---|---|---|---|---|---|---|---|---|
| Assets | 19.3 | 8.2 (7.5) | 21.9 | 10.6 (9.8) | 54.4 | 15.2 (7.6) | -16.9 | 14.9 (8.5) | -5.6 | 10.4 (9.7) |
| Loans | 3.0 | 1.9 (8.5) | 27.4 | 8.8 (8.8) | 60.9 | 19.9 (10.4) | 7.4 | 19.9 (9.5) | -12.2 | 7.5 (5.7) |
| Demand Deposits (IPC) | 3.5 | 0.9 (7.0) | 22.9 | 4.2 (8.0) | 55.8 | 14.6 (6.7) | -5.0 | 3.1 (8.4) | -18.0 | 1.8 (6.4) |
| Time Deposits (IPC) | 20.4 | 57.2 (65.8) | 11.8 | 17.1 (19.6) | 90.0 | 22.1 (22.6) | 18.5 | 31.1 (32.0) | -30.7 | 29.5 (26.1) |
| Total Deposits | 22.8 | 11.1 (6.2) | 21.7 | 10.9 (7.6) | 45.3 | 13.4 (7.3) | -12.6 | 10.0 (8.9) | -10.9 | 11.6 (10.2) |
| Capital | 9.6 | 7.4 (7.1) | 11.2 | 10.3 (8.7) | 51.9 | 11.4 (10.3) | 1.0 | 6.8 (5.3) | -29.5 | 7.5 (5.7) |

Rates of growth computed on an annual basis (December - December). Figures in parentheses are standard deviations.
Source: Reports of Condition, 1969-1974, FDIC.

The spurt growth year for Security was 1972. IPC time deposits increased by 90 percent, loans by 61 percent, IPC demand deposits by 56 percent, assets by 54 percent, capital by 52 percent, and total deposits by 45 percent. During 1973, Security began to contract as total assets declined by 17 percent and total deposits by 13 percent; however, its loans and IPC time deposits continued to expand. Finally, during 1974, all expansion stopped and all six of the variables listed in Table 7.11 declined, led by IPC time deposits which dropped off by 31 percent. Recall that from May until October of 1974 Franklin's financial difficulties were in the news almost continuously. The fact that Security did not experience greater deposit runoffs suggests that perhaps its financial difficulties were not widely known (or if they were known, uninsured depositors were confident that the bank would not be paid off if it failed).[12]

## 5. Summary and Conclusions

As the Comptroller predicted back in 1972, Security did emerge as an aggressive competitor in the metropolitan New York area. Unfortunately, the bank was *too* aggressive and the management team could not effectively handle the rapid expansion. The proximate cause of Security's downfall was an overextended real estate loan portfolio. However, like Hamilton, Security was poorly managed. The bank had embarked upon an aggressive expansionary program that was responsible for its *vulnerability*. Thus, the fundamental cause of Security's demise can be traced to a deliberate shift to a more aggressive banking posture, which for lack of a better term has been referred to as "go-go" banking. Go-go banking has been characterized by rapid expansion into new markets, aggressive liability management, and willingness to speculate, especially with real estate and construction loans. The major beneficiary of Security's go-go banking was Chemical Bank of New York, which for the bargain price of $40 million got over $1 billion in deposits and 86 banking offices.[13] As a result of the consolidation, the public interest may have been served in the short run because the "emergency situation" perceived by the banking authorities was eliminated; however, in the long run, the adverse effects of decreased competition and increased banking concentration may outweigh those short-run benefits. Finally, *prior to 1974,* there was only weak evidence from Security's financial statements regarding *clear* early-warning signals of the impending collapse. There was, however, enough "smoke" from adverse trends, poor management ratings, outlier characteristics, and changing bank policies to warrant a close investigation for the "fire."

## 7.4 UNITED STATES NATIONAL BANK OF SAN DIEGO: THE SECOND LARGEST FAILURE IN U.S. BANKING HISTORY

On October 18, 1973, the United States National Bank of San Diego (USNB) was declared insolvent by the Comptroller of the Currency. With approximately $1 billion in deposits, USNB's was, at the time, the largest bank failure in U.S. history. However, its reign as the all-time, heavyweight champion insolvent was short-lived; in slightly less than one year USNB was dethroned by Franklin National Bank of New York.

The purpose of this section is to study the circumstances surrounding USNB's collapse and to analyze its financial statements for any early-warning signals. The latter is accomplished by comparing USNB's performance with a group of 30 control banks located in California. The data analyzed are from balance sheets and income statements for the years 1969 to 1972. In addition, USNB is analyzed using a paired sample of problem and nonproblem banks for the 1969–1972 period.

### 1. Identification of USNB as a Problem Bank

On November 9, 1972, USNB was placed on the FDIC's problem-bank list in the "serious problem" category.[14] The Comptroller's examination, the so-called Martin I Report (based on the name of the national-bank examiner in charge of the examination), that led to this classification began on June 26, 1972, and was completed on September 12, 1972. The Martin I Report indicated that "classified" assets were 371 percent of capital and reserves, up from 25 percent of capital and reserves as of the September 13, 1971, examination report. Eighty-six percent of the classified assets and $113 million in standby letters of credit were obligations of business enterprises controlled by C. Arnhold Smith, his family, or business associates. The Martin I Report also indicated that Mr. Smith had knowingly withheld credit information relating to the classified loans to conceal their true quality.

Examinations prior to the Martin I Report apparently did not indicate that USNB should be classified as a problem bank. However, on April 16, 1969, *The Wall Street Journal* alleged that USNB was involved in financing some questionable deals in which private concerns controlled by C. Arnholt Smith (the President and Board Chairman of USNB), his friends, or his relatives reaped large and often quick profits on sales of land, small firms, and securities to Westgage-California Corporation, a conglomerate controlled by Mr. Smith. (On May 24, 1973, the Comptroller of the Currency forced Mr. Smith to resign the presidency and board chairmanship of USNB.) Even more indicting than the *Journal*'s report has been an investigation by the North American Newspaper Alliance (NANA), published in the Boston *Sunday Globe* (August 18, 1974), claiming that "all the facts exposed by the Martin examination had been known by the Comptroller's office for more than ten years."

On January 5, 1973, the Comptroller's office began another examination of USNB, the so-called Martin II Report. This examination, which was completed six months later, indicated that many of the Smith-related loans should now be classified as loss or doubtful, rather than substandard as in the Martin I Report. This deterioration in the perceived quality of USNB's loan portfolio (along with its liquidity implications) was a major concern to the FDIC. During June, as USNB's liquidity problem worsened, the Federal Reserve Bank of San Francisco was called upon to supply USNB's immediate liquidity needs. In July, as the banking authorities discussed USNB's fate, the Comptroller began a reexamination of USNB's portfolio of Smith-related loans. In late August, 1973, the Comptroller's office believed, based on the July examination, that USNB's insolvency was probable in the very near future and that there was little chance of a deposit assumption by another bank without the FDIC's financial assistance. Consequently, the FDIC began to consider seriously the alternative courses of action available under the Federal Deposit Insurance Act. The result was a deposit-assumption transaction with Crocker National Bank of San Francisco. Crocker's bid was $89.5 million, the highest of the three bids submitted. In return, Crocker received approximately $1,070 million in transferred deposit liabilities spread over 63 banking offices. The T-accounts describing the deposit-assumption transaction are presented in Table 7.12; important dates in USNB's collapse are presented in Table 7.13.

In less than fifteen months from its detection as a problem bank, USNB, the ninth largest bank in California and the 83rd largest bank in the United States (as of June 30, 1973), was closed. John J. Slocum (1974), then chief of the FDIC's division of liquidation, stated:

> The cause of [USNB's] closing was loss classifications exceeding capital, involving principally extensions to persons and entities controlled by or associated with the controlling stockholder and board chairman. This exhausted the capital structure and created a substantial deposit exposure.

### 2. Evidence from USNB's Financial Statements

This section focuses upon comparisons between USNB and (1) a control group of 30 California banks and (2) a paired sample of problem-nonproblem banks. Thus, USNB's performance is analyzed relative to

*Table 7.12*

T-Accounts for the USNB Deposit-Assumption Transaction

USNB
($ millions as of October 18, 1973)

| | | | |
|---|---|---|---|
| Assets | 1,266 | Deposits | 932 |
| Estimated "clean" | | | |
| assets | (854) | Capital and other | |
| | | Liabilities | 334 |
| Estimated "bad" | (412) | | |
| assets | | | |
| | | | |
| | 1,266 | | 1,266 |

CROCKER NATIONAL BANK
(marginal T-account, $ millions)

| | | | |
|---|---|---|---|
| USNB's clean assets* | 854 | Deposits | 923 |
| FDIC gross cash advance | 216 | Liabilities | 147 |
| Net advance | (126) | | |
| Premium paid to FDIC | (90) | | |
| | | | |
| | 1,070 | | 1,070 |

FDIC**
(marginal T-account, $ millions)

| | | | |
|---|---|---|---|
| Rejected assets | | Gross advance | 216 |
| (book values) | 412 | Other claims | 196 |
| | | | |
| | 412 | | 412 |

*Crocker had the privilege of returning any assets that turn out to be Smith-related and also was entitled to an errors-and-omissions clause.
**As of March 11, 1974, the FDIC's estimate of its eventual loss in the USNB receivership is $48.3 million.

other problem banks and relative to two alternative groups of nonproblem (control) banks.

The California control group consists of the 30 largest branch banks in California (as of June 30, 1973), excluding such outliers as Bank of America and foreign-controlled banks. Since statewide branching is so prevalent in California, the state was selected as the relevant geographic area from which to choose the control group. Moreover, using Califor-

*Table 7.13*

Important Dates in the USNB Story

| Date | Event |
|---|---|
| April 16, 1969 | *The Wall Street Journal* alleges that USNB is involved in financing some questionable deals in which private concerns controlled by C. Arnholt Smith (the President and Board Chairman of USNB), his friends, or his relatives reaped large and often quick profits on sales of land, small firms, and securities to Westgate-California Corporation, a conglomerate controlled by Mr. Smith. |
| December 11, 1970 | USNB's management is rated "Satisfactory" by examiner-in-charge Rogers; classified assets are 20.4 percent of capital and reserves. |
| September 13, 1971 | USNB's management is rated "Satisfactory" by examiner-in-charge Butler; classified assets are 25.3 percent of capital and reserves. |
| June 26, 1972 | Martin I Examination begins. |
| September 12, 1972 | Martin I Report is completed. USNB's management is rated "Poor"; classified assets are 371 percent of capital and reserves. |
| November 9, 1972 | USNB is placed on the FDIC's problem-bank list as a "serious problem" bank. |
| January 5, 1973 | Martin II examination begins. |
| May 24, 1973 | The Comptroller of the Currency forces C. Arnholt Smith to resign the presidency and board chairmanship of USNB. |
| June, 1973 | Martin II Report is completed. Many of the Smith-related loans are reclassified as loss or doubtful, rather than as substandard in the Martin I Report. The Federal Reserve Bank of San Francisco is called upon to supply USNB's immediate liquidity needs. |
| July, 1973 | The Comptroller's office begins a reexamination of USNB's portofolio of Smith-related loans and the three Federal banking agencies huddle to discuss USNB's fate, focusing upon the possibility of a deposit assumption *without* the FDIC's assistance. |
| August, 1973 | Based on the July examination, the Comptroller's office believes that USNB's insolvency is probable in the very near future and that there is little chance of a deposit assumption without the FDIC's financial assistance. |
| October 18, 1973 | USNB is closed by the Comptroller of the Currency and, with the FDIC's financial assistance, USNB's deposits and "clean" assets are assumed by Crocker National Bank of San Francisco. |
| August 18, 1974 | An investigation by the North American Newspaper Alliance, published in the *Boston Sunday Globe*, claims that "all the facts exposed by the Martin examination had been known by the Comptroller's office for more than ten years." |

nia as the relevant area has the advantage of controlling for state economic (e.g., demand factors) and banking (e.g., branching laws) variables.

The characteristics of the California control group in terms of asset size and number of banking offices are presented in Table 7.14. As of June 30, 1973, the average California control bank had total assets of $1,494 million spread over approximately 65 banking offices. The corresponding figures for USNB were $1,142 million and 63 banking offices. In terms of total resources, the largest bank in the control group had $10,530 million in total assets while the smallest bank had total resources of $100 million. In terms of number of banking offices, the most populous institution had 486 offices while the least populous bank had only three offices. The median-sized bank in the control group had approximately $175 million in total assets and approximately 16 banking offices. These two characteristics have right-skewed distributions.

Outlier tests are employed to identify the financial characteristics which distinguish USNB from the California control banks described above. These characteristics, mainly in the form of financial ratios, are derived from year-end balance sheets and income statements for the years 1969–1972. The statistical tests are designed to determine if USNB was an "outlier" in its California peer group. Since USNB was placed on the FDIC's problem-bank list on November 9, 1972 (it was closed on October 18, 1973), three (four) of the financial statements are preproblem (prefailure) observations.

In terms of size and number of banking offices, USNB was not a typical problem bank. It was a $1 billion institution with 63 banking offices. In contrast, the typical problem bank tends to be a unit bank with approximately thirty million dollars in total assets.[15] In addition, the average problem bank tends to be located in a small town or an agricultural area. The "country" nature of the average problem bank is indicated by the fact that in 1972, for example, loans to farmers accounted for approximately twenty percent of the typical problem bank's loan portfolio. In contrast, the corresponding figure for USNB was only 7.2 percent.

Since USNB was not a typical problem bank, comparisons between USNB and the paired sample of problem-nonproblem banks must be interpreted carefully. The structural differences between USNB and the typical problem bank were the major reason why the California control group was employed. The problem-bank group to be analyzed consists of 109 insured commercial banks (110 including USNB) identified as problem banks by the FDIC during 1972 (90 banks) and the first few months of 1973 (20 banks). Each problem bank was matched with a nonproblem (control) bank. The matching characteristics employed in selecting banks for the control group were: (1) geographic market area,

*Table 7.14*

Asset Size and Number of Banking Offices of the
California Control Banks, June 30, 1973

| Total Assets*<br>($ millions) | Frequency | Relative Frequency |
|---|---|---|
| 100 - 199 | 16 | .53 |
| 200 - 499 | 5 | .17 |
| 500 - 1,499 | 3 | .10 |
| 1,500 - 4,999 | 2 | .07 |
| 5,000 - 7,999 | 3 | .10 |
| More than 8,000 | 1 | .03 |
| Total | 30 | 1.00 |
| Mean $(\overline{X})$ | | $1,494 million |
| Standard Deviation (s) | | $2,792 million |
| Median (Md) | | $ 175 million |
| USNB | | $1,142 million |
| Coefficient of Variation $[v = s/(\overline{X})]$ | | 1.87 |
| Coefficient of Skewness $[k = 3(X\text{-}Md)/s]$ | | 1.42 |

| Number of Banking**<br>Offices | Frequency | Relative Frequency |
|---|---|---|
| 3 - 5 | 4 | .13 |
| 6 - 10 | 7 | .25 |
| 11 - 15 | 4 | .13 |
| 16 - 20 | 3 | .10 |
| 21 - 30 | 4 | .13 |
| 31 - 100 | 4 | .13 |
| 101 - 400 | 3 | .10 |
| More than 400 | 1 | .03 |
| Total | 30 | 1.00 |
| Mean $(\overline{X})$ | | 65 offices |
| Standard Deviation (s) | | 121 offices |
| Median (Md) | | 16 offices |
| USNB | | 63 offices |
| Coefficient of Variation $[v = s/(\underline{X})]$ | | 1.86 |
| Coefficient of Skewness $[k = 3(\overline{X} - Md)/s]$ | | 1.22 |

*As of December 31, 1973, there were 703 insured commercial banks (5.1 percent of the population of 13,733) with total deposits greater than $100 million.

**As of December 31, 1973, there were 9,297 insured commercial banks (67.7 percent of the population of 13,733) with only one banking office (i.e., unit banks).

(2) total deposits, (3) number of banking offices, and (4) Federal Reserve membership status. Data for these two groups (with USNB a member of the problem group) are analyzed to determine if USNB was more similar to the average problem bank or the average nonproblem bank. Year-end financial statements for the period 1969–1972 were scrutinized. The 1969–1971 data are preproblem observations.

### 3. Outlier Tests and Findings: USNB vs. the California Control Group

On a single-variable basis, 149 variables were screened for each of the years 1969–1972 for USNB and the 30 California control banks.[16] The tests compared USNB's variables with the means and standard deviations of the variables for the average control bank. Using a mean-plus-or-minus two-standard deviations test, only three variables were outliers in *each* of the years. The first variable was the ratio of deposits of states and political subdivisions to total deposits. On average, for the period 1969 to 1972, USNB derived 19.3 percent of its deposits from this source compared to 7.3 percent for the average California control bank.[17] The overwhelming majority of these deposits were in the form of time-and-savings deposits. The significance of this finding for identification of future problem banks is not obvious. However, a possible explanation for the phenomenon may have been C. Arnholt Smith's reputation as "Mr. San Diego of the Century" and hence his ability to attract the deposits of state and local governments to USNB.[18]

The second variable was the ratio of "customers' liability to this bank on acceptances outstanding" to total assets.[19] These "acceptances" are simply drafts or bills of exchange (i.e., orders to pay). On average, for the sample period, USNB held 2.1 percent of its assets in the form of these "acceptances" compared to 0.3 percent of the average California control bank. For USNB, the average dollar volume of these acceptances amounted to approximately $15 million. Since USNB had accepted these drafts or bills of exchange, it was obligated to pay them whether or not the customers kept their promises to supply the money before the instruments matured. In addition to these acceptances, USNB held about $113 million in so-called "standby" letters of credit, most of which were obligations of Smith-related business enterprises and were improperly booked and thus not s ubject to bank examiners' scrutinization.[20] The third variable was the ratio of "acceptances executed by or for account of this bank and outstanding" to total liabilities. Except for minor discrepancies, this variable was simply the bookkeeping counterpart of the previously described variable.

Let us now focus upon some of the variables that were less-distant outliers, but which had greater economic meaning for USNB's perfor-

*Table 7.15*

USNB's Operating Efficiency, 1969 - 1972

| Year | Average California Control Bank | | USNB |
|------|------|------|------|
| 1969 | 82.2 | (6.6) | 90.5 |
| 1970 | 83.3 | (7.3) | 90.5 |
| 1971 | 85.8 | (6.8) | 92.7 |
| 1972 | 85.8 | (7.6) | 101.2 |
| Average | 84.3 | (7.1) | 93.7 |

Figures in parentheses are standard deviations.
*Source: Reports of Income,* 1969–1972, FDIC.

mance. Consider first the ratio of total operating expense to total operating income (OEOI). The data for USNB and the average California control bank are presented in Table 7.15. These data indicate that USNB was relatively inefficient compared to the average California control bank. However, the most significant difference did not appear until 1972—after USNB already had been identified as a problem bank. Examination of the sources-and-uses-of-revenue data indicate that these two uses of revenue imposed a relatively heavier financial drain on USNB's operating income, namely, net occupancy for bank premises and interest on other borrowed money.[21] The data for these expense items are presented in Tables 7.16 and 7.17, respectively.

Over the period 1969 to 1972, USNB's net occupancy expense was roughly double that of the average California control bank. USNB's main office was located in the plush Westgate Plaza in San Diego, perhaps reflecting expense-preference behavior on the part of C. Arnholt Smith.[22] In addition, especially during 1969 and 1970, USNB in-

*Table 7.16*

USNB's Net Occupancy Expense as a Percentage of Total Operating Income

| Year | Average California Control Bank | | USNB |
|------|------|------|------|
| 1969 | 4.4 | (1.7) | 7.6 |
| 1970 | 4.5 | (1.6) | 8.2 |
| 1971 | 4.8 | (1.7) | 8.6 |
| 1972 | 4.8 | (2.0) | 8.1 |
| Average | 4.6 | (1.8) | 8.1 |

Figures in parentheses are standard deviations.
*Source: Reports of Income,* 1969–1972, FDIC.

*Table 7.17*

USNB's Interest on Other Borrowed Money
as a Percentage of Total Operating Income

| Year | Average California Control Bank | | USNB |
|------|------|------|------|
| 1969 | 0.5 | (1.0) | 4.7 |
| 1970 | 0.7 | (1.4) | 4.5 |
| 1971 | 0.2 | (0.6) | 1.4 |
| 1972 | 0.2 | (0.6) | 1.1 |
| Average | 0.4 | (0.9) | 2.9 |

Figures in parentheses are standard deviations.
*Source: Reports of Income,* 1969-1972, FDIC.

curred substantially higher interest payments on other borrowed money. Over the next two years, however, this drain on revenue was reduced significantly. In addition, during this period, USNB was a net debtor to the Federal-funds market. For example, during 1969, USNB spent 5.1 percent of its total operating income on purchases of Federal funds compared to 2.4 percent (standard deviation=3.0) for the average California control bank. In contrast, USNB generated only 0.2 percent of its revenue through the sale of Federal funds compared to 2.7 percent (standard deviation=2.7) for the average California control bank.

The loans-to-capital measure of adequate bank capital is presented in Table 7.18. The numerator of this ratio is total loans and discounts while the denominator is total capital accounts plus reserves for bad debt losses

*Table 7.18*

USNB's Ratio of Total Loans to Total Capital Plus Reserves

| Year | Average California Control Bank | | USNB |
|------|------|------|------|
| 1969 | 7.3 | (1.4) | 7.4 |
| 1970 | 7.4 | (1.6) | 8.1 |
| 1971 | 7.7 | (2.0) | 8.3 |
| 1972 | 8.0 | (2.0) | 7.2 |
| Average | 7.6 | (1.8) | 7.7 |

Figures in parentheses are standard deviations.
*Source: Reports of Income,* 1969–1972, FDIC.

Table 7.19

USNB's Return on Assets and Capital

| Year | Net Income as a Percentage of Total Assets (NIA) | | | Net Income as a Percentage of Total Capital (NIK) | | |
|---|---|---|---|---|---|---|
| | Average California Control Bank | | USNB | Average California Control Bank | | USNB |
| 1969 | 0.71 | (0.23) | 0.35 | 10.2 | (3.6) | 5.7 |
| 1970 | 0.73 | (0.31) | 0.37 | 10.6 | (3.6) | 6.8 |
| 1971 | 0.71 | (0.26) | 0.52 | 10.8 | (3.4) | 9.3 |
| 1972 | 0.67 | (0.32) | 0.46 | 10.3 | (4.0) | 7.5 |
| Average | 0.71 | (0.28) | 0.43 | 10.5 | (3.7) | 7.3 |

Figures in parentheses are standard deviations.
*Source: Reports of Income,* 1969–1972, FDIC.

on loans.[23] In the past, this ratio has been employed by the Comptroller of the Currency as a preliminary indicator of a nationally chartered bank's capital adequacy. It is clear that USNB's loan-volume (not loan-quality) measure of "capital adequacy" was quite similar to that of the average California control bank. Only after the fact did it become known that, in the estimation of the Comptroller's office (in 1972 and 1973), a significant number of these loans were of dubious quality. To test for loan quality, the ratio of net loan losses to total loans was used. However, the ratios gave no indication of USNB's poor loan quality. For example, in 1972, USNB's ratio was 0.42 percent compared to 0.79 percent for the California control group.

Two measures of USNB's profitability, NIA and NIK, are presented in Table 7.19. While USNB was less profitable than the average control bank over the four-year period, its NIA and NIK did improve over the years 1969 to 1971, until dropping off in 1972. On average, USNB was less profitable than about 68 percent of the California control banks.

Like Franklin, Hamilton, and Security, USNB grew rapidly in the years preceeding its demise. As of December 31, 1969, USNB had total *domestic* deposits of $424 million; by June 30, 1973, these deposits had more than doubled to $873 million. USNB's rates of growth of assets, deposits, and capital are presented in Table 7.20. On average, USNB grew only slightly faster than the average California control bank. However, the growth patterns of the variables were such that, except for 1972, USNB experienced both absolute and relative declines in its capital-asset and capital-deposit ratios.

*Table 7.20*
USNB's Rates of Growth, 1970 - 1972

| Year | Assets Control | | USNB | Deposits Control | | USNB | | Capital Control | | USNB |
|---|---|---|---|---|---|---|---|---|---|---|
| 1970 | 12.5 | (9.6)* | 11.3 | 15.3 | (10.1) | 18.8 | 6.6 | (6.0) | 3.7 |
| 1971 | 18.3 | (12.3) | 23.6 | 17.7 | (11.7) | 25.5 | 14.9 | (18.0) | 12.1 |
| 1972 | 16.9 | (14.1) | 34.8 | 18.5 | (15.7) | 31.4 | 12.9 | (10.5) | 45.6 |
| Average | 15.9 | (12.0) | 23.2 | 17.1 | (15.4) | 25.2 | 11.4 | (11.5) | 20.5 |

Figures in parentheses are standard deviations.
*Source: Reports of Condition and Income, 1969-1972, FDIC.*

### 4. USNB vs. the Paired Problem-Nonproblem Bank Sample

The findings reported in this section are based upon the following ten variables:

| Category | Variable |
|---|---|
| 1. Liquidity | 1. (Cash + U.S. Treasury Sec.)/Assets |
| 2. Loan Volume | 2. Loans/Assets |
| 3. Loan Quality | 3. Provision for Loan Losses/ Oper. Expense |
| 4. Capital Adequacy | 4. Loans/(Capital + Reserves) |
| 5. Operating Efficiency | 5. Operating Expense/ Operating Income |
| 6. Sources of Income (as a % of Total Income) | 6a. Interest and Fees on Loans |
| | b. Interest from U.S. Treas. Securities |
| | c. Interest on State & Local Obligations |
| 7. Uses of Income (as a % of Total Income) | 7a. Interest Paid on Deposits |
| | b. Other Expenses |

Data for these ten variables for the sample banks are presented in tables 7.21 and 7.22. The group means (see Table 7.21) and group dispersion matrices were found to be unequal in each of the four years. The inequality of the variance-covariance matrices requires that a quadratic discriminant function be used for classification purposes. In reclassifying the sample banks (i.e., replicating examiners ratings), about 75 percent of the banks were identified correctly in 1972.

In each of the years, USNB was assigned to the problem-bank group, meaning that its ten-variable profile (see Table 7.22) was more similar to the average problem bank than the average nonproblem bank. USNB's

## Table 7.21

Means and Standard Deviations of a Ten-Variable Profile for the Problem and Nonproblem (Control) Banks[a]

| Variables | 1969 Problem | 1969 Control | 1970 Problem | 1970 Control | 1971 Problem | 1971 Control | 1972 Problem | 1972 Control |
|---|---|---|---|---|---|---|---|---|
| Cash + U.S. Treasury Sec./Assets | 29.9 (11.5) | 30.3 (11.3) | 27.8 (10.7) | 30.1 (11.0) | 25.5* (9.5) | 28.7* (11.7) | 24.3 (8.1) | 26.9 (10.8) |
| Loans/Assets | 53.9* (11.1) | 49.3* (10.2) | 55.4* (9.6) | 48.9* (11.0) | 56.9* (9.1) | 47.8* (11.5) | 56.0* (9.8) | 47.8* (11.5) |
| Provisions for Loan Losses/Loans | 3.9 (4.7) | 3.2 (4.2) | 4.4* (4.9) | 2.8 (3.2) | 5.3* (5.2) | 2.8* (3.9) | 7.9* (8.6) | 2.5* (3.4) |
| Loans/Capital + Reserve | 648.3* (199.7) | 564.5* (182.6) | 692.2* (196.1) | 562.5* (184.6) | 768.9* (244.6) | 562.4* (185.3) | 838.6* (240.6) | 577.5* (188.5) |
| Operating Expense/Operating Income | 83.9* (10.9) | 78.5* (10.1) | 85.5* (8.7) | 78.6* (9.4) | 89.3* (11.1) | 81.8* (9.5) | 94.1* (15.2) | 82.4* (9.3) |
| Sources of Revenue (as a % of revenue) Loans | 64.7* (12.7) | 59.3* (10.1) | 65.8* (11.1) | 59.2* (10.5) | 68.8* (8.9) | 59.9* (11.1) | 69.8* (8.3) | 59.6* (11.6) |
| U.S. Treasury Securities | 15.7 (11.1) | 17.7 (10.9) | 13.7 (9.6) | 16.2 (10.5) | 12.1* (7.6) | 15.5* (10.7) | 10.4* (6.3) | 14.5* (10.7) |

229

## Table 7.21 (Cont.)

Means and Standard Deviations of a Ten-Variable Profile for the Problem and Nonproblem (Control) Banks[a]

| Variables | 1969 | | 1970 | | 1971 | | 1972 | |
|---|---|---|---|---|---|---|---|---|
| | Problem | Control | Problem | Control | Problem | Control | Problem | Control |
| State & Local Obligations | 3.8* | 5.4* | 4.6* | 6.3* | 5.0* | 7.1* | 4.9* | 7.3* |
| | (3.9) | (4.5) | (4.3) | (4.8) | (4.2) | (5.7) | (4.6) | (5.8) |
| Uses of Revenue (as a % of revenue) | | | | | | | | |
| Interest Paid on Deposits | 31.0 | 31.5 | 32.8 | 32.3 | 35.9 | 34.9 | 37.5 | 35.4 |
| | (9.8) | (11.0) | (8.6) | (10.2) | (9.2) | (10.1) | (8.0) | (10.5) |
| Other Expenses | 15.8* | 12.8* | 16.0* | 13.0* | 16.3* | 13.2* | 16.4* | 13.7* |
| | (7.1) | (4.7) | (6.7) | (5.1) | (6.4) | (5.4) | (5.2) | (5.2) |

[a] Variables measured as parentheses.
* Significantly different on a univariate basis at the 5 percent level. Figures in parentheses are standard deviations. The number of banks in each group is 110, except in 1972 when the number is 103.

*Table 7.22*

USNB's Ten Variable Profile

| Variables | 1969 | 1970 | 1971 | 1972 |
|---|---|---|---|---|
| Cash + U.S. Treasury Sec./Assets | 24.5 | 21.3 | 20.7 | 20.7 |
| Loans/Assets | 54.1 | 53.1 | 54.4 | 49.1 |
| Provisions for Loan Losses/ | | | | |
| Oper. Expense | 0.8 | 1.1 | 2.7 | 6.7 |
| Loans/Capital + Reserve | 738.7 | 799.3 | 834.0 | 716.7 |
| Operating Expense/ | | | | |
| Operating Income | 90.5 | 90.5 | 92.7 | 101.2 |
| Sources of Revenue (as a % | | | | |
| of revenue) Loans | 70.6 | 70.1 | 68.7 | 66.9 |
| U.S. Treasury Securities | 9.6 | 8.4 | 6.2 | 3.8 |
| State & Local Obligations | 2.8 | 3.8 | 7.2 | 8.5 |
| Uses of Revenue (as a % of revenue) | | | | |
| Interest Paid on Deposits | 34.3 | 34.5 | 40.4 | 42.9 |
| Other Expenses | 9.1 | 9.7 | 9.8 | 11.2 |

*Source:* Public Files and *Reports of Income and Condtion,* Federal Deposit Insurance Corporation. Variables are expressed as percentages.

probability of membership in the problem group for each year (1969–1972) was 52.47 percent, 75.61 percent, 78.24 percent, and 87.87 percent, respectively. Banks usually do not develop financial difficulties overnight; they tend to deteriorate gradually. USNB's data showed such a pattern: its data were more similar to the average future problem bank in 1969 and this similarity increased as the problem-identification date approached.

### 5. Failure-Prediction Results

Using the OEOI–IA linear failure-prediction models described in Chapter 5, USNB is predicted to have OEOI–IA characteristics more similar to the average failed bank than the average nonfailed bank. In this test, if a bank's Z-score is greater than zero, it is assigned to the failed-bank group. USNB's Z-scores for the first four years prior to failure are: 0.49 (1972), 0.48 (1971), 1.23 (1970), and 1.21 (1969). Thus, as early as midyear 1970 (the effective day for early-warning use of year-end 1969 data), USNB's accounting data are emitting early-warning signals. These findings are consistent with the problem-prediction results described in the previous section.

### 6. Market Information

Applying his market filter to USNB's stock-price data, Pettway (1978) finds problem-bank-list lead times of 45 weeks using his runs test and 33 weeks using his t-test. USNB was added to the FDIC's problem-bank list on November 9, 1972. Thus, by year-end 1971 at the earliest, USNB's market data are emitting early-warning signals. Since investors' expectations may be formed, at least in part, by their interpretation of a bank's accounting data, accounting early-warning signals generally are expected to lead market early-warning signals.

### 7. Summary Inference and Implication

Using the start of the Martin I examination (June 26, 1972) as the critical date for a meaningful early-warning signal, it must be concluded that there was some indication of USNB's impending collapse before that date. By December 31, 1972, the signals were clearer, but by then the examiners had already uncovered USNB's difficulties. Given the nature of these difficulties, exemplified by the fact that C. Arnholt Smith kept some of the bank's records at his personal residence to hide his manipulations from the banking authorities, it is perhaps surprising that any potential early-warning signals existed. USNB's demise was marked by two factors common to other *large* bank failures: (1) a rapid expansion and aggressive managerial policies in the years immediately preceding .failure and (2) a managerial situation characterized by a "one-man show."

## 7.5 SUMMARY AND CONCLUSIONS

This chapter has focused upon three banks that at one time held or were contenders for the all-time, heavyweight-champion, insolvent crown. Since their managers did not manifest either enough ineptitude and/or dishonesty, they did not produce "Rocky" scripts.

The root causes of bank failure can be traced to the quality and character of a banks' management. For example, regarding the USNB and Franklin failures, former Comptroller Smith stated, "U.S. National involved misuse of funds and other illegal activity and Franklin involved exceptional and extraordinarily inept management."[24] The failure of Hamilton National involved both of these factors; the main factor in Security Nation's downfall was simply poor management.

Two common factors in the failures of Franklin, Hamilton, Security, and USNB were (1) rapid expansion in the years preceding collapse and (2) concentration of power in the form of "one-man-show" leadership without adequate checks and balances. Franklin and Security were going to engulf the Big Apple; Hamilton was going to create a statewide banking system in Tennessee; and C. Arnholt Smith, "Mr. San Diego of the

Century," was going to use USNB to build a corporate empire for himself and his friends. The results speak for themselves.

Regarding early-warning signals, poorly-managed banks (e.g., Franklin) tend to generate stronger signals than dishonestly run institutions (e.g., USNB). The role of early-warning or surveillance systems is to attempt to identify *symptoms* of mismanagement and/or dishonesty. Of course, since the latter tends to be deliberately masked and therefore harder to uncover, there will always be a need for on-site bank inspections.

There are numerous lessons to be learned from the cases studied in this chapter and the previous one. First, for bank managers and boards of directors, significant changes in bank policies must be carefully analyzed and evaluated *before* being pursued. The management team should avoid trying to expand the bank beyond its capabilities. Size and growth should be secondary to the objectives of safety, efficiency, and profitability. Second, for the banking authorities and the Congress, the large bank failures and banking problems of the 1970s are not indicative of any *fundamental* weaknesses in the banking system. It would be a mistake to suggest otherwise and place *undue* restrictions on the system. Inequities and irregularities must be eliminated, but the system must not be strangled. The task of the bank regulators (in conjunction with the

Last National Nonproblem Bank & Trust

NINTH ILLUSTRATION

Congress) is to establish general guidelines, rules, and regulations to maintain public *confidence* in the banking system. Within such a framework, bankers should be permitted to shape their own destinies. Finally, for existing and would-be stockholders, *caveat emptor*.

## NOTES

1. For additional details about Hamilton's history and its collapse, see Milius (1976).

2. During 1974, the average insured commercial had ROE = 12.83 percent and ROA = 1.01 percent with PM = 13.56 percent, AU = 7.45 percent, and EM = 12.70. These figures were derived from the FDIC's *Bank Operating Statistics* (1974) using aggregate data. Note that the ROE identity holds only for individual bank data.

3. The ROE industry data for 1975 are: ROE = 11.07 percent, ROA = 0.86 percent, PM = 11.78 percent, AU = 7.30 percent, and EM = 12.87. Note the drop off in performance relative to 1974, see note 2 above.

4. *The Wall Street Journal* (January 13, 1975).

5. In a related study, Herzig-Marx (1977) concludes that bank-examination ratings and market-risk premiums contain basically the same information.

6. Security's net capital ratio (NCR, see Table 3.4) was estimated to be zero on the basis of this examination [i.e., its classified assets (loss + doubtful + substandard) were equal to its capital plus reserves for losses]. Based upon the previous exam (1-29-73), Security's NCR was 2.0.

7. The ratings vectors (see Chapter 3) were [6, 0, .4, U] in October and [6, 0, .6, U] in June. The previous ratings vector (from the January 29, 1973 exam) was [6, 2, .6, F]. The components of the ratings vector are [ACR, NCR, earnings-asset ratio, managerial rating].

8. "Security NB Seeking Recourse on Loans," *The American Banker* (April 10, 1974). Also in this article, Security issued a defense against criticism for lending to its auditors. It said the lending relationship was desirable and good business for the bank.

9. "Merger of Royal NB and Security National Allowed by Comptroller," *The American Banker* (April 7, 1972).

10. The construction and interpretation of a chi-square score is explained in the Appendix to Chapter 6.

11. During 1963, Security substantially reduced its tax-free municipals and shifted these funds into loans. Since deposits from state and political subdivisions declined by $226,564 during 1973, this portfolio shift probably was due to the fact that Security's pledging requirements had been reduced.

12. As of June 24, 1974, Security's total deposits were $1,419,878, of which 58 percent were estimated to be uninsured. By December 31, 1974, total deposits had dropped off only slightly to $1,333,966.

13. At the time of the acquisition, Security had 51 offices in Suffolk County, 20 in Nassau County, and 15 in New York City; Chemical had 13 offices in Suffolk, 16 in Nassau, and 145 in New York City.

14. Unless otherwise noted, many of the facts and figures used in this section are derived from former FDIC Chairman Wille's (1973) testimony before Congress on the USNB case.

15. The standard deviation corresponding to this 1972 figure is one hundred million dollars. The coefficient of variation (100/30) indicates a relatively large dispersion, and the nonnegativity asset constraint implies that the distribution is skewed to the right.

16. The number of categories of variables was considerably less than the total number of variables. For example, the capital-adequacy category alone had ten variables. Only single variable tests are reported here. See Sinkey (Spring 1975) for some multiple-variable tests.

17. By June 30, 1973, the figures were 28.9 percent and 7.9 percent, respectively. The standard deviation for the latter was 3.9 percent.

18. "How C. Arnholt Smith's Empire Came Apart," *Business Week* (October 27, 1973).

19. The numerator of this ratio is defined to include the liability to the reporting bank of its customers on drafts and bills of exchange which have been accepted by the reporting bank or by other banks for its account and which are outstanding, i.e., not held by the bank, on the date of the Condition Report. If held by the reporting bank, they should be reported as "Loans and discounts." In case a customer anticipates his liability to the bank on outstanding acceptances by paying the bank either the full amount of his liability or any part thereof in advance of the actual maturity of the acceptance, the bank should decrease the amount of the customers' liability on outstanding acceptances. If such funds are not received for immediate application to the reduction of the indebtedness to the bank or the receipt thereof does not immediately reduce or extinguish the indebtedness, then such funds held to meet acceptances must be reported as a demand-deposit item. The amount reported against this item should not include customers' liability on unused commercial and travelers' letters of credit issued under guaranty or against the deposit of security, i.e., not issued for money or its equivalent. *Instructions for the Preparation of Report of Condition on Form 64*, FDIC (1970), p. 9.

20. Effective September 15, 1974, all three Federal banking agencies adopted regulations governing the use of "standby" letters of credit (see FDIC News Release PR-18-74 dated August 9, 1974).

21. "Occupancy expense of bank premises, net" [report-of-income item 2(g)] represents the occupancy costs of banking premises whether owned by the bank, its consolidated building subsidiaries, or other consolidated subsidiaries. The item is calculated as "Gross occupancy expense" less "Rental income." Interest on other borrowed money" [report-of-income item(e)] includes interest and discount on bills payable, rediscounts, participation sales in pools of loans, and other instruments issued for the purpose of borrowing money other than federal funds purchased, securities sold under agreements to repurchase, sales of participations in pools of securities. For more detailed information of these items (and others) see *Instructions for the Preparation of Report of Income on Form 73*, FDIC (December, 1970).

22. See Edwards (1977) regarding expense-preference behavior in banking.

23. The loans-to-capital ratio [L/K] is the reciprocal of the capital-asset ratio [K/A] weighted by the loan-asset ratio [L/A]; that is, L/K = L/A[K/A]$^{-1}$. (I thank Paul Horovitz for this interpretation.) Note that this measure is very crude because it considers only the total volume of loans relative to capital; loan quality is ignored.

24. *The Wall Street Journal* (October 23, 1974).

Chapter 8

# *Commercial Banks and the REIT Debacle: A Three-Act Play (Comedic Tragedy)*

The safety of the bank requires it sternly to close its ears against the distress and piteous lamentations of its customers. It *must* refuse accommodations,—and just in proportion to its prosperity, must be the extent of its refusals. However, harsh the remedy, it is absolutely necessary; and if through an ill-judged pity or a false confidence in its own good fortune, this remedy is omitted, and accommodations are continued, the relief is only momentary; for the bank, if it continues to discount, must presently stop payment; and that stoppage not only puts a sudden period to its accommodations, but it involves the holders of its notes in the common misfortune.

Richard Hildreth
"The Received Theory of Banking"
*The History of Banks* (1837)

## 8.1 INTRODUCTION

Following the 1974 recession the "distress and piteous lamentations" of real estate investment trusts (REITs) were ringing in commercial bankers' ears. The bankers' ears *and* purse strings were not closed and the REITs were accommodated.

This chapter focuses upon the role commercial banks have played in the rise, the fall, and the rebound of the REIT industry. The story of the relationship can be viewed as a three-act play—one which has been a tragedy for the participants (the banks and the REITs) but a comedy to onlookers. Act One deals with the role that commercial-bank financing played in the rapid expansion of the REIT industry in the early 1970s. Act Two concentrates on the collapse of the REIT industry and the

The Accommodation Principle

The safety of the bank requires it sternly to close its ears against the distress and piteous lamentations of its customers. It must refuse accommodation . . .

TENTH ILLUSTRATION

scramble by the banks to keep a large part of the industry from going bankrupt. Act Three, which has yet to be completed, focuses upon the current state of the commercial bank-REIT debacle. The play is preceded by a primer on REITs.

## 8.2 WHAT IS AN REIT?

An REIT is simply another financial intermediary between surplus-spending units and deficit-spending units.[1] REITs channel funds from institutional and public investors into the real estate, mortgage, and construction markets. They supplement the more traditional sources of funds for these markets provided by commercial banks, thrift institutions, and life insurance companies. As of September 30, 1977, there were 219 REITs (or trusts) with total assets of $14.5 billion. The majority of REITs function as short-term construction and development trusts.

REITs, like mutual funds, were designed to expand the investment opportunities open to small savers. Unlike mutual funds, however, REITs are closed-end investment companies, as opposed to open-end investment companies (mutual funds). This simply means that trusts do not redeem shares on request as mutual funds do. A trust stockholder must sell his or her shares in the market to liquidate the investment. Like other stocks, the value (price) of an REIT share generally is determined by the trust's expected future earnings. The risk of the investment (i.e., the variability of the expected return, as measured by Beta for example) and the return largely will be determined by the quality of the REIT's management.

The modern REIT owes its existence to the Federal tax laws. When the corporate income tax rate increased significantly during World War II, real estate companies began lobbying to obtain the "pass-through" tax principle enjoyed by mutual funds. By 1960, the U.S. Congress passed such a law and, in 1961, the legislation (see *Internal Revenue Code*, Section 856-858) went into effect. Under the "pass-through" tax principle, an REIT is allowed a deduction for dividends paid to avoid double taxation of such income. In effect, net income distributed to REIT shareholders is exempt from Federal income taxes at the corporate level. (Shareholders' dividends are taxable, of course.) In addition, capital gains earned by a trust are not required to be distributed; but, if they are, they may be paid as capital gains and treated as such by shareholders. To qualify for the "pass-through" tax principle, an REIT must meet *(inter alia)* the following requirements: (1) asset holdings and income sources must be related primarily to real estate and (2) 90 percent or more of its annual net income must be distributed to shareholders as dividends.[2]

REITs are directed by trustees and administered by advisers. The trustees form the loan-and-investment policy-making body, while the advisers oversee daily operations and propose various investment projects to the trustees for their approval. The trustees, who are elected annually by the REIT's shareholders, usually have real estate, business, professional, or academic backgrounds. The advisers, who are under a negotiated contract with the trustees, mainly have financial backgrounds in mortgage banking, mortgage brokerage, real estate, finance, or insurance. In addition to providing financing for REITs, commercial banks frequently serve as REIT advisers.

In general, there are four types of REITs: (1) short-term mortgage trusts which finance the construction and development of housing, shopping centers, and office buildings; (2) long-term mortgage trusts which finance construction of apartments and commercial property; (3) equity trusts which invest in property ownership, where the major interest is gaining the rental income and possible appreciation of such properties as apartment buildings, shopping centers and office buildings, and (4) combination trusts which invest in one or more of the above areas. The last type is the most flexible since it enables trusts to modify their portfolio objectives with the changing real-estate market. Short-term construction and development loans are the most important investment category.

From 1961 to 1968, REITs sold about $350 million of securities to the public. As of 1968, there were about fifty trusts, most of which were relatively small and specialized in real property investments. At that time, only a few REITs concentrated on construction and development loans. With the tight money market and disintermediation of the 1969–1970 period, many savings and loan assocations and other mortgage-lending institutions curtailed or severely restricted their mortgage and real-estate investments. However, due to favorable stock market conditions, REITs were able to raise significant amounts of money through the sale of their equity securities and consequently their mortgage lending grew rapidly. At the start of 1969, total REIT assets were about $1 billion; by the end of 1973, they were approximately $20 billion. The size and growth of REIT total assets for the period of 1968–1977 are presented in Table 8.1.

As of mid-year 1977, REITs were located in every state in the Union and the total number of trusts was 219. As shown in Table 8.2, REIT

*Table 8.1*

Size and Growth of REIT Total Assets

| Year | Total Assets ($ billions) | Annual Percentage Growth |
|------|---------------------------|--------------------------|
| 1968 | 1.0 | — — |
| 69 | 2.0 | 100 |
| 70 | 4.7 | 135 |
| 71 | 8.1 | 72 |
| 72 | 14.2 | 75 |
| 73 | 20.2 | 42 |
| 74 | 21.0 | 4 |
| 75 | 19.2 | -9 |
| 76 | 16.5 | -15 |
| 77 II | 14.5 | -12* |

*Percentage decline for nine months.
Source: *REIT Statistics*, 1975-1977, and *REIT Fact Book, 1974*.

*Table 8.2*

Geographic Concentration of REIT Investments

Year-End 1974

| ($ millions) | | Percentage of All REIT Loans and Investments |
|---|---|---|
| Florida | $3,538.4 | 17.98% |
| Texas | 2,042.5 | 10.36% |
| California | 1,929.9 | 9.80% |
| Georgia | 1,115.6 | 5.69% |
| New York | 915.8 | 4.67% |
| TOTAL | $9,542.2 | 48.50% |

*Source: REIT Fact Book 1975, p. 42.*

investments are concentrated in five states: Florida, California, Texas, Georgia, and New York. These five states held 48.50 percent of all REIT loans and investments as of year-end 1974. Twenty-three trusts account for 42.3 percent of total REIT assets. However, the three-firm concentration ratio is only 9.12 percent. The three largest REITs are Continental Mortgage ($522.2 million), Corporate Property ($470.5 million), and Equitable Life ($394.4 million).[3]

## 8.3 ACT ONE: BANK FINANCING OF THE REIT EXPANSION

REITs obtain funds through the same channels used by other financial corporations, that is, the sale of securities and debentures, bank borrowing, and commercial paper. REITs, however, are subject to the IRS Code's preventing use of retained earnings as a source of funds. Since 1973, commercial banks have been the major supplier of funds to REITs through short-term credit lines, i.e., term loans of one- to three-year durations. The second most important source of funds is shareholders' equity. Other sources of funds include commercial paper, notes and debentures, and mortgages on property. By 1973, REITs were in the Eurodollar market. The REIT industry balance sheet as of June 30, 1977, is presented in Table 8.3. For comparison purposes, the industry balance sheet for three years earlier (June 30, 1974) is presented in Table 8.4.

*Table 8.3*

REIT Industry Balance Sheet
(June 30, 1977)

| Assets | ($ millions) | % | Liabilities + Equity | ($ millions) | % |
|---|---|---|---|---|---|
| First mortgages: | | | Commercial paper | 585.2 | 3.85 |
| Land and Development | $ 1,529.8 | 10.06 | Bank borrowings | 7,243.6 | 47.64 |
| Construction | 2,028.7 | 13.34 | Senior nonconvertible debt | 326.9 | 2.15 |
| Completed properties: | | | Sub. nonconvertible debt | 902.5 | 5.93 |
| 0-10 years | 951.7 | 6.26 | Convertible debt | 624.3 | 4.10 |
| 10+ years | 1,837.4 | 12.08 | Mortgages on property owned | 2,429.7 | 15.97 |
| Junior mortgages | 850.7 | 5.59 | Other liabilities | 346.8 | 2.28 |
| Loan loss allowance | (2,101.4) | (13.82) | Subtotal | 12,459.0 | 81.92 |
| Property owned | 9,126.6 | 60.01 | Shareholders' equity | 2,750.5 | 18.08 |
| Cash & other assets | 986.0 | 6.48 | | | |
| | $15,209.5 | 100.0 | | 15,209.5 | 100.0 |

*Source: REIT Statistics, 1977, II.*

242

*Table 8.4*

REIT Industry Balance Sheet
(June 30, 1974)

| Assets | ($ millions) | % | Liabilities + Equity | ($ millions) | % |
|---|---|---|---|---|---|
| First mortgages: | | | Commercial paper | $ 1,564.4 | 7.24 |
| Land loans | 988.3 | 4.57 | Bank term loans & | | |
| Development | 2,408.9 | 11.14 | revolving credits in use | 3,031.9 | 14.03 |
| Construction | 8,098.1 | 37.49 | Bank lines in use | 7,181.3 | 33.25 |
| Completed properties: | | | Senior nonconvertible debt | 356.5 | 1.65 |
| 0-10 years | 1,460.2 | 6.76 | Sub. nonconvertible debt | 1,052.7 | 4.87 |
| 10+ years | 1,827.4 | 8.46 | Convertible debt | 668.3 | 3.09 |
| Junior mortgages: | | | Mortgages on property owned | 1,551.4 | 7.18 |
| Land, devl., & construction | 339.9 | 1.57 | Other liabilities | 417.2 | 1.93 |
| Completed properties | 962.1 | 4.45 | Subtotal | $15,823.7 | 73.24 |
| Loan loss reserves | (246.6) | (1.14) | Shareholders' equity | 5,781.3 | 26.76 |
| Land leasebacks | 529.9 | 2.45 | | $21,605.0 | 100.0 |
| Property owned | 3,239.9 | 14.99 | | | |
| Cash & other assets | 1,999.7 | 9.26 | | | |
| | $21,605.0 | | | | |
| | | 100.00 | | | |

*Source: REIT Statistics, 1974: III*

A number of significant changes have occurred in the REIT industry balance sheet over the 1974–1977 period. On the asset side, five major changes took place. First, total assets declined by $6.4 billion (or 29.63 percent). Second, construction first mortgages declined by $6.1 billion (or 74.96 percent). Third, reserves for loan losses increased by $1.8 billion (or 751 percent). Fourth, property owned increased by $5.9 billion (or 182 percent). And fifth, REIT liquidity declined by $1.0 billion (or 51 percent). About 60 percent of the property owned by the REIT industry was acquired by or in lieu of foreclosures. These changes, of course, reflect the severe slump that occurred in the construction and real estate industries over this period.

On the liability side, four major changes occurred. First, use of commercial paper as a source of funds declined by about $1 billion. Access to the commercial-paper market is, of course, limited to the most credit-worthy businesses and, since the 1974 credit crunch, very few REITs have been rated as such. Second, while the total percentage of funds supplied by the commercial banking industry has remained the same (47 percent), the total dollar amount has declined by about $3 billion and the composition has changed. As of June 30, 1974, REITs had about $7 billion in bank credit lines in use, in addition to approximately three billion dollars in term loans or revolving credits in use. Three years later, total bank borrowings were only about $7 billion. Third, mortgages on property owned increased by $879 million. And fourth, shareholders' equity declined by slightly more than three billion dollars (a 52.43 percent decline). REIT shareholders and commercial banks (the major creditors to the REIT industry) have been the parties suffering the most financial damage from the collapse of the REIT industry.

The role that commercial banks have played in the expansion of the REIT industry is presented in Table 8.5. The figures for the years 1969–1971 include commercial paper. As of year-end 1972, commercial banks were supplying only 20.94 percent ($2.97 billion) of the total funds used by REITs. However, by year-end 1974, the percentage was 52.61 ($11.06 billion). Two and one-half years later, the figures were 47.60 percent and $7.24 billion.

In addition to providing the REIT industry with funds, commercial banks (mainly the largest ones) supply the industry with managerial resources in the form of adviserships. Recall that an adviser handles the daily operations of an REIT and recommends investment projects to the trustees. During the REIT "glory days," commercial banks were the major type of adviser affiliation. As of the fourth quarter of 1974, 39 commercial banks were REIT advisers with direct control over 32.2 percent of all REIT assets.[4]

Prior to 1973, commercial banks mainly supplied REITs with lines of credit. These lines mainly were used for three purposes: (1) to finance

*Table 8.5*

Commercial-Bank Financing of the REIT Industry

| Date | Funds Supplied (loans + credit lines) ($ billions) | % of Total Assets |
|------|------|------|
| 1968 IV | $ 0.09* | 8.74* |
| 1969 IV | 0.23* | 11.33* |
| 1970 IV | 0.80* | 16.91* |
| 1971 IV | 2.24* | 29.01* |
| 1972 IV | 2.97 | 20.94 |
| 1973 IV | 6.50 | 32.19 |
| 1974 IV | 11.06 | 52.61 |
| 1975 IV | 10.34 | 53.91 |
| 1976 IV | 8.47 | 51.18 |
| 1977 II | 7.24 | 47.60 |

*Indicates that commercial paper is included.
*Source: REIT Fact Book 1974* and *REIT Statistics,* 1975 I - 1977 II.

construction-and-development and other short-term mortgage loans; (2) as backup or reserve lines for commercial paper; and (3) to finance equity and long-term mortgage investments. The latter was employed to a lesser extent than the other two uses because of the greater risk of borrowing short and lending long.

As of year-end 1972, REIT bank lines in use were $2.4 billion. However, by December 31, 1973, lines in use had more than doubled to approximately $5.0 billion, equal to about one-half of the total lines available. As of the second quarter of 1974, REIT bank lines in use had peaked at $7.2 billion. At present, unused REIT credit lines are virtually nonexistent because they either have been drawn down or withdrawn by the banks.

As of year-end 1972, bank term loans to REITs were only about $500 million. However, by December 31, 1973, these loans had tripled and were $1.5 billion. Within the next twelve months, these loans more than tripled again as they totaled $5.3 billion. By year-end 1975, they were $8.3 billion. Bank term loans differ from bank lines of credit in that term loans are *formal* agreements which usually are callable prior to maturity if the customer fails to meet certain conditions. For example, such a condition might include a ceiling on an REIT's debt-equity ratio. REIT term loans usually were negotiated with more than one bank. Originally, such loans had maturities of five to seven years, but more recently, the maturities have been one to three years.

## 8.4 ACT TWO: THE COLLAPSE OF THE REIT INDUSTRY AND THE COMMERCIAL-BANK RESCUE

Over the period 1973 to 1974, the REIT industry's debt-equity ratio increased by 78 percent, from 1.8 to 3.2. This greater leverage was due to the substantial increase in the use of bank debt which rose from $3 billion (20.9 percent of total assets) to $11.1 billion (52.6 percent).[5] REITs turned toward commercial banks for funds because, as the economy and especially the construction industry slumped during 1974, the commercial-paper market, through which REITs had borrowed about $4 billion (as of year-end 1973) became very reluctant to accept REIT paper. Moody's rating service, which had evaluated the paper of many REITs, began to lower REIT ratings or to eliminate them completely. By the third quarter of 1974, REIT commercial paper in nine months had declined by $3 billion to $1 billion.

To prevent the REIT industry from going bankrupt, the banking system provided the liquidity for the orderly retirement of REIT commercial paper. The rescue operation was led by the ten largest banks, which had the most to lose, and was prodded along by the Federal Reserve, which did not want any more big banks in trouble. The vehicle for this rescue operation was the revolving-credit agreement. These "revolvers" were binding contractual agreements lasting from one to three years and locking all participatory banks into the same terms. Repaid principal was shared pro rata by all the banks so that no one was paid before another. Revolving-credit agreements are currently the most widely used credit arrangement between commercial banks and REITs. As shown in Table 8.6, nine major banks provided 51 percent of the $2.5 billion in credit negotiated by six troubled REITs.

During the REIT industry's commercial-paper crisis, some commercial banks were reluctant to help struggling REITs. For example, during the crisis 20 percent of the existing total bank lines of credit were canceled and some banks refused to participate in revolvers. However, the combined pressures of the REIT industry, major commercial banks, and the Federal Reserve forced some recalcitrant banks into participating in revolving-credit agreements.[6]

It is important to understand exactly what commercial banks have to lose as a result of REIT problems. Banks with loans to *troubled* REITs are experiencing three types of income loss. The first source of earnings reduction is loss of interest income. Most of the financial loss suffered by banks to date has been of this type. Troubled REITs are barely generating enough operating income to pay their *public* (subordinated) debtholders. Because the commercial bankers have been easily organized, they have been working closely with the troubled REITs trying to keep them afloat. These "workouts" have involved a restructuring of REIT

*Table 8.6*

Loans to Six Troubled REITs by Commercial Banks
($ millions as of Dec. 31, 1974)

| Bank | Chase Manhattan Mortgage & Realty Trust (41 banks) | Continental Mortgage Investors (83 banks) | First Mortgage Investors (100 banks) | Citizens & Southern Realty Investors (33 banks) | Builders Investment Group (49 banks) | Great American Mortgage Investors (71 banks) | Total |
|---|---|---|---|---|---|---|---|
| Chase Manhattan | 150.0 | 18.9 | 14.5 | 12.1 | 16.8 | 15.0 | 227.3 |
| Bankers Trust | 33.9 | 52.7 | 27.5 | 32.6 | 21.0 | 10.0 | 177.7 |
| First National of Chicago | 38.3 | 22.1 | 33.5 | 6.0 | 39.6 | 27.5 | 167.0 |
| First National City | 42.7 | | 28.5 | 24.1 | 28.0 | 23.2 | 146.5 |
| Continental Illinois Natl. | 43.9 | 28.3 | 33.5 | 18.1 | | 15.0 | 138.8 |
| Chemical | 27.7 | 42.7 | 34.8 | 12.1 | 7.0 | 10.0 | 134.3 |
| Manufacturers Hanover | 28.9 | 39.9 | 6.0 | 18.1 | 21.0 | | 113.9 |
| Bank of America | 27.7 | 10.5 | 8.0 | 18.1 | 21.0 | 25.0 | 110.3 |
| Morgan Guaranty | 27.7 | 16.8 | 5.0 | 24.1 | 8.4 | 10.0 | 92.0 |
| | | | | | | | |
| Total, nine banks | 420.8 | 231.9 | 191.3 | 165.3 | 162.8 | 135.7 | 1,307.8 |
| Other banks | 279.2 | 299.9 | 208.7 | 164.3 | 147.8 | 137.3 | 1,237.2 |
| | | | | | | | |
| TOTAL | 700.0 | 531.8 | 400.0 | 329.6 | 310.6 | 273.0 | 2,545.0 |

*Source: Fortune*, March 1975, p. 168.

bank debt (i.e., stretching maturities, reducing interest rates, relaxing financial requirements, and/or "swapping" debt for real assets). As a result of these agreements, the senior debt-holders (the banks) are receiving little or no interest while the junior debtholders are being paid interest in full. This situation has, of course, made bankers unhappy and they are attempting to impose tougher conditions on REITs and their public debtholders.[7]

The second source of income reduction is loss of principal. In general, the principal is threatened only if an REIT declares bankruptcy. Even then the banks, as senior creditors, have claims superior to holders of long-term subordinated debt, convertible debt, and equity. Moreover, most REIT loans are secured by real property which would be available for liquidation purposes. The reason banks are concerned about loss of principal is that some of them have REIT loans equal to or greater than their shareholders' equity. *Unexpected* loss of principal can lead to loss of income because such write-offs must be charged off against operating income (i.e., they are an operating expense). This is the type of loss that could produce the greatest source of income reduction. Over the past three years (1975–1977), banks have been writing off some REIT loans.

The third source of income reduction is greater potential loss because of REIT sponsorship. To protect their own reputations, some banks that sponsor an REIT may be tempted to be *too* generous with their financial assistance. For example (see Table 8.6), the largest REIT loan ($50 billion) was from Chase Manhattan Bank to its own trust. The increased risk exposure that common affiliation may produce is further illustrated by the First Wisconsin situation. In this case, First Wisconsin Mortgage Trust (an REIT) had to be bailed out by First Wisconsin Corporation (the parent holding company) and First Wisconsin National Bank (the major bank in FWC). On June 27, 1974, FWC agreed to (1) purchase loans involving losses of principal of approximately $4.5 million and (2) guarantee future losses of principal up to $5.5 million of its remaining loans. In addition, sponsorship may produce legal problems and expenses regarding alleged mismanagement of an REIT's assets, which also occurred in the First Wisconsin case.[8]

In the case of the bank-sponsored REITs, bankers are faced with a dilemma. That is, if a banking company does not come to the aid of its own REIT, the integrity of the company's name may suffer, not to mention its market value. Alternatively, if the banking company is too generous with its financial assistance, its earnings and hence its market value may be affected adversely. McConnell and Macias (1975), in a study for Keefe, Bruyette & Woods, Inc., claim that "the extent to which some bank holding companies have already gone to aid their REITs is far beyond the normal bounds of the traditionally conservative American

Banking Industry (p. i)." A bank-sponsored REIT can expect more assistance from its bank because (1) "family" problems usually are more worrisome than "nonfamily" problems and hence they get more attention and (2) a bank-sponsored REIT may have more opportunities for financial aid than a nonbank-sponsored one. Thus, banks that sponsor an REIT may be more susceptible to losses than banks that simply lend to REITs.

Among the 100 largest REITs, there are 39 bank-sponsored REITs. As of November 1975, 19 of these 39 banks had $127 million in loans to REITs, of which $18 million was to bank-sponsored REITs.[9] The REIT loan percentage of own to total ranged from 0.0 to 64.7 percent; the average was 27.0 percent.

In Table 8.7, total REIT loans by the ten largest U.S. banks are compared with their total loans outstanding (to measure concentration risk) and with their loan-loss reserves plus shareholders' equity (to measure insolvency risk). The data in the last column, showing REIT loans as a percentage of equity plus loan-loss reserves, are the most meaningful. On this basis, Bankers Trust (91.5 percent), First Chicago (88.1 percent), Chemical (86.6 percent), and Continental (79.5 percent) have the greatest risk exposure. The highest figure for the other six banks is 43.5 percent while the lowest is 27.0 percent. The four banks with greatest risk exposure also have the highest concentration of REIT loans in their loan portfolios (5–6 percent).

Amidst their REIT problems, the nation's largest banks also were threatened by the specter of New York City defaulting on its debt obligations. The combined REIT and New York City risk exposure of the six largest New York City banks is presented in Table 8.8. Risk is measured by combined NYC and REIT debt as a percentage of shareholder equity. If Bankers Trust and Chemical had to write off *all* of their NYC and REIT assets, a highly unlikely event, their equity capital would be wiped out. Assuming a ten percent charge-off, Chemical would lose 14.1 percent of its equity while Bankers Trust would lose 10.4 percent.[10]

## 8.5 ACT THREE: THE CURRENT STATE OF THE REIT-COMMERCIAL BANK DEBACLE

The final curtain on this comedic tragedy may not fall for another five to ten years. The plot in this final act has three dimensions: (1) the ability of bankers to arrange efficient "swaps" and to efficiently manage and unload the real properties they acquire; (2) the ability of the banks and the REITs to reach an agreement regarding the redemption of the subordinated debt held by the REITs; and (3) the state of the economy and, in particular, of the construction and real estate industries.

*Table 8.7*

REIT Risk Exposure of the Ten Largest U.S. Banks
(Dec. 31, 1974)

| Bank | Loans to REITs* (approximate) | Total Loans | Loans to REITs as a Percentage of: Valuation + Shareholders' Reserve | Equity |
|---|---|---|---|---|
| Bankers Trust | $600 | 4.9% | | 91.5% |
| First Chicago | 750 | 6.1 | | 88.1 |
| Chemical | 725 | 5.7 | | 86.6 |
| Continental Illinois | 700 | 5.5 | | 79.5 |
| Chase Manhattan | 725 | 2.6 | | 43.5 |
| Manufacturers Hanover | 375 | 2.4 | | 38.1 |
| Morgan | 400 | 2.8 | | 34.4 |
| Citibank | 750 | 2.1 | | 32.1 |
| BankAmerica | 550 | 1.8 | | 29.3 |
| Security Pacific | 175 | 1.9 | | 27.0 |

* $ millions. Except for the Morgan and Continental figures, the REIT loan amounts were approved by the respective banks.
*Source:* Drexel Burnham & Co.

*Table 8.8*

REIT and New York City Risk Exposure of the
Six Largest New York City Banks
($ millions, Sept. , 1974)

| Bank | NYC Bonds | MAC Bonds | REIT Loans | Total | Share-holders Equity | Risk (%) Ratio* |
|---|---|---|---|---|---|---|
| First National City | 175 | 171 | 750 | 1,096 | 2,390 | 45.9 |
| Chase Manhattan | 250 | 150 | 725 | 1,125 | 1,812 | 62.1 |
| Manufacturers Hanover | 175 | 107 | 375 | 657 | 1,077 | 61.0 |
| Morgan Guaranty | 150 | 68 | 400 | 618 | 1,269 | 48.7 |
| Chemical Bank | 225 | 110 | 718 | 1,053 | 746 | 141.1 |
| Bankers Trust | 75 | 71 | 600 | 746 | 718 | 103.9 |
| Average | 175 | 113 | 595 | 883 | 1,335 | 77.1 |

*Computed as "Total" column as a percentage of shareholder equity.
*Source: Congressional Record - House* (October 28, 1975), II 10347.

Beginning with the last dimension, a booming economy with moderate inflation would go a long way toward alleviating what ails both the REIT industry and banks with loans to troubled REITs. However, since the recovery from the 1974–1975 recession has been weaker than past recoveries, the prospects for a macroeconomic bail out do not appear bright. Although there have been some positive signs in the REIT industry's 1977 data (e.g., increased dividend payouts, greater investment and earnings opportunities, and new share offerings by a few REITs), its recovery has been about as sluggish and uncertain as the general economy. REIT industry data continues to be dominated by the troubled firms in the industry. Total industry assets ($14.5 billion as of 1977 III) are expected to continue shrinking into 1978 as some REITs swap loans and properties to repay bank debt.

The troubles that the REIT industry has experienced have been reflected by REIT stock prices. In 1974, REIT share prices declined more than those of any industry. In percentage points, eighteen of the twenty biggest losers on the New York Stock Exchange were REITs. The NAREIT share price index, which was started in January 1972 (=100), reached its peak at 103.32 in November of 1972.[11] By December 1974, it had reached its nadir at 16.87. As an indication of the "recovery" the industry has made since then, the index was 27.81 as of November 30, 1977. The January 31, 1978 index was 26.38.

Let us now focus upon the issue of REIT-bank "swaps." A swap is simply a forgiveness of debt in exchange for an asset. A hypothetical REIT-bank swap is illustrated in Table 8.9. In this example, the REIT's debt to the bank is eliminated for which the REIT gives to the bank an asset in the form of a mortgage or real property. The REIT is now a smaller entity. For the bank, the swap involves an exchange of one "bad" asset (the loan to the REIT) for another "bad" asset (the REIT's mortgage or property owned). In this example, the appraised value of the acquired asset is less than the value of the loan being canceled and the difference (called the "hit" in swap jargon) is charged off against the bank's loan-loss reserve.

The mechanics of arranging a swap go something like this. An REIT has some mortgages or properties (taken over from its borrowers) that it wants to unload. The REIT circulates this list of assets (usually with minimum asking prices) among its lender banks. The bankers review the swap list and, if any properties interest them, they inspect them and then bid on them. The bidding process requires the bank to estimate the future market values of the properties and the costs of maintaining the

*Table 8.9*

A Hypothetical REIT-Bank Swap: The Marginal T-Accounts

The Swamp & Desert Development Corp. (an REIT)

| Mortgage or Property Acquired | -$100M | Bank Debt | -$100M |
|---|---|---|---|
| | -$100M | | -$100M |

The Last National Bank

| REIT Loan | -$100M | Loan-loss reserve (the "hit") | -$10M |
|---|---|---|---|
| Mortgage or Property Acquired | $90M | | |
| | -$10M | | -$10M |

properties over some reasonable period of time. The bank's objective is to match the net proceeds from the sale of an acquired property (i.e., estimated market value minus carrying costs) with the amount of the discharged loan. Since the net proceeds usually are negative (a "hit"), the proper objective function is to minimize losses. One analyst has described a "successful swap" as one with a 17 percent "hit"; "hits" in the 20–25 percent range are said to be common occurrences.[12]

The swapping process and the reselling of acquired properties are costly and time consuming for the banks involved because, for the most part, they lack expertise in these areas. Consequently, many banks are turning to top real estate experts and other specialists for advice.[13] On balance, one has to question the wisdom of the entire swapping process. In many cases, it seems like the banks involved with troubled REITs are pouring "good money after bad." Be that as it may, the big banks have made swapping a major part of this REIT game plan. The goal of swapping is to salvage the bank's principal. The big banks have two motives for going the swap route. First, they want more control over the REIT situation and second, they think they can do a better loan-recovery job than the troubled REITs.

On the surface, swaps appear to be an ideal vehicle for REIT rehabilitation. However, since the banks are not interested in acquiring nonearning assets, swaps tend to strip troubled trusts of their *earning* assets. As a result, some REIT trustees have become concerned about their personal liability, if they permit a trust to be stripped.[14] The NAREIT estimates that over the period 1975 I to 1977 III more than $2 billion in REIT assets have been swapped with banks.

The last dimension of the third act focuses upon REIT redemption of publicly-held, *subordinated* debt. The fact that the debt is subordinated gives the banks (as senior creditors) veto power over any redemption plan. The bankers would appear to have three choices: (1) prohibit any redemption or refinancing; (2) allow a partial redemption (by cash and/or refinancing); and (3) permit the debt to be redeemed in full. The first and third courses of action are drastic measures the bankers probably will try to avoid. That is, prohibition more than likely would lead to bankruptcy and full redemption would ignore the bank's own interests. Thus, a middle course involving some form of partial redemption is most likely.

The schedule of future redemptions indicates the seriousness of the subordinated-debt problem. One of the most troubled REITs, Citizens and Southern Realty Investors, has a $29 million issue due in 1978. As of June 30, 1977, C&S Realty had $191 million in bank debt (78 percent of its total assets) and shareholders equity of −$14 million; its share price as of November 30, 1977 was 1.0.[15] The handling of C&S's redemption could set a precedence for future redemptions, which total $601.7 million over the years 1979–1982. The figures for the individual years are $135.1 million, $226.4 million, $51.1 million, and $189.1 million, respectively.[16] Tender offers, bankruptcy petitions, and other factors will modify these redemption figures, but the important point is that banks with loans to troubled REITs will have to make some difficult decisions regarding redemptions over the next few years.

## 8.6 ENCORE

The banking authorities and shareholders of banks with loans to troubled REITs will not be demanding a repetition of the commercial bank-REIT performance. The banks involved have been embarrassed by the whole REIT affair and their reputations as financial managers tarnished. They lent billions of dollars to REITs without carefully investigating what the trusts were going to do with the money. Since banks usually do not make direct loans in such a haphazard fashion, they should not have made indirect loans in such a manner. The banks and their shareholders have been and will be paying the price for this unwarranted and speculative expansion.

How could this REIT-bank fiasco have happened? Certainly, the worst recession since the Great Depression was a contributing factor. However, since estimating one's downside vulnerability (risk) is a fundamental part of financial analysis, the buck must stop at the desks of the banks' managers and directors. They simply made some bad decisions. This is obvious in retrospect. It is also obvious that the bankers overlooked and/or misjudged some basic economic considerations such as the ability of the economy to absorb such a large number of construction and development projects; the ability of the managers of the *infant* REIT industry (who in some cases were the bankers themselves since they were REIT advisers) to handle the rapid growth of the industry; and future building and energy costs. The bankers didn't do their homework and they got caught with their financial pants around their ankles—no wonder they are embarrassed.

Samuel Lefrak, the nation's largest builder and owner of apartment houses, sums up the REIT-bank situation this way:[17]

> Why didn't those usurers (i.e., the bankers) call me before? Now they're asking me questions about the guys they lent money to two years ago. Their properties are in trouble, so now they beg, "Sam, bail me out."

You can bet the bankers will talk to Sam before their next round of real-estate lending.

There are two lessons to be learned from the REIT difficulties of the 1970s. First, for the bankers, there is no substitute for sound credit management. And second, for the banking agencies, while identifying *symptoms* of poor credit management (i.e., bad loans) is important, it is more important to focus upon the policies and controls that produce such loans. The fact that the banking agencies appear to be moving in this direction is encouraging.

## NOTES

1. Before an acronym such as REIT or FDIC, the article *an* is used not *a*.

2. For the detailed requirements, see Sections 856–858 of the *Internal Revenue Code*.

3. On April 1, 1974, Continental asked for a halt in trading of its stock because it could not meet interest payments of $16.4 million and was defaulting on a $610 million revolving bank credit agreement. As of the third quarter of 1974, Continental had total assets of $823.3 million.

4. Not all trusts have advisers. Over the past few years, 20–40 percent of the total number of REITs have not had advisers. As of June 30, 1977, there were 87 REITs with no adviser, accounting for 34.2 percent (or $5.2 billion) of total industry assets.

5. By year-end 1976, the debt-equity ratio was 5.0, but this was due to the shrinkage of the equity base rather than to increased use of bank debt.

6. Equibank of Pittsburgh is an example of a bank that took a hard line but eventually was forced to soften its approach. See *Fortune* (March 1975), pp. 172–173.

7. For example, banks are attempting to get REITs to pledge assets as security for loans, see Carberry (1977).

8. For sponsored REITs, a potential conflict of interest arises because, although the trust and sponsor (e.g., bank) have for the most part separate and distinct shareholders (the Fed permits a holding company to own 5 percent of an REIT), the trust's and sponsor's managements overlap. As the First Wisconsin case illustrates, this potential conflict of interest can lead to litigation. A nonsponsored REIT is one that is independently managed.

9. These data were collected by Julia P. Gerdnic in a telephone survey of the 19 banks during November 1976.

10. During the first six months of 1976, Chemical Bank charged off $17 million of REIT loans.

11. NAREIT stands for the National Association of Real Estate Investment Trusts. The NAREIT index is based upon end of month prices of REITs whose shares are traded in the New York, American, and OTC markets. The figures presented in the text are from *REIT Statistics, 1977 II*.

12. See *Business Week* (October 11, 1976), pp. 53–56.

13. Ibid. and Foldessy (1976).

14. See Greer (1977) and his reference (p. 27) to the case of Investors Diversified Services.

15. *REIT Statistics, 1977 II*. See Table 8.6 for the composition of C&S's bank debt as of year-end 1974.

16. Tabulations by the *Realty Trust Review*, see Greer (1977), p. 25.

17. *The Bankers Magazine* (Spring 1975), p. 30.

# Chapter 9

# Bankers' Attitudes Toward the Bank-Examination Process and Major Issues in Banking

## 9.1 INTRODUCTION

This chapter presents the results of a survey conducted at the School for Bank Administration on August 5 and 6, 1976.[1] The purpose of the survey is to determine bankers' attitudes toward the bank-examination process and major issues in banking. The chapter consists of four parts. The first part briefly describes the typical survey respondent and the characteristics of his or her bank. (Detailed background information about the respondents' job titles and the characteristics of their banks is contained in the appendix of this chapter.) Respondents' attitudes toward the bank-examination process and the development of computer "early-warning" systems (for identifying potential "problem" banks) are presented in the second part. In the third part, respondents' attitudes toward major issues in banking such as electronic banking, removal of Regulation Q ceilings, and payment of interest on demand deposits are analyzed. The chapter ends with a summary-and-conclusions section followed by the survey questionnaire.

## 9.2 THE TYPICAL SURVEY RESPONDENT

The typical survey respondent is a middle-or top-level banker with the title of Cashier and/or Vice President, a person who is making (or who will be making in the future) important managerial decisions. The typical respondent's bank is a state-chartered unit one located in a rural or non-SMSA area and having total deposits between $10 million and $50

A Banker's Early-Warning System

FRANK AND ERNEST                                                by Bob Thaves

Reprinted by permission of Newspaper Enterprise Association.

ELEVENTH ILLUSTRATION

million. Thus, the typical respondent's bank is representative of the average U.S. commercial bank.

## 9.3 SURVEY FINDINGS

### *1. The Bank-Examination Process and "Early-Warning" Systems*

The purpose of the first part of the survey is to determine bankers' attitudes toward the bank-examination process and computerized "early-warning" systems. Regarding the bank-examination process, the following four questions are asked.

1. Do you think bank examinations are necessary for maintaining the "safety and soundness" of individual banks
   Answers: Yes__78__ No__4__ No Opinion__1__

The respondents are overwhelmingly in favor of the need for bank examinations. Seventy-eight out of 82 (95 percent) answer yes.

2. Do you think detailed loan evaluations should comprise the major part of a bank examination?
   Answers: Yes__48__ No__29__ No Opinion__6__

The traditional on-site bank examination mainly focuses upon a detailed analysis of a bank's loan portfolio. As documented in Chapter 2, if a bank has a large volume of adversely classified assets (mainly "substandard" loans) relative to its capital and reserves, the banking agencies tend to classify it as a "problem bank." Although a majority of the respondents (62.3 percent of those having an opinion) think detailed loan evaluations should comprise the major part of a bank examination, this is 32.7 percentage points less than the vote for bank examinations.

Combining the answers to the previous two questions and generalizing to the population of bankers, it is concluded that bankers are over-whelmingly in favor of the need for bank examinations. However, one out of three bankers think detailed loan evaluations should *not* be the major focus of a bank examination.

The next two questions focus upon contact with bank examiners and the competency of examiners.

    3. Have you ever had any contact with a bank examiner?
        Answers:    Yes _81_    No _1_    Not Applicable _1_
    4. Do you think bank examiners are competent?
        Answers:    Yes _57_    No _7_    No Opinion _5_
                 Yes & No _13_          Not Applicable _1_

All but one of the respondents lacked contact with a bank examiner. (The National Bank Examiner in the group answered "Not Applicable" to these two questions.) Only 9.0 percent of the respondents with an opinion think bank examiners are *not* competent, while 74.0 percent think examiners are competent. Thirteen respondents (17 percent of those with an opinion) feel that a simple "yes" or "no" is inadequate for describing examiners' competency and answered "yes & no." These respondents probably had contact with both competent and incompetent examiners and/or with examiners competent in some examination areas but not in others.

Although not solicited, a number of respondents provided written opinions concerning the competency of bank examiners. The basic thrust of these comments focused upon the "inexperience" and/or "lack of training" of some examiners. For example, two respondents who considered the Comptroller's examiners to be *competent* added, respectively, "banks serve as a training ground for the majority of examiners" and "most of the time they send us trainees." Two respondents who regarded the Comptroller's examiners to be *incompetent* stated, respectively, "in general, too many inexperienced examiners" and "many are inexperienced, possibly need more training so that they do not stop the operations of the bank." Four respondents who thought the FDIC examiners were *competent* mentioned, respectively, (1) "supervisory (examiners) normally competent, but not below that level;" (2) "junior examiners are hard to work with and lack experience;" (3) "some (examiners) lack accounting training and they follow book procedures too strictly—most do not understand day-to-day banking problems"; and (4) "in our area, examiners have greatly improved in the past three years—their examinations have become much more constructive." Finally, one respondent who considered Federal Reserve examiners to be *competent* wrote "(examiners) have not had the experience they need."

Generalizing, the important point is that 3 out of 4 bankers think that examiners are competent and only 1 out of 10 think they are not competent. However, there is some dissatisfaction among bankers about the lack of "experience" and "training" of some examiners.

Regarding computerized "early-warning" systems for identifying potential problem banks, the following two questions are asked:

1. Would you favor reforming the bank-examination process along the lines suggested in this course?
   Answers: Yes__78__ No__2__ No Opinion__3__
2. Do you think computerized "early-warning systems" should be used to aid in scheduling bank examinations?
   Answers: Yes__76__ No__5__ No Opinion__2__

These two questions are somewhat similar. The similarity is intentional to check for consistency of answers and to allow those who dislike my reform proposal still to show a preference for early-warning systems. The reform proposal I suggested in the course is:

All banks are analyzed by a computerized early-warning system *prior* to their examinations. Existing problem banks and banks "flagged" by the computer are examined *before* nonproblem and nonflagged banks. In addition, those banks examined first are inspected *more intensively* than those at the "safety-and-soundness" end of the queue.

Regarding the traditional bank examination and its focus on loan evaluations, the basic premise is that such examinations for every bank in every year are not necessary. However, on-site bank inspections are not eliminated. On the contrary, every bank is inspected *at least* once a year to check for the factors that have been the major causes of bank failures (e.g., insider transactions, brokered funds, fraud, embezzlement, etc.). These mandatory inspections require much less time and money than the traditional bank examination. Known problem banks and banks flagged as in need of special supervision are given more detailed and thorough bank inspections. These inspections included detailed loan evaluations only in certain cases. To summarize, this inspection system requires substantial human input and analysis; it is not a machine-sans-man system. The major chances include (1) increased computer analysis as a filtering mechanism for identifying banks with financial difficulties and (2) reallocation of human resources (a) away from detailed loan evaluations and toward more productive areas and (b) away from "safe and sound" banks and toward "problem" banks.

Seventy-eight out of 80 respondents (3 had no opinion) favor this reform proposal. Regarding the second question, 76 out of 81 respondents (2 had no opinion) favor the use of computerized early-warning systems to aid in scheduling bank examinations.

Generalizing from these responses, it is clear that bankers are in favor of the innovations and reforms the banking authorities are making in the bank-examination process. In terms of implementation, the Comptroller's National Bank Surveillance System (NBSS; see Chapter 4) is near completion as an operational examination mechanism. At the FDIC, considerable early-warning research and trend analysis has been conducted and recently an Integrated Monitoring System (IMS), designed to monitor bank performance between examinations, was instituted. At the Federal Reserve, the Division of Banking Supervision and Regulation was realigned recently to improve supervisory functions. Finally, several state banking agencies, most notably the Illinois State Banking Commission, have attempted to implement surveillance or early-warning mechanisms.

### 2. Major Issues in Banking

The last part of the survey asks respondents about thirteen major issues in banking. The issues and answers (ranking from most favored to least favored) are presented in Table 9.1. Respondents are asked whether

Table 9.1

Major Issues in Banking

| Issue | Favor | Oppose | Undecided | No Answer | Favor / (Favor + Oppose) (%) |
|---|---|---|---|---|---|
| 1. Electronic Banking | 81 | 2 | 0 | 0 | 97.6 |
| 2. One Consolidated Federal Banking Agency | 50 | 30 | 0 | 3 | 62.5 |
| 3. Increased Disclosure of Banking Data | 47 | 31 | 1 | 4 | 60.3 |
| 4. Removal of Regulation Q Ceilings | 39 | 36 | 1 | 7 | 52.0 |
| 5. Operation of U.S. Banks in Foreign Countries | 37 | 35 | 1 | 10 | 51.4 |
| 6. Continued Bank Holding Company Expansion and Diversification | 29 | 47 | 0 | 7 | 38.1 |
| 7. Unlimited State-Wide Branching | 27 | 54 | 0 | 2 | 33.3 |
| 8. Payment of Interest on Checking Accounts | 22 | 59 | 0 | 2 | 27.2 |
| 9. Public Disclosure of Bank-Exam Data | 22 | 60 | 0 | 1 | 26.8 |
| 10. Operation of Foreign Banks in U.S. | 15 | 60 | 1 | 7 | 20.0 |
| 11. Public Disclosure of So-called Problem-Bank Lists | 14 | 67 | 0 | 2 | 17.3 |
| 12. Granting Checking Account Powers to SLAs | 12 | 69 | 0 | 2 | 14.6 |
| 13. Branching Across State Boundries | 11 | 71 | 0 | 1 | 13.4 |

they "favored" or "opposed" the particular issue. The respondents are most in favor of electronic banking (97.6 percent) and least in favor of permitting branching across state boundaries (13.4 percent).

Arranging the 13 issues into the following six categories:

1. Innovation (issue 1)
2. Regulatory Reform (issue 2),
3. Disclosure (issues 3, 9, 11),
4. Competition (issues 4, 7, 8, 12, 13),
5. Holding Company Movement (issue 6), and
6. Foreign Banking (issues 5, 10),

the respondents are in favor of innovation, regualtory reform, and some disclosure but oppose competition and continued holding company expansion and diversification. Regarding foreign banking, the respondents oppose the operation of foreign banks in the U.S. but favor the operation of U.S. banks in foreign countries.

On a disaggregated basis (e.g., deposit size), a further breakdown of the attitudes reported in Table 9.1 are presented below. Using a total-deposits cutoff point of $50 million (16 respondents are associated with banks with deposits greater than or equal to $50 million, while 66 respondents are associated with banks with deposits less than $50 million, see Table 2 in the Appendix) and a "majority decision rule," only two major differences in attitudes are observed. First, the majority of the "large" bankers (56.3 percent) favor expansion of the holding-company movement (issue 6) while only 30.3 percent of the "small" bankers favor this issue.[2] Second, the majority of "small" bankers (59.1 percent) oppose the operation of U.S. banks in foreign countries (issue 5) while the majority of "large" bankers (62.5 percent) favor this proposition. Although both "large" and "small" bankers are in favor of a monolithic banking authority (issue 2) and increased disclosure of banking data (issue 3), "large" bankers are more strongly in favor of these positions (i.e., 81.3 percent versus 56.1 percent and 87.5 percent versus 50.0 percent, respectively). Except for the public disclosure of bank-examination data (issue 9), which both groups oppose (although "large" bankers are less strongly opposed—43.8 percent versus 22.7 percent), "large" and "small" bankers closely agree on the other issues.

About 1 out of 3 survey respondents (see Table 3 in the Appendix) are affiliated with a bank holding company. Regarding issue 6, continued bank holding company expansion and diversification, the majority of affiliated bankers favor this movement (17 of 27 or 63 percent) while the majority of nonaffiliated bankers oppose it (38 of 55 or 69.1 percent).

Regarding the expansion of banking offices (issues 7 and 13), the respondents oppose both unlimited state-wide branching (66.7 percent) and branching across state boundaries (86.6 percent). However, separating the bankers on the basis of branching structure (unit versus branch, see Table 3 in the Appendix), exactly 50 percent of the branch bankers (15 of 30) favor unlimited state-wide branching while only 23.1 percent of the unit bankers favor such a structure. Regarding branching across state boundries, both branch and unit bankers oppose this proposition (83.3 percent and 88.5 percent, respectively). Since branching across state boundries would impair the concept of a dual-banking system, the negative vote against such a branching structure implies a vote in favor of dual banking.

Although all possible permutations and combinations of survey responses are not explored, a further breakdown of attitudes on the basis of region of the country, origin of charter, and Federal banking authority reveal only one additional significant difference. That is, with regard to the increased disclosure of banking data (issue 3), respondents whose banks are members of the Federal Reserve System oppose increased disclosure (21 of 33 or 63.6 percent) while nonmember bankers favor it (37 of 49 or 75.5 percent). Since the Federal Reserve has never been accused (by Wright Patman, Ralph Nader, and others) of being an extremely open institution, the member bankers' penchant for "secrecy" may be a reflection of the Fed's wishes for privacy.

In closing, there is no indication across any of the various subgroups explored that increased banking competition is favored by any particular subgroup. Of the five issues related to competition (4, 7, 8, 12, 13), only the removal of Regulation Q ceilings (issue 4) is favored by the majority of the survey respondents and then just barely (52.0 percent). Although some of these issues have been labeled for some time as "an idea whose time has come," banking legislative history indicates that (because of strong lobbying efforts) bankers usually get what they want. Thus, these survey findings can be interpreted as an indicator of the changes that are most likely to occur in the commercial-banking industry over the next few years.

## 9.4 SUMMARY AND CONCLUSIONS

This chapter has focused upon the results of a survey regarding the bank-examination process and major issues in banking. The survey was conducted at the School for Bank Administration during August of 1976. Eighty-two bankers and one National Bank Examiner participated in the survey.

The typical survey respondent is a middle- or top-level banker with the title of Cashier and/or Vice President. The typical respondent's bank is a state-chartered unit bank located in a rural or non-SMSA area and having between $10 million and $50 million in total deposits.

The survey findings indicate: (1) bank examinations are important and bank examiners are competent; (2) early-warning systems and examination reforms should be introduced into bank supervision; (3) electronic banking, one consolidated Federal banking agency, and some disclosure should be *encouraged;* and (4) increased competition (in terms of relaxed branching restrictions, removal of Reg Q ceilings, payment of interest on demand deposits, and granting of checking account powers to SLAs), continued holding company expansion and diversification, and foreign banking should be *discouraged.*

Because the U.S. commercial-banking industry operates in a quasi-regulated environment, many of the changes that occur in the industry require prior approval of either the U.S. Congress or the U.S. banking authorities, or both. Moreover, since the banking industry has a very strong lobby, commercial bankers have been able, for the most part, to control their environment and to shape it to suit their own special interests.[3] With this in mind, the survey findings can be regarded as a barometer of the changes most likely to occur in the banking system over the next few years.

# APPENDIX

# BACKGROUND INFORMATION

## 1. Respondents' Job Titles

The job titles of the 83 survey respondents are presented in Table 9.2. Except for one respondent, who is a National Bank Examiner, all of the respondents are bank employees. The most frequent job-title responses are "Cashier" or "Vice President and Cashier" with 25 (30.2 percent) and 20 (24.1 percent) responses, respectively. Overall, the title of "Cashier" is associated with 45 of the respondents (54.2 percent) while the title "Vice President" is associated with 28 of the respondents (33.7 percent). The important point is that the survey respondents are middle- or top-level bank employees who are making (or who will be making in the future) managerial decisions.

## 2. Characteristics of the Respondents' Banks

The deposit size, branching structure, holding-company affiliation, location, and Federal regulatory agency of the respondents' banks are presented in this section. The deposit-size classes are presented in Table 9.3.

*Table 9.2*
Job Titles for 83 Survey Respondents

| Job Title | Number | Percent |
|---|---|---|
| Cashier | 25 | 30.2 |
| Vice President and Cashier | 20 | 24.1 |
| Assistant Vice President | 11 | 13.3 |
| Vice President | 8 | 9.6 |
| Auditor | 6 | 7.2 |
| Assistant Cashier | 3 | 3.6 |
| Operations Officer | 2 | 2.4 |
| Other | 8 | 9.6 |
| Total | 83 | 100.0 |

The cashier category included two respondents who are "Cashier and Secretary"; one who is "Cashier and Assistant Trust Officer"; and one "Cashier and Operations Officer." The assistant vice-president category includes three respondents with additional titles of "Comptroller," "Auditor," and "Branch Manager," respectively. The vice-president category includes one "Executive Vice President," one "Vice President and Operations Chief," one "Vice President and Comptroller," one "Vice President - Secretary - "other" category includes the following eight job titles: (1) Comptroller, (2) Branch Manager, (3) Banking Officer/Assistant Branch Manager, (4) Control Division Manager and Personnel, (5) Regional Representative, Business Development, (6) Accounting Officer, (7) Business Loan Officer, and (8) National Bank Examiner.

The majority of the respondents' banks (71.1 percent) have total deposits in the $10 million to $50 million size category. Except for the absence of very large banks, the distribution of the respondents' banks is quite similar to that for the population of insured commercial banks. For example, in the $10 million to $25 million deposit class, the percentage

*Table 9.3*
Total Deposits of Respondents' Banks*

| Total Deposits ($ millions) | Banks Number | Percent |
|---|---|---|
| 0 - 9.9 | 7 | 8.5 |
| 10 - 24.9 | 31 | 37.8 |
| 25 - 49.9 | 28 | 34.1 |
| 50 - 99.9 | 13 | 15.8 |
| 100 - 249.9 | 2 | 2.5 |
| 250 - 499.9 | 1 | 1.3 |
| Total | 82 | 100.0 |

*Excludes respondent who is a National Bank Examiner.

*Table 9.4*
Branching Structure and Holding-Company Affiliation

|  | Affiliated | Unaffiliated | Total* |
|---|---|---|---|
| Unit | 15 | 37 | 52 |
| Branch | 12 | 18 | 30 |
| Total* | 27 | 55 | 82 |

*Excludes respondent who is a National Bank Examiner.

of respondent banks is 37.4 compared to 32.6 percent for the population (as of December 31, 1974).

The branching structure and holding-company affiliation of the respondents' banks are presented in Table 9.4. Thirty-seven of the respondents' banks (45.1 percent) are nonaffiliated unit banks while 15 institutions (18.3 percent) are unit banks affiliated with holding companies. Of the 30 branch banks, 12 have holding company affiliations and 18 do not. Finally, there are nine banks affiliated with one-bank holding companies and 18 with multibank holding companies.

The number of states and the number of respondents from each state are presented in Table 9.5. Twenty-eight states are represented with seventeen states having more than one respondent. One respondent indicated a multistate affilation and one respondent (not the National Bank Examiner) left the answer space blank. Forty-one of the respondents

*Table 9.5*
Number of States and the Number of Respondents from each State

| 1. Alabama | 3 | 16. Missouri | 3 |
|---|---|---|---|
| 2. Arkansas | 1 | 17. New Jersey | 1 |
| 3. California | 1 | 18. New Mexico | 2 |
| 4. Florida | 4 | 19. North Dakota | 1 |
| 5. Georgia | 6 | 20. Ohio | 3 |
| 6. Illinois | 6 | 21. Oklahoma | 2 |
| 7. Indiana | 4 | 22. Oregon | 3 |
| 8. Iowa | 6 | 23. Pennsylvania | 1 |
| 9. Kentucky | 1 | 24. South Dakota | 1 |
| 10. Louisiana | 2 | 25. Texas | 8 |
| 11. Maine | 1 | 26. Virginia | 2 |
| 12. Massachusetts | 1 | 27. West Virginia | 1 |
| 13. Michigan | 5 | 28. Wisconsin | 8 |
| 14. Minnesota | 3 | 29. Multi-State* | 1 |
| 15. Mississippi | 1 | 30. Blank | 1 |

*Indicated as California, Illinois, Massachusetts, and New York.

*Table 9.6*

Survey: Attitudes Towards The Bank-Examination Process

and Major Issues in Banking

I.  Background Information

    A.  Your bank title or position is  _____.

    B.  Your Federal Bank agency is (check one)

          \_\_\_\_\_Comptroller of the Currency

          \_\_\_\_\_Federal Reserve

          \_\_\_\_\_FDIC

    C.  The approximate size of you bank is

          _____Total deposits (millions of dollars)

    D.  Is your bank a unit or branch bank? (Check one and if branch, list number of branches)  D' Holding-Company Affilation (check one)

          \_\_\_\_\_Unit or           \_\_\_\_\_None

          \_\_\_\_\_Number of branches    \_\_\_\_\_1-BHC

                             \_\_\_\_\_Multi-BHC

    E.  Location parameters

        1.  State (give name) _____

        2.  SMSA (check one) \_\_\_\_\_Yes    \_\_\_\_\_No

II.  The Bank-Examination Process

    A.  Do you think that bank examinations are necessary for maintaining the "safety and soundness" of individual banks? (check one)
        \_\_\_\_\_ Yes    \_\_\_\_\_ No    \_\_\_\_\_ No opinion

    B.  Would you favor reforming the bank-examination process along the lines suggested in this course? (check one)
        \_\_\_\_\_ Yes    \_\_\_\_\_ No    \_\_\_\_\_ No opinion

    C.  Do you think that detailed loan evaluations should comprise the major part of a bank examination? (check one)
        \_\_\_\_\_ Yes    \_\_\_\_\_ No    \_\_\_\_\_ No opinion

    D.  Do you think that computerized "early-warning systems" should be used to aid in scheduling bank examination? (check one)
        \_\_\_\_\_ Yes    \_\_\_\_\_ No    \_\_\_\_\_ No opinion

    E.  Have you ever had any contact with a bank examiner? (check one)
        \_\_\_\_\_ Yes    \_\_\_\_\_ No    \_\_\_\_\_ No opinion

    F.  Do you think that bank examiners are competent? (check one)
        \_\_\_\_\_ Yes    \_\_\_\_\_ No    \_\_\_\_\_ No opinion

III.  Major Issues in Banking

    A.  What is your opinion regarding the following issues: (check one for each issue)

        1.  Electronic banking    \_\_\_\_\_ Favor    \_\_\_\_\_ Oppose

        2.  Removal of Regulation Q Ceilings    \_\_\_\_\_ Favor    \_\_\_\_\_ Oppose

        3.  Payment of interest on checking accounts    \_\_\_\_\_Favor    \_\_\_\_\_Oppose

        4.  Unlimited state-wide branching    \_\_\_\_\_ Favor    \_\_\_\_\_Oppose

        5.  Branching across state boundaries    \_\_\_\_\_ Favor    \_\_\_\_\_ Oppose

        6.  Continued bank holding company expansion and diversification
            \_\_\_\_\_ Favor    \_\_\_\_\_ Oppose

        7.  One consolidated federal banking agency    \_\_\_\_\_ Favor    \_\_\_\_Oppose

        8.  Increased disclosure of banking data    \_\_\_\_\_ Favor    \_\_\_\_\_ Oppose

        9.  Public disclosure of bank-exam data    \_\_\_\_\_ Favor    \_\_\_\_\_ Oppose

        10.  Public disclosure of so-called problem-bank lists
             \_\_\_\_\_ Favor    \_\_\_\_\_ Oppose

        11.  Operation of foreign banks in the U.S.    \_\_\_\_\_ Favor    \_\_\_\_Oppose

        12.  Operation of U.S. banks in foreign countries
             \_\_\_\_\_ Favor    \_\_\_\_\_ Oppose

        13.  Granting checking-account powers to SLAs    \_\_\_\_\_ Favor    \_\_\_\_Oppose

Thank You

(49.4 percent) are from the following states: Texas (8), Wisconsin (8), Georgia (6), Illinois (6), Iowa (6), Michigan (5), Florida (4), and Indiana (4). Alabama, Minnesota, Missouri, Ohio, and Oregon have three respondents each, while Louisiana, New Mexico, Oklahoma, and Virginia have two respondents each. As an additional locational parameter, the survey respondents indicate whether or not their bank is located in a Standard Metropolitan Statistical Area (SMSA). Twenty-one of the respondents indicate their bank is located in an SMSA while 33 indicate a non-SMSA location. Twenty-eight of the respondents do not know if their bank is in an SMSA or not, which probably indicates that their bank is not located in an SMSA.

Regarding the respondents' Federal banking agency, 49 respondents list the Federal Deposit Insurance Corporation, 27 give the Comptroller of the Currency, and six check the Federal Reserve. Since nationally chartered banks are required to join the Federal Reserve System, 55 of the respondents' banks (67 percent) are state-chartered institutions.

To summarize, the *typical* respondents' bank is a state-chartered unit bank located in a rural or non-SMSA area and having total deposits between $10 million and $50 million.

## NOTES

1. The School for Bank Administration is sponsored by the Bank Administration Institute and held each summer at the University of Wisconsin, Madison.

2. Eight of the 16 "large" bankers are affiliated with holding companies.

3. According to Senator Proxmire "[The bank lobby] is very sophisticated. It's viewed as the toughest, strongest lobby in Washington." See Hume (1978).

# Chapter 10

# *Epilogue*

## 10.1 MAJOR THEMES AND CONCLUSIONS

The major themes and conclusions of the book are:

1. Problem and failed institutions are not new banking phenomena. They have existed for centuries. Only recently have they been widely publicized.

2. Over recent years most banks that have failed were identified as "problem banks" by the banking authorities prior to their collapse. Why were they allowed to fail? The goal of bank regulation and supervision is *limited* failure prevention. Only if the closing of a malperforming bank is perceived as jeopardizing the "safety and soundness" of the banking system (e.g., Franklin National) should its demise be *postponed*. Marginal banks should fail.

3. For all practical purposes "problem banks" are those with low "net capital ratios" (NCR). The NCR is dominated by the volume of "substandard" loans and has been successful in anticipating recent bank failures, both large and small ones.

4. The performance buck stops at the desks of a bank's managers and directors. Inept and/or dishonest managers and directors have been the major cause of financial difficulties in commercial banks.

5. The four largest U.S. bank failures (defined to include the emergency merger of Security National) all occurred during the "go-go" banking era of the 1970s. The policies of these banks were marked by shifts from "conservative" banking to "go-go" banking in the years prior to failure and their top management frequently was described as a "one-man show."

6. Although the 1974 recession contributed to the REIT-bank crisis of the 1970s, sloppy management and misconceptions on the part of

268

the banks involved were the *sine qua non* for the crisis. The banks simply misjudged and/or failed to investigate some basic economic and financial factors.

7. Banks' financial statements contain useful information for constructing "early-warning" mechanisms. Such systems can be used to *complement* the traditional, on-site bank examination by providing information to guide the timing, scope, and intensity of a bank's examination. The use of early-warning or surveillance mechanisms should enable the banking agencies to allocate *(more efficiently)* their scarce examination resources and perhaps to identify potential problem banks more quickly.

8. The number of variables required to develop a reasonably accurate early-warning system appears to be relatively small. Depending upon the number and composition of the sample banks and the sample period, from two to seven variables have been effective. The information content of these variables usually is collapsed into some index (measuring, e.g., probability of failure) via a multivariate statistical technique such as discriminant analysis, arctangent regression, or logit analysis. One drawback of these techniques is their perplexity to the layperson (examiner), who is expected to use the information. Thus, a prerequisite for implementation is that the system and its information be digestible by the prospective users. The Comptrollers's NBSS tends to meet this requirement; however, NBSS does not qualify as a statistical model. Application of the New York Fed's early-warning functions in the entire Federal Reserve System is the closest thing to an operational surveillance model in U.S. bank supervision today.

## 10.2 PROBLEM-BANK PUBLICITY: SCYLLA, CHARYBDIS, CASSANDRA, AND ROCKEFELLER

Over the years 1973–1977, commercial banks have received a great deal of publicity—much of it unfavorable. David Rockefeller, chairman of Chase Manhattan Bank (surely an unbiased observer), contends that problem-bank coverage by the media has been imbalanced. In a speech to the Economic Club of New York, Mr. Rockefeller said:

As to perspective, I think the "problem banks" episode is an example of the media's failure to provide the public with enough information to intelligently assess an issue. For example:

When banks chose to stay with their borrowers during the recession rather than set off a long chain of foreclosures and bankruptcy, not to mention job losses, that would have plunged the country into a major depression—few journalists offered this perspective. When banks were caught between the Scylla of congressional demands for credit allocation to socially responsible borrowers and the Charybdis of political cries for conservative lending policies—the media offered scant perspective. Even today, with the banking system well on the road to full recovery from as severe and deep a recession as we have had in 40 years—there is little, if any, perspective from the Cassandra commentators who told us about the "problem banks."[1]

## Chase's Rockefeller Between Scylla and Charybdis

TWELFTH ILLUSTRATION

Ironically Rockefeller's bankruptcy scenario does not apply to troubled REITs. Each REIT is simply a pool of financial assets without substantial industrial operations. Thus, from a social standpoint, if the banks had pulled the plug on troubled REITs, few members of the labor force would have been made idle and no shortage of products or services would have been ensued. On balance, except for possible effects on the public's confidence in the banking system, REITs' bankruptcies would have had a minimal ripple effect in the economy.

## 10.3 BORED BY THE BANK FLAP

Rockefeller's criticism of the press coverage of so-called problem banks is not without merit. More than a year before Rockefeller made his speech, I expressed similar sentiments in a letter (dated February 12, 1976) to the editor of *The Wall Street Journal:*

Dear Sirs:

I applaud your editorial "Bored by the Bank Flap" (February 10, 1976). Having analyzed "problem banks" and worked on the development of an "early-warning" system at the FDIC for the past four years, I am familiar with so-called problem banks. Your editorial placed a much needed perspective on the "bank flap." The real problem for the banking agencies is how to measure a bank's risk exposure. The "flap" that has been reported deals with the relationship between a bank's examiner-classified assets and its capital and reserves. A bank with a high volume of classified assets relative to its capital and reserves, say 80 percent, probably will make its agency's "watch" list. Part of the problem is that classifying a bank's loans into various risk categories is a highly subjective process. In addition, because of the conservative weighting scheme applied to the various risk classes, the banking agencies tend to overstate a bank's true risk exposure. For example, a bank's classified assets mainly will consist of "substandard" loans, examiners' least risky classification. However, in calculating a bank's capital adequacy, these substandard loans will receive the same weight as the more risky "doubtful" and "loss" classifications.

Problem banks frequently are said to be suffering from "inadequate capital." The traditional remedy for such a situation is to "jawbone" a bank into increasing its capital. During a recent Senate Banking Committee hearing, Senator Proxmire, with the proverbial ass' jawbone in hand, told Comptroller Smith, "I'm not asking you to apply it ruthlessly (the capital-adequacy standard for large banks). Apply it in a namby-pamby way. Play the violin and sing while you're doing it. Just do it."

Imprecise capital standards and definitions of what are problem banks are the basic issues in the current "bank flap." (Related issues focus upon disclosure and regulatory reform.) My research efforts have deemphasized, but not excluded, the role of capital in evaluating a bank's "safety and soundness." In my mind, a banks' earnings record is the best indicator of its soundness. If a bank can make risky loans *and* maintain its "bottom-line" performance, more power to it. A bank with a good earnings record will be able to generate capital both internally and externally.

## 10.4 JAWBONING: COOKIE AND CAPITAL BOTH START WITH "C"

The "Cookie Monster" is one of the muppets on the television show *Sesame Street*. He (or is it she?) has an insatiable appetite for cookies. The Cookie Monster's bag is jawboning for cookies. e.g., "I want cookie!" Since he never seems to suffer from "cookie inadequacy" (or "inadequate cookie"), the banking authorities should study his jawboning techniques. The Cookie Monster's favorite song is:

C is for cookie that's good enough for me.
Yea, C is for cookie that's good enough for me.
Oh, cookie cookie cookie starts with C.

Since capital is also a C word, the transition to bank jawboning is straightforward, even for the banking authorities. As Senator Proxmire plays the violin, the "Capital Monster" sings:

C is for capital that's good enough for me.
Yea, C is for capital that's good enough for me.
Oh, capital capital capital starts with C.

If banks still refuse to increase their capital, let them eat cookies.

## 10.5 THE NEW CZAR'S ATTITUDE TOWARD PROBLEM BANKS

G. William Miller, recently appointed by President Carter to replace Arthur Burns as chairman of the Board of Governors of the Federal Reserve System, also has been bored by the bank flap. According to Miller, "Congress has been unnecessarily concerned about bank regulation and problem banks."[2] A fellow director of the Boston Federal Reserve Bank thinks that Miller will succeed in explaining to Congress how bank regulators should work. (What an accomplishment that would be!) John Hunter, Jr., another Boston Fed director says, "I think he [Miller] would say that we don't need more bank controls, but that existing controls need to be made to function properly."[3]

## 10.6. HOW TO USE AN EARLY-WARNING SYSTEM: IF I WERE BANKING CZAR

If I were banking czar, I would issue the following guidelines to my Department of Supervision and Examination *and* publish them for the public:

1. Problem and failed banks have existed for a long time and will continue to exist in the future. Our job is to keep such institutions, especially failed ones, at a level consistent with maintaining confidence in the rest of the banking system. Accordingly, the actual number of failures or problems during any period of time isn't important, as long as the confidence factor is maintained. To maintain confidence in the banking system, we must carry out our Congressional mandate to assure safe and sound banking practices. Since confidence can be destroyed by ignorance and/or misrepresentation of facts, it is imperative that the public understand such concepts as problem bank, deposit insurance, payoff versus assumption, "clean assets" in a failed bank, etc. We don't want the adverse publicity of the 1970's to undermine the public's confidence in the banking system. Keeping the public educated and informed is a major factor in maintaining confidence.

2. Supervision and examination procedures will be directed toward preventing, monitoring, and eliminating the dishonest, incompetent, and inequitable elements in banking. If we do an effective job in these areas, we will maintain confidence in the banking system. Our supervision-and-examination arsenal will consist of two main weapons (1) computerized early-warning mechanisms and (2) on-site bank inspections. Alternative early-warning models will be employed as screening devices to schedule on-the-spot bank inspections. Regarding the traditional bank examination and its focus on loan evaluations, the basic premise will be that such examinations for every bank in every year are not necessary. On-site bank inspections will not be eliminated. On the contrary, every bank will be inspected *at least* once a year to check for violations of laws and regulations, unfair lending practices (e.g., "redlining" and other forms of discrimination), and other irregular and anticompetitive banking practices. These mandatory inspections will, of course, require much less time and money than the traditional bank examination. Known "problem banks" and banks that have been flagged as in need of special supervision or potentially in need of special supervision will be given more detailed and thorough bank inspections. These inspections will be designed to pinpoint problems and potential remedies. Peer-group analyses (and hence peer-group pressure) will be used in explaining actual and potential problem areas. In some cases, even traditional loan evaluations will be made. However, loan evaluations and criticisms should be handled delicately so as not to encourage discriminatory lending practices. Although our inspection system will have a "bottom-line" focus (banks are given monopoly power, in varying degrees depending upon their particular market, and hence, they should be able to generate a reasonable profit), we will not be myopic in this

regard. For example, if a bank has low earnings because it is providing "full service" to all of its customers, this will be given appropriate weight. In contrast, if a bank has low earnings because of self-serving and/or incompetent managers and/or directors, this will be given appropriate weight also, but with a negative sign. Moreover, in cases where banks have appeared to abuse their monopoly power, we will encourage greater competition. Clearly, our inspection system will require substantial human input and analysis; it will not be a machine-sans-man system. The major changes will include (1) increased computer analysis as a filtering mechanism for identifying banks with financial difficulties and (2) reallocation of human resources (a) away from detailed loan evaluations and toward more productive areas and (b) away from "safe and sound" banks and toward "problem banks."

## 10.7 FUTURE EARLY-WARNING RESEARCH

Accounting, market, and examination information is available for identifying banks with financial difficulties. The on-site examination has been and still is the cornerstone of the bank-supervisory process. Four decades ago Secrist (1938) suggested that bank accounting data be used to distinguish sound from unsound banking. Only recently, however, have the banking authorities attempted to make more efficient use of these data in the form of early-warning or surveillance systems. The "efficient-market hypothesis" contends that all relevant information on the future performance of any asset is included and properly discounted in its current price. If the market for banks with actively traded securities is efficient, information about potential problems at a bank is transmitted into the bank's security price. To date, the banking agencies have not attempted to use market information in the bank-supervisory process.

Accounting, market, and examination reports are the informational flows available for identifying banks with financial difficulties. They are important research areas, with the market territory being the least explored. A *complete* early-warning or surveillance mechanism should employ all of these informational sources.

## 10.8 A LAST REFLECTION

The years 1973–1977 have been turbulent and trying ones for the U.S. banking and financial system. While a weaker system might have collapsed, the U.S. system did not. On balance, I stand by my testimony made before the Committee on Banking, Housing and Urban Affairs (U.S. Senate, March 11, 1977), ". . . the [U.S.] banking system is relatively healthy and the banking agencies have done an adequate job of carrying out their statutory responsibility to assure a safe and sound banking system."

## NOTES

1. "Notable & Quotable," *Wall Street Journal* (June 22, 1977).
2. Ulman (1977), p. 3.
3. Ibid.

## REFERENCES

Addington, L. H., *The Blitzkrieg Era and the German General Staff, 1865–1941*, New Brunswick, N.J.: Rutgers University Press, 1971.

Altman, E. I., "Some Estimates of the Cost of Lending Errors for Commercial Banks," Salomon Brothers Center for the Study of Financial Institutions, Working Paper No. 85, 1976.

———, "The Development of a Performance-Prediction System for Savings and Loan Associations," Invited Research Working Paper No. 10, Federal Home Loan Bank Board, Washington, D.C., December 1975.

———, "Comments on Franklin National," Annual Meeting of the Southern Finance Association, New Orleans, 1975.

———, "Financial Ratios, Discriminant Analysis, and the Prediction of Corporate Bankruptcy," *Journal of Finance*, September 1968, pp. 589–609.

———, R. Avery, R. A. Eisenbeis, and J. F. Sinkey, Jr., *Applications of Classification Techniques in Business, Banking, and Finance*, Greenwich, Conn., JAI Press, 1979.

———, and R. A. Eisenbeis, "Financial Applications of Discriminant Analysis: A Clarification," Salomon Brothers Center for the Study of Financial Institutions, Working Paper No. 79, 1976.

———, R. G. Haldeman, and P. Narayanan, "ZETA Analysis: A New Model to Identify Bankruptcy Risk of Corporations," *Journal of Banking and Finance* 1, 1977, pp. 29–54.

*(The) American Banker* (various issues).

Anderson, R. E., "1974–1975: Banking's Stability in Two Dark Years," *Journal of Commercial Bank Lending*, December 1976, pp. 10–18.

*Annual Report*, Federal Deposit Insurance Corporation, Washington, D.C. (various issues).

*Annual Report*, Federal Reserve Bank of New York, 1974, pp. 21–26.

Aplido, V. P., and T. G. Gies, "Capital Adequacy and Commercial Bank Failure," *The Bankers Magazine*, Summer 1972, pp. 24–30.

Babcock, C., "Problem Banks Rising," *The Washington Post*, February 6, 1976.

Barnett, R. E., "Anatomy of a Bank Failure," *The Magazine of Bank Administration*, April 1972, pp. 20–23, 43.

———, "Remarks on the Economy, Banking, and Bank Regulation," *FDIC News Release,* PR-37-76, May 5, 1976.

———, "The FDIC: Bank Examination and Supervision," *FDIC News Release,* PR-94-76, November 11, 1976.

Benston, G. J., "Bank Examination," *The Bulletin,* Nos. 89–90, New York University, Graduate School of Business, May 1973.

———, "How We Can Learn From Past Bank Failures," *The Bankers Magazine,* Winter 1975, pp. 19–25.

———, and J. T. Marlin, "Bank Examiners' Evaluation of Credit: An Analysis of the Usefulness of Substandard Loan Data," *Journal of Money, Credit and Banking,* February 1974, pp. 23–44.

Bloch, E., *The Setting of Standards of Supervision for Savings and Loan Associations,* Washington, D.C.: Federal Home Loan Bank Board, July 1969.

Bremer, C. D., *American Bank Failures,* New York: Columbia University Press, 1935.

Brimmer, A. F., "Expanding Money Markets and the Evolution of Central Bank Responsibilities: The Federal Reserve and the Failure of Franklin National Bank," 1975–1976 Lecture Series on Contemporary Business, New York: New York University, February 25, 1976.

———, and F. R. Dahl, "Growth of American International Banking: Implications for Public Policy," *Journal of Finance,* May 1975, pp. 341–363.

Burns, A. F., "Maintaining the Soundness of Our Banking System," *Monthly Review,* Federal Reserve Bank of New York, November 1974, pp. 263–267.

*Business Week,* "How C. Arnholt Smith's Empire Came Apart," October 27, 1973, pp. 85–89.

———, "Are Swaps the Way Out for the Banks," October 11, 1976, pp. 53–56.

Calame, B. E., "Self-Dealing Tycoon," *The Wall Street Journal,* April 16, 1969.

Carberry, J., "Tottering Trusts," *The Wall Street Journal,* June 1, 1977, p. 38.

Cates, D. C., "Can Bank Condition Be Externally Judged," *Journal of Commercial Bank Lending,* May 1975, pp. 2–18.

Cole, D. W., "Return on Equity Model for Banks," *The Bankers Magazine,* Autumn 1974, pp. 40–47.

*Congressional Record-House,* October 28, 1975.

Cooley, W. W., and P. R. Lohnes, *Multivariate Data Analysis,* New York: John Wiley & Sons, 1971.

De Roover, R., *the Medici Bank: Its Organization, Operations, and Decline,* New York: New York University Press, 1948.

Eisenbeis, R. A., "Financial Early Warning Systems: Status and Future Directions," *Issues in Bank Regulation,* Summer 1977, pp. 8–12.

———, "Pitfalls in the Application of Discriminant Analysis in Business Finance, and Economics," *Journal of Finance,* June 1977, pp. 875–900.

———, and R. B. Avery, *Discriminant Analysis and Classification Procedures: Theory and Applications,* Lexington, Mass.: D. C. Heath and Company, 1972.

———, "Two Aspects of Investigating Group Differences in Linear Discriminant Analysis," *Decision Sciences,* October 1973.

*Federal Deposit Insurance Act,* U.S. Congress, 1934.

FDIC, "Bank Examiners' Orientation Course," Washington, D.C., 1973.

———, "Instructions for the Preparation of Report of Condition on Form 64," Washington, D.C., 1970.

*FDIC News Releases* (various issues), Washington, D.C.

Federal Reserve Bank of Richmond, "Recent Bank Failures—Why?" *Monthly Review,* September 1965, pp. 2–5.

*Federal Supervision of State and National Bank,* Comptroller General of the United States, Washington, D.C., 1977.

Foldessy, E. P., "Citibank Enlists Top Real Estate Experts to Real Recoup Funds Tied to Property," *The Wall Street Journal,* December 1, 1976.

———, "The Examiners," *The Wall Street Journal,* September 9, 1976.

Gambs, C. M., "Bank Failures: An Historical Perspective," *Monthly Review,* Federal Reserve Bank of Kansas City, June 1977, pp. 10–20.

Gerdnic, J. P., and J. F. Sinkey, Jr., "A Look at the REIT Industry and Its Relationship with Commercial Banks," Executive Summary No. 75-4, FDIC, Washington, D.C., 1975.

Gibson, W. E., "Deposit Insurance in the U.S.: Evaluation and Reform," *Journal of Financial and Quantitative Analysis,* March 1972 pp. 1575–1594.

Gilbert, A., "Bank Failures and Public Policy," *Monthly Review,* Federal Reserve Bank of St. Louis, November 1975, pp. 7–15.

Golembe, C. H., "Bank Failures and All That," Vol. 1974–1978, Washington, D.C.: C. H. Golembe Associates Inc.

Greer, P., "Grim Third Act Looms in REIT Drama," *Financier,* May 1977, pp. 25–29.

Guttentag, J. M., "Reflections on Bank Regulatory Structure and Large Bank Failures," *Proceedings of a Conference on Bank Structure and Competition," Federal Reserve Bank of Chicago, 1975.*

Hall, C. B., *"Revised Regulatory Examinations and Their Impact on the Lending Function," Journal of Commercial Bank Lending,* September 1976, pp. 30–37.

———, "Update: Changes in the Loan Examination and Reporting Process," *Journal of Commercial Bank Lending,* December 1976, pp. 34–42.

Hammond, B., *Banks and Politics in America,* Princeton, N.J.: Princeton University Press, 1957.

Hanweck, G. A. "Predicting Bank Failures." Financial Studies Section, Board of Governors, Washington, D.C., November, 1977.

———, "Using a Simulation Model Approach for the Identification of Problem Banks," Financial Studies Section, Board of Governors, Washington, D.C., August, 1977.

———, "Identifying Failing Banks and Bank Holding Companies: A Comparison of Publicly Available Data with that from Confidential Sources," *Proceedings of a Conference on Bank Structure and Competition,* Federal Reserve Bank of Chicago, 1976.

*Haskins & Sells Study 1974–75,* New York: Haskins & Sells, 1975.

Herzig-Marx, C., "Comparing Market and Regulatory Assessments of Bank Condition," Paper presented at the Southern Finance Association Annual Meeting, November 3, 1977.

Hildreth, R., *The History of Banks,* Boston: Hilliard Gray & Co., 1837; reprinted by Augustus M. Kelley Publishers, New York, 1968.

Hilkert, R. N., "The Muddle in Bank Supervision," *Business Review,* Federal Reserve Bank of Philadelphia, June 1964.

Hill, G. W., "Why 67 Insured Banks Failed: 1960–1974," Washington, D.C.: FDIC, 1975.

Holland, R. C., "Bank Holding Companies and Financial Stability," *Journal of Financial and Quantitative Analysis,* November 1975, pp. 577–587.

Horovitz, P. M., "Failures of Large Banks: Implications for Banking Supervision," *Journal of Financial and Quantitative Analysis,* November 1975, pp. 589–601.

Hume, C. R., "He Believes Banks, Regulators Too Cozy," *The Atlanta Journal and Constitution,* January 2, 1978, p. 6-A.

Joy, O. M., and J. O. Tollefson, "On the Financial Applications of Discriminant Analysis," *Journal of Financial and Quantitative Analysis,* December 1975, pp. 723–239.

Kane, E. J., "Short-Changing the Small Saver: Federal Government Discrimination Against Small Savers During the Vietnam War," *Journal of Money, Credit and Banking* 2, November 1970, pp.513–522.

———, "All for the Best: The Federal Reserve Board 60th Annual Report," *The American Economic Review,* December 1974, pp. 835–850.

———, "Can FDIC Regulation Deliver Us from Self-Dealing?" *The Bankers Magazine,* Autumn 1976, pp. 13–15.

Kane, T. P., *The Romance and Tragedy of Banking,* New York: The Bankers Publishing Co., 1923.

Kaufman, G. G., "Preventing Bank Failures," *Compendium of Major Issues in Bank Regulation,* Washington, D.C.: Government Printing Office, May 1975, pp. 769–796.

Kessler, R., "Citibank, Chase Manhattan on U.S. Problem List," *The Washington Post,* January 11, 1976.

Klisten, E., "The New OES Rating System," *Federal Home Loan Bank Board Journal,* December 1971, pp. 8–13, 27, 29.

Korobow, L., and D. P. Stuhr, "Toward Early Warning of Changes in Banks' Financial Condition: A Progress Report," *Monthly Review,* Federal Reserve Bank of New York, July 1975, pp. 157–165.

———, ———, and D. Martin, "A Probabilistic Approach to Early Warning of Changes in Bank Financial Condition," *Monthly Review,* Federal Reserve Bank of New York, July 1976, pp. 187–94.

———, "A Nationwide Test of Early Warning Research in Banking," *Quarterly Review,* Autumn 1977, Federal Reserve Bank of New York, pp. 37–52.

Kurtz, R. D., and J. F. Sinkey, Jr., "Bank Disclosure Policy and Procedures, Adverse Publicity, and Bank Deposit Flows," *Journal of Bank Research.* Autumn 1973, pp. 177–184.

Leavy, H. L., "Early Warning System—New Supervisory Tool," *FHLBB Journal,* September, 1969, pp. 12, 14.

Leff, G., "Should Deposit Insurance Be 100 Percent?" *The Bankers Magazine,* Summer 1976, pp. 23–29.

*Manual of Examination Policies,* Washington, D.C.: FDIC, 1976.

Martin, D., "Logit Analysis and Early-Warning Systems for Bank Supervision," *Journal of Banking and Finance,* forthcoming.

Mayer, M., *The Bankers,* New York: Weybright & Talley, 1974.

Mayer, T., "A Graduated Deposit Insurance Plan," *Review of Economics and Statistics,* February 1965, pp. 114–116.

———, "Should Large Banks Be Allowed to Fail," *Journal of Financial and Quantitative Analysis,* November 1975, pp. 603–610.

McConnell, C. E., and W. S. Macias, "Bank Loans to REITs: How Serious the Problem?" New York: Keefe Bruyette, & Woods Inc., May 2, 1975.

Means, L. B., and T. L. Zearley, "Financial Modeling as a Decision-Making Tool," *FHLBB Journal,* November 1975, pp. 25–30.

Meyer, P. A., and H. W. Pifer, "Prediction of Bank Failures," *Journal of Finance,* September 1970, pp. 853–868.

Milius, P., "How the Hamilton Failed," *The Bankers Magazine,* September 1976, pp. 79–82.

Mingo, J., S. A. Rhoades, and B. Wolkowitz, "Risk and its Implications for the Banking System," *The Magazine of Bank Administration,* February 1976, pp. 52–58 and Part II, March 1976, pp. 43–47.

National Industrial Conference Board, *The Banking Situation in the United States,* New York, 1932.

Orgler, Y. E., "A Credit-Scoring Model for Commercial Loans," *Journal of Money, Credit and Banking,* November 1970, pp. 435–445.

Pettway, R. H., "Potential Insolvency, Market Efficiency, and Bank Regulation of Large Commercial Banks," Paper presented at the Eastern Finance Association Annual Meeting, Atlanta, 1978.

*REIT Fact Book,* National Association of Real Estate Investment Trusts, Washington, D.C., 1974 and 1975.

*REIT Statistics,* National Association of Real Estate Investment Trusts, Washington, D.C., 1974–1977.

Robertson, R. M., *The Comptroller and Bank Supervision,* The Office of the Comptroller of the Currency, Washington, D.C., 1968.

Robertson, W., "How the Bankers Got Trapped in the REIT Disaster," *Fortune,* March 1975, pp. 113–115, 168–169, 172–176.

Rockefeller, D., "Problems, Perspectives and Responsibilities," The Chase Manhattan Bank, New York, March 15, 1977. Address at the Economic Club of New York, New York.

Roll, R., "A Critique of the Asset Pricing Theory's Tests," *Journal of Financial Economics* 4, 1977, pp. 129–176.

Rose, P. S., and W. L. Scott, "Risk in Commercial Banking: Evidence from Postwar Bank Failures," *Southern Economic Journal,* July 1978, pp. 90–106.

Rose, S., "What Really Went Wrong at Franklin National," *Fortune,* October 1974, pp. 118–121, 220, 223–227.

Salem, G. M., and N. M. Singer, "Bank Loans to REITs: Facts vs. Misconceptions," February 5, 1975, New York: Drexel Burnham & Co.

———, "Bank Loans to REITs," February 25, 1975, New York: Drexel Burnham & Co., a follow-up of their note of February 5.

Samuelson, P., *Economics* (8th edition), New York: McGraw-Hill Book Co., 1970, p. 249.

Santomero, A. M., and J. D. Vinso, "Estimating the Probability of Failure for the Banking System," *Journal of Banking and Finance,* forthcoming.

Secrist, H., *National Bank Failures and Nonfailures,* Bloomington, Ind.: The Principia Press, 1938.

Schall, L. D., and C. W. Haley, *Introduction to Financial Management,* New York: McGraw-Hill Book Co., 1977.

Scheibla, S., "Big Bank Failure," "Letters of Discredit?", and "Good Money After Bad," *Barron's,* April 1, April 8, and September 9, 1974, respectively.

Sinkey, J. F., Jr., "The Bank-Examination Process and Major Issues in Banking: A Survey," *The Bankers Magazine,* May–June 1978, pp. 43–45.

———, "Identifying 'Problem' Banks: How do the Banking Authorities Measure a Bank's Risk Exposure," *Journal of Money, Credit, and Banking, May 1978,* pp. 184–193. This paper is a condensed version of FDIC Working Paper No. 76-2, "Bank Capital, Loan Evaluations, and 'Problem' Banks," Washington, D.C.

———, "Identifying Large Problem/Failed Banks: The Case of Franklin National Bank of New York," *Journal of Financial and Quantitative Analysis,* December 1977, pp. 779–800.

———, "Problem and Failed Banks, Bank Examinations, and Early-Warning Systems: A Summary," in *Financial Crises* (E. I. Altman and A. W. Sametz, eds.), New York: Wiley-Interscience, 1977, pp. 24–47.

———, "The Collapse of Franklin National Bank of New York," *Journal of Bank Research,* Summer 1977, pp. 113–122.

———, Statement on the Condition of the U.S. Banking System and the Effectiveness of Bank Supervision, Committee on Banking, Housing and Urban Affairs, U.S. Senate, March 11, 1977. Reprinted in the *Congressional Record.*

———, "REITs and Commercial Banks: An Update," Executive Summary No. 75-9, Washington, D.C.: FDIC, 1975.

———, "Adverse Publicity and Bank Deposit Flows: The Cases of Franklin National Bank of New York and United States National Bank of San Diego," *Journal of Bank Research,* Summer 1975, pp. 109–112.

———, "Early-Warning System: Some Preliminary Predictions of Problem Commercial Banks," *Proceedings of a Conference on Bank Structure and Competition,* May 1975, pp. 85–91.

———, "The Failure of United States National Bank of San Diego: A Portfolio and Performance Analysis," *Journal of Bank Research,* Spring 1975, pp. 8–24.

———, "A Multivariate Statistical Analysis of the Characteristics of Problem Banks," *Journal of Finance,* March 1975, pp. 21–36.

———, "The Way Problem Banks Perform," *The Bankers Magazine,* Autumn 1974, pp. 40–51.

———, "The Effects of Foreign Operations on the Safety and Soundness of Large Commercial Banks," unpublished FDIC Memorandum, August 28, 1974.

———, and D. A. Walker, "Problem Banks: Identification and Characteristics," *Journal of Bank Research,* Winter 1975, pp. 208–217.

Slocum, J. J., "Liquidity Banks," speech delivered before the Ninth District Bank Examiners' Conference, Federal Reserve Bank of Minneapolis, December 7, 1973. Reprinted in the *American Banker,* March 22, 1974.

——, "Why 57 Insured Banks Did Not Make It—1960 to 1972," *Journal of Commercial Bank Lending,* August 1973, pp. 44–56.

Straub, P. A., and R. McDavid, "REITs: A Background Analysis and Recent Industry Developments, 1961–1974," Economic Staff Paper 75-No. 1, Securities and Exchange Commission, Washington, D.C., February 1975.

Stuhr, D. P., and R. Van Wicklen, "Rating the Financial Condition of Banks: A Statistical Approach to Bank Supervision," *Monthly Review,* Federal Reserve Bank of New York, September 1974, pp. 233–238.

Sullivan, L., *Prelude to Panic,* Washington, D.C.: Statesmen Press, 1936.

Tussing, A. D., "The Case for Bank Failures," *The Journal of Law and Economics,* October 1967, pp. 129–147.

Ulman, N., "Miller Emerges as Pragmatic Activist in Speeches and Talks with Associates, *The Wall Street Journal,* December 20, 1977, p. 3.

U.S. Congress, House Committee on Banking Currency and Housing, Subcommittee on Domestic Monetary Policy, "An Act to Lower Interest Rates and Allocate Credit," Hearings on H. R. 212 (February 4–6, 1975), 94th Congress, First Session, Washington, D.C.: Government Printing Office, 1975. (Statements and information relating to Franklin appear on pages 200–273.)

Upham, C. B., and E. Lamke, *Closed and Distressed Banks,* Washington, D.C.: The Brookings Institution, 1934.

Verbrugge, J. A., and J. F. Sinkey, Jr., "Major Issues Facing the Savings and Loan Industry," *FHLBB Journal,* November, 1977, pp. 30–33.

Wagman, R., and S. Engelmayer, "The Nation's Biggest Bank Failure," *Boston Sunday Globe,* August 18, 1974. Investigation by North American Newspaper Alliance.

*The Wall Street Journal,* "Notable and Quotable," June 22, 1977.

——, "Bored by the Bank Flap," editorial, February 10, 1976.

Weaver, A. S., and C. Herzig-Marx, "A Comparative Study of the Effect of Leverage on Risk Premiums for Debt Issues of Banks and Bank Holding Companies," Department of Research, Federal Reserve Bank of Chicago, Research Paper No. 78-1.

Welles, C., "The Needlessly High Cost of Folding Franklin National," *New York Magazine,* November 18, 1974, pp. 71–72, 74, 76–78, 81.

Weston, J. F., and E. F. Brigham, *Managerial Finance,* Hinsdale, Ill.: The Dryden Press, 1975.

Wille, F., Letter to Sentor Proxmire regarding the FDIC's identification and treatment of banks experiencing financial difficulties, February 5, 1976. Available from the FDIC's Information Office, Washington, D.C. 20429.

——, "FDIC 1975: Source of Strength Within the American Banking System," Washington, D.C.: FDIC, March 11, 1975.

——, "The FDIC and Franklin National Bank: A Report to the Congress and All FDIC-Insured Banks," FDIC Press Release 69-74. Reprint of an address before the 81st Annual Convention of the Savings Bank Association of New York State, Boco Raton, Fla., November 23, 1974.

————, "United States National Bank," Statement before the Subcommittee on Bank Supervision and Insurance Committee on Banking and Currency, House of Representatives, November 27, 1973, reprinted as FDIC Press Release 85-73.

Wojnilower, A. M., *The Quality of Bank Loans,* Occasional Paper 82, New York: National Bureau of Economic Research, 1962.

Wu, H. K. "Bank Examiner Criticisms, Loan Defaults, and Bank Loan Quality," *Journal of Finance,* September 1969, pp. 697–705.

# Index

Addington, L. H., 69
Altman, E. I., 76–77, 89, 100, 127, 189–192
American Bank & Trust of Orangeburg,
    S.C., 38, 132
American Bankers Associations, 17, 21
Anti-redlining, 27
    (*See also* Redlining)
Assets, 49, 253

Banchi Grossi, 1
Banchi in Mercato, 1
Bank entry, restricting, 28
Bank failures, 268–271, 273–274
    Early Warning System, 134–143
    financial characteristics, 101–143
    prevention (*See also* EWS)
        monitoring, 27
        restricted entry, 27–28
    rate, 7–8, 10
    record, 5–6
    (*See also* Failed banks)
Bank of America, 1, 33, 84, 220
Bank of the Commonwealth of Detroit, 38,
    56–57
Bank of Italy in San Francisco, 1
Bank management, 2–3, 8–10, 12, 17–18,
    19, 28, 45–48, 50, 57–58, 88–89, 120,
    148–150, 177, 215, 263
Bank notes, 3–5
Bank performance measures, 106–119
Bank of Picayune, Mississippi, 57
Bank regulation, 27, 32, 40, 44, 58–60
    (*See also* Banking authorities)

Bankers Trust Co., 33, 249
Banking Act of 1933, 14
Banking Act of 1935, 32
Banking authorities, 5, 10, 17, 18, 23,
    27–32, 40, 45, 48, 49, 70–71, 88,
    257–260, 268, 271–272, 274–275
    (*See also* Bank regulation, safety and
        soundness goal)
Banks:
    capital, 48–51, 60–63, 124
    examination process, 256–263
    examination purposes, 28, 48, 148
    holding companies, 27, 33–34, 43, 47–
        48
    House Committee on Banking and
        Currency, 9–10
    insured-nonmember 25, 33
    loan-evaluation process, 48–51, 60–63
    national, 24–25, 32, 35
    non-insured, 25, 34–35
    Senate Banking Committee, 14
    state-member, 25–26
    state's rights, 24
    (*See also* Commercial banks, Bank
        management, Failed and problem
        banks, Bank failures, Banking
        authorities, Bank regulation)
Barnett, R. E., 62
Bartell, Robert, 88
Benston, G. J., 45
Berkshire Bank, Pittsfield, Mass., 4
Beta, 186–192
    Franklin's, 188–192
Boston Exchange Office, 3

Bremer, C. D., 10–13, 23, 71
  overbanking-failure, hypothesis, 11–12
Brigham, Eugene, 94
Brimmer, A. F., 148, 154, 160
Burns, Arthur F., 21–23, 26, 33, 272

California Banking Commission, 88
Cambiatori, 1
Capital adequacy of failed banks, 124–127
Capital Asset Pricing Model (CAPM),
  186–192
Capital ratios:
  FDIC's, 51–53, 55–57, 124, 268
  "predictor" of failures, 55–57
  weighted, 51–53
Centennial Bank of Philadelphia, 128
Chase Manhattan Bank, 18, 248, 269
Chemical Bank of New York, 153, 177, 199,
  205, 209, 217, 249
Citibank, 18, 42, 44, 179–185
Citicorp, 42–44
Citizens and Southern National Bank,
  201
Citizens and Southern Realty Investors,
  253–254
Cole, D. W., 98
Colwell, William, 3–5
Commercial bank (*See also* Banks, Failed and
  problem banks, Bank failures, EWS,
  FDIC, deposits, Federal Reserve)
  establishment of U.S. National Banking
    System, 5
  first, 1
  history, early, 1–5
Competition in laxity, 11, 13, 21–27
Comptroller of the Currency, 5, 10, 12,
  23–24, 34, 43, 46, 67, 199, 202, 205,
  208, 217, 218
  (*See also* NBSS)
Conference on Financial Crises, May, 1977,
  134
Cooley, W. W., 117
Crocker National Bank of San Francisco,
  219
Currency Act of 1863, 5
  (*See also* National Bank Act)

Deposit assumption, 34–39, 146, 152–154,
  200

Deposit Insurance National Bank (DINB),
  38–39
Deposit Insurance System, 32–34
  assumptions, 34–39, 146, 152–154,
    200
  fund, 39–40
  payoffs, 34–39, 152
  termination, 30–32
  variable premium, 71
Deposit payoffs, 34–39, 152
de Roover, R., 1–2
Dexter, Andrew, 3–5, 19
Discriminant analysis, 53–55, 58, 73–74,
  124, 127
  assumptions, 73–75
  purposes, 74
  regression analysis, 11, 73
  tests: multiple-variable, 127–133,
    143–144
  seven-variable, 181–184, 269
  single-variable, 165–177
  two-variable, 177–181
  (*See also* Early Warning Systems)
Dual Banking, 24–26

Early Warning System (EWS), 256, 269,
  273–275
  definition and origin, 67–79
  failure prediction model, 87, 127–143
  Franklin National Bank, 163–184
  Hamilton National Bank, 203
  how to use, 272–274
  lead time, 72
  multiple discriminant analysis, 73–90
    outlier technique (peer-group analysis),
      83–87
    standard two-group approach, 73–87
  policy-enforcement area, 73
  purposes and potential advantages,
    70–72
  Security National Bank, 212–215
  USNB, 222–225
Economy and relationship to problem
  banks, 57–63
Edge Act Corporations, 26
Eisenbeis, R. A., 76–77
Equal-credit opportunity, 27
Equity, 44, 48
European-American Bank and Trust
  Company (EAT&T), 153–154

FDI Act:
  Section 8(a), 29–32
  Section 8(b), 29–32
  Section 8(e), 29–32
  Section 8(g), 31–32
  Section 13(3), 35, 152
  Rule 2.2, 37
  Rule 2.3, 37
  Section 13(c), 38
  Section 11, 39
FDIC, 17, 24, 70–71, 79–80, 82–90
  Annual Report 1974, 35, 37, 157
  deposit assumption, 34–38, 146, 152, 200
  Deposit Insurance Fund, 39–40, 48
  Deposit Insurance National Bank
    (DINB), 38–39
  deposit payoff, 34–38, 152
  Division of Bank Supervision (DBS), 18,
    69, 140
  enforcement actions, 29–32
  Establishment Act, 32
  failure prevention goal, 32–34
  fiduciary obligation, 35–36
  financial assistance to failing bank, 38
  Integrated Monitoring System (IMS), 90,
    260
  losses, 80–82
  Manual of Examination policies (1976),
    48–52
  Net Capital Ratio, 51–53, 55–57, 124, 268
  Office of Management Systems (OMS), 69
  problem bank list, 46
  problem banks; ratings:
    Other Problems (OPs), 18, 140
    Potential Payoffs (PPOs), 18, 140, 150
    Serious Problems (SPs), 18, 140
  report on Security National, 208
  report on USNB, 219
  "selective-withdrawal" program, 25
  termination-of-deposit insurance, 31–32
  variable deposit-insurance premium, 71
Failed banks:
  average size, 6–8
  data and methods, 101–105
  definition, 18
  financial characteristics, 101–143
    capital adequacy, 124–127
    data and methods, 101–105
    failure prediction models, 127–133
  pre-deposit insurance failures, 5–8
    causes, 8–14

post-deposit insurance failures, 15–17
  causes, 17–18
  rate, 7–10
  record, 5–6
  (*See also* Problem banks;
    Deposit-insurance system;
    Management, Substandard loans;
    Failure prevention; Early Warning
    Systems; Bank failures)
Failure-prediction models, 127–133
Farmers Exchange Bank, Glocester, R.I.,
  3
Federal funds, 120, 138, 148, 154, 172, 182,
  203, 215
Federal Home Loan Bank Board, 89
Federal Reserve, 23–24, 25–26, 28, 46, 73,
  87–90, 136, 148–150, 154, 157–158,
  202, 269
Federal Reserve Bank of New York, 87–90,
  136, 148–151, 269
Financial characteristics of problem and
  failed banks, 101–143
Financial ratios, 92–101
  liquidity, 94–96, 100
  leverage, 94, 96–97, 100
  activity, 94, 97–98, 100
  profitability, 94, 98–100, 120
  (*See also* Ratio analysis)
First Chicago Bank, 249
First National Bank of Attica, N.Y., 9
First National Bank of Rio Grande City,
  29
First National City Bank, 153, 177
First State Bank, 104
First State Bank and Trust Co. of Rio
  Grande City, Texas, 29, 128–129
First Tennessee Bank, N. A., 199
First Tennessee National Bank (now First
  Tennessee Bank, N.A.), 199
First Tennessee National Corporation,
  199
First Wisconsin Corporation, 248
First Wisconsin Mortgage Trust, 248
First Wisconsin National Bank, 248
Franklin National Bank of New York, 5, 15,
  23, 34, 36, 37, 38, 56, 83, 127, 146–192,
  198, 206, 210, 218, 227, 232–233, 268
Franklin New York Corporation (FNYC),
  148–150
Free-banking era, 10–11
Free-banking laws, 5–6

Gibson, W. E., 39
Glass bill, 32
Glass-Steagall Act, 14

Haldeman, R. G., 100
Hamilton Bancshares, Inc., 199, 201–202
Hamilton Factors, Inc., 199
Hamilton Financial Services, Inc., 199
Hamilton Mortgage Corp., 199, 201–205
Hamilton National Associates, 201
Hamilton National of Chattanooga, 56, 105,
  127, 132, 199–205, 212, 215–217, 227,
  232–233, 268
Hanweck, G. A., 87
Haskins & Sells Study, 84–87
Heimann, John G., 43
Herzig-Marx, C., 73, 192
Hildreth, Richard, 1, 237
Hilkert, R. N., 23
Hill, G. W., 17–18
Holding companies, 27, 33–34, 43, 47
Horowitz, P. M., 16, 38
House Committee on Banking & Currency,
  9–10

Illinois State Banking Commission, 135
Inflation, 3, 16, 33
International banking, 162–163
International City Bank and Trust, 132

"Jawboning," 29, 272
Joy, O. M., 77–78, 81
Jurisdictional tangle, 21–26, 40, 67,
  157–158

Kane, E. J., 155–157
Kane, T. P., 9
Keefe, Bruyette and Woods, Inc., 248
Keefe, Harry, 146, 185, 209
Korobow, L., 87

Lachenbruch "holdout" classification
  technique, 55
Laurel Bank of Kansas City, 39
Lefrak, Samuel, 254

Loans, substandard, 44, 45, 49–51, 53–56,
  62–63, 71, 120, 124, 171, 209, 268
Lohnes, P. R., 117

Marcias, W. S., 248
Macroeconomic stabilization policy, 27, 33,
  39
Management, 2–3, 5, 8–10, 12, 17–18, 19,
  28, 45–48, 50, 57–58, 88, 120,
  148–150, 177, 215, 263
Martin, D., 87, 124
Martin I Report (of USNB), 218, 232
Martin II Report (of USNB and Smith
  loans), 218
Mayer, M., 1
Mayer, T., 71
Manufacturers Hanover Trust Company,
  153
McConnell, C. E., 248
Medici Bank, 1–2
Merchants National Bank of Washington,
  D.C., 9–10
Mergers, 26, 27, 163, 205
Miller, G. William, 272
Morgan Guaranty Trust Company, 154,
  177–185
Multiple-variable tests of bank soundness,
  127–133

Narayanan, P., 100
National Bank Act, 5
National Bank Surveillance System (NBSS),
  73, 84–87, 90, 125–127, 148–151, 154,
  260, 269
National Industrial Conference Board,
  Study, 8, 12
New York City crises, 163, 249
New York Clearing House Association, 154

Orgler, Y. E., 163

Da Panzano Bank, 1
Performance measurement systems, 202,
  210–212, 215, 224–227
Problem banks:
  asset condition, 45
  bank performance measures, 106–119

definition, 18–19, 45
  Other Problem (OP), 18–19, 34, 44, 45,
    46, 58, 60, 140
  Potential Payoff (PPO), 18, 45, 46–47,
    58, 140, 150
  Serious Problem (SP), 18–19, 45, 46, 58,
    60
  financial characteristics, 101–143
  financial ratios and comparative analysis,
    92–101
  identifying large banks, 56–57, 140–144
  publicity, 269–271
  relationship to the economy, 57–63
  (*See also* Failed banks, Management,
    Substandard loans)
Problem bank publicity, 269–271
Problem identification of banks:
  large, 56–57, 140–144
  small, 57, 67–69


REIT, 17, 33, 163, 206, 237–255, 268, 271
ROE decomposition analysis, 94, 98–99,
    120–123, 203–205
Ratio analysis:
  activity, 94, 97–98, 100
  analysis definition, 92–94
  FDIC's capital ratio, 51–53, 55–57, 124,
    268
  leverage, or debt, 94, 96–97, 100
  liquidity, 94–96, 100
  net capital, 44, 49, 55–57, 268
  profitability, 94, 98–100, 120
  (*See also* Financial ratio)
Reconstruction Finance Act, 14
Redlining, 273
  (*See also* Anti-redlining)
Regulation Q, 262
Repurchase Agreements (REPOS), 203
Robertson, R. M., 23
Rockefeller, David, 269–271
Rose, P. S., 89
Rose, S., 154, 210
Roth, Arthur, 158–159
Royal National Bank of New York, 209–210


Samuelson, P., 33
Santomero, A. M., 124

Saxon, James J., 23, 160
School for Bank Administration, 256, 262
Scott, W. L., 89
Secrist, Horace, 67–69, 70
Securities Exchange Commission, (SEC),
    154
Security Market Line (SML), 161
Security National Bank of Long Island, 56,
    163, 177–185, 199, 205–217, 232–233,
    268
Senate Banking Committee, 14
Sharpstown State Bank, Texas, 36
Slocum, John J., 219
Smith, C. Arnhold, 3, 199, 218–219, 224,
    232
Smith, James E., 34, 232, 271
Stagflation, 33
"States' rights," 24
Stuhr, D. P., 87
Subordinated debt, 253
Substandard loans, 49–51, 53–56, 62–63,
    71, 120, 124, 171, 209, 268
Swope Parkway National Bank, 39, 104


Talcott National Corporation, 148
Tollefson, J. O., 77–78, 81


United States National Bank of San Diego
    (USNB), 3, 5, 15, 23, 37, 56, 69, 70, 82,
    83, 84, 148, 163–164, 199, 206, 209,
    218–233, 268
Unity Bank in Roxbury, Mass., 38


Van Wicklen, R., 87
Variable deposit-insurance premium, 71
Venango National Bank of Franklin, Penn.,
    9–10
Vinso, J. D., 124


Weston, J. F., 94
Willie, Frank, 18, 34, 155, 209


Youmans, N. Rountree, 201–202

# HOME

A Play

by

DAVID STOREY

SAMUEL FRENCH

LONDON

NEW YORK SYDNEY TORONTO HOLLYWOOD